T
Bed & Breakfast
Directory

1993-1994 Edition

The Christian Bed & Breakfast Directory

1993-1994 Edition

Edited by Karen Carroll

A BARBOUR BOOK

ISBN 1-55748-341-8

Published by   Barbour and Company, Inc.
P.O. Box 719
Uhrichsville, Ohio 44683

Table of Contents

How To Use This Book

Have you dreamed of spending a few days in a rustic cabin in Alaska? Would you like to stay in an urban town house while taking care of some business in the city? Would your family like to spend a weekend on a midwestern farm feeding the pigs and gathering eggs? Maybe a romantic Victorian mansion in San Francisco or an antebellum plantation in Mississippi is what you've been looking for. No matter what your needs may be, whether you are traveling for business or pleasure, you will find a variety of choices in the 1993-94 edition of *The Christian Bed & Breakfast Directory*.

In the pages of this guide, you will find nearly 1,000 bed and breakfasts, small inns, and homestays. All of the information has been updated from last year's edition, and many entries are listed for the first time. Although every establishment is not owned or operated by Christians, each host has expressed a desire to welcome Christian travelers.

The directory is designed for easy reference. At a glance, you can determine the number of rooms available at each establishment and how many rooms have private (PB) and shared (SB) baths. You will find the name of the host or hosts, the price range for two people sharing one room, the kind of breakfast that is served, and what credit cards are accepted. There is also a "Notes" section to let you know important information that may not be included in the description. These notes correspond to the list at the bottom of each page. The descriptions have been written by the hosts. The publisher has not visited these bed and breakfasts and is not responsible for inaccuracies.

It is recommended that you make reservations in advance. Many bed and breakfasts have small staffs or are run single-handedly and cannot easily accommodate surprises. Also, ask about taxes, as city and state taxes vary. Remember to ask for directions, and if your special dietary needs can be met, and confirm check-in and check-out times.

Whether you're planning a honeymoon (first or second!), family vacation, or business trip, *The Christian Bed & Breakfast Directory* will make any outing out of the ordinary.

Karen Carroll, editor

Barbour Books would like to hear about your adventures—both memorable and forgettable—so our next edition will better serve your needs. Just drop a line to the attention of *The Christian Bed & Breakfast Directory,* Barbour & Company, Inc., P.O. Box 719, Uhrichsville, Ohio 44683. We appreciate your help!

Alabama

FOREST HOME

Pine Flat Plantation Bed & Breakfast

P.O. Box 33, Route 1, 36030
(205) 471-8024; (205) 346-2739

Pine Flat Plantation Bed and Breakfast was built in 1825 by an ancestor of the present owner. This country comfortable home has recently been lovingly restored and warmly decorated with cheerful fabrics and interesting antiques. Located just minutes off I-65 between Grennville and Pine Apple, Alabama, this plantation home provides a relaxed, romantic country setting for weary travelers, hunters who want more than just a hunt, or city folks looking for a peaceful place to unwind.

Hosts: Jane and Greg Inge
Rooms: 5 (3PB;2SB) $60-75
Full Breakfast
Credit Cards: None
Notes: 2, 7, 10, 12

LEEDS

Bed and Breakfast Birmingham

Route 2, Box 275, 35094
(205) 699-9841

This is a reservation service for the state of Alabama with bed and breakfasts in Anniston, Decatur, Fort Payne, Huntsville, Birmingham, Arab, Franklin, Spanish Fort, and Muscle Shoals. Meals vary. Horse boarding, stalls, pasture, and trails on property in Birmingham area only. Kay Red Horse, coordinator.

Pine Flat Plantation Bed and Breakfast

MONTGOMERY

Red Bluff Cottage

551 Clay St., P.O. Box 1026, 36101
(205) 264-0556

This raised cottage, furnished with family antiques, is high above the Alabama River in Montgomery's Cottage Hill district near the state Capitol, Dextor Avenue, King Memorial Baptist Church, the first White House of the Confederacy, the Civil Rights Memorial, and Old Alabama Town. It is convenient to the Alabama Shakespeare Festival Theater, the Museum Of Fine Arts, and the expanded zoo.

Hosts: Mark and Anne Waldo
Rooms: 4 (PB) $55
Full Breakfast
Credit Cards: None
Notes: 2, 5, 7, 12

NOTES: Credit cards accepted: A Master Card; B Visa; C American Express; D Discover Card; E Diners Club; F Other; 2 Personal checks accepted; 3 Lunch available; 4 Dinner available; 5 Open all

Alaska

ANCHORAGE

Alaska Bed and Breakfast

320 East 12th Avenue, 99501
(907) 279-3200

This cozy home in downtown Anchorage is within easy walking distance of downtown shops, restaurants, museum, and other points of interest. A large, fenced-in back yard offers flowers and picnic table for a restful place to relax. Kitchen and laundry privileges are available. A longtime Alaskan, your hostess can provide much information about the beautiful state of Alaska.

Host: Joy Young
Rooms: 3 (1PB; 2SB) $45-60
Continental Breakfast
Credit Cards: A, B, C, D
Notes: 2, 5, 7, 11

Bed and Breakfast on the Park

602 West 10th Ave., 99501
(907) 277-0878

Three charming rooms with private baths in a converted log cabin church on the Park Trip in downtown Anchorage. Within walking distance to shops, churches, museums, restaurants, and all activities in the park. Off street parking. Beautiful setting.

Hosts: Helen and Stella
Rooms: 3 (PB) $100
Continental Breakfast
Credit Cards: None
Notes: 2, 5, 8, 12

Bed and Breakfast on the Park

Green Bough Bed and Breakfast

3832 Young Street, 99508
(907) 562-4636

Established in 1981 to practice the art of Christian hospitality, Green Bough is Anchorage's oldest independent bed and breakfast home. We have remodeled the kitchen and baths. Slip into freshly ironed sheets, and awaken to freshly brewed coffee and home-baked

year; 6 Pets welcome; 7 Children welcome; 8 Tennis nearby; 9 Swimming nearby; 10 Golf nearby; 11 Skiing nearby; 12 May be booked through travel agent

breads. Amiable felines are available for petting. Your hosts are 25-year Alaskan residents and are involved in evangelical ministries. We offer special rates for families and missionaries.

Hosts: Jerry and Phyllis Jost
Rooms: 5 (2PB; 3SB) $45-60
Continental Breakfast
Credit Cards: None
Notes: 2, 5, 7, 8, 9, 10, 11, 12

Hillcrest Haven Bed and Breakfast

1449 Hillcrest Drive, 99503
(907) 274-3086; FAX (907)   276-8411

The recipient of several awards for exceptional service from Anchorage's visitor bureau, this European-style guest house is blessed with the finest views of Anchorage, Denali Cook Inlet, and spectacular sunsets. Located in a secluded wilderness setting, it is convenient to downtown, buses, restaurants, shopping, and airport.

Host: Linda M. Smith
Rooms: 5 (2 PB; 3 SB) $56-68
Continental Breakfast
Credit Cards: A , B, C, D, E
Notes: 2, 5, 8, 9, 11

A Homestay at Homesteads

Mailing address: Box 771283, Eagle River, 99577
(907) 272-8644; (907) 694-8644

Enjoy a breathtaking view surrounded by wilderness, yet close to Anchorage. We know where to hike, pick berries, and fish. Let us make all your Alaska travel arrangements. The wilderness trailhead across the creek can be seen from our flower-lined porch in the summer and is perfect for cross-country skiing in the winter. Breakfast is served with a view of two glaciers or Denali.

Host: Sharon Kelly
Rooms: 3 (1PB; 2SB)
Full Breakfast
Credit Cards: None
Notes: 2, 5, 9, 10, 11, 12

Hospitality Plus

7722 Anne Circle, 99504-4601
(907) 333-8504

A comfortable home, delightful and thematically decorated rooms, caring and knowledgeable hosts, sumptuous breakfasts elegantly served, a mountain range within reach, a profusion of wildflowers and moose in the yard. Add to that years of various Alaskan adventures, a Hungarian refugee's escape story, exceptional tour and guiding experience, an avid fisherman, storytelling experts, and artistic achievements, and then sum it all up in one word: HOSPITALITY. It doesn't get better than this.

Hosts: Charlie and Joan Budai
Rooms: 3 (1PB; 2SB) $50-75
Full Breakfast
Credit Cards: None
Notes: 5, 7, 8, 10, 11, 12

NOTES: Credit cards accepted: A Master Card; B Visa; C American Express; D Discover Card; E Diners Club; F Other; 2 Personal checks accepted; 3 Lunch available; 4 Dinner available; 5 Open all

DOUGLAS

Windsock Inn
Bed and Breakfast

P. O. Box 240223, 99824-0223
(907) 364-2431

Only three families have owned and occupied this historic home built in 1912 in the heart of Douglas, five minutes from downtown Juneau. Pioneer hosts are now retired and spend a portion of the winters south but return each spring to share their Alaskan experience and hospitality with bed and breakfast clientele from all over the world.

Hosts: Julie and Bob Isaac
Rooms: 2 (SB) $45-50
Full Breakfast
Credit Cards: None
Notes: 2, 7, 8, 9, 10, 11, 12

Windsock Inn Bed and Breakfast

FAIRBANKS

Alaska's 7 Gables
Bed and Breakfast

P. O. Box 80890, 99708
(907) 479-0751

Historically, Alaska's 7 Gables was a fraternity house. It is within walking distance of the University of Alaska, Fairbanks campus, yet near the river and airport. The spacious 10,000 square-foot Tudor-style home features a floral solarium, a foyer with antique stained-glass and an indoor waterfall, cathedral ceilings, wedding chapel, conference room, and dormers. A gourmet breakfast is served daily. Other amenities include cable TV and phones, library, laundry facilities, jacuzzis, bikes, canoes, and skis. Suites are available.

Hosts: Paul and Leicha Welton
Rooms: 9 (4PB; 4SB) $45-95
Full Breakfast
Credit Cards: A, B, D, E
Notes: 2, 5, 7, 9, 10, 11, 12

Hillside
Bed and Breakfast

310 Rambling Road, 99712
(907) 457-2664

Experience authentic Alaskan decor and hospitality in contemporary comfort with a beautiful, wooded location. Spacious rooms, full sourdough breakfasts, laundry facilities, in-room TVs, private kitchenette. Only seven minutes from downtown and close to popular attractions. The hosts have lived several years in the Alaskan bush, as well as in Fairbanks. Non-smoking only.

Hosts: Tim and Deb Vanasse
Rooms: 2 (SB) $45-55
Full Breakfast
Credit Cards: None
Notes: 2, 5, 6, 7, 11, 12

year; 6 Pets welcome; 7 Children welcome; 8 Tennis nearby; 9 Swimming nearby; 10 Golf nearby; 11 Skiing nearby; 12 May be booked through travel agent

HOMER

Homer Bed and Breakfast/ Seekins

Box 1264, 99603
(907) 235-8996

Spectacular panoramic view of beautiful Koclenar Bay. Glaciers and mountains. Yummy breakfasts served in our rustic Alaskan home, with art-native doll collection. Truly Alaskan. Each unit has cable TV, kitchens with pots, pans, dishes, popcorn poppers, popcorn, coffee, and tea. Daily maid service. Outdoor wood-heated sauna, occasional moose, birds at feeder, flowers. We are also a referral service for other apartments, suites, and cabins. Fishing, boats and land sight-seeing available. Hosts moved here from Wisconsin and Minnesota in 1969.

Hosts: Floyd and Gert Seekins
Rooms: 8 (6PB; 2SB) $50-95
Full Breakfast
Credit Cards: A, B
Notes: 2, 5, 6, 7, 8, 9, 10, 11, 12

Patchwork Farm Bed and Breakfast

36170 Sunshine Drive, 99603
(907) 235-7368

This established bed and breakfast home is in a peaceful, rural setting with fishing and sight-seeing just minutes away. This is the perfect place for a long-needed rest or a quiet hike on our nature trail. A children's dream. With so much to explore, they will keep busy for hours. During the winter months, enjoy cross-country skiing on a groomed 15-kilometer ski trail. Afterwards, enjoy conversation beside a toasty fire with a cup of steaming coffee, tea, or cider.

Hosts: Robert and Kim Avera
Rooms: 3 (2PB; 1SB) $60-80
Full Breakfast
Credit Cards: None
Notes: 2, 5, 7, 11

JUNEAU

Pearson's Pond Luxury B & B

4541 Sawa Circle, 99801
(907) 789-3772

Private studio/suites on scenic pond. Hot tub under the stars, rowboat, bicycles, BBQ, guest kitchenette. Complimentary capuccino, fresh breads, gourmet coffee, popcorn. Near glacier, fishing, rafting, skiing, ferry, airport, and Glacier Bay departures. Smokefree. Quiet, scenic, and lots of privacy in fully equipped studio with private entrance and deck. In-room dining and TV, VCR, and stereo tapes provided. Hosts will make all travel, tours, excursion arrangements. Guests say it's a definite "10"...where expectations are quietly met. AAA three-diamond award winner.

Hosts: Steve and Diane Pearson
Rooms: 3 (1PB; 2SB) $69-148
Full (self-serve) Breakfast
Credit Cards: A, B, E
Notes: 2, 5, 8, 9, 11, 12

NOTES: Credit cards accepted: A Master Card; B Visa; C American Express; D Discover Card; E Diners Club; F Other; 2 Personal checks accepted; 3 Lunch available; 4 Dinner available; 5 Open all

Swiss Chalet Bed and Breakfast

P. O. Box 1734, 99664
(907) 224-3939

See Seward and stay one block from the Seward highway at Mile .1 on the road to Exit Glacier where a clean, cozy chalet offers comfortable beds and a tasty breakfast. From Swiss Chalet, it is a short ride to the boat harbor where charters for fishing and Kenai Fjords tours are available in magnificent Resurrection Bay and beyond. Swiss Chalet is located within a short walk of Le Barn Appetit, a delightful, natural food restaurant and bakery.

Hosts: Stan Jones and Charlotte Freeman-Jones
Rooms: 4 (2PB; 2SB) $50
Full Breakfast
Credit Cards: A, B
Notes: 2, 12

The White House Bed and Breakfast

SEWARD

The White House B&B

P.O. Box 1157, 99664
(907) 224-3614

This 5,000 square foot home is surrounded by a panoramic mountain view. One-half of the home is for guest use. Country charm abound with quilts and hand crafts. Guest TV room and fully equipped kitchen is in common area. Breakfast is self-serve buffet in guest dining area. The Historical Iditarod Trail close by. Also the famed Kenai Fjords National Park is accessed by road or boat.

Hosts: Tom and Annette Reese
Rooms: 5 (3PB; 2SB) $40-55 (winter) $55-75 (summer)
Continental Breakfast
Credit Cards: A, B
Notes: 2, 5, 7, 11, 12

SITKA

Karras Bed and Breakfast

230 Kegwonton Street, 99835
(907) 747-3985

A warm welcome will be yours at our bed and breakfast overlooking Sitka Sound, the picturesque fishing fleet, and the Pacific Ocean. You can walk to Sitka's main historic attractions, dining, and shopping areas. Bus service is available from the airport or ferry to our home. We have a room for lounging, reading, visiting, and watching the endless marine traffic.

Hosts: Pete and Bertha Karras
Rooms: 4 (S2B) $43.20 & up, plus tax
Full Breakfast
Credit Cards: C
Notes: 2, 5, 7

year; 6 Pets welcome; 7 Children welcome; 8 Tennis nearby; 9 Swimming nearby; 10 Golf nearby; 11 Skiing nearby; 12 May be booked through travel agent

THORNE BAY

Boardwalk Wilderness Lodge

P.O. Box 19121, 99919
(907) 828-3918

May-September fully-guided and family operated fishing lodge features Alaska's best fresh and saltwater fishing and crabbing. Flightseeing. Tours. Deluxe accommodations. Bed and Breakfast available only during off-season.

Hosts: Sid and Kathy Cook
Rooms: 4 (SB) $270 (off season) $1400
(May-Sept. day & night includes meals, guide, lodging and transportation)
Full Breakfast
Credit Cards: A, B
Notes: 2, 3, 4, 5, 7, 12

WASILLA

Yukon Don's

HC 31 5086, 99654
(907) 376-7472

This 10,000-square foot converted cow barn is one of Alaska's finest bed and breakfast inns and has been selected as one of the Top 50 Inns in America by *Inn Times* in 1991. Located near the old town site of Matanuska and just 40 minutes from Anchorage, we offer the finest view in the Matanuska Valley. Each of our rooms is theme decorated. A full-color brochure is available on request.

Hosts: Diane and Art Mongeau
Rooms: 5 (1PB; 4SB) $50-80
Continental Breakfast
Credit Cards: None
Notes: 2, 5, 7, 9, 10, 11, 12

NOTES: Credit cards accepted: A Master Card; B Visa; C American Express; D Discover Card; E Diners Club; F Other; 2 Personal checks accepted; 3 Lunch available; 4 Dinner available; 5 Open all

Arizona

BISBEE

Park Place
Bed and Breakfast

200 East Vista, 85603
(602) 432-3054 evening; (800) 388-4388
daytime

This pleasant 5,000-square-foot home offers a three-course breakfast, spacious rooms, terraces, early morning hot coffee, jogging park, tennis, golf; is close to Mexico.

Hosts: Bob and Janet Watkins
Rooms: 4 (2PB; 2 SB) $40-60
Full Breakfast
Credit Cards: A, B
Notes: 2, 5, 8, 10

CORNVILLE

Pumpkinshell Ranch
Bed and Breakfast

11005 E. Johnson Road, 86325
(602) 634-4797

This new, large solar home is set in the middle of four acres in a secluded country setting. Rooms have private en

trances and twin, queen, or king beds. Enjoy the distinguished architecture with luxurious decor, a deck overlooking waterfalls, the pond in the back yard, private library, and restful atmosphere. Indian cliff dwellings are nearby.

Hosts: Kay and Terry Johnson
Rooms: 2 (PB) $65-70
Full Breakfast
Credit Cards: A, B
Notes: 2, 5, 7, 9

FLAGSTAFF

Comfi Cottages
of Flagstaff

1612 N. Aztec, 86001
(602) 774-0731; (602) 779-2236

Near the Grand Canyon, great for families. Five individual cottages with antiques and English country motif. Three cottages are two-bedroom, one bath; one is a one-bedroom honeymoon cottage; one is a large three-bedroom, two baths. Fully equipped with linens, towels and blankets. Kitchens have dishes, pots, pans, coffee pot, etc. Ready-to-prepare breakfast foods in fridge. Color

year; 6 Pets welcome; 7 Children welcome; 8 Tennis nearby; 9 Swimming nearby; 10 Golf nearby; 11 Skiing nearby; 12 May be booked through travel agent

cable TV and telephone. Bicycles on premises, washer and dryer available, and picnic and barbecue grills at each cottage.

Hosts: Ed and Pat Wiebe
Rooms: 8 (7PB; 1SB) $65-95
Full Breakfast
Credit Cards: A, B
Notes: 2, 5, 7, 8, 9, 10, 11, 12

PHOENIX

Westways Private Resort Inn

P.O. Box 41624, 85080
(602) 582-3868

Westways was fashioned after the world's finest five star resorts, with one exception...only four to six private guest rooms! Arizona contemporary Spanish Mediterranean design, located in easy to reach northwest Phoenix, adjacent to Thunderbird Park and Arrowhead Ranch on-one plus designer landscaped acre. Interior is designer decorated for guest comfort and amenities include, leisure room, satellite and large screen TV, VCR, table games, stereo, mini ping-pong, library and fireplace. Each morning a complimentary "Ranchette" breakfast is served. Unparalleled simple elegance! Resplendently decorated in rich colors and textures, each guest room provides the kind of amenities you would expect from a premier resort.

Hosts: Darrell Trapp
Rooms: 6 (PB) $49-122 (varies seasonally)
Full Breakfast (summer—continental plus)

Credit Cards: A, B, C
Notes: 2, 3, 4, 5, 8, 9, 10, 12

SEDONA

Bed and Breakfast at Saddle Rock Ranch

255 Rock Ridge Drive, 86336
(602) 282-7640

History...Romance...Antiques...Elegance. Centrally located Historic Landmark estate with panoramic vistas. Romantic rooms feature private baths, antiques, canopied beds, fieldstone fireplaces and superb views. Private guest parlor. Hillside grounds feature a sparkling pool with jacuzzi, spa, view decks, flower gardens, birds and wildlife. Guest refrigerator, microwave, plentiful ice and BBQ available. Your warm, friendly hosts provide scrumptious breakfasts, famous oatmeal cookies, afternoon snacks. Hiking, horseback riding, fishing, tennis and golf nearby. Five minutes to shops, galleries and restaurants.

Hosts: Fran and Dan Bruno
Rooms: 3 (PB) $95-125
Full Breakfast
Credit Cards: None
Notes: 2, 5, 8, 9, 10, 11

Westways Private Resort Inn

NOTES: Credit cards accepted: A Master Card; B Visa; C American Express; D Discover Card; E Diners Club; F Other; 2 Personal checks accepted; 3 Lunch available; 4 Dinner available; 5 Open all

TEMPE

Mi Casa Su Casa Bed and Breakfast

P. O. Box 950, 85280-0950
(602) 990-0682; (800) 456-0682 reservations;
FAX (602) 990-0950

Our reservation service has over 130 inspected and approved homestays, guest cottages, ranches, and inns in Arizona, Utah, and New Mexico. Listings include Ajo, Apache Junction, Bisbee, Cave Creek, Cottonwood, Clarkdale, Dragoon, Flagstaff, Mesa, Paradise Valley, Phoenix, Prescott, Scottsdale, Tempe, Tucson, Yuma, and other cities in Arizona; Alburquerque, Carlsbad, Los Cruces, Ramah, Silver City, and Santa Fe, New Mexico; Moab, Monroe, Monticello, Salt Lake City, Springdale, and St. George, Utah. Private and shared baths ranging from $25 to $125. Full or continental breakfast. Ruth Young, coordinator.

TUCSON

Casa Alegre Bed and Breakfast

316 E. Speedway, 85705
(602) 628-1800

Casa Alegre is a distinguished 1915 craftsman style bungalow, located minutes from the University of Arizona and downtown Tuscon. Each of the four guest rooms has been lovingly furnished with unique pieces that reflect the highlights of Tuscon's history. Every morning, guests awaken to a scrumptious full breakfast and spend their relaxing time in the Inn's serene patio and pool area or by the rock fireplace in the formal living room during the cool winter months.

Host: Phyllis Florek
Rooms: 4 (PB) $65-80
Full Breakfast
Credit Cards: A, B
Notes: 2, 5, 8, 9, 10, 11, 12

El Presidio Bed and Breakfast Inn

297 North Main Avenue, 85701
(602) 623-6151; (501) 297-8764 (at night)

Experience southwestern charm in a desert oasis with the romance of a country inn. Garden courtyards with Old Mexico ambience of lush, floral displays, fountains, and cobblestone surround richly appointed guest house and suites. Enjoy antique decors, robes, complimentary beverages, fruit, snacks, TVs, and telephones. A Victorian adobe, the award-winning inn is in a historic district close to downtown. Walk to restaurants, museums, and shops, art district. Mobil 3 - star rated.

Hosts: Patti Toci
Rooms: 4 (PB) $65-105
Full Breakfast
Credit Cards: None
Notes: 2, 5, 8, 9, 10, 11, 12

year; 6 Pets welcome; 7 Children welcome; 8 Tennis nearby; 9 Swimming nearby; 10 Golf nearby; 11 Skiing nearby; 12 May be booked through travel agent

Arkansas

CALICO ROCK

Happy Lonesome Log Cabins
HC 61, Box 72, 72519
(501) 297-8211; (501) 297-8764 (at night)

Log cabins in the Ozark National Forest, decorated with the past in mind, but offering modern comforts. The sleeping loft and hide-a-bed accommodate four, with kitchenette, bath, living area with wood stove. Cabins are unhosted for maximum privacy and provided with coffee, milk, cereal, and homemade bread. Panoramic river view, near Ozark Folk Center, Blanchard Caverns, antique shops, live music shows, trout fishing, hiking.

Host: Carolyn S. Eck
Rooms: 5 (3PB; 2SB) $45
Full Breakfast
Credit Cards: A, B, D
Notes: 2, 5, 7, 12

Happy Lonesome Log Cabins

EUREKA SPRINGS

Heart of the Hills
5 Summit, 72632
(501) 253-7468

This historic Victorian home is in a quaint town nestled into the Ozark Mountains. Wake up to a scrumptious breakfast, enjoy a gorgeous four-block walk to shops, museums, and galleries, catch a trolley for a spin around the area, or relax in the jacuzzi. Rooms have antiques with a Victorian decor. Come, experience a "touch of true, Southern hospitality."

Host: Jan Jacobs Weber
Rooms: 4 (PB) $70-119
Full Breakfast
Credit Cards: A, B
Notes: 5, 7, 9, 10,

The Heartstone Inn and Cottages
35 Kingshighway, 72632
(501) 253-8916

This award-winning, nine-room inn is located in the historic district and has turn-of-the-century charm with all mod-

---

NOTES: Credit cards accepted: A Master Card; B Visa; C American Express; D Discover Card; E Diners Club; F Other; 2 Personal checks accepted; 3 Lunch available; 4 Dinner available; 5 Open all

ern conveniences. Two charming cottages are also available. Antiques, fresh flowers, private entrances, air conditioning, cable TV. King, queen, and double beds. "Best breakfast in the Ozarks," *The New York Times*, 1989.

Hosts: Iris and Bill Simantel
Rooms: 9 plus 2 cottages (PB) $58-105
Full Breakfast
Credit Cards: A, B, C, D
Closed Christmas through January
Notes: 2, 7, 12

Red Bud Manor

7 Kingshighway, 72632
(501) 253-9649

This quaint Victorian country bed and breakfast inn is located on the historic loop in Eureka Springs, Arkansas. Built in 1891, the inn has off-street parking and the historic trolley, which stops in front of the inn, will take guests to the historic Victorian town. All the guest rooms have private entrances, private baths, cable TV, and refrigerators. Some rooms have queen size beds, jacuzzi tubs, and are decorated with antiques.

Host: Shari Bozeman
Rooms: 3 (PB) $65-97
Full Breakfast
Credit Cards: A, B
Notes: 2, 5

Ridgeway House

28 Ridgeway, 72632
(501) 253-6618; (800) 477-6618

Prepare to be pampered! Sumptuous breakfast elegantly served, luxurious rooms, antiques, flowers, desserts, quiet street within walking distance of eight

churches, five-minute walk to historic downtown, trolley one block. Porches, decks, private jacuzzi suite for anniversaries/honeymoons. All my guests are VIPs! Open all year.

Host: Linda Kerkera
Rooms: 5 (3PB; 2SB) $69-99
Full Breakfast
Credit Cards: A, B, C
Notes: 2, 5, 7, 12

Singleton House

11 Singleton, 72632
(501) 253-9111

This old-fashioned Victorian with a touch of magic is whimsically decorated and has an eclectic collection of treasures and antiques. Breakfast is served on the balcony overlooking a fantasy garden and fish pond. Walk to the historic district, shops, and cafes. Passion play and Holy Land tour reservations can be arranged. A guest cottage is also available. An innkeepers' apprenticeship program is also available.

Host: Barbara Bavron
Rooms: 5 (PB) $65-75/ Cottage, No Breakfast, $95
Full Breakfast
Credit Cards: A, B, C, D
Notes: 2, 5, 7, 9, 10, 12

Willow Ridge Luxury Lodging

85 Kingshighway, 72632
(501) 253-7737; (800) 467-1737

Enjoy a Victorian aura, a glimpse of the 1920s, or relaxing country charm. Lo-

---

cated on 14 wooded acres adjacent to the Eureka Springs chamber of commerce visitors' center, Willow Ridge takes advantage of the natural terrain so that rooms on each story have a ground-level entry and parking. Each upper-story room has a private balcony. Recreational facilities are nearby.

Hosts: Roy and Patricia Manley
Rooms: 7 (PB) $125
Continental Breakfast
Credit Cards: A, B, D
Notes: 5, 12

FAYETTEVILLE

Hill Avenue Bed and Breakfast

131 S. Hill, 72701
(501) 444-0865

This century old home is located in a residential neighborhood near the University of Arkansas, downtown square, and Walton Art Center. This inn is the only licensed Bed and Breakfast in Fayetteville. Comfortable common areas and a large porch are available to guests. Breakfast is served on the porch or in the formal dining room.

Hosts: Cecila and Dale Thompson
Rooms: 3 (PB) $40
Full Breakfast
Credit Cards: None
Notes: None

Hill Avenue Bed and Breakfast

GASSVILLE

Lithia Springs Lodge

R1, Box 77A, 72635
(510) 435-6100

Lovingly restored early Ozark health lodge six miles southwest of Mountain Home in north central Arkansas. Fishing, boating, canoeing in famous lakes and rivers. Scenic hills and valleys, caverns; Silver Dollar City, Branson, Eureka Springs within driving distance. Enjoy the walk in meadow and woods and browse through the adjoining Country Treasures Gift Shop.

Hosts: Paul and Reita Johnson
Rooms: 5 (3PB; 2SB) $40-45
Full Breakfast
Credit Cards: None
Notes: 2, 7 (over 7), 8, 9, 10

HARDY

Olde Stonehouse B&B Inn

511 Main St., 72542
(501) 856-2983

Historic native Arkansas stone house with large porches lined with jumbo rocking chairs provides the perfect place to relax and watch the world go by. Each room is individually and comfortable furnished with antiques. Central heat and air, ceiling fans, queen beds, private baths. In-town location, block from Spring River and the unique shops of Old Hardy Town. Breakfast is a treat, like Grandma used to make, gourmet but hearty! Evening snacks. Spe-

NOTES: Credit cards accepted: A Master Card; B Visa; C American Express; D Discover Card; E Diners Club; F Other; 2 Personal checks accepted; 3 Lunch available; 4 Dinner available; 5 Open all

cial occasion packages available. Murder mystery dinner parties and packages, gift certificates. Three country music theaters, golf courses, horseback riding, canoeing and fishing nearby. Attractions: Mammoth Springs State Park, Grand Gulf State Park, Evening Shade, AR, Arkansas Traveler Theater.

Hosts: David and Peggy Johnson
Rooms: 5 (PB) $55-85
Full Breakfast
Credit Cards: A, B, D
Notes: 2, 3, 4, 5, 8, 9, 10, 12

California

ALAMEDA

Garratt Mansion

900 Union St., 94501
(510) 521-4779

This 1893 Victorian halts time on the tranquil island of Alameda. Only 15 miles to Berkeley or downtown San Francisco. We'll help maximize your vacation plans or leave you alone to regroup. Our rooms are large and comfortable, and our breakfasts are nutritious and filling.

Hosts: Royce and Betty Gladden
Rooms: 6 (3PB; 3SB) $75-125
Full Breakfast
Credit Cards: A, B, C, E
Notes: 2, 5, 7, 8, 9, 10, 12

Garratt Mansion

ALBION

Fensalden Inn

P.O. Box 99 , 95410
(707) 937-4042

Overlooking the Pacific Ocean from twenty tree-lined pastoral acres, Fensalden Inn offers a quiet respite for the perfect getaway. A former stage-coach way station, the inn offers a restful, yet interesting stay for the traveler. There are eight guest quarters; some are suites with fireplaces and kitchens, all have private baths with showers or tubs. Come and whale watch, join the deer on a stroll through our meadow, or just relax and enjoy!

Hosts: Scott and Francis Brazil
Rooms: 8 (PB) $95-140
Full Gourmet Breakfast
Credit Cards: A, B
Notes: 2, 5, 8, 9, 10, 12

NOTES: Credit cards accepted: A Master Card; B Visa; C American Express; D Discover Card; E Diners Club; F Other; 2 Personal checks accepted; 3 Lunch available; 4 Dinner available; 5 Open all

ANGWIN

Forest Manor

415 Cold Springs Road, 94508
(707) 965-3538

Tucked among the forest and vineyards of famous Napa wine country is this secluded 20-acre English Tudor estate, described as " one of the most romantic country inns . . . a small exclusive resort." Enjoy the scenic countryside near hot air ballooning, hot springs, lake, and water sports. Fireplaces, verandas, 53-foot pool, spas, spacious suites (one with Jacuzzi), refrigerators, coffee makers, home-baked breakfast. Hosts are former medical missionaries.

Hosts: Harold and Corlene Lambeth
Rooms: 3 (PB) $99-179 off-season; $119-199 in-season
Expanded Continental Breakfast
Credit Cards: A, B
Notes: 2, 5, 8, 9, 12

APTOS

Apple Lane Inn

6265 Soquel Drive, 95003
(408) 475-6868; (800) 649-8988

This secluded 1870s Victorian is set on a hill overlooking acres of gardens, meadows, orchards, a romantic gazebo, and flowering gardens. Each room is unique with period antiques, quilts, and authentic decor. A lavish country breakfast is served in the parlor. Enjoy the game room, darts, croquet, horseshoes, and player piano. Pick apples to feed the horses or gather fresh eggs and produce from the gardens. Walk to the beach. Just minutes from Santa Cruz.

Hosts: Douglas and Diana Groom
Rooms: 5 (3 PB; 2 SB) $70-125
Full Breakfast
Credit Cards: A, B, D
Notes: 2, 5, 8, 10

AUBURN

Power's Mansion Inn

164 Cleveland Avenue, 95603
(916) 885-1166

This magnificent mansion was built with the Power's family gold mine fortune, and no expense was spared to make it an elegant showcase. The legendary, century-old Victorian has been restored to the grandeur of yesteryear with individually decorated rooms filled with antique furniture. Each room has a private bath, phone and television. A delicious, full breakfast is served every morning.

Hosts: Tina and Tony Verhaart/ Owners: Jean and Arno Lejnieks
Rooms: 11 (PB) $75-160
Full Breakfast
Credit Cards: A, B, C
Notes: 2, 5, 6, 7, 8, 9, 10, 12

BISHOP

The Chalfont House

213 Academy, 93514
(619) 872-1790

This 1900 semi-Victorian, two-story house includes country antique furnishings and handmade quilts. There are five rooms and two suites. Tea is served

year; 6 Pets welcome; 7 Children welcome; 8 Tennis nearby; 9 Swimming nearby; 10 Golf nearby; 11 Skiing nearby; 12 May be booked through travel agent

in the afternoon; ice cream sundaes are served in the evenings. Enjoy TV, VCR, library, and a fireplace in the parlor. Central air and ceiling fans. No smoking.

Hosts: Fred and Sally Manecke
Rooms: 7 (PB) $60-90
Full Breakfast
Credit Cards: C
Notes: 2, 5, 7, 8, 9, 10, 11, 12

CALISTOGA

Calistoga Wishing Well Inn

2653 Foothill Blvd (Hwy 128), 94515
(707) 942-5534

A country estate among vineyards with elegant period interiors. Situated on four acres in a historical setting. Enjoy your gourmet breakfast featuring home-grown fruits and preserves, and complimentary wine and hors d'oerves poolside with a magnificent view of Mt. St. Helena or on your private sun deck. Fireplace in the parlor and cottage. Jacuzzi under the stars; all private baths. Near mud baths, balloon rides, wineries.

Hosts: Marina and Keith Dinsmoor
Rooms: 3(PB) $120-150
Full Breakfast
Credit Cards: A, B, C
Notes: 2, 5, 7, 8, 9, 10, 12

Hillcrest Bed and Breakfast

3225 Lake County Highway, 94515
(707) 942-6334

My home is your home. Hillcrest offers a million-dollar view of Napa Valley, swimming, hiking, fishing, and a fireplace. The owner's family has been on this piece of land since 1860. Her great, great grandfather established a winery and vineyards in 1882, which the home overlooks. Rooms have balconies, and the home is filled with heirlooms from the family mansion that burned down in 1964. There is a mini-museum of silver, china, art, and furniture.

Host: Debbie O'Gorman
Rooms: 6 (3 PB; 3 SB) $45-90
Continental Breakfast
Credit Cards: None
Notes: 2, 5, 8, 9, 10, 11, 12

Quail Mt. B&B

4455 North St. Helena Hwy, 94515
(707) 942-0316

A secluded, romantic 3-guest room B & B located on 26 heavily wooded acres 300 feet above Napa Valley. All king size beds, private baths and decks. A swimming pool, hot tub, and picnic facilities on premises. A full breakfast is served in the guest common room, decks that wrap around the house, or in winter, in the formal dining room that has a fireplace. Reservation deposit required.

Hosts: Alma and Don Swiers
Rooms: 3 (PB) $100-130
Full Breakfast
Credit Cards: A, B
Notes: 2, 8, 10, 12

NOTES: Credit cards accepted: A Master Card; B Visa; C American Express; D Discover Card; E Diners Club; F Other; 2 Personal checks accepted; 3 Lunch available; 4 Dinner available; 5 Open all

Scarlett's Country Inn

3918 Silverado Trail, 94515
(707) 942-6669

This secluded 1890 farmhouse set in the quiet of green lawns and tall pines that overlook vineyards has three exquisitely appointed suites, one with a fireplace. Breakfast is served in your room or by the woodland swimming pool. Close to wineries and spas, we offer private baths, queen beds, private entrances, air conditioning, and afternoon refreshments.

Hosts: Scarlett and Derek Dwyer
Rooms: 3 (PB) $95-150
Continental Breakfast
Credit Cards: None
Notes: 2, 5, 7, 8, 9, 10, 12

Scarlett's Country Inn

CAMBRIA

The Pickford House Bed and Breakfast

2555 MacLeod Way, 93428
(805) 927-8619

Enjoy antiques, claw foot tubs with showers, oak pullchain toilets, only seven miles from Hearst Castle. Wine is served at 5:00 P.M. for guests. Three rooms have fireplaces; all rooms have in-room TVs and king or queen beds. Near beaches. Gift certificates available. Third person any age $20. Reservations needed. Well-behaved children welcome. Check in after 3PM, check out 11 AM.

Host: Anna Larsen
Rooms: 8 (PB) $85-120 plus tax
Full Breakfast
Credit Cards: A, B
Notes: 2, 5, 7

CAMINO

Camino Hotel B&B

P.O. Box 1197, 4103 Carson Road, 95709
(916) 644-7740

Turn of the century loggers' barracks. Artfully restored with large parlor, storm porch and ten guest rooms. Located in the Apple Hill region of California's gold country. Thirteen wineries, 12 Christmas tree farms, and 46 apple orchards nearby. Walking distance to community church, restaurant and playground.

Hosts: Paula Nobert and John Eddy
Rooms: 10 (4PB; 6SB) $65-85
Full Breakfast
Credit Cards: A, B, C, D
Notes: 2, 3, 4, 5, 7, 8, 9, 10, 11, 12

CARLSBAD

Pelican Cove Inn

320 Walnut, 92008
(619) 434-5995

This romantic inn is located 200 yards from the beach and features eight room,

year; 6 Pets welcome; 7 Children welcome; 8 Tennis nearby; 9 Swimming nearby; 10 Golf nearby; 11 Skiing nearby; 12 May be booked through travel agent

all with: private baths (some spas), feather beds, down comforters, fireplaces, and TVs. An extended continental breakfast that can be enjoyed in your room, the gazebo, or the oceanview deck is included. Excellent restaurants and shopping are within walking distance.

Hosts: Scott and Betsy Buckwald
Rooms: 8 (PB) $85-150
Extended Continental Breakfast
Credit Cards: A,B, C
Notes: 2, 5, 8, 9, 10, 12

CARMEL

San Antonio House

P.O. Box 3683, 93921
(408) 624-4334

San Antonio House is a charming early Carmel home that brings back memories of Carmel as an artists' village. There are four suites, all with private entrances, private baths, and woodburning fireplaces. All of the rooms open onto an enchanting garden. Three blocks from downtown shopping and restaurants and one block from the beach. San Antonio House is a unique and romantic getaway in a quiet neighborhood.

Hosts: Sarah Anne & Richard Lee
Rooms: 4 (PB) $110-155
Expanded Continental Breakfast
Credit Cards: A,B
Notes: 2, 5, 10, 12 (winter only)

Sunset House

P.O. Box 1925 (Camino Real between 7th and Ocean), 93921

(408) 624-4884

Sunset House is a romantic inn, located on a quiet residential street, capturing the essence of Carmel. Experience the sound of the surf, being close to the beach and yet only two blocks away from quaint shops, restaurants and galleries that make Carmel famous. A special breakfast tray is brought to the room, allowing guest to relax and enjoy the glow of the fire and the beauty of the view. Each room is uniquely decorated to insure guests an enjoyable stay.

Hosts: Camille and Dennis Fike
Rooms: 3 (PB) $110-150
Continental Breakfast
Credit Cards: None
Notes: 2, 5, 7, 8, 9, 10

CARMEL VALLEY

The Valley Lodge

Carmel Valley Road at Ford Road, Box 93, 93924
(408) 659-2261; (800) 641-4646

A warm Carmel Valley welcome awaits the two of you, a few of you, or a small conference. Relax in a garden patio room or a cozy one- or two-bedroom cottage with fireplace and kitchen. Enjoy a sumptuous continental breakfast, our heated pool, sauna, hot spa, and fitness center. Tennis and golf are nearby. Walk to fine restaurants and quaint shops of Carmel Valley village, or just listen to your beard grow.

Hosts: Peter and Sherry Coakley
Rooms: 31 (PB) $95-135; $155 one-bedroom cottage; $235 two-bedroom cottage
Expanded Continental Breakfast
Credit Cards: A, B, C

NOTES: Credit cards accepted: A Master Card; B Visa; C American Express; D Discover Card; E Diners Club; F Other; 2 Personal checks accepted; 3 Lunch available; 4 Dinner available; 5 Open all

Notes: 2, 5, 6 (extra fee), 7, 8, 9 (on premises), 10, 12

CLOVERDALE

Ye Olde' Shelford House

29955 River Road, 95425
(707) 894-5956; (800) 833-6479

This 1885 country Victorian is located in the heart of wine country, with six beautifully decorated rooms with family antiques, fresh flowers, homemade quilts, and porcelain dolls by Ina. A gourmet breakfast is served in our delightful dining room. We will make reservations for you at one of the many good restaurants nearby. Before you retire, you can enjoy the many games in the recreation room, then get into the hot tub to relax after a busy day.

Hosts: Ina and Al Sauder
Rooms: 6 (PB) $85-110
Full Breakfast
Closed January
Credit Cards: A, B, C, D
Notes: 2, 7, 8, 9, 10

COLUMBIA

Fallon Hotel

Washington Street, 95310
(209) 532-1470

Since 1857 the Fallon Hotel in the historic Columbia State Park has provided hospitality and comfort to travelers from all over the world. It has been authentically restored to its Victorian grandeur, and many of the antiques and furnishings are original to the hotel. We welcome you to come visit our Fallon Hotel, Fallon Theater, and old-fashioned ice cream parlor for a taste of the Old West.

Host: Tom Bender
Rooms: 14 (13 PB; 1 SB) $50-90
Continental Breakfast
Credit Cards: A, B, C
Notes: 2, 5 (wkends only Jan-March), 7, 10, 11

ELK

Elk Cove Inn

6300 South Highway 1, P.O. Box 367, 95432
(707) 877-3321

This 1883 Victorian is nestled atop a bluff overlooking the ocean. Enjoy wide vista views amid the relaxed and romantic setting of a rural village. Behind the main house are four cabins, two with fireplace and skylights. The main house, where a full breakfast is served in the dining rooms, has three large ocean-view rooms, a parlor, and deck. There is access to a driftwood strewn beach and numerous scenic trails for hiking and biking nearby.

Host: Hildrun-Uta Triebess
Rooms: 8 (PB) $108-138
Full Breakfast
Credit Cards: None
Notes: 2, 5, 8, 10

FAWNSKIN

The Inn at Fawnskin B & B

880 Canyon Road, P.O. Box 378, 92333
(909) 866-3200

Beautiful custom log home with knotty pine interior located on the quiet north shore of Big Bear Lake on an acre of land among towering pine trees. Living room with big rock fireplace, baby grand piano and comfy furniture. Library. Game room with 50-inch wide-screen TV, full-size pool table, movie library and game table. Full delicious home-made breakfast served in front of another brick fireplace. Four lovely guest rooms.

Hosts: G.B. and Susan Sneed
Rooms: 4 (2PB; 2SB) $75-155
Full Breakfast
Credit Cards: A, B
Notes: 2, 3, 4, 5, 8, 9, 10, 11, 12

The Inn at Fawnskin

FERNDALE

The Gingerbread Mansion

400 Berding Street, P. O. Box 40, 95536
(707) 786-4000

Trimmed in gingerbread and surrounded by a formal English garden, the Gingerbread Mansion, circa 1899, is an elegant Queen Anne Eastlake-style Victorian. Completely decorated in antiques, the Victorian theme is carried throughout the four parlors, dining room, and nine guest rooms. The Gingerbread Mansion is located in the state historic landmark village of Ferndale, offering three blocks of shops, galler-

ies, a repertory theater, and museum. The coast, redwoods, hiking trails, and more are nearby.

Host: Ken Torbert
Rooms: 9 (PB) $85-185
Expanded Continental Breakfast
Credit Cards: A, B, C
Notes: 2, 5, 10, 12

FISH CAMP

Karen's Bed and Breakfast

P.O. Box 8, 1144 Railroad Avenue, 93623
(209) 683-4550; (800) 346-1443 (U.S. and Canada)

Two miles from Yosemite National Park on Highway 41. Open year round. Enjoy cozy country comfort nestled amid the towering pines and whispering cedars at 5,000 feet. Step into your delightfully decorated room with individual temperature control. Luxuriate in your private bathtub or shower. Eat heartily of a bountiful country breakfast served by candlelight or the tasty tidbits and beverages at tea time. Fine dining and horseback riding nearby.

Hosts: Karen Bergh and Lee Morse
Rooms: 3 (PB) $85
Full Breakfast
Credit Cards: None
Notes: 2, 5, 7, 9, 10, 11, 12

FORT BRAGG

Grey Whale Inn

615 Main St., 95437
(707) 964-0640

Handsome four-story Mendocino Coast

NOTES: Credit cards accepted: A Master Card; B Visa; C American Express; D Discover Card; E Diners Club; F Other; 2 Personal checks accepted; 3 Lunch available; 4 Dinner available; 5 Open all

Landmark since 1915. Cozy rooms to expansive suites, all have private baths, ocean, garden or hill, or town views. Some have fireplaces, TV, one has jacuzzi tub, all have phones. Recreation Area: Pool table/library, fireside lounge, TV theatre. Sixteen person conference room. Full buffet breakfast features blue-ribbon breads. Friendly, helpful staff. Relaxed seaside charm, situated 6 blocks to beach. Celebrate your special occasion on the fabled Mendocino Coast!

Hosts: John & Colette Bailey
Rooms: 14 (PB) $82.50-154
Full Breakfast
Credit Cards: A ,B, C, D
Notes: 2,5,7,8,9,10,12

Pudding Creek Inn
700 North Main, 95437
(707) 964-9529; (800) 227-9529

Two lovely 1887 Victorian homes adjoined by a lush garden court offer comfortable and romantic rooms. Your stay includes buffet breakfast in two dining rooms with fresh fruit, juice, main dish, and tantalizing homemade coffee cakes served hot. Antiques, fireplaces, personalized sight seeing assistance. Near scenic Skunk Train excursion through the Redwoods, beaches, dining, shops, galleries, hiking, tennis, and golf.

Hosts: Garry and Carole Anloff
Rooms: 10 (PB) $65-125
Full Breakfast

Credit Cards: A, B, C, D
Notes: 5 (by prior arrangement), 8, 9, 10, 12

GEYSERVILLE

Campbell Ranch Inn
1475 Canyon Road, 95441
(707) 857-3476

A 35-acre country setting in the heart of the Sonoma wine country offers a spectacular view, beautiful gardens, tennis court, swimming pool, hot tub, and bicycles. We have five spacious rooms with fresh flowers, fruit, king beds, and balconies. Full breakfast is served on the terrace, and we offer an evening dessert of homemade pie or cake.

Hosts: Mary Jane and Jerry Campbell
Rooms: 5 (PB) $100-145
Full Breakfast
Credit Cards: A, B
Notes: 2, 5, 10, 12

GUALALA

North Coast Country Inn
34591 South Highway 1, 95445
(707) 884-4537; (800) 995-4537

Picturesque redwood buildings on a forested hillside overlook the Pacific Ocean. The large guest suites feature fireplaces, decks, mini-kitchens, and authentic antique furnishings. Enjoy the romantic hot tub under the pines and the beautiful hilltop garden with gazebo. Near beaches, hiking, golf, tennis, horseback riding, state parks, and restaurants.

Hosts: Loren and Nancy Flanagan

Rooms: 4 (PB) $115
Full Breakfast
Credit Cards: A, B, C
Notes: 2, 5, 8, 10, 12

HALF MOON BAY

Old Thyme Inn

779 Main Street, 94019
(415) 726-1616

The Inn has 7 guest rooms, all with
private baths. We are a restored 1899
Queen Anne Victorian, located on historic Main Street in the downtown area.
Some rooms have fireplaces and double
size whirlpool tubs. The theme is our
English-style herb garden; all rooms
are named after herbs. Atmosphere is
friendly and informal. We serve beverages in the evening and a hearty breakfast each morning. Nearby activities
include: Golf, whale-watching,
tidepools, shopping. Many fine restaurants are close-by, some within walking distance.

Hosts: George and Marcia Dempsey
Rooms: 7 (PB) $65-210
Full Breakfast
Credit Cards: A, B
Notes: 2, 5, 8, 9, 10, 12

HEALDSBURG

Frampton House Bed and Breakfast

489 Powell Avenue, 95448
(707) 433-5084

This 1908 Victorian in the heart of wine
country offers two large rooms with
skylights, queen beds, tubs for two, and

views. Also, there is a small, romantic
retreat with two skylights, private deck,
and fabulous views. The sitting room
has a fireplace. Pool, spa, sauna,
ping-pong, bikes. Privacy and personalized attention with casual ambience.

Host: Paula Bogle
Rooms: 3 (PB) $70-95
Full Breakfast
Credit Cards: A, B
Notes: 2, 5, 7 (over 12), 8, 9, 10, 12 (10%)

Healdsburg Inn on the Plaza

110 Matheson Street, 95448
(707) 433-6991; (800) 491-2327

Come to a quiet place in the center of
town where history and hospitality
meet. Fireplaces, sunrise colors, good
things baking, and classical music all
add to the special feeling of the little
hotel. We have gift shops and a bakery
on the street floor. Breakfast is served
in the sun-filled solarium.

Host: Genny Jenkins
Rooms: 9 (PB) $75-155
Full Breakfast
Credit Cards: A, B
Notes: 2, 5, 8, 9, 10

HOMEWOOD

Rockwood Lodge

5295 West Lake Boulevard, 96141-0226
(916) 525-5273 or 800-LE TAHOE; FAX (916)
525-5949

Set back in the tall trees on the wooded
west shore of Tahoe, the lodge blends
in with its surroundings. There is his-

tory and elegance in this region, and Rockwood is a remnant of the "old Tahoe" and has all the requisites for a special sojourn: knotty pine walls, huge stone fireplace, sitting room, and an intimate atmosphere. Homey touches add to the enjoyment of a stay at Rockwood. This is the way a mountain chalet ought to be.

Host: Louis Reinkens
Rooms: 4 (2 PB; 2 SB) $90-200
Full Breakfast
Credit Cards: None
Notes: 2, 5, 8, 9, 10, 11,12

IONE

The Heirloom

214 Shakeley Lane, P.O. Box 322, 95640
(209) 274-4468

Travel down a country lane to a spacious, romantic English garden and a petite Colonial mansion built circa 1863. The house features balconies, fireplaces, and heirloom antiques, along with a gourmet breakfast and gracious hospitality. Located in the historic gold country, close to all major northern California cities. The area abounds with antiques, wineries, and historic sites.

Hosts: Melisande Hubbs and Patricia Cross
Rooms: 6 (4 PB; 2 SB) $50-85
Full Breakfast
Credit Cards: None
Closed Thanksgiving and Christmas
Notes: 2, 5, 10, 11, 12

JACKSON

Gate House Inn

1330 Jackson Gate Road, 95642
(209) 223-3500; (800) 841-1072

The Gate House Inn is a charming turn-of-the-century Victorian in the country on one acre of garden property with a swimming pool. Rooms are decorated with Victorian and country furnishings. One room has a fireplace, and the private cottage has a wood-burning stove. Walk to fine restaurants and historic sites. Three-star Mobil rated.

Hosts: Stan and Bev Smith
Rooms: 5 (PB) $75-105
Full Breakfast
Credit Cards: A, B, D
Notes: 2, 5, 7 (over 12), 8, 9, 10, 11, 12

JULIAN

Julian Gold Rush Hotel

2032 Main Street, P.O. Box 1856, 92036
(619) 765-0201; (800) 734-5854

Built almost 100 years ago by a freed slave and his wife, the hotel still reflects the dream and tradition of the genteel hospitality of the Victorian era. The "Queen of the Back Country" has the distinction of being the oldest continuously operating hotel in southern California. Listed on the National Register of Historic Places.

Hosts: Steve and Gig Ballinger
Rooms: 18 (5 PB; 13 SB) $64-145

year; 6 Pets welcome; 7 Children welcome; 8 Tennis nearby; 9 Swimming nearby; 10 Golf nearby; 11 Skiing nearby; 12 May be booked through travel agent

Full Breakfast
Credit Cards: A, B, C
Notes: 2, 5, 7, 8, 12

Julian Gold Rush Hotel

LAGUNA BEACH

Eiler's Inn

741 South Coast Highway, 92651
(714) 494-3004

Twelve rooms with private baths and a courtyard with gurgling fountain and colorful blooming plants are within walking distance of town and most restaurants; one-half block from the beach.

Hosts: Henk and Annette Wirtz
Rooms: 12 (PB) $100-130
Full Breakfast
Credit Cards: A, B, C
Notes: 2, 5, 8, 9, 10, 12

LAKE ARROWHEAD

Bluebelle House
Bed and Breakfast

263 South State Highway 173, P. O. Box 2177, 92352
(714) 336-3292; (800) 429-BLUE California

The cozy elegance of European decor in an alpine setting welcomes you to Bluebelle House. Guests appreciate immaculate housekeeping, exquisite breakfasts, warm hospitality, and relaxing by the fire or out on the deck. Walk to charming lakeside village, boating, swimming, and restaurants. Private beach club and ice skating are nearby; winter sports 30 minutes away.

Hosts: Rick and Lila Peiffer
Rooms: 5 (3 PB; 2 SB) $75-110
Full Breakfast
Credit Cards: A, B
Notes: 2, 5, 9, 11

LODI

Wine and Roses
Country Inn

2505 W. Turner Rd., 95242
(209) 334-6988; FAX (209) 334-6570

Nestled in a secluded five acre setting of towering trees and old-fashioned flower gardens, our inn is a beautiful, charming and romantic 90-year-old historical estate that has been converted to an elegant country inn with 9 guest rooms and a special 2-room suite with terrace. Handmade comforters, antiques, collectibles, fresh flowers, library, evening refreshments, delightful breakfast. Full restaurant featuring "wine country" dining for lunch, dinner and Sunday brunch. Lake with boating, swimming, fishing, golf, tennis, shopping, museum, zoo within 5 minutes. Delta Waterways, Old Sacramento Gold Country within 30 minutes.

Hosts: Kris Cromwell, and Del & Sherri Smith

NOTES: Credit cards accepted: A Master Card; B Visa; C American Express; D Discover Card; E Diners Club; F Other; 2 Personal checks accepted; 3 Lunch available; 4 Dinner available; 5 Open all

Rooms: 10 (PB) $79-125
Full Breakfast
Credit Cards: A, B, C
Notes: 2, 3, 4, 5, 7, 8, 9, 10, 12

LONG BEACH

Lord Mayor's Inn

435 Cedar Avenue, 90802
(310) 436-0324

An award-winning historical landmark, the 1904 home of the first mayor of Long Beach invites you to enjoy the ambience of years gone by. Rooms have 10-foot ceilings and are decorated with period antiques. Each unique bedroom has its private bath and is accessible to a large sundeck. Full breakfast is served in the dining room or deck overlooking the garden. Located near beaches, close by major attractions, within walking distance of convention and civic center and special events held downtown. The right touch for the business and vacation traveler.

Hosts: Laura and Reuben Brasser
Rooms: 5 (PB) $85-95
Full Breakfast
Credit Cards: A, B, C
Notes: 2, 5, 7, 9

LOS OSOS

Gerarda's Bed and Breakfast

1056 Bay Oaks Drive, 93402
(805) 528-3973

Gerarda's three-bedroom ranch-style home is comfortably furnished and of-fers wonderful ocean and mountain views from the elaborate flower gardens in front and back. Gerarda speaks five languages and will welcome you warmly. She cooks a wonderful family-style breakfast. You will be only a few miles from state parks, Morro Bay, Hearst Castle, San Luis Obispo, universities, and a shopping center.

Host: Gerarda Ondang
Rooms: 3 (1 PB; 2 SB) $30-45
Full Breakfast
Credit Cards: None
Notes: 2, 5, 8, 9, 10

LOTUS

Golden Lotus Bed and Breakfast

1006 Lotus Road, P.O. Box 830, 95651
(916) 621-4562

This 1857 country pre-Victorian, surrounded by flower and herb gardens, has six bedrooms, each decorated in a completely different style—early gold miner's quarters, oriental, secret garden, pirate's cabin, room of wishes, etc. Breakfast is served in extensive library or 1855 adjacent building. Inn has frontage on South Fork of America River and is one mile from Marshall Gold Discovery Park. Whitewater rafting is available. Antique store on site.

Hosts: Bruce and Jill Smith
Rooms: 6 (PB) $80-95 ($10 off weekdays)
Full Breakfast
Credit Cards: None
Notes: 2, 3, 4, 5, 7 (over 10) , 12

---

year; 6 Pets welcome; 7 Children welcome; 8 Tennis nearby; 9 Swimming nearby; 10 Golf nearby; 11 Skiing nearby; 12 May be booked through travel agent

MARIPOSA

Finch Haven

4605 Triangle Road, 95338
(209) 966-4738 (voice and FAX)

A quiet country home on 9 acres with panoramic mountain views. Birds, deer, and other abundant wildlife. Two rooms, each with private bath and private deck. Queen and twin beds. Nutritious breakfast. In the heart of the California Gold Rush Country near historic attractions. Convenient access to spectacular Yosemite Valley and Yosemite National Park. A restful place to practice Mark 6:31 and to enjoy Christian hospitality.

Hosts: Bruce and Carol Fincham
Rooms: 2 (PB) $65
Continental Plus
Credit Cards: A,B, C
Notes: 2, 5, 8, 9, 10, 11, 12

Meadow Creek Ranch B&B Inn

2669 Triangle Road, 95338
(209) 966-3843

Our 1858 historical ranch house has been compared to European inns. A restful, friendly atmosphere of trees and meadows await you. The old chicken coop is now a cozy country cottage with private bath, English fireplace, clawfoot tub and the sound of the old waterwheel turning out by the barn. You will enjoy our family style breakfast. Visit Yosemite National Park and travel the gold country.

Hosts: Bob and Carol Shockley (Owners)
Rooms: 4 (2PB; 3SB) $75-95
Full Country Breakfast
Credit Cards: A, B, C
Notes: 2, 5, 7 (12 and older) , 8, 9, 10, 11, 12

Oak Meadows, too Bed and Breakfast

5263 Highway 140 North, P. O. Box 619, 95338
(209) 742-6161

Just a short drive to Yosemite National Park, Oak Meadows, too is located in the historic Gold Rush town of Mariposa. Oak Meadows, too was built with New England architecture and turn-of-the-century charm. A stone fireplace greets you upon arrival in the guest parlor, where a continental-plus breakfast is served each morning. All rooms are furnished with handmade quilts, brass headboards, and charming wallpapers. Central heat and air conditioning.

Hosts: Frank Ross and Karen Black
Rooms: 6 (PB) $69-89
Expanded Continental Breakfast
Credit Cards: A, B
Notes: 2, 5, 11, 12 (10%)

MCCLOUD

McCloud Guest House

606 West Colombero Drive, P.O. Box 1510, 90657
(916) 964-3160

This lovely, old country home was built in 1907 and has been restored to its former glory by the owners/hosts. Five

---

NOTES: Credit cards accepted: A Master Card; B Visa; C American Express; D Discover Card; E Diners Club; F Other; 2 Personal checks accepted; 3 Lunch available; 4 Dinner available; 5 Open all

large bedrooms are individually decorated. Each has its own bath, three with
claw foot tubs. It is situated on parklike
grounds with rolling lawns, giant oaks,
and flowers stretching around the
16-foot wraparound veranda.

Hosts: Bill and Patti Leigh, Dennis and Pat
Abreu
Rooms: 5 (PB) $75-90
Expanded Continental Breakfast
Credit Cards: A, B
Notes: 2, 4, 5, 9, 10, 11

MENDOCINO

Blair House Inn
45110 Little Lake Rd, P.O. Box 1608, 95460
(707) 937-1800

Blair House is a Victorian home situated in the heart of Mendocino. All
rooms have queen size beds with
handcrafted quilts. Some rooms can
accommodate a third person or a child.
Oriental rugs grace the floors throughout the house. Antiques, Swedish and
early American furnishings complete
the elegance of this "Grand Dame" of
the Victorian era. Smoking is permitted on the porch and in the garden only.
This is the home featured as Jessica
Fletcher's home in the TV series, *Murder, She Wrote.*

Host: Norm Fluhrer
Rooms: 5 (3PB; 2SB) $70-125
Continental Breakfast
Credit Cards: A, B
Notes: 2, 5, 6, 7, 8, 10, 12

John Dougherty House
571 Ukiah Street, P. O. Box 817, 95460
(707) 937-5266

The historic John Dougherty House was
built in 1867 and is one of the oldest
houses in Mendocino. Located on land
bordered by Ukiah and Albion Streets,
the inn has some of the best ocean and
bay views in the village. Steps away
from great restaurants and shopping,
but years removed from 20th-century
reality. The inn is furnished with period
country antiques. Cottages, cabin, and
water tower.

Hosts: David and Marion Wells
Rooms: 6 (PB) $95-140
Expanded Continental Breakfast
Credit Cards: None
Notes: 2, 5

Mendocino Village Inn
44860 Main Street, Box 626, 95460
(707) 937-0246

Fog, fireplaces and Frog pond. Beach
trails, hearty breakfasts and good company. Feline follies and coastal whimsy.

Hosts: Bill and Kathleen Erwin
Rooms: 13 (11 PB; 2 SB) $65-185
Full Breakfast
Credit Cards: None
Notes: 2, 5, 8, 10

MT. SHASTA

Mt. Shasta Ranch Bed and Breakfast
1008 W. A. Barr Road, 96067
(916) 926-3870

The inn is situated in a rural setting with
a majestic view of Mt. Shasta and features a main lodge, carriage house, and

year; 6 Pets welcome; 7 Children welcome; 8 Tennis nearby; 9 Swimming nearby; 10 Golf nearby; 11
Skiing nearby; 12 May be booked through travel agent

cottage. Group accommodations are available. Our breakfast room is ideally suited for seminars and retreats with large seating capacity. The game room includes piano, Ping-Pong, pool table, and board games. Guests also enjoy an outdoor Jacuzzi. Nearby recreational facilities include alpine and Nordic skiing, fishing, hiking, mountain bike rentals, surrey rides, and museums. Call for pastor's discount.

Hosts: Bill and Marry Larsen
Rooms: 9 (4 PB; 5 SB) $55-75
Cabin: 1
Full Breakfast
Credit Cards: A, B, C
Notes: 2, 5, 7, 8, 9, 10, 11, 12

NAPA

Hennessey House Bed and Breakfast

1727 Main Street, 94559
(707) 226-3774

Hennessey House, a beautiful Eastlake-style Queen Anne Victorian located in downtown Napa, is listed in the National Register of Historic Places. It features antique furnishings, fireplaces, whirlpools, patios and a sauna. The dining room, where a sumptuous breakfast is served, features one of the finest examples of a hand-painted stamped tin ceiling in California. Just a short walk to the wine train!

Hosts: Lauriann and Andrea
Rooms: 10 (PB) $75-150
Full Breakfast
Credit Cards: A, B, C
Notes: 2, 5, 7, 10, 12

La Belle Epoque

1386 Calistoga Avenue, 94559
(707) 257-2161

This elegantly antique-filled Queen Anne Victorian is enhanced by a profusion of vintage and contemporary stamped glass. The inn has six tastefully decorated guestrooms, each with private bath, one with a cozy fireplace. A full gourmet-style breakfast is served each morning, either in the formal dining room by the fireside or in the plant-filled sunroom. Complimentary wine and appetizers served nightly in the wine room/cellar. Easy walk to Old Town Napa's shops, wine train, and opera house.

Hosts: Merlin and Claudia Wedepohl (owners)
Rooms: 6 (PB) $108-140
Full Gourmet Breakfast
Credit Cards: A, B, C, D
Notes: 2, 5, 8, 9, 10, 12

NEWPORT BEACH

Doryman's Oceanfront Inn B&B

2102 W. Oceanfront, 92663
(714) 675-7300

Romance, luxury, and resounding elegance await you at this spectacular oceanfront Victorian B & B. Enjoy intimate sunsets overlooking the vast Pacific. Hot cocoa and English butter cookies at bedtime and a complimentary breakfast brought right to your room. Rooms feature canopy beds, touch button fireplaces, Italian marble bathrooms with sunken jacuzzi tubs. Victorian and French country style antiques throughout; candlelit dinners upon request.

Hosts: Michael and Laura Palitz
Rooms: 10 (PB) $135-275
Delux Continental Breakfast
Credit Cards: A, B, C
Notes: 2, 3, 4, 5, 8, 9, 10, 11, 12

OAKHURST

Ople's Guest House
41118 Highway 41, 93644
(209) 683-4317

Set on a hill and half hidden by trees is the rambling style house where Yosemite travelers make a stop for the night. The easy-going atmosphere, the clean and pleasant accommodations, and affordable rates make Ople's Guest House a favorite in Oakhurst. Families are welcome, and guests may enjoy a fireplace and TV in the livingroom. You will appreciate the guest house that offers off-street parking and wheelchair access.

Host: Ople Smith
Rooms: 3 (SB) $40
Continental Breakfast
Credit Cards: A, B, D, F
Notes: 2, 5, 7, 8, 9, 10, 11, 12

PACIFIC GROVE

Gatehouse Inn Bed and Breakfast
225 Central Avenue, 93950
(800) 753-1881

Built in 1884, the historic Gatehouse Inn is a seaside Victorian home, with distinctive rooms, stunning views, private baths, fireplaces, patios, delicious breakfasts, afternoon wine and cheese. Walk to the ocean, Cannery Row, Monterey Bay Aquarium, shops and restaurants, 10 minutes from Carmel, Pebble Beach and world renowned golf courses.

Hosts: Doug and Kristi Aslin
Rooms: 8 (PB) $95-170
Full Breakfast
Credit Cards: A, B, C
Notes: 2, 5, 10, 12

The Gatehouse Inn Bed and Breakfast

Roserox Country Inn By-The-Sea
557 Ocean View Blvd. , 93950
(408) 373-7673

This historic 1904 mansion sits on the edge of the Pacific Ocean shoreline. The charming, four-story inn offers eight guest rooms with ocean views, beautifully decorated with designer linens and high, brass beds. Slippers to take home, imported French water, and a country breakfast will entice you. The famous cheese and wine hour is observed in the parlor around a cozy fireplace. Walk to Monterey Bay Aquarium, John Steinbeck's Cannery Row, swimming, golf, fishing, and whale watching.

year; 6 Pets welcome; 7 Children welcome; 8 Tennis nearby; 9 Swimming nearby; 10 Golf nearby; 11 Skiing nearby; 12 May be booked through travel agent

Hosts: Dawn and Vyette Browncroft
Rooms: 8 (SB) $126-206
Full Breakfast
Credit Cards: None
Notes: 2, 5, 8, 9, 10, 12

PALMSPRINGS

Casa Cody Bed and Breakfast Country Inn

175 South Cahuilla Road, 92262
(619) 320-9346

A romantic, historic hideaway is nestled against the spectacular San Jacinto Mountains in the heart of Palm Springs Village. Completely redecorated in Santa Fe decor, it has 17 ground-level units consisting of hotel rooms, studio suites, and one- and two-bedroom suites with private patios, fireplaces, fully equipped tiled kitchens. Cable TV and private phones; two pools; secluded, tree-shaded whirlpool spa.

Hosts: Therese Hayes and Frank Tysen
Rooms: 17 (PB) $35 summer midweek; $160 winter weekend
Continental Breakfast
Credit Cards: A, B, C
Notes: 2, 5, 6 (limited), 7 (limited), 8, 9, 10, 11

Sakura Japanese Bed and Breakfast

1677 N Via Miracestee at the corner of Vista Chino, 92262
(619) 327-0705

Unique, Japanese style inn, shoui windows, lanterns, kimonos, futons, garden. Japanese and American full breakfast; Japanese and vegetarian dinners served by request. Low cost B & B tours of Japan, Shiatsu Japanese accupressure massage, Japanese video movies. Over 80 golf courses in the area, as well as hiking, biking, tramway ride, tennis, horseback riding, hot air ballooning, and plenty of fine shops and restaurants. Winter daytime temperatures between 70 and 85 degrees.

Hosts: George and Fumiko Cebra
Rooms: 5 (SB) $45-65 (summer) $65-75 (October 1 - June 31)
Full Breakfast
Credit Cards: C
Notes: 2, 4, 5, 7, 8, 9, 10, 11, 12

PLACERVILLE

River Rock Inn

1756 Georgetown Drive, 95661
(916) 622-7640

Innkeeper Dorothy Irvin welcomes you to the gold country's River Rock Inn. Its comfortable rooms, tastefully furnished with antiques, front on the spacious deck with uninterrupted view of the river. The large living room encourages you to relax with TV, conversation or listening to the sounds of the river. Gold Mine tours, Marshall State Park, fishing, hiking, whitewater rafting are all available nearby. Hot tub on premises to relax in after activities.

Host: Dorothy Irvin
Rooms: 4 (2PB; 2 (half baths)) $75-90
Full Breakfast
Credit Cards: None
Notes: 2, 5, 7, 9, 10, 11, 12

NOTES: Credit cards accepted: A Master Card; B Visa; C American Express; D Discover Card; E Diners Club; F Other; 2 Personal checks accepted; 3 Lunch available; 4 Dinner available; 5 Open all

POINT REYES STATION

Carriage House
Bed and Breakfast

325 Mesa Road, P.O. Box 1239, 94956
(415) 663-8627

Adjacent to the Point Reyes National Seashore, one hour north of San Francisco. Built in the 1920s and recently remodeled into two peaceful spacious suites. Bedrooms with queen bed, living room with fireplace, queen size sleeping couch, single daybed. Full baths, complete kitchens, TV, outdoor BBQs. Families welcome, childcare available with advance notice. Over 100 miles of nearby trails for hiking, bicycling, horseback riding, bird watching, beach combing and whale watching. Suite can accommodate 5.

Host: Felicity Kirsch
Rooms: 2 (PB) $100-120
Choice of Continental or Full Breakfast
Credit Cards: None
Notes: 2, 5, 7, 8, 10, 12

The Tree House

73 Drake Summit, P.O. Box 1075, 94956
(415) 663-8720

The Tree House sits close to all the most interesting points of this beautiful community. The beaches, the lighthouse, the visitor center of the National Seashore and the numerous hiking trails...you can enjoy your evening eating out, or just stay at the Tree House and Bar B Que some oysters and sip wine by the fire.

Host: Lisa Pastel
Rooms: 3 (PB) $80-95
Full Breakfast
Credit Cards: None
Notes: 2, 5, 6, 7

ST. HELENA

Bartels Ranch
and Country Inn

1200 Conn Valley Road, 94574
(707) 963-4001; FAX (707) 963-5100

Situated in the heart of the world-famous Napa Valley wine country is this secluded, romantic, elegant country estate overlooking a "100-acre valley with a 10,000-acre view." Honeymoon "Heart of the Valley" suite has sunken Jacuzzi, sauna, shower, stone fireplace, and private deck with vineyard view. Romantic, award-winning accommodations, expansive entertainment room, poolside lounging, personalized itineraries, afternoon refreshments, pool table, fireplace, library and terraces overlooking the vineyard. Bicycle to nearby wineries, lake, golf, tennis, fishing, boating, mineral spas and bird watching.

Host: Jami Bartels
Rooms: 4 (PB) $99-275
Expanded Continental Breakfast
Credit Cards: A, B, C, D
Notes: 2, 3, 4, 5, 8, 9, 10, 12

Cinnamon Bear
Bed and Breakfast

1407 Kearney Street, 94574
(707) 963-4653

year; 6 Pets welcome; 7 Children welcome; 8 Tennis nearby; 9 Swimming nearby; 10 Golf nearby; 11 Skiing nearby; 12 May be booked through travel agent

Cinnamon Bear is furnished in the style of the 1920s with many fine antiques. Gleaming hardwood floors and Oriental carpets add to its unique elegance. Relax in front of the fireplace in the living room, or watch the world go by on the spacious front porch. Puzzles, games, and books are available in the parlor for your enjoyment, or peruse a selection of local menus.

Host: Genny Jenkins
Rooms: 4 (PB) $75-150
Full Breakfast
Credit Cards: A, B
Notes: 2, 5, 8, 9, 10

Erika's Hillside
285 Fawn Park, 94574
(707) 963-2887

You will be welcomed with warm, European hospitality when you arrive at this hillside chalet that is more than 100 years old. Just two miles from St. Helena, you will find a peaceful and romantic, wooded country setting with a view of vineyards and wineries. The spacious, airy rooms have private entrances and bath, fireplace, and hot tub. Continental breakfast and German specialties are served on the patio or in the garden room.

Host: Erika Cunningham
Rooms: 3 (PB) $65-165
Continental Breakfast
Credit Cards: C
Notes: 2, 5, 7, 8, 9, 10, 12

SAN FRANCISCO

Amsterdam Hotel
749 Taylor Street, 94108
(415) 673-3277; (800) 637-3444; FAX (415) 673-0453

Originally built in 1909, the hotel reflects the charm of a small European hotel. It is situated on Nob Hill, just two blocks from the cable car.

Host: Orisa
Rooms: 31 (26 PB; 5 SB) $49-70
Continental Breakfast
Credit Cards: A, B, C
Notes: 5, 8, 9, 11

Casa Arguello
225 Arguello Boulevard, 94118
(415) 752-9482

Comfortable rooms in this cheerful, elegant flat are only 15 minutes from the center of town in a desireable residential neighborhood convenient to Golden Gate Park, the Presidio, Gold Gate Bridge, restaurants, and shops. Public transportation is at the corner.

Hosts: Emma Baires and Marina McKenzie
Rooms: 5 (3 PB; 2 SB) $50-75
Expanded Continental Breakfast
Credit Cards: None
Notes: 2, 5, 7, 8, 9, 10

The Chateau Tivoli Bed and Breakfast Inn
1057 Steiner Street, 94115
(415) 776-5462; (800) 228-1647

The chateau is a landmark mansion built in 1892. Guests experience a time travel journey back to San Francisco's

---

NOTES: Credit cards accepted: A Master Card; B Visa; C American Express; D Discover Card; E Diners Club; F Other; 2 Personal checks accepted; 3 Lunch available; 4 Dinner available; 5 Open all

golden age of opulence. Choose from five rooms, two with fireplaces, and two suites; all with phones. Breakfast is served in guest rooms or in the dining room. Near shops, restaurants, opera, and symphony. Reservation deposit required.

Hosts: Rodney, Willard, and Shiobhan
Rooms: 7 (5 PB; 2 SB) $80-200
Full Breakfast; Continental breakfast weekdays
Credit Cards: A, B, C
Notes: 2, 5, 7, 8, 9, 10, 12

The Monte Cristo
600 Presidio Avenue, 94115
(415) 931-1875

The Monte Cristo has been a part of San Francisco since 1875, located two blocks from the elegantly restored Victorian shops, restaurants, and antique stores on Sacramento Street. There is convenient transportation to downtown San Francisco and to the financial district. Each room is elegantly furnished with authentic period pieces.

Host: George Yuan
Rooms: 14 (11 PB; 3 SB) $63-108
Full Buffet Breakfast
Credit Cards: A, B, C, D, E
Notes: 5, 7, 12

SAN GREGORIO

Rancho San Gregorio
Route 1, Box 54, 94074 (hwy 84)
(415) 747-0810; FAX (415) 747-0184

Five miles inland from the Pacific Ocean is an idyllic rural valley where Rancho San Gregorio welcomes travelers to share relaxed hospitality. Picnic, hike, or bike in wooded parks or on ocean beaches. Our country breakfast features local specialties. Located 45 minutes from San Francisco, Santa Cruz, and the bay area.

Hosts: Bud and Lee Raynor
Rooms: 4 (PB) $65-135
Full Breakfast
Credit Cards: A, B, C
Notes: 2, 5, 7, 10

SANTA BARBARA

Blue Quail Inn and Cottages
1908 Bath Street, 93101
(800) 676-1622 U.S.A.; (800) 549-1622
California

Cottages and suites in a delightfully relaxing country setting are close to town and beaches. A delectable full breakfast, afternoon light hors d'oeuvres, and evening sweets and hot spiced apple cider are served. Guests have use of our bicycles. Three blocks to Sansum Clinic and Cottage Hospital. Picnic lunches and gift certificates available. Off-season midweek and extended-stay discounts.

Host: Jeanise Suding Eaton
Rooms: 9 (PB) $74-165
Full Breakfast
Credit Cards: A, B, C
Notes: 2, 3, 5, 7, 8, 9, 10, 12

Chesire Cat Inn Bed and Breakfast
36 W. Valerio Street, 93101
(805) 569-1610

---

year; 6 Pets welcome; 7 Children welcome; 8 Tennis nearby; 9 Swimming nearby; 10 Golf nearby; 11 Skiing nearby; 12 May be booked through travel agent

Victorian elegance in Southern California seaside village. The Cheshire Cat is conveniently situated near theaters, restaurants and shops. Decorated exclusively in Laura Ashley papers and linens, the sunny guest rooms have private baths; some with jacuzzis, balconies. Free bicycles are available for guest use. Collectibles, English antiques, and fresh flowers enhance your stay in beautiful Santa Barbara.

Host: Christine Dunstan (owner) Margaret Goeden (manager)
Rooms: 14 (PB) $79-190 Midweek, $119-249 Weekend
Full Breakfast
Credit Cards: A, B
Notes: 2, 5, 7, 8, 9, 10, 12

Long's Seaview Bed and Breakfast

317 Piedmont Road, 93105
(805) 687-2947

This ranch-style home overlooking Santa Barbara has views of the ocean and Channel Islands. The guest room with private entrance is furnished with antiques and king bed. A huge patio and gardens are available. Near all attractions, beach, and Solvang. Your friendly host will be happy to provide you with maps and information about the area.

Host: LaVerne Long
Room: 1 (PB) $70-75
Full Breakfast
Credit Cards: None
Notes: 2, 7 (over 10), 8, 9, 10

The Old Yacht Club Inn

431 Corona Del Mar Drive, 93103
(805) 962-1277; (800) 549-1676 California
(800) 676-1676 U.S.A.; FAX (805) 962-3989

The inn at the beach! These 1912 California craftsman and 1925 early California-style homes house nine individually decorated guest rooms furnished with antiques. Bicycles, beach chairs, and towels are included, and an evening social hour is provided. Gourmet dinner is available on Saturdays.

Hosts: Nancy, Sandy, and Lu
Rooms: 9 (PB) $65-140
Full Breakfast
Credit Cards: A, B, C, D
Notes: 2, 4 (Saturdays), 5, 7, 8, 9, 10, 12

Parsonage Bed and Breakfast

1600 Olive St., 93101
(805) 962-9336

Queen Anne Victorian built in 1892. Spectacular honeymoon suite. Views of the ocean, city and mountains. Period furnishing create a unique and elegant atmosphere throughout the house and in each individually decorated room. Generous homemade breakfast served on the sundeck or in the formal dining room by the cozy fireplace.

Host: Holli Harmon
Rooms: 6 (PB) $70-185
Full Breakfast
Credit Cards: A, B, C
Notes: 2, 5, 8, 9, 12

NOTES: Credit cards accepted: A Master Card; B Visa; C American Express; D Discover Card; E Diners Club; F Other; 2 Personal checks accepted; 3 Lunch available; 4 Dinner available; 5 Open all

Simpson House Inn

121 East Arrellaga, 93101
(805) 963-7067; (800) 676-1280

Secluded on one acre of English gardens, this beautiful Eastlake-style Victorian home, circa 1874, is just a five-minute walk to Santa Barbara's restaurants, theaters, museums, and shops. Lovingly restored, it is elegantly appointed with antiques, English lace, Oriental carpets, large comfortable beds with goose down comforters, fresh flowers, and claw foot tubs. Enjoy fresh California juices and fruits, the finest of coffees and teas, and homemade breads. Rooms with fireplaces and private decks overlooking gardens.

Hosts: Gillean Wilson, Linda, and Glyn Davies
Rooms: 12 (PB) $75-150
Full Breakfast
Credit Cards: A, B, C, D
Notes: 2, 5, 8, 9

Valli's View

Valli's View

340 N. Sierra Vista Rd., 93108
(805) 969-1272

You'll love this beautiful home, its gardens, sunny patios, shady deck, and ever changing mountain views. The charming guest room has color TV and private bath. The spacious back patios offer lounges for sunning and porch swings for relaxing. A shady fern garden surrounds the deck that overlooks mountains and valley. In the evening relax in the living room around grand piano and fireplace. This is a place God has blessed us with and we enjoy sharing it with others.

Hosts: Valli and Larry Stevens
Rooms: 1 (PB) $75
Full Breakfast
Credit Cards: None
Notes: 2, 5, 6 (outside), 7 ,8 ,9 ,10 ,12

SANTA CRUZ

Babbling Brook Inn

1025 Laurel Street, 95060
(408) 427-2437; (800) 866-1131;
FAX (408) 427-2457

The foundations of the inn date back to the 1790s when padres from the local mission built a grist mill to take advantage of the stream to grind corn. In the 19th century, a water wheel generated power for a tannery. Then a few years later, a rustic log cabin was built, which remains as the heart of the inn. Most of the rooms are chalets in the garden, surrounded by pines and redwoods, cascading waterfalls, and gardens.

Host: Helen King
Rooms: 12 (PB) $85-135
Full Breakfast
Credit Cards: A, B, C, D, E
Notes: 2, 5, 8, 9, 10, 12

year; 6 Pets welcome; 7 Children welcome; 8 Tennis nearby; 9 Swimming nearby; 10 Golf nearby; 11 Skiing nearby; 12 May be booked through travel agent

The Darling House, A Bed and Breakfast Inn by the Sea

314 West Cliff Drive, 95060
(408) 458-1958; (800) 458-1958

This 1910 oceanside architectural masterpiece designed by William Weeks is lighted by the rising sun through beveled glass and Tiffany lamps. The spacious lawns, rose gardens, citrus orchard, towering palms, and expansive ocean-view verandas create colorful California splendor in an atmosphere of peaceful elegance. Stroll to secluded beaches, lighthouse, wharf, and boardwalk. Complimentary gourmet dinner weekdays except holidays.

Hosts: Darrell and Karen Darling
Rooms: 8 (2 PB; 6 SB) $85-225
Continental Breakfast
Credit Cards: A, B, C, D
Notes: 2, 4, 5, 7, 8, 9, 10, 12

SEAL BEACH

The Seal Beach Inn and Gardens

212 Fifth Street, 90740
(310) 493-2416

Just outside Los Angeles and 20 miles from Disneyland, nestled in a charming beachside community, is The Seal Beach Inn, French Mediterranean in style. Our Old World inn is surrounded by wrought iron balconies and lush gardens. The rooms vary, but all are furnished with antiques, hand-painted tiles, and lace comforters. Sit by the fireplace in our library, or listen to the fountains. Suites and all the services of a fine hotel are available.

Hosts: Marjorie Bettenhausen and Harty Schmaehl
Rooms: 23 (PB) $108-175
Full Breakfast
Credit Cards: A, B, C, D, F
Notes: 3, 5, 6 (by arrangement), 8, 9, 10, 11, 12

SONOMA

Sparrow's Nest Inn

424 Denmark St., 95476
(707) 996-3750

Sparrow's Nest Inn is a charming country cottage in the historic town of Sonoma. It is near the lovely town square and 45 minutes from the glorious Golden Gate Bridge. Surrounded by private flower gardens and patio, the one-bedroom cottage includes a small kitchen, breakfast nook, living room with phone and cable television, and bathroom. The decor is light, pleasing and comfortable English country style. We hope to make your visit enjoyable and memorable!

Hosts: Thomas and Kathleen Anderson
Rooms: 1 (single cottage) (PB) $85-105
Both Full and Continental Breakfast available
Credit Cards: A, B
Notes: 2, 5, 6 (by special arrangement), 7 (over 10 yrs old), 10

NOTES: Credit cards accepted: A Master Card; B Visa; C American Express; D Discover Card; E Diners Club; F Other; 2 Personal checks accepted; 3 Lunch available; 4 Dinner available; 5 Open all

SOQUEL

Blue Spruce Inn

2815 S. Main Street, 95073
(408) 464-1137 or (800) 559-1137

Spa tubs, fireplaces, quiet gardens and original local art foster relaxation for our guests. Our 1875 frame house, located near the north coast of the Monterey Bay, blends the flavor of yesterday with the luxury of today. Enjoy a hike in the redwoods, bike through the coastal fields, walk to outstanding restaurants. Fresh and unpretentious as a sea breeze, professional personal attention is our hallmark.

Hosts: Pat and Tom O'Brien
Rooms: 5 (PB) $80-125
Full Breakfast
Credit Cards: A, B, C
Notes: 2, 5, 8, 9, 10, 12

SPRINGVILLE

Annie's Bed and Breakfast

33024 Glore Dr., 93625
(209) 539-3827

Situated on 5 acres in the beautiful Sierra Foothills, this inn features beautiful antiques, feather beds and handmade quilts. Full Country Breakfast is prepared on an antique wood cookstove. The host has a custom saddle shop and a horse training facility on the property. Guests are welcome to come out and watch. Annie's is a great place to relax and enjoy the peace and quiet of country life.

Hosts: John and Annie Bozanich
Rooms: 3 (PB) $75-85
Full Breakfast
Credit Cards: A, B, C, E
Notes: 2, 4, 5, 8, 9, 10, 12

SUMMERLAND

Summerland Inn

2161 Ortega Hill Road, P. O. Box 1209, 93067
(805) 969-5225

Located minutes from beautiful Santa Barbara, this newly built New England-style bed and breakfast is a must for southern California travelers. Enjoy ocean views, fireplace rooms, brass and four-poster beds, country folk ark, biblical quotations, and Christian motifs. Christian reading material is available. All rooms include cable TV and free local calls.

Host: James Farned
Rooms: 11 (PB) $55-130 (10% discount to
Christian Bed and Breakfast Directory patrons)
Continental Breakfast
Credit Cards: A, B, C, E
Notes: 2, 5, 7, 8, 9, 10

SUSANVILLE

The Roseberry House

609 North Street, 96130
(916) 257-5675

The Roseberry House was built in 1902. It has unique Victorian styling and spacious upstairs rooms. Breakfast is served in the large formal dining room, while early-morning coffee is available in the upstairs hall. Chocolates and other treats are served in the evening, and bicycles are available for guests to use. We have

year; 6 Pets welcome; 7 Children welcome; 8 Tennis nearby; 9 Swimming nearby; 10 Golf nearby; 11 Skiing nearby; 12 May be booked through travel agent

warm summer days, spectacular autumn colors, and often a white Christmas.

Hosts: Bill and Maxine Ashmore
Rooms: 4 (PB) $50-70
Full Breakfast
Credit Cards: A, B, C
Notes: 2, 5, 8, 9, 10, 11

SUTTER CREEK

Sutter Creek Inn

75 Main Street, P.O. Box 385, 95685
(209) 267-5606; (209) 267-0642

The inn is known for its fireplaces, hanging beds, and private patios. All rooms have private baths and electric blankets. All guests gather 'round the kitchen fireplace to enjoy a hot breakfast. A large library in the livingroom invites guests to while away the time before afternoon refreshments.

Host: Jane Way
Rooms: 19 (PB) $45-135
Full Breakfast
Credit Cards: None
Notes: 2, 5, 7, 8, 9, 10, 11, 12

Oak Hill Ranch Bed and Breakfast

TOULUMNE

Oak Hill Ranch Bed and Breakfast

18550 Connally Ln, P.O. Box 307, 95379
(209) 928-4717

A real treat awaits you here in a traditional Victorian home bed and breakfast, providing all the comforts, amenities and pampering you naturally expect. Located in California's famed gold country near Yosemite and State Historic Parks at 3,000 feet elevation on our 56 wooded acres, we are minutes from winter and summer recreation resorts and super shopping centers. A full country breakfast is included in our moderate rates. Private baths, queen beds, fireplaces. Charming Victorian decor in four bedrooms and private cottage.

Hosts: Sanford and Jane Grover
Rooms: 5 (3PB; 2SB) $67-110
Full Breakfast
Credit Cards: None
Notes: 2, 5, 8, 9, 10, 11

TRINIDAD

Trinidad Bed and Breakfast

560 Edwards Street, P. O. Box 849, 95570
(707) 677-0840

Our Cape Cod-style home overlooks beautiful Trinidad Bay and offers spectacular views of the rugged coastline and fishing harbor below. Two suites, one with fireplace, and two upstairs bedrooms are available. We are surrounded by dozens of beaches, trails, and Redwood National Parks; within walking distance of restaurants and shops. Breakfast delivered to guests staying in suites, while a family-style breakfast is served to guests in rooms. Closed Monday and Tuesday, November 1 to February 28.

Hosts: Paul and Carol Kirk
Rooms: 4 (PB) $105-145

NOTES: Credit cards accepted: A Master Card; B Visa; C American Express; D Discover Card; E Diners Club; F Other; 2 Personal checks accepted; 3 Lunch available; 4 Dinner available; 5 Open all

Expanded Continental Breakfast
Credit Cards: A, B, D
Notes: 2, 5

UKIAH

Vichy Hot Springs Resort and Inn

2605 Vichy Springs Road, 95482
(707) 462-9515

Vichy Springs is a delightful two-hour drive north of San Francisco. Historic cottages and rooms await with delightful vistas from all locations. Vichy Springs features naturally sparkling 90-degree mineral baths, a communal 104-degree pool, and Olympic-size pool, along with 700 private acres with trails and roads for hiking, jogging, picnicking, and mountain bicycling. Vichy's idyllic setting is a quiet, healing environment.

Hosts: Gilbert and Marjorie Ashoff
Rooms: 14 (PB) $110-160
Full Breakfast
Credit Cards: A, B, C, D, E, F
Notes: 2, 5, 7, 8, 9, 10, 12

VENTURA

La Mer

411 Poli Street, 93001
(805) 643-3600

Built in 1890, this is a romantic European getaway in a Victorian Cape Cod home. A historic landmark nestled on a green hillside overlooking the spectacular California coastline. The distinctive guest rooms, all with private entrances, are each a European adventure, furnished in European antiques to capture the feeling of a specific country. Bavarian buffet-style breakfast and complimentary refreshments; midweek packages; horse carriage rides.

Host: Gisela Flender Baida
Rooms: 5 (PB) $80-155
Full Breakfast
Credit Cards: A, B
Notes: 2, 5, 8, 9, 10, 12

WESTPORT

Howard Creek Ranch

P. O. Box 121, 95488
(707) 964-6725

Howard Creek Ranch is a historic 1867 oceanfront farm bordered by miles of beach and mountains in a wilderness area. Flower gardens, antiques, fireplaces, redwoods, a 75-foot swinging foot bridge over Howard Creek, cabins, hot tub, sauna, cold pool, and nearby horseback riding are combined with comfort, hospitality, and good food.

Hosts: Charles and Sally Grigg
Rooms: 9 (6 PB; 3 SB) $60-110
Full Breakfast
Credit Cards: A, B
Notes: 2, 5, 6 (by arrangement), 7 (by arrangement)

WHITTIER

Coleen's California Casa

P. O. Box 9302, 90608
(310) 699-8427

Coleen's California Casa is located less than five minutes from the freeway in a quiet residential area. There is a lovely view of the city from the front deck. After a day's outing, enjoy hors

year; 6 Pets welcome; 7 Children welcome; 8 Tennis nearby; 9 Swimming nearby; 10 Golf nearby; 11 Skiing nearby; 12 May be booked through travel agent

d'oeuvres. Dinner is also available if requested in advance. Children are welcome here, and the house is convenient to Disneyland, Knott's Berry Farm, and most Los Angeles attractions.

Host: Coleen Davis
Rooms: 3 (PB) $60-85
Full Breakfast
Credit Cards: None
Notes: 2, 3, 4, 5, 7, 8, 9, 10

YOUNTVILLE

Bordeaux House

6600 Washington Street, 94599
(707) 944-2855

The formal red brick building is nestled in lush gardens like a building half-English, half-French. Bordeaux House is well off the main Napa Valley highway but quickly accessible to it, and is only a little more than one hour from San Francisco. In the spacious rooms, ornamentation has been kept to a minimum. Individual patios provide leisurely views across the sea of vines.

Rooms: 6 (PB) $95-120
Continental Breakfast
Credit Cards: A, B, C, D, E
Notes: 5, 12

Sybron House

7400 St. Helena Hwy, 94599
(707) 944-2785

Victorian style home with spectacular hilltop location, set in very heart of the Napa Valley. All guest rooms have high brass ceilings, queen beds, private baths and are tastefully decorated with antiques. Guests enjoy a large common

area room complete with grand piano, fireplace, wet bar, library, sunroom, balcony, and panoramic view. Private tennis court available to all guests. Tennis pro available for private lessons and tennis packages. Secluded, yet conveniently located to everything.

Hosts: Cheryl Maddox and Sybil Maddox
Rooms: 4 (PB) $115-160
Expanded Continental Breakfast
Credit Cards: A, B, C
Notes: 2, 8, 9, 10, 12

YUBA CITY

Moore Mansion Inn

560 Cooper Ave., 95991
(916) 674-8559

Constructed in the early 1920s by Charles Moore, owner of the Omega Gold Mine, a craftsman cottage that has retained its original atmosphere. Oak paneling, leaded glass windows, French doors and original brass all add to the ambience of the seventeen-room, historically rich home. Five beautifully decorated sleeping rooms and ample off-street parking.

Hosts: Peggy Harden
Rooms: 5 (PB) $65-85
Full Breakfast
Credit Cards: A, B
Notes: 5, 7, 8, 9, 10, 12

NOTES: Credit cards accepted: A Master Card; B Visa; C American Express; D Discover Card; E Diners Club; F Other; 2 Personal checks accepted; 3 Lunch available; 4 Dinner available; 5 Open all

Colorado

ALLENSPARK

Allenspark Lodge

184 Main, 80510
(303) 747-2552

A classic high mountain bed and breakfast, nestled in a flower-starred village.
Comfortable rooms, warm hospitality
and magnificent surroundings make our
historic, cozy, beautifully remodeled
lodge the ideal place for that vacation
weekend, reception, reunion or retreat.
Let the magic begin! Hot tub, continental breakfast, hospitality and game room,
near Rocky Mountain National Park.

Hosts: Mike and Becky Osmun
Rooms: 14 (5PB; 9SB) $39.95-74.95
Continental Breakfast
Credit Cards: A, B, D
Notes: 2, 3, 4, 5, 7, 11, 12

ASPEN

Little Red Ski Haus

118 East Cooper, 81611
(303) 925-3333

We are a quaint historic lodge that has
had only one owner for 30 years. The
100-year-old Victorian house has additional rooms for a total of 21 bedrooms.

Christian hosts look forward to welcoming Christian groups to their lodge.
Rates vary depending on number of
guests and private or shared baths.

Hosts: Marge Babcock Rily and Jeannene
Babcock
Rooms: 21 (4 PB; 17 SB) $70-110
Continental Breakfast in summer/fall
Includes Full Breakfast
Credit Cards: A, B, C
Notes: 7, 8, 9, 10, 11

BOULDER

Briar Rose Bed and Breakfast

2151 Arapahoe Ave, 80302
(303) 442-3007

Elegant small inn close to University of
Colorado and downtown. Unique
rooms have period antiques, featherbed
comforters, fresh flowers and good
books. Friendly attentive service includes afternoon and evening tea with
our own shortbread cookies. Big breakfast served in dining room or on sun
porch.

Hosts: Margaret and Bob Weisenbach
Rooms: 9 (PB) $80-105
Expanded Continental Breakfast
Credit Cards: A, B, C, E
Notes: 2, 5, 7, 8, 10, 11, 12

---

year; 6 Pets welcome; 7 Children welcome; 8 Tennis nearby; 9 Swimming nearby; 10 Golf nearby; 11
Skiing nearby; 12 May be booked through travel agent

BRECKENRIDGE

Allaire Timbers Inn

9511 Hwy #9, South Main St., PO Box 4653,
80424
(303) 453-7530; (800) 624-4904

Breckenridge's distinctive new mountain inn. Nestled in the trees at the south end of Main Street, this log house offers uniquely decorated guest rooms. Two suites boast private fireplace and hot tub. Relax by a crackling fire in the log and beam Greatroom. Unwind in the outdoor spa overlooking spectacular views of Breckenridge and Ten Mile Range. Gourmet breakfasts. Wheelchair accessible.

Hosts: Jack and Kathy Gumph
Rooms: 10 (PB) $95-210
Full Breakfast—ski season; Continental
Breakfast—summer
Credit Cards: A, B, C, D
Notes: 2, 5, 10, 11, 12

CASCADE

Eastholme
Bed and Breakfast

4445 Haggerman St., P.O. Box 98, 80809
(719) 684-9901

This charming 1885 Victorian structure, nestled in the Pikes Peak mountain village of Cascade, is the perfect headquarters for a Colorado vacation. Located just six miles west of Colorado Springs, only fifteen minutes from downtown, Eastholme is midway between the Air Force Academy and Cripple Creek, making it close to everywhere. A designated landmark, Eastholme received Colorado's Historical Preservation Award for 1989. Features include forty-foot porch and balcony, guest parlor, kitchen, hiking trails, affordable.

Hosts: Harland and Joanne Jacobson
Rooms: 6 (4PB; 2SB) $44-69
Full Breakfast
Credit Cards: None
Notes: 2, 5, 12

COLORADO SPRINGS

Holden House—1902
Bed and Breakfast Inn

1102 West Pikes Peak Avenue, 80904
(719) 471-3980

This historic 1902 storybook Victorian and 1906 carriage house are filled with antiques and family treasures. Five lovely guest rooms (three suites) boast feather pillows, individual decor, period furnishings, and queen beds. Suites include fireplaces and "tubs for two." Centrally located just one mile west of downtown near the historic district, shopping, restaurants, and attractions, the inn is in a residential area. The romance of the past with the comforts of today.

Hosts: Sallie and Welling Clark
Rooms: 5 (PB) $60-90
Full Breakfast
Credit Cards: A, B, C, D
Notes: 2, 5, 8, 9, 10, 11

NOTES: Credit cards accepted: A Master Card; B Visa; C American Express; D Discover Card; E Diners Club; F Other; 2 Personal checks accepted; 3 Lunch available; 4 Dinner available; 5 Open all

DENVER

Castle Marne - A Luxury Urban Inn

1572 Race Street, 80203
(303) 331-0621

Come fall under the spell of one of Denver's grandest historic mansions. Your stay at the Castle Marne combines old-world elegance with modern-day convenience and comfort. Each guest room is a unique experience in pampered luxury. All rooms have private baths. Afternoon tea and a full gourmet breakfast are served in the cherry paneled dining room. Castle Marne is a certified Denver Landmark and on the National Register of Historic Structures.

Hosts: The Parker Family
Rooms: 9 (PB) $80-155
Full Breakfast
Credit Cards: A, B, C, D, E, F
Notes: 2, 3, 4, 5, 8, 9, 10, 11, 12

Queen Anne Inn

2147 Tremont Place, 80205
(303) 296-6666; (800) 432-INNS

Two Queen Anne Victorians facing Benedict Park in the Clement Historic District in downtown Denver. Private baths, phones, fresh flowers, classical music in all rooms. Air conditioned. Free parking. Most honored B&B in Colorado.

Host: Tom King
Rooms: 14 (PB) $75-150

Expanded Continental Breakfast
Credit Cards: A, B, C, D,
Notes: 2, 5, 8, 9, 10, 11, 12

DOLORES

Mountain View Bed and Breakfast

28050 County Road P, 81323
(303) 882-7861; (800) 228-4592

Mountain View is located halfway between Cortez and Dolores in the four corners area of southwestern Colorado. We are 12 miles from the entrance to Mesa Verde National Park, 6 miles from the Dolores River and McPhee Reservoir and 8 miles from the beautiful San Juan National Forest and its 14,000-foot peaks. The lodge itself is situated on the east slope of the Montezuma Valley on 22 wooded acres with canyon, stream, hiking trails, large lawn, decks and porches all around.

Hosts: Brenda and Cecil Dunn
Rooms: 6 (PB) $45-55
Full Breakfast
Credit Cards: A, B
Notes: 2, 5, 7, 9, 10, 12

DURANGO

Country Sunshine Bed and Breakfast

35130 Highway 550 North, 81301
(303) 247-2853; (800) 383-2853

This spacious ranch home on the Animas River has Ponderosa pines, quilts, and

year; 6 Pets welcome; 7 Children welcome; 8 Tennis nearby; 9 Swimming nearby; 10 Golf nearby; 11 Skiing nearby; 12 May be booked through travel agent

an informal atmosphere. It is a safe place for children and adults. A spacious hot springs spa is available to relax in, and there are plenty of common areas. The friendly hosts are in their fourth season.

Hosts: Jim and Jill Anderson
Rooms: 6 (PB) $70-85
Full Breakfast
Credit Cards: A, B
Notes: 2, 7, 10, 12

Logwood Bed and Breakfast—The Verheyden Inn

35060 U. S. Highway 550, 81301
(303) 259-4396

Built in 1988, this 4800-square-foot red cedar log home sits on 15 acres amid the beautiful San Juan Mountains and beside the Animas River. Guest rooms are decorated with a southwestern flair. Homemade country quilts adorn the country made queen size beds. Private baths in all guest rooms. A large river rock fireplace warms the elegant living and dining areas in the winter season. Award-winning desserts are served in the evening. Pamper yourselves; come home to LOGWOOD.

Host: Debby and Greg Verheyden
Rooms: 5 (PB) $65-75
Full Breakfast
Credit Cards: A, B
Notes: 2, 5, 7 (over six), 9, 10, 11, 12

GEORGETOWN

The Hardy House Bed and Breakfast Inn

605 Brownell, P. O. Box 0156, 80444
(303) 569-3388

The Hardy House, with its late-19th-century charm, invites you to relax in the parlor by the pot-bellied stove, sleep under feather comforters, and enjoy a savory breakfast. Georgetown is only 55 minutes from Denver and the airport. Surrounded by mountains, it boasts unique shopping, wonderful restaurants, and close proximity to seven ski areas.

Host: Sarah Schmidt
Rooms: 4 (PB) $57-72
Full Breakfast
Credit Cards: A, B
Notes: 2, 5, 7 (over 7), 11

GREEN MOUNTAIN FALLS

Outlook Lodge Bed and Breakfast

Box 5, 6975 Howard St., 80819
(719) 684-2303

A quaint lodge nestled at the foot of Pike's Peak. Built in 1889 as the parsonage for the Church of the Wildwood. Features stained-glass windows and hand-carved balustrades. Rooms furnished with brass beds and other antiques. Rates include a full breakfast. Nearby swimming, hiking, tennis, fishing, horseback riding, restaurants and shopping. Outlook Lodge provides

---

NOTES: Credit cards accepted: A Master Card; B Visa; C American Express; D Discover Card; E Diners Club; F Other; 2 Personal checks accepted; 3 Lunch available; 4 Dinner available; 5 Open all

nostalgia with a relaxing atmosphere.

Hosts: Hayley and Patrick Moran
Rooms: 9 (6PB; 3SB) $50-75
Full Breakfast
Credit Cards: A, B
Notes: 2, 5, 7, 8, 9

LEADVILLE

Wood Haven Manor
807/809 Spruce, 80461
(719) 486-0210; (800) 748-2570

Enjoy the taste and style of Victorian Leadville by stepping back 100 years in this beautiful home located on the prestigious "Banker's Row." Each room is distinctively decorated in Victorian style with private bath. One suite with whirlpool tub. Spacious dining room, comfortable living room with fireplace. Historic city with a backdrop of Colorado's highest mountains.

Hosts: Bobby and Jolene Wood
Rooms: 8 (7PB; 1SB) $60
Full Breakfast
Credit Cards: A, B, C, D
Notes: None

OURAY

Ouray 1898 House
322 Main Street, P. O. Box 641, 81427
(303) 325-4871

This 90-year-old house has been completely renovated and combines the el-egance of the 19th century with the comfortable amenities of the 20th century. Each room features a TV and a spectacular view of the San Juan Mountains from its deck. Eat a health-conscious, full breakfast on antique china. Jeep rides, horseback riding, and the city's hot spring pool are a few of the local diversions.

Hosts: Lee and Kathy Bates
Rooms: 4 (PB) $58-78
Full Breakfast
Credit Cards: A, B
Notes: 2, 7, 9

PAGOSA SPRINGS

Davidson's Country Inn
Box 87, 81147
(303) 264-5863

Davidson's Country Inn is a three-story log house located at the foot of the Rocky Mountains on 32 acres. The inn provides a library, a playroom, a game room, and some outdoor activities. A two-bedroom cabin is also available. The inn is tastefully decorated with family heirlooms and antiques, with a warm country touch to make you feel at home. Two miles east of Highway 160.

Hosts: Gilbert and Evelyn Davidson
Rooms: 7 (4 PB; 3 SB) $38-62
Full Breakfast
Credit Cards: A, B
Notes: 2, 5, 7, 8, 9, 10, 11, 12

---

year; 6 Pets welcome; 7 Children welcome; 8 Tennis nearby; 9 Swimming nearby; 10 Golf nearby; 11 Skiing nearby; 12 May be booked through travel agent

PINE

Meadow Creek Bed and Breakfast

13438 Hwy 285, 80470
(303) 838-4167

Nestled in pines and aspens on 35 acres and restores in 1988, this 1929 mountain bed and breakfast offers a relaxing, romantic, friendly getaway. There are six bedrooms, common room with fireplace, jacuzzi, sauna, decks, gazebo, and good home cooking. Family owned and operated, we are pleased to share this little piece of "God's Country." New this year is "The Room in the Meadow," a private, detached room with fireplace, jacuzzi tub, king bed, lots of windows, and lots of privacy.

Hosts: Pat and Dennis Carnahan; Judy and Don
Rooms: 7 (PB) $74-109
Full Breakfast
Credit Cards: A, B
Notes: 2, 4, 5, 10, 11, 12

PONCHA SPRINGS

Jackson Hotel Bed and Breakfast

P.O. Box 457, 220 S. Main Street, 81242-0457
(719) 539-4861

The Jackson was built in 1878 as a stagestop where a number of notable people of the times stayed. The rooms are furnished much as they originally were. We are located in the heart of some of the best white water rafting in the summer and Colorado skiing in the winter as well as hunting and fishing. Also located in the hotel is an antique shop.

Hosts: Russell and Judy Conrod
Rooms: 8 (SB) $38
Continental Breakfast
Credit Cards: A, B
Notes: 2, 5, 7, 9, 10, 11

PUEBLO

Abriendo Inn

300 West Abriendo Avenue, 81004
(719) 544-2703

Experience the comfort, style, and luxury of the past in rooms, delightfully furnished with antiques, crocheted bedspreads, and brass and four-poster beds. Breakfast is always hearty, home-baked, and served in the oak wainscoted dining room or one of the picturesque porches. Located within walking distance of restaurants, shops, and galleries...all in the heart of Pueblo. A classic bed and breakfast inn listed with the National Register of Historic Places.

Hosts: Kerrelyn and Chuck Trent
Rooms: 7 (PB) $48-89
Full Breakfast
Credit Cards: A, B, C, D, E
Notes: 2, 5, 7 (over 7), 8, 10, 11, 12

SALIDA

Gazebo Country Inn

507 E. 3rd, 81201
(719) 539-7806

A 1901 restored Victorian home, with

NOTES: Credit cards accepted: A Master Card; B Visa; C American Express; D Discover Card; E Diners Club; F Other; 2 Personal checks accepted; 3 Lunch available; 4 Dinner available; 5 Open all

magnificent deck and porch views. Gourmet breakfast and private baths. Located in the heart of the Rockies. Whitewater rafting on the Arkansas River and skiing at the Monarch Mountain Lodge are a few of the amenities. We are committed to your comfort and relaxation.

Hosts: Don and Bonnie Johannsen
Rooms: 3 (PB) $45-55
Full Breakfast
Credit Cards: None
Notes: 2, 5, 8, 9, 10, 11, 12

SILVERTON

Christopher House Bed and Breakfast

821 Empire Street, P. O. Box 241, 81433
(303) 387-5857 June-September;
(904) 567-7549 October-May

This charming 1894 Victorian home has the original, golden oak woodwork, parlor fireplace, and antiques throughout. All bedrooms offer comfortable mattresses, wall-to-wall carpeting, and

a mountain view. Guests are warmly welcomed with mints and fresh wildflowers. A full breakfast is served to Christian and Irish music. Conveniently located only four blocks from the town's narrow-gauge train depot, Old West shops, restaurants, and riding stables. Guest transportation to and from the train depot is available.

Hosts: Howard and Eileen Swonger
Rooms: 4 (1 PB; 3 SB) $42-52
Full Breakfast
Credit Cards: None
Notes: 2, 7, 8, 10, 12

WINTER PARK

Mulligan's Mountain Inn

P.O. Box 397, 80482
(303) 887-2877

Nestled in the beautiful Rocky Mountains, this cozy home is a quiet getaway. We are surrounded by year round activity with skiing in the winter and golfing and hiking in the summer. On the premises is an outdoor hot tub and recreation room with pool table, darts, and Nintendo. A full home-cooked breakfast is served each morning. You can expect quiet surroundings, a beautiful view, and friendly hospitality.

Hosts: Fred and Shirley Mulligan
Rooms: 4 (SB) $45-70
Full Breakfast
Credit Cards: None
Notes: 2, 5, 9, 10, 11

year; 6 Pets welcome; 7 Children welcome; 8 Tennis nearby; 9 Swimming nearby; 10 Golf nearby; 11 Skiing nearby; 12 May be booked through travel agent

Connecticut

CLINTON

Captain Dibbel House
21 Commerce Street, 06413
(203) 669-1646

Our 1886 Victorian, just two blocks from the shore, features a wisteria-covered, century-old footbridge and gazebo on our half-acre of lawn and gardens. Spacious living room and bedrooms are comfortably furnished with antiques and family heirlooms, fresh flowers, fruit baskets, home-baked treats. There are bicycles, nearby beaches, and marinas to enjoy.

Hosts: Helen and Ellis Adams
Rooms: 4 (PB) $65-85
Full Breakfast
Credit Cards: A, B, C, D
Notes: 2, 8, 9, 10, 12

CORNWALL BRIDGE

The Cornwall Inn
Route 7, 06754
(203) 672-6884; (800) 786-6884

The Cornwall Inn is a charming country inn dating back to 1810. Rooms are decorated with antiques and king or queen beds. Enjoy fine, country dining in a relaxed candlelit atmosphere or on the terrace in-season overlooking the pool. The inn is located in the northwest corner of Connecticut with the Housatonic River nearby for fly fishing, canoeing, and tubing. Hiking, biking, antiquing, skiing, auto racing, and foliage bring many travelers.

Hosts: Lois, Emily, Robyn, Ron, and Brian
Rooms: 13 (12 PB; 1 SB) $50-100
Full Breakfast
Credit Cards: A, B, C, D
Notes: 2, 3, 4, 5, 6, 7, 8, 9, 10, 11, 12

NOTES: Credit cards accepted: A Master Card; B Visa; C American Express; D Discover Card; E Diners Club; F Other; 2 Personal checks accepted; 3 Lunch available; 4 Dinner available; 5 Open all

GLASTONBURY

Butternut Farm

1654 Main Street, 06033
(203) 633-7197

This 18th-century architectural jewel is furnished in period antiques. Prize-winning dairy goats, pigeons, and chickens roam in an estate setting with trees and herb gardens. The farm is located ten minutes from Hartford by expressway; one and one-half hours to any place in Connecticut.

Host: Don Reid
Rooms: 2 (PB); Suite (PB); Apartment (PB)
$65-85
Full Breakfast
Credit Cards: A, B, C
Notes: 2, 5, 7, 8, 9, 10, 11

MIDDLEBURY

Tucker Hill Inn

96 Tucker Hill Road, 06762
(203) 758-8334

Charming New England Colonial. In an earlier incarnation it was a tea room at a trolley stop. Large spacious guest rooms with their own cozy sitting room. Nearby is antiquing, and summer and winter activities are available.

Host: Susan Cebelenski
Rooms: 4 (2PB; 2SB) $55-80
Full Breakfast
Credit Cards: A, B, C
Notes: 2, 5, 7, 8, 9, 10, 12

MYSTIC

Harbour Inne and Cottage

Edgemont Street, 06355
(203) 572-9253

Harbour Inn and Cottage is located in downtown Mystic, overlooking the Mystic River. The Inne has several rooms, each containing a double size bed, color cable TV, air conditioning, and a private bathroom. The Inne also has a kitchen that is open to all guests, and a common room with a fireplace.

The cottage can sleep up to six people. It has a bedroom with two beds, and a fireplace. There is also a sofabed in the kitchen/living room for two more people. The cottage also has a private bath and its own parking.

Host: Charley Lecouras, Jr.
Rooms: 4 (plus 3 room cottage) (PB) $45-85
(cottage: $125-175)
No meals provided, but guests have full use of kitchen to prepare own meals.
Credit Cards: None
Notes: 5, 6, 7, 8, 9, 10

NEW MILFORD

The Heritage Inn of Litchfield County

34 Bridge Street, 06776
(203) 354-8883; FAX (203) 350-5543

Located in the center of the village of New Milford, the Heritage Inn is a

---

year; 6 Pets welcome; 7 Children welcome; 8 Tennis nearby; 9 Swimming nearby; 10 Golf nearby; 11 Skiing nearby; 12 May be booked through travel agent

painstakingly restored 1800s tobacco barn, which the region is famous for. All 20 rooms are tastefully designed in a rich, traditional decor with color cable TV and telephone. It is within walking distance of shops, restaurants, movies, and the historical town green. Come, relax in this beautiful building, enjoy our hearty breakfast in the morning, and unwind in the Litchfield hills.

Host: Deana Berry
Rooms: 20 (PB) $69-94
Full or Continental Breakfast
Credit Cards: A, B, C
Notes: 2, 5, 6, 7, 8, 9, 10, 12

OLD LYME

Old Lyme Inn

85 Lyme Street, 06371
(203) 434-2600

This 1850s Victorian country inn has 13 guest rooms all with private baths, telephones, clock radios, air-conditioning, and a complimentary continental breakfast. Located in the historic district of this art colony, The Old Lyme Inn is known nationally and internationally for its romantic setting and

outstanding food. Near Mystic, Essex, and the Connecticut shoreline.

Host: Diana Field Atwood
Rooms: 13 (PB) $95-140
Continental Breakfast
Credit Cards: A, B, C, D, E
Notes: 2, 3, 4, 5, 6, 7, 8, 9, 10, 12

OLD MYSTIC

Red Brook Inn

P. O. Box 237, 06372
(203) 572-0349

Nestled on seven acres of old New England wooded countryside, bed and breakfast lodging is provided in two historic buildings: the Haley Tavern, circa 1740, is a restored center-chimney colonial tavern. The Crary Homestead, circa 1770, is a Colonial built by sea captain Nathaneil Crary. Each room is appointed with period furnishings, including canopy beds, and there are many working fireplaces throughout the inn. A hearty breakfast is served family style in the ancient keeping room. Enjoy a quiet, colonial atmosphere near

Old Lyme Inn

NOTES: Credit cards accepted: A Master Card; B Visa; C American Express; D Discover Card; E Diners Club; F Other; 2 Personal checks accepted; 3 Lunch available; 4 Dinner available; 5 Open all

Mystic Seaport Museum, antique shops, and aquarium. Colonial dinner weekends are also available November and December. No smoking.

Host: Ruth Keyes
Rooms: 11 (PB) $95-169
Full Breakfast
Credit Cards: A, B
Notes: 5, 7, 8, 9, 10

RIDGEFIELD

Epenetus Howe House
91 N. Salem Rd., 06877
(203) 438-HOWE

Preserved Dutch Colonial home, circa 1725, located in Historic Ridgefield, just 1 1/2 hours from New York City and 30 minutes from Stamford and White Plains. Two antique furnished rooms. Warm, inviting, restful atmosphere.

Hosts: Diane and John Armato
Rooms: 2 (SB) $85
Hearty Continental Breakfast
Credit Cards: A, B, C
Notes: 2, 5, 7, 8, 9, 10, 12

SOMERSVILLE

The Old Mill Inn
63 Maple Street, P.O. Box 443, 06072
(203) 763-1473

This gracious, old New England home

has twin or double beds, cable TV, phone, refrigerator, stereo, fireplace, and books everywhere. The beautiful muraled dining room with a glass wall overlooks the lawn and its surrounding gardens, flowering trees, and shrubs. It is convenient to shopping, restaurants, airport, and many other attractions.

Hosts: Ralph and Phyllis Lumb
Rooms: 4 (2 PB; 2 SB) $54-60
Expanded Continental Breakfast
Credit Cards: None
Notes: 2, 5, 8, 9, 10, 12

THOMPSON

A Taste of Ireland
47 Quaddick Road, 06277
(203) 923-2883

Charming country cottage circa1780 on National Historic Registry. Fireplaced sitting room. Home library of Irish literature and Celtic music. Hosts well-versed in assisting guests in genealogy research and travel planning to "the old sod." Authentic imported foods and beverages complete the full breakfast served in atrium room overlooking gardens and lovely stone walls. Home is located in quiet corner of N.E. Connecticut—a nature lover's retreat area.

Hosts: Elaine Chicoine and husband Jean
Rooms: 2 (1PB; 1SB) $50-65
Full Irish Breakfast
Credit Cards: None
Notes: 2, 5, 7, 9, 10, 11, 12

---

year; 6 Pets welcome; 7 Children welcome; 8 Tennis nearby; 9 Swimming nearby; 10 Golf nearby; 11 Skiing nearby; 12 May be booked through travel agent

Delaware

NEW CASTLE

William Penn Guest House

206 Delaware Street, 19720
(302) 328-7736

Visit historic New Castle and stay in a charmingly restored home, circa 1692, close to museums and major highways.

Hosts: Richard and Irma Burwell
Rooms: 4 (1 PB; 2 SB) $45-65
Continental Breakfast
Credit Cards: None
Notes: 2, 7, 8

SMYRNA

The Main Stay

41 S. Main Street, 19977
(302) 653-4293

Traditional white clapboard colonial townhouse is situated in the heart of historic area. Antique furniture, oriental rugs, needle work and patch work quilts are decor, depending on the season. Sun porch, open porch and fireplace are for relaxing. Laundry facilities available. Coffe and tea always on tap.

Host: Phyllis E. Howarth
Rooms: 3(SB) $45
Full Gourmet Breakfast
Credit Cards: None
Notes: 8, 10

WILMINGTON

Bed and Breakfast Delaware

Box 177, 3600 Silverside Road, 19810

Bed and Breakfast Delaware is a reservation service offering quality accomodations in a large choice of inns and guesthouses in the Brandywine Valley. We also cover beaches, national parks, wildlife areas, in Maryland and Pennsylvania. Full or continental breakfasts available.

District of Columbia

Adams Inn

1744 Lanier Place Northwest, 20009
(202) 745-3600

This turn-of-the-century town house is in a neighborhood with many ethnic restaurants and has comfortable, homestyle furnishings. Near transportation, convention sites, government buildings, and tourist attractions.

Hosts: Gene and Nancy Thompson
Rooms: 25 (12PB; 13SB) $45-90
Expanded Continental Breakfast
Credit cards: A, B, C, E
Notes: 2, 5, 7, 12

The Reeds

P. O. Box 12011, 20005
(202) 328-3510

Built in the late 1800s, this large Victorian home features original wood paneling, including a unique oak staircase, stained glass, chandeliers, Victorian-style lattice porch, and art nouveau and Victorian antiques and decorations. The house has been featured in the *Washington Post* and the *Philadelphia Inquirer* and as part of "Christmas at the Smithsonian." It is located ten blocks from the White House at historic Logan Circle.

Hosts: Charles and Jackie Reed
Rooms: 6 (1PB; 5SB) $55-85
Expanded Continental Breakfast
Credit Cards: A, B, C, E
Notes: 2 (two weeks in advance only), 5, 7, 8, 9

Florida

AMELIA ISLAND

Elizabeth Pointe Lodge

98 South Fletcher, 32034
(904) 277-4851

The main house of the lodge is constructed in an 1890s Nantucket shingle style with a strong maritime theme, broad porches, rockers, sunshine, and lemonade. Located prominently by the Atlantic Ocean, the inn is only steps from often deserted beaches. Suites are available for families. A newspaper is delivered to your room in the morning, and breakfast is served overlooking the ocean.

Hosts: David and Susan Caples
Rooms: 20 (PB) $85-115
Full Breakfast
Credit Cards: A, B, C
Notes: 2, 3, 4, 5, 7, 8, 9, 10, 12

The Phoenix's Nest On Amelia

619 S. Fletcher Avenue, 32034
(904) 277-2129

A seaside retreat. Our suites are private, restful, gracious, romantic, interesting and fun. All bedrooms have an ocean view. There are bikes, boogie boards, videos and 250-year-old magazine collection here. Golf, tennis, charter fishing, museums, shopping and a fort within a 5 mile radius. You can, however, do absolutely nothing while you're here and do it with dignity!

Host: Hariett Johnston Fortenberry
Rooms: 4 private suites (PB) $65-85
Continental Breakfast
Credit Cards: A, B
Notes: 2, 5, 6, 7, 8, 9, 10, 12(10%)

The Phoenix's Nest on Amelia

NOTES: Credit cards accepted: A Master Card; B Visa; C American Express; D Discover Card; E Diners Club; F Other; 2 Personal checks accepted; 3 Lunch available; 4 Dinner available; 5 Open all

COLEMAN

The Son's Shady Brook Bed and Breakfast

P. O. Box 551, 33521
(904) PIT-STOP (748-7867)

Come for a refreshing change in a rural setting that is easy to find. This modern house on 21 secluded, wooded acres overlooking a springfed creek offers solitude with tranquility and therapeutic, picturesque surroundings. This is a relaxing retreat for the elderly, newlyweds, handicapped, and others. The bedrooms are beautifully decorated. Enjoy the piano, library, fireplace, and more. Within one hour of Orlando and Tampa.

Host: Jean Lake Martin
Rooms: 4 (PB) $50-60
Full Breakfast
Credit Cards: A, B, C
Notes: 2, 3 (by arrangement), 4 (by arrangement), 5, 8, 9, 10

DAYTONA BEACH

Captain's Quarters Inn

3711 South Atlantic Avenue, 32127
(904) 767-3119; (800) 332-3119

Daytona's first bed and breakfast directly on the Atlantic Ocean has oceanfront suites in a quiet section of Daytona. "Your home away from home" is our motto. Enjoy private balconies, complete kitchens, guest laundry, daily newspapers, unique gift shop, pool heated to 80 degrees, fishing pier next door, and all new decorated rooms. Close to shopping.

Host: Becky Sue Morgan and family
Rooms: 26 (PB) $75-195
Full Breakfast
Credit Cards: A, B, C, D
Notes: 2, 3, 5, 7, 8, 9, 10, 12

HOLMES BEACH

Harrington House

5626 Gulf Drive, 34217
(813) 778-5444

Centrally located on Anna Maria Island, in the small city of Holmes Beach, overlooking the Gulf of Mexico, Harrington House awaits your visit. The largest three-story home on the island was constructed in 1925 for the first mayor of Holmes Beach. Flower gardens, inground pool and beachfront swimming are attractive features you'll find at Harrington House. Our great room lends itself to reading, watching TV, listening to music, or just sitting and talking, creating new friends or getting acquainted with old ones. Christmastime is especially festive at Harrington House. Rooms are gorgeously decorated, each with its own atmosphere. Breakfast served on the porch overlooking the sea or in the formal dining room.

Hosts: Jo and Frank Davis
Rooms: 11 (PB) $59-149
Credit Cards: A, B
Notes: 2, 5, 8, 9, 10, 12

---

year; 6 Pets welcome; 7 Children welcome; 8 Tennis nearby; 9 Swimming nearby; 10 Golf nearby; 11 Skiing nearby; 12 May be booked through travel agent

INDIAN SHORES

Meeks Bed and Breakfast on the Gulf Beaches
19418 Gulf Blvd #407, 34635
(813) 596-5424

Beach! Pool! Sunsets! Enjoy your stay in this beach condo overlooking the Gulf of Mexico. A beach cottage is sometimes available. Choose your breakfast, then bask in the sun, swim in the gulf, and catch spectacular sunsets from your balcony. Dine at nearby seafood restaurants and visit the local seabird sanctuary, sunken gardens, and the Dali Museum. Other nearby attractions are Busch Gardens in Tampa and sponge diving in Tarpon Springs. This B&B is located between Clearwater and St. Petersburg Beach, only two hours from Walt Disney World. Your hostess is a real estate broker.

Host: Greta and Bob Meeks
Rooms: 2 (1PB; 1SB) $50-60
Full Breakfast
Credit Cards: None
Notes: None

JUPITER

Innisfail
134 Timber Lane, 33458
(407) 744-5905

A contemporary ranch framed by palm trees, Innisfail—Gaelic for "the abode of peace and harmony"—doubles as a gallery. The vanNoordens are sculptors, and guests are welcome to watch them work in their home studio. While you don't have to be an art lover to visit, it helps to be a pet lover; Katherine and Luke's four-footed family comprises three dogs and two cats. Jupiter has wonderful beaches, but you can get an equally good tan using the vanNoorden's swimming pool. In the morning, your choice of full or continental breakfast.

Hosts: Katherine and Luke vanNoorden
Rooms: 1 (PB) $50(June-Oct), $60(Nov-May)
Full and Continental Breakfast available
Credit Cards: None
Notes: 2, 4, 5, 6, 7, 8, 9, 10,

KEY WEST

Papa's Hide Away
309 Louisa Street, 33040
(305) 294-7709

Secluded private getaway. Lush tropical gardens. Heated pool and jacuzzi. Bright, spacious (sleeps four) studios: kitchenette, private bath and patio, AC, cable TV. Cottage: 2 bedroom, one beath, full kitchen, living room, dining room (sleeps six), AC, cable TV, wrap-around porch. Walking distance to beach and historic downtown. Bikes for rent available. Owners serve with tender loving care.

Hosts: Shawn and Sandy McBratine
Rooms: 5 studios and 1 cottage (PB) $75-125
Continental Breakfast
Credit Cards: A, B, C, D
Notes: 5, 7, 8, 9, 10, 12

NOTES: Credit cards accepted: A Master Card; B Visa; C American Express; D Discover Card; E Diners Club; F Other; 2 Personal checks accepted; 3 Lunch available; 4 Dinner available; 5 Open all

LAKELAND

Sunset Motel & R.V. Park

2301 New Tampa Highway, 33801
(813) 683-6464

This resort motel with pool and recreation room is central to Cyprus Gardens, Disneyworld, Sea World, Universal Studios, Busch Gardens, and more. Walk to banks and shopping. TV, telephone and refrigerator in all rooms; microwaves and grills available; kitchenettes, apartments, suites.

Hosts: Eunice, John, Will, and Bill
Rooms: 14 (PB) $50
Continental Breakfast (on request)
Credit Cards: A, B
Notes: 5, 7, 9, 10, 12

LAKE WALES

Chalet Suzanne Country Inn and Restaurant

3800 Chalet Suzanne Dr., 33853
(813)676-6011; (800) 433-6011

Listed on the National Register of Historic Places, Chalet Suzanne has been family owned and operated since 1931. It is on 100 acres in a fairy tale setting. Thirty guest rooms have all the amenities. Our four-star restaurant serves breakfast, lunch and dinner. We also have gift shops, a ceramic studio, swimming pool, soup cannery, and lighted airstrip. We are proud to say that our soups accompanied Jim Irwin on Apollo

15. Ask about our mini vacation for two.

Hosts: Carl and Vita Hinshaw
Rooms: 30 (PB) $105-185
Full Breakfast
Credit Cards: A, B, C, D, E, F
Notes: 2, 3, 4, 5, 6, 7, 8, 9, 10, 12

MARATHON

Hopp-Inn Guest House

5 Man-O-War Drive, 33050
(305) 743-4118; FAX (305) 743-9220

Established in 1981, this guest house is located in the heart of the Florida Keys and looks out on the ocean. Breakfast often includes homemade muffins or banana bread. We are convenient to Key West, Dolphin Research Center, and all water activities. We also have charter fishing packages available aboard the *Sea Wolf.* Also 1 and 2 bedroom villas.

Hosts: Joe and Joan Hopp
Rooms: 5 (PB) $55-75
Full Breakfast
Credit Cards: A, B
Notes: 8, 9, 10, 12

MIAMI

Miami River Inn

118 SW South River Drive, 33130
(305) 325-0045

Enjoy a turn-of-the-century environment overlooking Miami's vibrant riverfront and downtown. Our forty-one rooms (thirty-eight with private

year; 6 Pets welcome; 7 Children welcome; 8 Tennis nearby; 9 Swimming nearby; 10 Golf nearby; 11 Skiing nearby; 12 May be booked through travel agent

bath), each individually decorated and furnished with antiques, include touch-tone telephones, TV, and central air conditioning and heat. Our pool and jacuzzi are surrounded by lush tropical gardens. Complimentary breakfast and afternoon tea are served daily. The lobby contains a library of historical publications about Miami and menus from restaurants in the river district.

Host: Sallye Jude
Rooms: 41 (38PB; 3SB) $75
Continental Breakfast
Credit Cards: A, B, C, D, E
Notes: 5, 7, 8, 9, 10, 12

NEW SMYRNA BEACH

Night Swan Intracoastal Bed and Breakfast

512 South Riverside Drive, 32168
(904) 423-4940

Come watch the pelicans, dolphins, sailboats, and yachts along the Atlantic Intracoastal Waterway from our beautiful front room, our wraparound porch, or your room. Our spacious three-story home has kept its character and charm of 1906 in the Historic District of New Smyrna Beach, with its central fireplace and its intricate, natural wood in every room. We are located between Daytona Beach and Kennedy Space Center, on the Indian River, just two miles from the beach.

Hosts: Chuck and Martha Nighswonger
Rooms: 5 (PB) $49-89
Expanded Continental Breakfast
Credit Cards: A, B
Notes: 2, 5, 8, 10, 12

The Riverview Hotel

103 Flagler Avenue, 32169
(904) 428-5858

A charming, elegantly restored 1885 hotel adjoins the award-winning Riverview Charlie's Restaurant. We are located on the Intracoastal Waterway and just a short walk to the area's finest beach. Breakfast is served in your room.

Hosts: Jim and Christa Kelsey
Rooms: 18 (PB) $63-150
Expanded Continental Breakfast
Credit Cards: A, B, C, D, E, F
Notes: 3, 4, 5, 7, 8, 9, 10, 12

ORLANDO

The Courtyard at Lake Lucerne

211 North Lucerne Circle, East, 32801
(407) 648-5188; (800) 444-5289

A unique property made up of three historic buildings furnished with antiques and surrounding a tropically landscaped brick courtyard, this establishment is located in the historic district on the southern edge of downtown Orlando, convenient to everything central Florida has to offer. Rooms have phones and cable TV; two suites have double Jacuzzis and steam showers.

Hosts: Charles and Paula Meiner
Rooms: 22 (PB) $65-150
Expanded Continental Breakfast
Credit Cards: A, B, C
Notes: 2, 5, 6, 7, 8, 9, 12

NOTES: Credit cards accepted: A Master Card; B Visa; C American Express; D Discover Card; E Diners Club; F Other; 2 Personal checks accepted; 3 Lunch available; 4 Dinner available; 5 Open all

Perri House Bed and Breakfast
10417 State Road 535, 32836
(407) 876-4830; (800) 780-4830

Perri House is a quiet, private, and secluded country estate home conveniently nestled in 20 acres in the backyard of the Walt Disney World Resort area of Orlando! Because of its outstanding location, Perri House provides easy access to all that Disney and Orlando have to offer. Each guest room has its own private bath and private outside entrance, TV, telephone, and ceiling fan. After a day or evening of activities, arrive home to a relaxing pool and spa. An upscale continental breakfast awaits you each morning and features giant sweet muffins, breads, cereals, and fruit. After ten years of owning and operating their own restaurant and nightclub, Nick and Angi know how to offer a unique blend of cordial hospitality, comfort, and friendship!

Hosts: Nick and Angi Perretti
Rooms: 4 (PB) $65-75
Continental Breakfast
Credit Cards: A, B, C, D
Notes: 2, 5, 7, 8, 9, 10, 12

The Rio Pinar House
532 Pinar Drive, 32825
(407) 277-4903

Located in the quiet Rio Pinar golf community 30 minutes from Disney World, Sea World, and Universal Studios, the Rio Pinar House features comfortable rooms. A full breakfast is served in the formal dining room or on the screened-in porch overlooking the yard.

Hosts: Victor and Delores Freudenburg
Rooms: 3 (PB) $45-55
Full Breakfast
Credit Cards: None
Notes: 2, 5, 7, 8, 10, 12

PALM BEACH

Palm Beach Historic Inn
365 So. County Road, 33480
(407) 832-4009

Palm Beach Historic Inn is a charming, beautifully restored landmark building. All rooms have private baths, A/C and cable TV. We are perfectly located—one block from the beach, 2 blocks from world famous Worth Avenue, minutes from the airport and water sports of every kind, cruises, golf, tennis, jai-lai, croquet, polo, comedy clubs, supper clubs, exciting nightlife, cultural events and performing arts of every kind. Walking distance from fabulous galleries, spectacular shopping and exquisite dining.

Hosts: Ruth and Franklin Frank
Rooms: 17 (PB) seasonal rates
Continental Breakfast

year; 6 Pets welcome; 7 Children welcome; 8 Tennis nearby; 9 Swimming nearby; 10 Golf nearby; 11 Skiing nearby; 12 May be booked through travel agent

Credit Cards: A, B, C
Notes: 5, 7, 8, 9, 10, 12

PENSACOLA

Homestead Inn

7830 Pine Forest Road, 32526
(904) 944-4816

Featuring Lancaster, Pennsylvania,
Amish-Mennonite recipes at our Victorian restaurant. Our rooms have wood
floors, poster beds, fireplaces and garden tubs. Outdoor pool.

Hosts: Neil and Jeanne Liechty
Rooms: 6 (PB) $59-79
Full Breakfast
Credit Cards: A, B, C
Notes: 2, 5

ST. AUGUSTINE

Castle Garden B&B

15 Shenandoah Street, 32084
(904) 829-3839

Stay at a Castle and be treated like
royalty! Relax and enjoy the peace and
quiet of "royal treatment" at our newly
restored 100-year-old Castle of Moorish
Revival design where the only sound
you'll hear is the occasional roar of a
cannon shot from the old fort 200 yards
to the south, or the creak of solid wood
floors. Awaken to the aroma of freshly
baked goodies as we prepare a full,
mouth-watering, country breakfast just
like "mom used to make." The unusual
coquina stone exterior remains virtu-
ally untouched, while the interior of
this former Castle Warden Carriage
House boasts two magnificent bridal
suites complete with soothing in-room
jacuzzi, sunken bedrooms and all of
life's little pleasures! Amenities: complimentary wine, chocolates, bikes, and
private parking.

Host: Bruce L. Kloeckner
Rooms: 6 (PB) $49-150
Full Breakfast
Credit Cards: A, B, C, D
Notes: 2, 5, 7, 10, 12

Old Powder House Inn

38 Cordova Street, 32084
(800) 447-4149; (904) 824-4149

Towering pecan and oak trees shade
verandas with large rockers to watch
the passing horse and buggies. An
introduction to a romantic escape in the
charming turn-of-the-century Victorian
inn. Amenities include high tea, hors
d'oeuvres, Jacuzzi, cable TV, parking,
bicycles, family hospitality, picnics,
special honeymoon packages, anniversaries, and birthdays.

Rooms: 9 (PB) $59-99
Full Breakfast
Credit Cards: A, B
Notes: 2, 5, 7, 8, 9, 10, 12

SAINT PETERSBURG

Mansion House

105 5th Ave. NE, 33701
(813) 821-9391

Proprietors Alan and Suzanne left Wales
in February of 1991 to embark on a

NOTES: Credit cards accepted: A Master Card; B Visa; C American Express; D Discover Card; E
Diners Club; F Other; 2 Personal checks accepted; 3 Lunch available; 4 Dinner available; 5 Open all

remodeling venture of a turn-of-the-century southern home in St. Petersburg. Alan, interested in water color painting, woodwork and design, used his skills to the full, whilst Suzanne cleverly coordinated the interiors to achieve a Floridian-style B&B with an English flair. Located within walking distance of marina, pier, museums, sunken gardens. Excellent shopping and superb beaches.

Hosts: Suzanne and Alan Lucas
Rooms: 6 (PB) $55-60
Full English Breakfast
Credit Cards: A, B
Notes: 2, 5, 7, 8, 9, 10, 12

SEBASTIAN

The Davis House
607 Davis St., 32958
(407) 589-4114

When you visit the charming Sebastian/Vero beach area, plan to stay at The Davis House, the only inn of its kind in Indian River County. Whether here for business or pleasure, you'll be sure to enjoy our efficiency suites, continental breakfast every morning and our very reasonable rates. Each suite contains a modern kitchenette complete with microwave, dinnerware and utensils, a full bath, a king size bed, generous closet space, sleeper sofa, cable TV and telephone. Gathering room serves as a social area where guests can play cards, watch TV or just relax. Or you may choose to unwind in the jacuzzi with sun deck, surrounded by privacy fences and lush tropical landscaping. No matter how long you plan to stay, we can accommodate you!

Host: Steven Wild
Rooms: 12 (PB) $48-79
Continental Breakfast
Credit Cards: A, B
Notes: 2, 5, 7, 8, 9, 10, 12

VENICE

The Banyan House
519 South Harbor Drive, 34285
(813) 484-1385

Experience the Old World charm of one of Venice's historic Mediterranean homes, circa 1926, on the gulf coast. Relax in the peaceful atmosphere of our lovely courtyard dominated by a huge banyan tree. This provides an unusual setting for the garden patio, pool, and Jacuzzi. Central to shopping, beaches, restaurants, and golf. Complimentary bicycles.

Hosts: Chuck and Susan McCormick
Rooms: 9 (7 PB; 2 SB) $49-89
Continental Breakfast
Credit Cards: None
Notes: 2, 5, 7 (over 12), 9

year; 6 Pets welcome; 7 Children welcome; 8 Tennis nearby; 9 Swimming nearby; 10 Golf nearby; 11 Skiing nearby; 12 May be booked through travel agent

Georgia

ATLANTA

Beverly Hills Inn

65 Sheridan Drive, Northeast, 30305
(404) 233-8520; (800) 331-8520

A charming European-style hotel with 18 suites uniquely decorated with period furnishings offers fresh flowers, continental breakfast, and the little things that count. We're a morning star, not a constellation; a solitary path, not a highway. Only some will understand, but then, we don't have room for everybody!

Hosts: Bonnie and Lyle Klienhans
Rooms: 18 (PB) $74-120
Continental Breakfast
Credit Cards: A, B, C, E
Notes: 2, 5, 6, 7, 8, 9, 10, 12

Oakwood House B&B

951 Edgewood Ave. NE, 30307
(404) 521-9320

Just two miles from Downtown Atlanta, in the city's first suburbs, oakwood welcomes you with four guest rooms— each with a new private bath and each equally furnished to compliment the house's 1911 post-Victorian style, including original woodwork and hundreds of books. On mild days, breakfast is served on the deck overlooking a huge backyard oak tree that predates the neighborhood. The hosts live next door, offering attentive service and privacy. It's a short walk to Little 5 Points, Atlanta's Soho. Nearby are the Carter Presidential library, Martin Luther King, Jr., grave site, stadium, Omni, World Congress Center and Underground Atlanta. No smoking indoors.

Hosts: Judy and Robert Hotchkiss
Rooms: 4 (PB) $65-85
Expanded Continental Breakfast
Credit Cards: A, B
Notes: 2, 5, 7, 12

Shellmont
Bed and Breakfast Lodge

821 Piedmont Avenue, Northeast, 30308
(404) 872-9290

Built in 1891, Shellmont is on the National Register of Historic Places and is a City of Atlanta Landmark Building. A true Victorian treasure of carved wood-

---

NOTES: Credit cards accepted: A Master Card; B Visa; C American Express; D Discover Card; E Diners Club; F Other; 2 Personal checks accepted; 3 Lunch available; 4 Dinner available; 5 Open all

work, stained and leaded glass, and unique architecture located in midtown, Atlanta's restaurant, theater, and cultural district, one mile from downtown. It is furnished entirely with antiques.

Hosts: Ed and Debbie McCord
Rooms: 5 (PB) $65-90
Continental Breakfast
Credit Cards: A, B, C
Notes: 2, 7 (limited), 8, 9, 10

Shellmont Bed and Breakfast Lodge

COMMERCE

The Pittman House

81 Homer Street, 30529
(906) 335-3823

A gracious, white Colonial built around 1890 is completely furnished with period antiques. If our furnishings are inspiring, visit our antique shop next door. Also, you may enjoy one of Tom's hand-carved Old World Santas. A discount shopping mall is only five minutes away.

Hosts: Tom and Dot Tomberlin
Rooms: 4 (2 PB; 2 SB) $45-65
Full Breakfast
Credit Cards: A, B
Notes: 2, 5, 7, 10, 11, 12

GAINESVILLE

The Dunlap House

635 Green Street, 30501
(706) 536-0200

The Dunlap House, built in 1910, is located in the historic section of Gainesville, Georgia, and is on The National Register of Historical Places. In 1985, it was renovated as a luxury Bed and Breakfast inn. Each room has private bath, telephone, TV, and is furnished in period reproduction furniture. Some rooms have fireplaces. A continental breakfast and late afternoon refreshments are served. The atmosphere is of Southern living where each guest is treated as in our home.

Hosts: Ann and Ben Ventress
Rooms: 9 (PB) $85-130
Continental Breakfast
Credit Cards: A, B, C
Notes: 2, 5, 10, 12

HAMILTON

Wedgwood Bed and Breakfast

P. O. Box 115, Highway 27 and Mobley, 31811
(706) 628-5659

Wedgwood is located 5.5 miles south of world-famous Callaway Gardens, 20 miles from Roosevelt's Little White House in Warm Springs, and 18 miles from Columbus. This 1850 home radiates the warmth, friendliness, and enthusiasm of your hostess. The inside is Wedgwood blue with white stenciling.

year; 6 Pets welcome; 7 Children welcome; 8 Tennis nearby; 9 Swimming nearby; 10 Golf nearby; 11 Skiing nearby; 12 May be booked through travel agent

Spacious rooms are comfortably furnished with period antiques. Personalized service and complimentary refreshments. No smoking.

Host: Janice Neuffer
Rooms: 3 (PB) $63-73
Full Breakfast
Credit Cards: None
Notes: 2, 5, 7, 8, 9, 10, 12

HELEN

Chattahoochee Ridge Lodge

P.O. Box 175, 30545
(800) 476-8331 or (706) 878-3144

Alone on a woodsy mountain above a waterfall, a mile from downtown, the lodge has five new rooms and suites (kitchens and fireplaces) with private entrances, TV, AC, free phones and jacuzzi; plus double insulation and back-up solar for stewards of the earth. You'll like the quiet seclusion, large windows, and deep-rock water. We'll help you plan great vacation days, including Bob's oom-pah band at a German restaurant. Decor includes wide-board knotty pine, brass beds, wall-to-wall carpet, and paddle fans.

Hosts: Mary and Bob Swift
Rooms: 5 (PB) $40-65
Continental Breakfast
Credit Cards: A, B, C, D
Notes: 2, 5, 7, 8, 9, 10, 12

Chattahoochee
Ridge Lodge

Dutch Cottage Bed and Breakfast

P.O. Box 757, 30545
(706) 878-3135

Located in a beautiful Alpine Village in the mountains of north Georgia—a tranquil waterfall and ivy-covered hillside lead to this European-style Bed and Breakfast located in an idyllic wooded setting. Choose from 3 comfortable rooms, each with private bath, AC and TV, or a charming hilltop honeymoon chalet. Full breakfast buffet. Walk to town. Open May through October.

Hosts: Bill and Jane Vander Werf
Rooms: 3 (4) (3PB; 1SB) $50-75
Notes: 2, 7, 8, 9, 10

Habersham Hollow Country Inn and Cabins

Route 6, Box 6208, 30523
(706) 754-5147

This peaceful oasis of solitude and serenity is nestled in the northeast Georgia mountains. A five-minute drive from Alpine Helen, it is a place of quiet, simple pleasures and genuine warmth and charm. The elegant country bed and breakfast has secluded, cozy cabins with fireplaces. The relaxed, casual, friendly atmosphere will make you feel as though you were in the country home of old friends.

Hosts: C. J. and Maryann Gibbons
Rooms: 4 (PB) $75-95
Full Breakfast
Credit Cards: A, B
Notes: 2, 5, 6, 7, 8, 9, 10, 11

NOTES: Credit cards accepted: A Master Card; B Visa; C American Express; D Discover Card; E Diners Club; F Other; 2 Personal checks accepted; 3 Lunch available; 4 Dinner available; 5 Open all

Hoffbrauhaus Inn

1 Main Street, 30545
(404) 878-2248; (800) 257-8528

Bavarian decor. All rooms have one queen bed, telephone, color cable TV, VCR. Two rooms have private balconies overlooking the Chattahoochee River. Breakfast is served in your room, and we have a full service lounge and dining room downstairs. Walk to Alpine Village, shopping, entertainment, fishing, and Octoberfest.

Host: Chris Hammersen
Rooms: 4 (PB) $35-95
Continental Breakfast
Credit Cards: A, B, C, D, E, F
Notes: 2, 3, 4, 5, 8, 9, 10, 12

HEPHZIBAH

Into the Woods

176 Longhorn Road, 30815
(706) 554-1400

Near Augusta, this charmingly restored, southern home circa 1880 offers four bedrooms, 2 and 1/2 baths and is nestled on a wooded four acre site. Refurbished with antiques of the same period. Gracious porches add to your stay here. A full country breakfast is served in a sunny dining area.

Hosts: Robert Risser
Rooms: 4 (2PB; 2SB) $55-65
Full Breakfast
Credit Cards: A, B
Notes: 2, 4 (upon request), 5, 7, 8, 9, 10

MOUNTAIN CITY

York House, Inc.

P. O. Box 126, 30562
(800) 231-YORK (9675)

This lovely 1896 bed and breakfast inn has a country flair and is listed on the National Register of Historic Places. It is nestled among the beautiful north Georgia mountains and is close to recreational activities. Completely renovated, the 13 guest rooms are decorated with period antiques and offer cable color TV. Guests begin their day with a continental breakfast served on a silver tray.

Hosts: Chad and Heather Andrews (owners-
Phyllis and Jimmy Smith)
Rooms: 13 (PB) $64-79
Continental Breakfast
Credit Cards: A, B, C, D
Notes: 2, 5, 7, 8, 9, 10, 11, 12

SAUTEE

Wood Haven Chalet

Rt. #1, Box 1086, Covered Bridge Road, 30571
(706) 878-2589

Located in a secluded mountain setting on Covered Bridge Road, this charming chalet is only a few minutes drive from the Alpine village of Helen, Georgia. You can choose an upper bedroom with an antique double bed located near an inside balcony where there is a grand piano for sing alongs. Also a lower single unit with a private deck and entrance and bath including a color TV, fireplace and cooking facilities. A deluxe continental breakfast is served for

year; 6 Pets welcome; 7 Children welcome; 8 Tennis nearby; 9 Swimming nearby; 10 Golf nearby; 11 Skiing nearby; 12 May be booked through travel agent

all in the dining area.

Hosts: Van and Ginger Wunderlich
Rooms: 3 (1PB; 2SB) $55-65
Expanded Continental Breakfast
Credit Cards: None
Notes: 2, 5, 10

SAVANNAH

Jesse Mount House

209 West Jones Street, 31401
(912) 236-1774; (800) 347-1774

Located in the heart of Savannah's historic district, this antebellum house beckons you to enjoy the comfort and opulence loved by the original owner, Jesse Mount. Built in 1854, this luxurious brick house is a fine example of classic Georgian architecture. Amenities include access to private garden, bowls of fresh fruit and candies, guest-controlled AC, a central location, tour and restaurant information, private baths and telephone, cable TV and bicycles.

Host: Howard Crawford
Rooms: 1-3 bedroom suite (PB) $120(2)-185(8)
Continental Breakfast
Credit Cards: None
Notes: 2, 5, 12

THOMSON

1810 West Inn

254 North Seymour Dr. NW, 30824
(706) 595-3156

1810 West Inn is a rambling Peidmont style restored farmhouse and accompanying renovated country houses that offer 19th century ambience with 20th-century conveniences. Just off I-20 near Augusta. Relax among antique furnishings, inviting country kitchen and large screened-in veranda that overlooks twelve landscaped acres. Private, perfect for retreats.

Host: Virginia White
Rooms: 10 (PB) $45-65
Expanded Continental Breakfast
Credit Cards: A, B, C
Notes: 2, 5, 7, 8, 9, 10, 12

Hawaii

Hale Kai

111 Honolii Pali, 96720
(808) 935-6330; FAX (808) 935-8439

Christian hosts offer their beautiful, four star, modern bed and breakfast on the bluff facing the ocean, surfing beach, and Hilo Bay. Hale Kai is just two miles from downtown Hilo. Guests are treated as family. We were recently selected as "one of the 100 top bed and breakfasts in U.S.A. and Canada." Explore the entire island from this location: Rainbow Falls, three miles away; botanical gardens, 3 miles away; Volcano Park, 30 miles away; Waipo Valley, 32 miles away; fish auction, three miles away; snorkeling, 4 miles away. Also available is a cottage with living room, bedroom, kitchen and bath. Also has a swimming pool and jacuzzi.

Host: Evonne Bjornen
Rooms: 5 plus cottage (PB) $85-98
Full Breakfast
Credit Cards: None
Notes: 2, 5, 7 (over 12), 8, 9, 10, 12

Papaya Paradise Bed & Breakfast

395 Auwinala Road, 96734
(808) 261-0316

Private, quiet, tropical and near all attractions. Swim in the 20X40 pool. Relax in the jacuzzi. Stroll Kailua Beach (a beautiful 4 miles of white sandy beach offering all kinds of water sports). Enjoy a full breakfast on the lanai surrounded by Hawaiian plants, trees and flowers with Mount Olomona in the background. Rooms with private bath, private entry, air conditioning, TV and refrigerator. Just 20 miles from Waikiki and the Honolulu airport. Three- night minimum stay.

Hosts: Bob and Jeanette Martz
Rooms: 2 (PB) $65-70
Full Breakfast
Credit Cards: None
Notes: 5, 7 (over 8), 8, 9, 10

---

year; 6 Pets welcome; 7 Children welcome; 8 Tennis nearby; 9 Swimming nearby; 10 Golf nearby; 11 Skiing nearby; 12 May be booked through travel agent

KAUAI—PRINCEVILLE

Hale 'Aha

3875 Kamehameha Drive, P. O. Box 3370, 96722
(800) 826-6733

"Where the East meets the West." The Garden Island of the Pacific. Lovely new guest house. Enjoy this beautiful home on the golf course overlooking the ocean. Send for colored brochure or call toll free. Christian hosts.

Hosts: Herb and Ruth Bockelman
Rooms: 4 (PB) $80; $190 suites
Continental Breakfast
Credit Cards: None
Notes: 2, 5, 8, 9, 10, 12

LAHAINA

The Guesthouse

1620 Ainakea Road, 96761
(808) 661-8085; (800) 621-8942

Conveniently located between the historic whaling town of Lahaina and the beach resort of Kaanapali, The Guesthouse offers a choice of five guest rooms, each with a different touch of Aloha. All have air-conditioning, TV, refrigerators, and a private jacuzzi has been added to our honeymoon suites. Enjoy the conveniences of home with our modern kitchen and laundry facilities. Relax at poolside or take a short stroll to the beach. We know your visit will be special, so expect outstanding accommodations at moderate price.

Hosts: Fred and Tanna Branum
Rooms: 5 (PB) $60-95
Full Breakfast
Credit Cards: A, B, C, F
Notes: 2, 5, 8, 9, 10, 12

MAUI-HAIKU

Haikuleana Bed and Breakfast

555 Haiku Road, 96708
(808) 575-2890

Experience the real feeling of "Aloha" in an 1850s plantation home. Set in the agricultural district close to waterfalls and secluded beaches. Haikuleana is a convenient way station for visitors headed to Hana and the Haleakala Crater. Swimming ponds, the world's best windsurfing and golf course are all nearby. Fred completely renovated the house. You'll admire its high ceilings, plank floors, porch and lush tropical gardens. The cool Hawaiian rooms are furnished with drapes, ticking comforters, wicker and antiques.

Host: Frederick J. Fox
Rooms: 4 (PB) $80-85
Full Breakfast
Credit Cards: None
Notes: 2, 5, 7 (over 6), 8, 9, 10

NOTES: Credit cards accepted: A Master Card; B Visa; C American Express; D Discover Card; E Diners Club; F Other; 2 Personal checks accepted; 3 Lunch available; 4 Dinner available; 5 Open all

OAHU—KANEOHE

Emma's Guest Rooms
47-600 Hui Ulili Street, 96744
(808) 239-7248; FAX (808) 239-7224

Located in beautiful Temple Valley on Oahu's lush windward shore. The valley is guarded by mountains filled with bird songs, peace, and tranquility.

Emma's is centrally located and convenient to Oahu's finest beaches, visitor attractions, modern shopping mall, and numerous restaurants. Guest kitchenette, dining, and TV lounge.

Hosts: Emma and Stan Sargeant
Rooms: 3 (PB) $45
Continental Breakfast
Credit Cards: A, B, C, D
Notes: 2, 5, 8, 9, 10

Idaho

COEUR D'ALENE

Cricket on the Hearth

1521 Lakeside Avenue, 83814
(208) 664-6926

Cricket on the Hearth, Coeur d'Alene's first bed and breakfast inn, has a touch of country that gives the inn a "down home" aura. Each of the five guest rooms is furnished in theme, from romantic to unique. After a relaxing weekend around the inn with its two cozy fireplaces and delicious full breakfast, guests are sure to find staying at Cricket on the Hearth habit forming.

Hosts: Al and Karen Hutson
Rooms: 5 (3 PB; 2 SB) $45-75
Full Breakfast
Notes: 2, 5, 8, 9, 10, 11

Katie's Wild Rose Inn

5150 Couer d'Alene, 83814
(208) 765-9474; (800) 328-9474

Looking through the pine trees to Lake Coeur d'Alene, Katie's Wild Rose Inn is a haven for the weary traveler. Only 600 feet from the public dock and beach road, the inn has four cozy rooms, one with its own Jacuzzi. Guests can relax in the family room beside the fireplace or enjoy a game of pool. A full breakfast is served on the deck or in the dining room where you can admire the view.

Hosts: Joisse and Lee Knowles
Rooms: 4 (2 PB; 2 SB) $65-85
Full Breakfast
Credit Cards: A, B
Notes: 2, 5, 9, 10, 11

LEWISTON

Shiloh Rose B&B

3414 Selway Dr., 83501
(208) 743-2482

The Shiloh Rose, decorated in a warm, country-Victorian style, offers a spacious three-room suite as your home away from home. Lace curtains, fragrant potpourri and fresh roses in season invite you to linger. Have your morning coffee in the sitting room with a real wood-burning stove. Browse through the overflowing bookshelves, enjoy the TV/VCR...or the grand piano. A complete breakfast is served in the dining room or on the deck overlooking the valley. The views are fantastic.

Host: Dorothy A. Mader
Rooms: 1 (PB) $65-70
Full Breakfast
Credit Cards: A, B
Notes: 2, 5, 7 (over 10), 8, 9, 10, 11

NOTES: Credit cards accepted: A Master Card; B Visa; C American Express; D Discover Card; E Diners Club; F Other; 2 Personal checks accepted; 3 Lunch available; 4 Dinner available; 5 Open all

Illinois

BARRINGTON

Barbara B's Bed and Breakfast

P. O. Box 1415, 60010
(708) 526-8876

Barbara B's Bed and Breakfast features a warm and inviting atmosphere in a country setting overlooking a conservation area. Breakfast is served on a screened-in porch or in the dining room. Guests can relax by a roaring fire amid antiques or walk to a nearby lake.

Hosts: Les and Barbara Ayres
Room: 1 (PB) $45
Full Breakfast
Credit Cards: None
Notes: 2, 5, 7, 8, 9, 11, 12

CARLYLE

Country Haus

1191 Franklin, 62231
(618) 594-8313

Country Haus is a comfortable 1890s Eastlake-style home. Located one mile from Carlyle Lake, there are a number of outdoor activities to choose from such as sailing, boating, skiing, fishing, and hiking. A museum and specialty shop are within walking distance. A gift shop is located on the premises, and lunch and dinner are available by advance reservation. Each room is individually decorated, and TV and stereo are ready for our guests to use in the downstairs library. A Jacuzzi is located on the first floor.

Hosts: Ron and Vickie Cook
Rooms: 4 (PB) $45-55
Full Breakfast
Credit Cards: A, B, C
Notes: 2, 3, 4, 5, 7, 8, 9, 10, 11

CHAMPAIGN

Barb's Bed and Breakfast

606 S. Russell, 61821
(217) 356-0376

This cozy cottage is situated in a quiet, attractive neighborhood with easy access to the University of Illinois. The twin cities and nearby communities offer many interesting things to see and do. Antique shops, museums, bike trails, and a wide variety of restaurants are all

---

year; 6 Pets welcome; 7 Children welcome; 8 Tennis nearby; 9 Swimming nearby; 10 Golf nearby; 11 Skiing nearby; 12 May be booked through travel agent

close by. The comfortable guest rooms, featuring handmade quilts, antiques and ceiling fans share a parlor with a fireplace.

Hosts: Barb and Merle Eyestone
Rooms: 2 (SB) $45
Hearty Continental Breakfast
Notes: 2, 7 (over 12), 8, 9, 10

EVANSTON

The Margarita European Inn

1566 Oak Avenue, 60201
(708) 869-2273

The romantic at heart will truly enjoy this modest and charming European-style inn in Evanston, the home of Northwestern University. Relax in the grand parlor with the morning paper or in the roof garden at sunset. Explore the numerous antique and specialty shops nearby. On rainy days, curl up with a novel from our wood-paneled English library, or indulge in a culinary creation from our critically acclaimed northern Italian restaurant, Va Pensiero.

Hosts: Barbara and Tim Gorham
Rooms: 49 (15PB; 34SB) $40-80
Continental Breakfast
Credit Cards: A, B, C
Notes: 2, 3, 4, 5, 7, 8, 9, 10, 12

GALENA

Avery Guest House

606 South Prospect Street, 61036
(815) 777-3883

This pre-Civil War home located near Galena's main shopping and historic buildings is a homey refuge after a day of exploring. Enjoy the view from our porch swing, feel free to play the piano, watch TV, or join a table game. Sleep soundly on comfortable queen beds, then enjoy our hearty continental breakfast in the sunny dining room with bay window. Mississippi river boats nearby.

Hosts: Flo and Roger Jensen
Rooms: 4 (S2B) $45-60
Expanded Continental Breakfast
Credit Cards: A, B
Notes: 2, 5, 7, 8, 9, 10, 11, 12

Belle Aire Mansion

11410 Route 20 West, 61036
(815) 777-0893

Belle Aire Mansion guest house is a pre-Civil War Federal home surrounded by 11 well-groomed acres that include extensive lawns, flowers, and a block-long, tree-lined driveway. We do our best to make our guests feel they are special friends.

Hosts: Jan and Lorraine Svec
Rooms: 5 (PB) $65-135
Full Breakfast
Credit Cards: A, B, D
Notes: 2, 7, 8, 10, 11

Brierwreath Manor Bed and Breakfast

216 North Bench Street, 61036
(815) 777-0608

Brierwreath Manor, circa 1884, is just one block from Galena's Main Street and has a dramatic and inviting wrap-

NOTES: Credit cards accepted: A Master Card; B Visa; C American Express; D Discover Card; E Diners Club; F Other; 2 Personal checks accepted; 3 Lunch available; 4 Dinner available; 5 Open all

around porch that beckons to you after a hard day. The house is furnished in an eclectic blend of antique and early American. You'll not only relax but feel right at home. Central air conditioning, ceiling fans, and cable TV add to your enjoyment.

Hosts: Mike and Lyn Cook
Rooms: 3 (PB) $70-80
Full Breakfast
Credit Cards: None
Notes: 2, 5, 8, 9, 10, 11

Colonial Guest House

1004 Park Avenue, 61036
(815) 777-0336

Built in 1826, this 21-room mansion has 11 outside doors, 5 large porches, 1 four-room penthouse that overlooks the city, and 3 rooms with kitchens. It is one block off Main Street. This house is loaded with antiques and has operated as a guest house for 33 years.

Host: Mary Keller
Rooms: 6 (PB) $50-60
Continental Breakfast
Credit Cards: None
Notes: 2, 5, 7 (small), 8, 9, 10, 11,

HIGHLAND

Phyllis' Bed and Breakfast

801 9th St., 62249
(618) 654-4619

Highland, known as "Neu-Schweizerland," is located just 30 miles east of St. Louis. The inn was built around the turn of the century and is close to town square, stores, shops, and restaurants. In the square is a gazebo where festivals and music concerts are held in the summer. At Christmas time, the square and gazebo are decorated for the season. Points of interests include Latzer Homestead, Lindendale Park/fairgrounds, Wicks Organ Company, and other fascinating landmarks. Each room is uniquely decorated. No smoking or alcoholic beverages permitted.

Hosts: Bob and Phyllis Bible
Rooms: 3 (PB) $40-55
Hearty Continental Breakfast
Credit Cards: A, B
Notes: 2, 5, 8, 9, 10

Phyllis' Bed and Breakfast

NAPERVILLE

Harrison House Bed and Breakfast

26 North Eagle Street, 60540
(708) 420-1117

Harrison House Bed and Breakfast, circa 1911, is a warm and friendly guest house 25 miles west of Chicago. Four antique-filled air conditioned guest rooms, one with a Jacuzzi. Walk to the train, great shops, wonderful restaurants, and historic sites. Homemade chocolate chip cookies, fresh flowers,

year; 6 Pets welcome; 7 Children welcome; 8 Tennis nearby; 9 Swimming nearby; 10 Golf nearby; 11 Skiing nearby; 12 May be booked through travel agent

gourmet coffee and a scrumptious breakfast. Prepare to be pampered!

Hosts: Neal and Lynn Harrison; Bette Coulter
Rooms: 4 (PB) $78-138 (midweek discounts available)
Full Breakfast on weekends; continental breakfast on weekdays
Credit Cards: A, B, C
Notes: 2, 8, 9, 10, 11

NAUVOO

Mississippi Memories
Rural Route 1, Box 291, 62354
(217) 453-2771

Located on the banks of the Mississippi, this gracious home offers lodging and elegantly served full breakfasts. In quiet, wooded surroundings, it is just two miles from historic Nauvoo, with its dozens of restored Mormon-era homes and shops. Two decks offer spectacular sunsets, drifting barges, and bald eagle watching.

Hosts: Marge and Dean Starr
Rooms: 5 (2 PB; 3 SB) $45-59
Full Breakfast
Credit Cards: A, B
Notes: 2, 5, 7, 8, 9. 10

OAKLAND

Inn on the Square
3 W. Montgomery, 61943
(217) 346-2289

Located 20 minutes from Eastern Illinois University, Charleston, The Inn on the Square specializes in fine food and friendly atmosphere. Best of all is the return of Bed and Breakfast tourism.

Blending the old with the new, we offer you warm hospitality and simple country pleasures, as well as historical sites, recreational activities, shopping excursions, and plain old sittin' and rockin'. Features three upstairs bedrooms comfortably furnished for country living and each with its own private bath. Come visit us!

Hosts: Gary and Linda Miller
Rooms: 3 (PB) $45-50
Full Breakfast
Credit Cards: A, B
Notes: 2, 3 (Mon-Sat), 4 (Fri, Sat, Sun 11-2), 5, 7, 9, 10, 12(15%)

Inn on the Square

PEORIA

Ruth's Bed and Breakfast
1506 West Alta Road, 61615
(309) 243-5977

Guest rooms share a bath in this private home. Enjoy family atmosphere. Children are welcome. There are two acres to roam near family restaurants and within 20 minutes of city attractions. Reservations required.

Hosts: Ruth and William Giles
Rooms: 3 (SB) $30
Continental Breakfast
Credit Cards: None
Notes: 2, 5, 7, 10

NOTES: Credit cards accepted: A Master Card; B Visa; C American Express; D Discover Card; E Diners Club; F Other; 2 Personal checks accepted; 3 Lunch available; 4 Dinner available; 5 Open all

Indiana

BRISTOL

Tyler's Place
19562 St. Rd. 120, 46507
(219) 848-7145

Originally the home of the Raber greenskeeper, Tyler's Place offers a pleasant view of the 27-hole rolling golf course and plenty of warm Hoosier hospitality. The common room is decorated with an Amish flavor. Breakfast is served in the sun room and evenings are enjoyed around the backyard fire ring. Conveniently situated minutes from the 80-90 toll road.

Host: Esther Tyler
Rooms: 3 (2PB; 1SB) $45-75
Full Breakfast
Notes: 2, 5, 8, 9, 10, 11

CORYDON

The Kintner House Inn
101 South Capitol Street, 47112
(812) 738-2020

AAA rated, this completely restored inn, circa 1873, is on the National Register of Historic Places and is furnished with Victorian and country antiques. It features five fireplaces and serves a full breakfast in the dining room. The staff prides itself on personal attention and guests' comfort. Private baths.

Host: Mary Jane Bridgwater
Rooms: 15 (PB) $35-89
Full Breakfast
Credit Cards: A, B, C, D, E
Notes: 2, 5, 8, 9, 10, 11

CRAWFORDSVILLE

Davis House
1010 W. Wabash Ave., 47933
(317) 364-0461

You'll enjoy the unique colonial atmosphere of this 1870 country mansion. Located in a quiet neighborhood, convenient to Wabash College and several local museums. Renovated in 1940, this historic home combines the original grace with the modern guest conveniences. Common rooms available for group meetings. Limited smoking.

Hosts: Jan and Dave Stearns
Rooms: 5 (PB) $49-65

---

year; 6 Pets welcome; 7 Children welcome; 8 Tennis nearby; 9 Swimming nearby; 10 Golf nearby; 11 Skiing nearby; 12 May be booked through travel agent

Full Breakfast
Credit Cards: A, B, C, D
Notes: 2, 5, 7, 12

Davis House

DANA

Castle B&B

214 Maple, P.O. Box 532, 47847
(317) 665-3282

In small-town America, Dana, Indiana, still has that quality of neighboring as a way of life. A Victorian motif is evident within the Castle. The Rose Room and the West Room are shaded by ancient maples. The Castle has welcomed generations of families within its walls since 1894. Your visit, too, will be a special event.

Host: Marilyn L. Fisher
Rooms: 2 (SB) $40
Continental Breakfast
Credit Cards: A, B
Notes: 2, 5, 7

GOSHEN

Timberidge
Bed and Breakfast

16801 SR 4, 46526
(219) 533-7133

The Austrian chalet white pine log home is nestled in the beauty of the quiet woods, just two miles from Goshen and near many local points of interest. Our guests enjoy the privacy of a master suite. A path through the woods is frequented by birds, squirrels, deer. Nearby are Amish farms where field work is done by horse-drawn equipment. Timberidge offer the best of city and country—close to town, yet removed to the majestic beauty of the woods that evokes a love of nature and a reverence of God's creation. AC and TV.

Hosts: Edward and Donita Brookmyer
Rooms: 1 (PB) $60
Full and Continental Breakfast Available
Credit Cards: None
Notes: 2, 5, 7, 8, 9, 10

GREENCASTLE

The Walden Inn

2 Seminary Square, P.O. Box 490, 46135
(317) 635-2761

Gracious hospitality reminiscent of a similar time is the experience of guests at Walden Inn. It's a philosophy that envelops you the moment you arrive. You'll discover an atmosphere that is warm and unpretentious where guests feel comfortable with our special amenities, distinctive cuisine and personal service. Because Walden Inn has just 55 guest rooms, our staff can provide the individual attention to detail that cannot be found in larger facilities.

Hosts: Steve
Rooms: 55 (PB) $49-80
Full and Continental Breakfast Available
Credit Cards: A, B, C, D, E, F
Notes: 2, 3, 4, 5, 6, 7, 8, 9, 10, 12

NOTES: Credit cards accepted: A Master Card; B Visa; C American Express; D Discover Card; E Diners Club; F Other; 2 Personal checks accepted; 3 Lunch available; 4 Dinner available; 5 Open all

HAGERSTOWN

The Teetor House

300 West Main Street, 47346
(317) 489-4422; for reservations call (800) 824-4319

This elegant, historic mansion on ten landscaped acres in a quaint, small town caters to travelers for business or pleasure. Affordable luxury. Fine restaurants and many antique stores are nearby. The house is fully air conditioned and offers many unique amenities. Five miles north of I-70 in east-central Indiana, a one-hour drive from Dayton, Ohio, and Indianapolis.

Hosts: Jack and JoAnne Warmoth
Rooms: 4 (PB) $70-85
Full Breakfast
Credit Cards: A, B
Notes: 2, 4 (by arrangement), 5, 7, 8, 9, 10, 12

HARTFORD CITY

De'Coys'
Bed and Breakfast

1546W 100N, 47348
(317) 348-2164

Located just west of Hartford City, Indiana, De'Coys' Bed and Breakfast offers its clients extraordinary attractive guest rooms with many special "Hoosier" touches. Guests enjoy a relaxed rural atmosphere in an old restored country home enriched with many amenities not customary to the typical hotel or motel setting. Each room demonstrates its own character, featuring antique furnishings and comfortable arrangements. An overnight stay includes a complimentary breakfast consisting of homemade specialties served from the thrasher kitchen.

Hosts: Chris and Tiann Coy
Rooms: 5 (1PB; 4SB) $44-50
Full Breakfast
Credit Cards: None
Notes: 2, 5, 7, 10

HUNTINGTON

Purviance House

326 South Jefferson, 46750
(219) 356-4218; (219) 356-9215

Built in 1859, this beautiful home is on the National Register of Historic Places. It features winding cherry staircase, ornate ceilings, unique fireplaces, and parquet floors and has been lovingly restored and decorated with antiques and period furnishings to create a warm, inviting atmosphere. Amenities include TV in rooms, snacks, beverages, kitchen privileges, and library. Near recreational areas with swimming, boating, hiking, and bicycling. Historic tours available. One-half hour from Fort Wayne; two hours from Indianapolis.

Hosts: Bob and Jean Gernand
Rooms: 4 (2 PB; 2 SB) $40-60
Full Breakfast
Credit Cards: None
Notes: 2, 5, 7, 8, 9, 10

Purviance House

---

year; 6 Pets welcome; 7 Children welcome; 8 Tennis nearby; 9 Swimming nearby; 10 Golf nearby; 11 Skiing nearby; 12 May be booked through travel agent

KOONTZ LAKE

Koontz House Bed and Breakfast

Rural Route 3, Box 592, 46574
(219) 586-7090

Come enjoy the beautiful home Sam Koontz built, circa 1880, on the west edge of 387-acre Koontz Lake with swimming area and boat dock. The house features large, airy bedrooms with color TV. A lakeside restaurant, marina, boat rental, and antique shops are all within walking distance. Potato Creek State Park is 12 miles away, Christmas shop and paraplanes are 60 miles away.

Hosts: Les and Jan Davison
Rooms: 4 (SB) $30-60
Full Breakfast
Credit Cards: None
Notes: 2, 5, 7, 8, 9, 10, 11, 12

LAGRANGE

The 1886 Inn

P. O. Box 5, 46761
(219) 463-4227

The 1886 Inn bed and breakfast is filled with historic charm and elegance. Every room is aglow with old-fashioned beauty. It is the finest lodging in the area, yet affordable. Ten minutes from Shipshewana flea market.

Hosts: Duane and Gloria Billman
Rooms: 5 (3 PB; 2 SB) $69-89
Expanded Continental Breakfast
Credit Cards: A, B
Notes: 2, 5, 8, 10

METAMORA

The Thorpe House Country Inn

Clayborne Street, P.O. Box 36, 47030
(317) 932-2365; (317) 647-5425

Visit the Thorpe House in historic Metamora, where the steam engine still brings passenger cars and the grist mill still grinds cornmeal. Spend a relaxing evening in this 1840 canal town home. Rooms are tastefully furnished with antiques and country accessories. Enjoy a hearty breakfast before visiting more than 100 shops in this quaint village. Our family-style dining room is also open to the public.

Hosts: Mike and Jean Owens
Rooms: 4 plus two-room suite (PB) $60-100
Full Breakfast
Credit Cards: A, B, D
Notes: 2, 3, 4, 6, 7, 10, 12

MIDDLEBURY

Bee Hive Bed and Breakfast

Box 1191, 46540
(219) 825-5023

Come visit Amish country and enjoy Hoosier hospitality. The Bee Hive is a two-story, open floor plan with exposed hand-sawed red oak beams and a loft. Enjoy our collection of antique farm machinery and other collectibles. Snuggle under handmade quilts and

---

NOTES: Credit cards accepted: A Master Card; B Visa; C American Express; D Discover Card; E Diners Club; F Other; 2 Personal checks accepted; 3 Lunch available; 4 Dinner available; 5 Open all

wake to the smell of freshly baked muffins.

Hosts: Herb and Treva Swarm
Rooms: 3 (SB) $49.50-60
Full Breakfast
Credit Cards: A, B
Notes: 2, 5, 7, 8, 10, 11

The Lookout Bed and Breakfast

14544 CR 12, 46540
(219) 825-9809

Located in the Amish country of northeast Indiana. Near the Menno-Hof (Amish-Mennonite Information Center); Shipshewana auction and flea market; antique, craft, and gift shops; famous restaurants; and the 1832 Bonneyville Mill. Enjoy the spectacular view with a country-style breakfast in the sunroom. Swim in the private pool, or walk the wooded trails.

Hosts: Mary-Lou and Jim Wolfe
Rooms: 5 (3 PB; 2 SB) $50-70
Full Breakfast
Credit Cards: A, B
Notes: 2, 5, 7, 9, 10, 11

Patchwork Quilt Country Inn

11748 CR2, 46540
(219) 825-2417

Relax and enjoy the simple grace and charm of our 100-year-old farmhouse. Sample our country cooking with homemade breads and desserts. Tour our back roads, and meet our Amish friends. Buy handmade articles, then return to the inn and rest in our quaint guest rooms.

Host: Maxine Zook and Susan Thomas
Rooms: 9 (SB) $50.95-95
Full Breakfast
Credit Cards: A, B
Closed first two weeks of January, holidays, Sundays
Notes: 2, 3, 4, 8, 10, 11

RED BOILING SPRINGS

Armour's Red Boiling Springs Hotel

321 East Main, 37150
(615) 699-2180

Armour's Hotel is one of three remaining historical hotels from a well-known booming mineral resort era of Red Boiling Springs heyday. The newly renovated building is furnished with antiques reflecting the turn of the century. Mineral baths are available on premises. Family style meals are served by reservations only. Group retreats are welcome. No television or telephones in rooms to interrupt your visits.

Hosts: Brenda and Bobby Thomas
Rooms: 20 (PB) $65
Full Breakfast and Dinner Included
Credit Cards: None
Notes: 2, 3, 4, 5, 7, 8

Armour's Red Boiling Springs Hotel

year; 6 Pets welcome; 7 Children welcome; 8 Tennis nearby; 9 Swimming nearby; 10 Golf nearby; 11 Skiing nearby; 12 May be booked through travel agent

SALEM

Lanning House & 1920 Annex

206 E. Poplar St., 47167
(812) 883-3484

The Lanning House & 1920 Annex is a part of the John Hay Center which included the John Hay home, museum and pioneer village. John Hay was Lincoln's secretary. Salem is 35 miles north of Louisville, 25 miles north of the old state capitol, 40 miles west of Madison and 25 miles from Spring Mill State Park. Approved by the Indiana Bed and Breakfast Association.

Host: Jeanette Hart
Rooms: 7 (3PB; 4SB) $30-50
Full Breakfast
Credit Cards: None
Notes: 2, 5, 7

SHIPSHEWANA

Morton Street Bed and Breakfast

140 Morton Street, P. O. Box 775, 46565
(219) 768-4391; (800) 447-6475

Remember when beds were made of white iron and were piled high with homemade quilts? You'll enjoy the attention you receive from the staff as they give you that "welcome home" feeling! Located within easy walking distance of all shops, the flea market, and the Buggy Wheel Restaurant.

Hosts: Joel & Kim Mishler and Esther Mishler
Rooms: 10 (PB)

Full Breakfast
Credit Cards: A, B, D
Notes: 2, 5, 7

TIPPECANOE

Bessinger's Hillfarm Wildlife Refuge Bed and Breakfast

4588 State Road 110, 46570
(219) 223-3288

This cozy log home overlooks 285 acres of rolling hills, woods, pasture fields, and marsh with 41 islands. It is ideal for geese and deer year-round. This farm features hiking trails with beautiful views, picnic areas, and benches tucked away in a quiet area. Varied seasons make it possible to canoe, swim, fish, bird-watch, hike, and cross-country ski. Start with a country breakfast and be ready for an unforgettable experience.

Hosts: Wayne and Betty Bessinger
Rooms: 3 (PB) $55-65
Full Breakfast
Credit Cards: None
Notes: 2, 4, 5, 9

WARSAW

White Hill Manor

2513 East Center Street, 46580
(219) 269-6933

This restored English Tudor mansion has hand-hewn oak beams and leaded-glass windows. Eight elegant bedrooms have phone, TV, and air conditioning. A conference room and a luxurious suite with spa bath are also available.

NOTES: Credit cards accepted: A Master Card; B Visa; C American Express; D Discover Card; E Diners Club; F Other; 2 Personal checks accepted; 3 Lunch available; 4 Dinner available; 5 Open all

Breakfast is served on the dining porch that is furnished with wicker. Adjacent to Wagon Wheel Theatre and Restaurant. Lake recreation and wonderful antique shops are nearby. Corporate discount.

Host: Gladys Deloe
Rooms: 8 (PB) $75-112
Full Breakfast
Credit Cards: A, B, C, D
Notes: 2, 5, 7, 8, 9, 10

WINONA LAKE

Gunn Guest House
904 Park Avenue, 46590
(219) 267-7552

The Gunn Guest House is located in the heart of historic Winona Lake. This Victorian home built in 1903 has beveled glass window and some rooms with eight sides. The Homer

Rodeheaver Auditorium, Grace College and Seminary, a beach and picnic area are attractions within walking distance. Wagon Wheel Theater, Biblical Gardens, and numerous antique shops are also nearby. The picturesque town park, which includes a beach and picnic area, is within walking distance.

Host: Delores Gunn
Rooms: 3 (SB) $40
Full Breakfast
Credit Cards: None
Notes: 2, 5, 7, 8, 9, 10, 11

Gunn Guest House

---

year; 6 Pets welcome; 7 Children welcome; 8 Tennis nearby; 9 Swimming nearby; 10 Golf nearby; 11 Skiing nearby; 12 May be booked through travel agent

Iowa

AMANA COLONIES

Die Heimat Country Inn

Main Street, Homestead, 52236
(319) 622-3937

Die Heimat Country Inn is located in
the historic Amana Colonies. It was
built in 1854 and is listed on the National Register of Historic Places. The
inn is decorated with locally handcrafted walnut and cherry furniture, with
many homemade quilts and antiques
throughout.

Hosts: Don and Sheila Janda
Rooms: 19 (PB) $36-65
Full Breakfast
Credit Cards: A, B, D
Notes: 2, 5, 6, 7, 8, 9, 10, 11

Die Heimat Country Inn

BURLINGTON

Lakeview Bed and Breakfast

RR#5, Box 734, 52601
(319) 752-8735 or (800) 753-8735

Built from the ruins of the county's third
oldest home, the elegant country mansion stands where stagecoach passen-
gers once slept. Now your retreat to
Lakeview is a mix of the old and the
new on 30 acres of magnificent country
charm. The house features crystal chandeliers, an abundance of antiques and
collectibles, and a circular staircase.
Outdoors you can enjoy a swim in our
pool, fishing on our 3-acre lake stocked
with catfish, large-mouthed bass, and
bluegill; or just spend time making
friends with our family of miniature
horses. Guests can also take advantage
of our large video library of noted Christian speakers.

Hosts: Jack and Linda Rowley
Rooms: 4 (PB) $45-60
Expanded Continental Breakfast
Credit Cards: A, B
Notes: 2, 5, 8, 9, 10, 12

NOTES: Credit cards accepted: A Master Card; B Visa; C American Express; D Discover Card; E
Diners Club; F Other; 2 Personal checks accepted; 3 Lunch available; 4 Dinner available; 5 Open all

CALMAR

Calmar Guesthouse

Rural Route 1, Box 206, 52132
(319) 562-3851

Newly remodeled, this century-old Victorian home was built by attorney John B. Kaye and has stained glass, antiques, and upstairs and downstairs sitting rooms with cable TV. It is located close to Bily Clocks in Spillville, the smallest church, Spook Cave, Niagara Cave, Lake Meyer, bike trails, golf courses, a community college, Norwegian museum, and Luther College in Decorah. Breakfast is served in the formal dining room. Bicycle trails are nearby.

Hosts: Art and Lucille Kruse
Rooms: 5 (SB) $35-45
Full Breakfast
Credit Cards: A
Notes: 2, 5, 8, 9, 10, 11

CLERMONT

Mill Street Bed and Breakfast

505 Mill Street, P. O. Box 34, 52135
(319) 423-5531

Mill Street Bed and Breakfast is a ranch-style home with central air conditioning. Near excellent restaurant and gift shops. Enjoy Montauk, canoeing, and fishing.

Hosts: Roger and Lois Amundson
Rooms: 2 (PB) $35
Full Breakfast
Notes: 2, 5, 7, 8, 9, 10

DUBUQUE

Another World—Paradise Valley Inn

P.O. Box 2, 52001
(800) 388-0942

A secluded log inn resembling a ski chalet minutes from heritage bicycle trail, Scandinavian Mountain Ski Area, Mississippi River and riverboat rides, antique shopping, Dubuque's downtown attractions and supperclubs. Special features include private baths, fireplace, TVs, kitchen, outdoor hot tub. Experience "romance at its best" in our valentine red heart-shaped bubble Luv tub showcased at many of America's leading resorts.

Hosts: Karen and Gene Parker
Rooms: 4 (PB) $75-150
Full Breakfast
Credit Cards: A, B
Notes: 2, 5, 7, 11, 12

The Mandolin Inn

199 Loras Boulevard, 52001
(319) 556-0069; (800) 524-7996

This unusual 1908 Edwardian has original oil paintings on the dining room walls and an Italian tile fireplace. Ideally located in the historic section of Dubuque, it is surrounded by magnificent turn-of-the-century churches, private homes, and historically significant government buildings.

Host: Jan Oswald
Rooms: 8 (6 PB; 2 SB) $65-100
Full Breakfast
Credit Cards: A, B, C, D
Notes: 2, 5, 7, 8, 9, 10, 11, 12

---

year; 6 Pets welcome; 7 Children welcome; 8 Tennis nearby; 9 Swimming nearby; 10 Golf nearby; 11 Skiing nearby; 12 May be booked through travel agent

FOREST CITY

The 1897 Victorian House

306 South Clark St., 50436
(515) 582-3613

Offering you hospitality in this turn-of-the-century Queen Anne Victorian home, as a guest at The 1897 Victorian House, you may choose from four beautifully decorated bedrooms, each with a private bath. Breakfast, included in your room rate, is served every morning in our dining room, and we specialize in "homemade" food. An antique shop is located on premises, and tours of various local interests are available. Gift certificates are available. Come relax in Forest City, a quiet yet progressive rural community.

Hosts: Richard and Doris Johnson
Rooms: 3 (PB) $50-70
Full Breakfast
Credit Cards: A, B
Notes: 2, 3&4 (by reservation), 5, 7 (by arrangement), 10, 12

IOWA CITY

Haverkamp's Linn St. Homestay B&B

619 N Linn St., 52245
(319) 337-4363

Enjoy the warmth and hospitality in our 1908 Edwardian home filled with heirlooms and collectibles. Only a short walk to downtown Iowa City and the University of Iowa main campus, and a short drive to the Hoover Library in West Branch, to the Amish in Kalona,

and to the 7 Amana Colonies.

Hosts: Dorothy and Clarence Haverkamp
Rooms: 3 (SB) $30-40
Credit Cards: None
Notes: 2, 5, 7, 8, 9, 12

LAKE VIEW

Marie's Bed and Breakfast

969 7th St., P.O. Box 817, 51450
(712) 657-2486

Modern all-brick ranch style home offers two bedrooms, one with a queen size bed, the other an extra long double bed and a single electric bed, all with a shared bath. Breakfast is your choice—full or continental. Marie's Bed and breakfast is handicapped accessible! Summer and weekly rates available. Only one block from the 950-acre beautiful Blackhawk Lake.

Hosts: Roy and Marie Werkmeister
Rooms: 2 (1PB; 1SB) $35-45 (winter-summer rates)
Choice of Full or Continental Breakfast
Credit Cards: None
Notes: 2, 3, 4, 5, 6 (except cats), 8, 9, 10, 11

LEIGHTON

Leighton-Pella Heritage House

1345 Highway 163-48MM, 50143
(515) 626-3092

This lovely 1918 farm home has TVs and central air conditioning. The Victorian room is filled with antique furniture and an old pump organ. Located near Pella, famous for Tulip Time the second week of May, historical tours are available to experience a touch of Holland. Dutch shops and a gourmet restaurant, and many antique shops are nearby. Near Red Rock Dam recreation areas. Hunters are welcome; lots of pheasant and quail, facilities to dress game and freezer space for storage. Member IBBIA.

Host: Iola Vander Wilt
Rooms: 3 (1 PB; 2 SB) $35-50
Full Breakfast
Credit Cards: None
Closed January
Notes: 2, 6, 7, 8, 9, 10, 11

MARENGO

Loy's Farm Bed and Breakfast

Rural Route 1, Box 82, 52301 (I-80 exit 216 North)
(319) 642-7787

This beautiful, modern home is on a working grain and hog farm with quiet and pleasant views of rolling countryside. A farm tour is offered with friendly hospitality. The large recreation room includes a pool table, table tennis, and shuffleboard. Swing set and sand pile are in the large yard. Close to the Amana Colonies, Tanger Mall, Kalona, Iowa City, West Branch, and Cedar Rapids. I-80, Exit 216 north one mile.

Host: Loy and Robert Walker
Rooms: 3 (1PB; 2 SB) $45-60
Full Breakfast
Notes: 2, 4 (by arrangement), 5, 6 (caged), 7, 8, 9, 10, 12

PELLA

Avondgloren (Sunset View)

R.R. #3, P.O. Box 65, 50219-0065
(515) 628-1578

Our charming brick home is ideally situated 1 1/2 miles southwest of Pella and 1 1/2 mile Northwest of Red Rock Dam. It is on an acreage with a view of both sunset and sunrise. It has decorating accents of live plants inside for your year-round enjoyment, as well as flower gardens outside true to the Dutch heritage. Also, a family room with a TV and fireplace is available for your use. Central air conditioning. A back deck with a lovely country view can also be used for your leisure time enjoyment. Credit Cards are only used to hold your room. Payment for stay paid with cash or check in order to keep room rates low.

Hosts: Henry and Luella M. Bandstra
Rooms: 3(SB) $45-55
Full Breakfast
Notes: 2, 5, 8, 10

SPENCER

Hannah Marie Country Inn

4070 So. HWY 71, 51301
(712) 262-1286; (712) 332-7719

Capture the grandeur of country. A pretty country-Victorian home, circa 1910. Once again visit the home-in-your-heart. A grandma's house. Cro-

year; 6 Pets welcome; 7 Children welcome; 8 Tennis nearby; 9 Swimming nearby; 10 Golf nearby; 11 Skiing nearby; 12 May be booked through travel agent

quet, rocking chairs, hammocks, air-conditioned, softened water. Near Iowa Great Lakes, West Bend, Grotto. Seen in *Iowan Home and Away (AAA)* and *Better Homes and Gardens' Country Inns Cookbook,* and *Country Woman.* Des Moines Registered Readers selected "Best B&B in Iowa" 1990. Also selected in "Best Fifty Inns" by *Inn Times.*

Host: Mary Nichols
Rooms: 3 (PB) $55-65
Full Breakfast
Credit Cards: A, B, C
Notes: 2, 3, 4, 7, 8, 9, 10, 12

STRATFORD

Hooks Point Farmstead

RR 3495 Hooks Point Drive, 50249
(515) 838-2781; (800) 383-7062

One hour north of Des Moines, 20 minutes west of I-35, near Boone and Scenic Valley RR, is this inviting 1904 homestay with old-fashioned warmth and modern comforts. Featherbeds, full breakfast, and opportunities for on-premises gourmet dining, backwood picnics, bicycling, canoeing, and antiquing. This is a working grain farm.

Hosts: Marvin and Mary Jo Johnson
Rooms: 3 (2 PB; 1 SB) $45-90
Full Breakfast
Credit Cards: A, B
Notes: 2, 4, 5, 7, 8, 9, 10, 11, 12

TIPTON

Victorian House

508 E. 4th St., 52772
(319) 886-2633

Rare, unique 1883 Eastlake-stick style Victorian on the National Register of Historic Places featuring Fresco paintings, vinegar style painting, impressive entryway furnished with an abundance of antiques and restored to the grandeur of the 1880s. Located in a small, quiet friendly town of many Victorian style homes, 9 churches and tree-lined streets located in the hub of S.E. Iowa. Come feel at home and enjoy our full, delicious breakfast. Reservations recommended.

Hosts: Lowell and Dee
Rooms: 4 (PB) $65(weekends) - $60(weekday)
2nd nite $10 off
Closed Jan and Feb
Full Breakfast
Credit Cards: A, B
Notes: 2, 4, 8, 9, 10, 12

WASHINGTON

Quiet Sleeping Rooms

125 Green Meadows Drive, 52353
(319) 653-3736

Modern home with all the conveniences. Private entrance, electric heat, air conditioned, shower with soft water, queen size bed, refrigerator, etc.

Hosts: Lois and Glen Williams
Rooms: 2 (1PB; 1SB) $30-35
Choice of Full or Continental Breakfast
Credit Cards: None
Notes: 2, 5, 6, 7, 8, 9, 10, 12

NOTES: Credit cards accepted: A Master Card; B Visa; C American Express; D Discover Card; E Diners Club; F Other; 2 Personal checks accepted; 3 Lunch available; 4 Dinner available; 5 Open all

WEBSTER CITY

Centennial Farm Bed and Breakfast

1091 220th Street, 50595
(515) 832-3050

Centennial Farm is a bed and breakfast homestay located on a working farm that has been in the family since 1869. Guests may gather their own eggs and take a ride in a 1929 Model A pickup truck, if desired. In a quiet location near several good antique shops. Member of Iowa Bed and Breakfast Innkeepers Association, Inc. Air conditioned. Twenty-two miles west of I-35 at Exit 142 or Exit 144.

Hosts: Tom and Shirley Yungclas
Rooms: 2 (SB) $35
Full Breakfast
Credit Cards: None
Notes: 2, 5, 7, 8, 9, 10

Kansas

ATWOOD

Goodnite at Irenes'

703 South Sixth, 67730
(913) 626-3521

Enjoy old-fashioned hospitality in a clean, comfortable home. Relax on an outdoor deck, hearing the birds sing while viewing the country pasture. Guests are welcome to enjoy the patio, large back yard, and the family room with TV and phone. We specialize in homemade continental or country style breakfast. Hunters welcome, but no hunting privileges. Non-smokers preferred.

Host: Irene E. Holste
Rooms: 2 (1 PB; 1 SB) $35
Full or Continental Breakfast
Credit Cards: None
Notes: 2, 5, 6, 7, 9

CASSODAY

The Sunbarger Guest House

R.R. #1, 66842
(316) 735-4499

Enjoy privacy and comfort of charming turn-of-the-century guest house set on spacious grounds, surrounded by wooded, bluestem pasture, longhorn cattle, and quarter horses. Within a mile of Cassoday, Interstate 35 Turnpike exit, real cowtown, and gateway to scenic Flinthills. Catered meals to your taste. Artists, antiques, cowboys abound! Half of payment required to reserve room.

Hosts: Dale and Judy Remsberg
Rooms: 4 (2PB; 2SB) $45
Continental Breakfast
Credit Cards: None
Notes: 2, 3, 4, 5

GREAT BEND

Peaceful Acres Bed and Breakfast

Rt. 5, Box 153, 67530
(316) 793-7527

Enjoy a mini-farm, sprawling, tree-shaded old farmhouse furnished with some antiques. If you like quiet, and peace, chickens, goats, guineas, kittens in the spring, and the old-fashioned hospitality, you need to come and visit us. Breakfast will be fixed from home-grown products. We are near historical areas, Sante Fe Trail, Ft. Larned, Cheyenne Bottoms, zoo and tennis courts.

Hosts: R. Dale and Doris J. Nitzel
Rooms: 3 (SB) $30
Full Breakfast
Credit Cards: None
Notes: 2, 5, 6, 8, 12

HALSTEAD

Heritage Inn
300 Main Street, Box 43, 67056
(316) 835-2118

The Heritage Inn offers the charm of the 1920s with the conveniences of the 1990s. Each room is beautifully decorated and has cable TV, refrigerator, individual heating and air conditioning. Breakfast is served in our cozy hotel cafe. While enjoying a leisurely breakfast, you can swap stories with other guests, or get acquainted with local business people.

Hosts: Jim and Geri Hartong
Rooms: 5 (PB) $29
Full Breakfast
Credit Cards: A, B
Notes: 2, 3, 4, 5, 7, 8, 10

LINDSBORG

Swedish Country Inn
112 West Lincoln, 67456
(913) 227-2985

The Swedish Country Inn is an authen-
tic Swedish bed and breakfast. There are 19 rooms furnished with Swedish-pine imported furniture and handmade quilts. Each room has a TV and phone. A full buffet Scandinavian breakfast is served. Use of sauna and bicycles is included. We have a small gift shop just off the lobby and are only one-half block off Main Street where there are wonderful shops and art galleries.

Hosts: Nick and Joan Wilson
Rooms: 19 (PB) $45-75
Full Breakfast
Credit Cards: A, B
Notes: 2, 5, 7, 8, 9, 10

VALLEY FALLS

The Barn Bed and Breakfast Inn
Rural Route 2, Box 87, 66088
(913) 945-3225

In the rolling hills of northeast Kansas, this 100-year-old barn has been converted into a bed and breakfast. Sitting high on a hill with a beautiful view, it has a large indoor heated pool, fitness room, three living rooms, king and queen beds in all rooms. We serve you supper, as well as a full breakfast, and have three large meeting rooms available.

Hosts: Tom and Marcella Ryan
Rooms: 20 (PB) $57-72
Full Breakfast and Supper
Credit Cards: A, B, C, D
Notes: 2, 3, 4, 5, 7, 8, 9, 10, 12

year; 6 Pets welcome; 7 Children welcome; 8 Tennis nearby; 9 Swimming nearby; 10 Golf nearby; 11 Skiing nearby; 12 May be booked through travel agent

Kentucky

BARDSTOWN

Kenmore Farms
1050 Bloomfield Rd., US 62E, 40004
(502) 348-8023

Circa 1860. This Victorian-style home on 170 acres features antique furniture, oriental rugs, poplar floors and a cherry banister. The bed linens are authentic period pieces decorated with lace. The inn serves a full Kentucky country breakfast. The champion saddle horse, Beau Brummel, lived at the farm.

Hosts: Dorothy and Bernie Keene
Rooms: 3 (PB) $70
Full Breakfast
Credit Cards: None
Notes: 2, 5, 7 (over 12), 8, 9, 10

Pineapple Inn

GEORGETOWN

Log Cabin Bed and Breakfast
350 North Broadway, 40324
(502) 863-3514

This authentic log cabin has two bedrooms, fireplace, kitchen/family room, air conditioning. Georgetown is a quiet, historic town five miles north of the Kentucky Horse Park and 12 miles north of Lexington. Facilities are completely private.

Hosts: Clay and Janis McKnight
Cabin: 1 (PB) $64
Expanded Continental Breakfast
Credit Cards: None
Notes: 2, 5, 6, 7, 8, 9, 12

Pineapple Inn
645 S. Broadway, 40324
(502) 868-5453

Located in beautiful Georgetown, Kentucky, our beautiful home, built in 1876, is on The National Historic Register. Country French dining room, large living room. Three bedrooms with private baths upstairs. Grandma's Room, full bed, Victorian Room, full bed, Ameri-

---

NOTES: Credit cards accepted: A Master Card; B Visa; C American Express; D Discover Card; E Diners Club; F Other; 2 Personal checks accepted; 3 Lunch available; 4 Dinner available; 5 Open all

cana Room, twin beds, Main floor room, queen size bed with canopy. Shared bath. Home is furnished with antiques. Very beautifully decorated. Full breakfast served.

Hosts: Muriel and Les
Rooms: 4 (3PB; 1SB) $60
Full Breakfast
Credit Cards: None
Notes: 2, 5, 8, 9, 10

GLENDALE

Petticoat Junction Bed and Breakfast

223 High Street, P.O. Box 36, 42740
(502) 369-8604

Our accommodations provide the utmost in comfort and relaxation. Unwind in the homey atmosphere of a beautifully renovated 1870s farmhouse furnished with antiques, vintage linens and a blend of country and Victorian decor. Meet new friends or cherish those quiet times alone with someone special. Awaken to the mouth-watering aroma of fresh-perked coffee and a hearty Southern-style breakfast. Come be our guests and experience our quaint hospitality.

Hosts: Jack and Rachel Holman
Rooms: 6 (4PB; 2SB) $60-75
Full Breakfast
Credit Cards: None
Notes: 2, 5, 7, 12 –

Petticoat Junction Bed and Breakfast

HARRODSBURG

Canaan Land Farm B&B

4355 Lexington Rd., 40330
(606) 734-3984

Step back in time to a house nearly 200 years old. Canaan Land B&B is an historic home, circa 1795. Rooms feature antiques and feather beds, full breakfast and true southern hospitality. This is a working sheep farm with lambing November and March. Your host is a shepherd/attorney, and your hostess is a handspinner/artist. Farm is secluded and peaceful. Close to Shaker Village. This is a non-smoking B&B.

Hosts: Fred and Theo Bee
Rooms: 3 (PB) $65-75
Full Breakfast
Credit Cards: None
Notes: 2, 5, 7 (strictly supervised by parents), 9, 10

LOUISVILLE

The Victorian Secret Bed and Breakfast

1132 South First Street, 40203
(502) 581-1914

"Step inside and step back 100 years in time" describes this three-story, Victorian brick mansion in historic Louisville. Recently restored to its former elegance, the 110-year-old structure offers spacious accommodations, high ceilings and original woodwork. The Louisville area, rich in historic homes, will also tempt railbirds and would-be jockeys to make a pilgrimage to the

year; 6 Pets welcome; 7 Children welcome; 8 Tennis nearby; 9 Swimming nearby; 10 Golf nearby; 11 Skiing nearby; 12 May be booked through travel agent

famous track at Churchill Downs, Home of the Kentucky Derby.

Hosts: Nan and Steve Roosa
Rooms: 6 (2PB; 4SB) $48-68
Continental Breakfast
Credit Cards: None
Notes: None

MIDDLESBORO

The Ridge Runner Bed and Breakfast

208 Arthur Heights, 40965
(606) 248-4299

This 1891 Victorian home is furnished with authentic antiques and nestled in the Cumberland Gap Mountains. A picturesque view is enjoyed from a 60-foot front porch. A relaxed, peaceful atmosphere; you are treated like a special person. Five minutes from Cumberland Gap National Historic Park, 12 miles from Pine Mountain State Park, 50 miles from Knoxville, Tennessee.

Host: Susan Richards
Rooms: 5 (2 PB; 3 SB) $40-45
Full Breakfast
Credit Cards: A, B
Notes: 2, 5

PADUCAH

Ehrhardt's Bed and Breakfast

285 Springwell Lane, 42001
(502) 554-0644

Our brick Colonial ranch home is lo-cated just one mile off I-24, which is noted for its lovely scenery. We hope to make you feel at home in antique-filled bedrooms and a cozy den with a fireplace. Nearby are the beautiful Kentucky and Barkley lakes and the famous Land Between the Lakes area.

Hosts: Eileen and Phil Ehrhardt
Rooms: 2 (SB) $35
Full Breakfast
Credit Cards: None
Notes: 2, 7 (over 12), 8, 9, 10

STEARNS

Marcum-Porter House

P.O. Box 369, 42647
(606) 376-2242; (606) 748-9070; (502) 223-3368

Located in the heart of the Big South Fork National Recreation Area, this charming early 20th century house offers gracious accommodations for discriminating guests with interests in history and unspoiled scenic beauty. Gourmet breakfast in formal dining room. Spacious grounds. Nearby attractions include the Big South Fork Scenic Railway, 9-hole golf course, swimming pool, local history museum, hiking, whitewater rafting and fishing on wild rivers and streams and Cumberland Falls State Park.

Hosts: Pat Porter Newton/Charles and Sandra Porter
Rooms: 4 (1PB; 3SB) $45-65
Gourmet Breakfast
Credit Cards: A, B
Notes: 2, 7, 8, 9, 10

NOTES: Credit cards accepted: A Master Card; B Visa; C American Express; D Discover Card; E Diners Club; F Other; 2 Personal checks accepted; 3 Lunch available; 4 Dinner available; 5 Open all

WILMORE

Scott Station Inn Bed and Breakfast

305 East Main St., 40390
(606) 858-0121

The Scott Station Inn is located in downtown, historic Wilmore, Kentucky, just three blocks from famous Asbury College, Asbury Seminary and only minutes from Shakertown, Fort Harrod and Lexington, Kentucky. Beautifully refurbished in 1990, this 100-year-old farmhouse has kept the charm of an old Kentucky home. Our inn has six rental rooms; three with shared baths ($39) and three with private baths ($49). We welcome pastor-staff and Sunday school retreats.

Hosts: Kathy and Tom Hunsberger (minister)
Rooms: 6 (3PB; 3SB) $39-49
Full Breakfast
Credit Cards: A, B
Notes: None

Scott Station Inn Bed and Breakfast

Louisiana

CARENCRO

La Maison de Campagne, Lafayette B&B

825 Kidder Road, 70520
(318) 896-6529; (800) 368-7308

The "country house" is a turn-of-the-century country Victorian nestled on nine acres of old live oak and pecan trees fifteen minutes from downtown Lafayette. All guest rooms are individually decorated with antiques and private baths. Experience the *joie de vive*, the joy of life of the Cajun culture in the music, food and festivals— all within a 30-mile radius. Full complimentary country gourmet breakfast included.

Hosts: Fred and Joeann McLemore
Rooms: 3 (PB) $75
Full Breakfast
Credit Cards: A, B
Notes: 2, 5, 9

NEW ORLEANS

St. Charles Guest House

1748 Prytania Street, 70130
(504) 523-6556

A simple, cozy, and affordable pension in the Lower Garden District on the streetcar line is 10 minutes to downtown and the French Quarter. Continental breakfast is served overlooking a charming pool and patio complete with banana tree. Tours are available from our lobby.

Hosts: Joanne and Dennis Hilton
Rooms: 30 (26 PB; 4 SB) $30-65
Continental Breakfast
Credit Cards: None
Notes: 2 (in advance), 5, 7, 8, 9

NOTES: Credit cards accepted: A Master Card; B Visa; C American Express; D Discover Card; E Diners Club; F Other; 2 Personal checks accepted; 3 Lunch available; 4 Dinner available; 5 Open all

PORT VINCENT

Tree House in the Park

Mailing address: 16520 Airport Road,
Prairieville, 70769
1-800-Le Cabin (1-800-532-2246)

Tree House in the Park is a Cajun cabin
in the swamp. Private entrance, queen
size waterbed, private hot tub on
sundeck, steps down to pool. Island
with gazebo. Boat slip, fishing dock,
double kayak. No smoking.

Host: Fran Schmieder
Rooms: 2 (PB) $100
Full Breakfast and Supper
Credit Cards: A, B
Notes: 2, 5, 9, 12

WHITE CASTLE

Nottoway Plantation Inn and Restaurant

Louisiana Highway 1, P.O. Box 160, 70788
(504) 545-2730; (504) 545-9167; FAX (504)
545-8632

Built in 1859 by John Randolph, a
wealthy sugar cane planter, Nottoway
is a blend of Italianate and Greek Revival styles. Nottoway is the largest
remaining plantation home in the South.
Its guest rooms are individually decorated with period furnishings.

Hosts: Cindy Hidalgo and Faye Russell
Rooms: 13 (PB) $125-250 (10 rooms, 3 suites)
Full Breakfast
Credit Cards: A, B, C, D
Closed Christmas Day
Notes: 2, 3, 4, 5, 8, 9, 10, 12

Maine

ANDOVER

Andover Arms Family Style Bed and Breakfast

Newton Street, P.O. Box 387, 04216-0387
(207) 392-4251

Discover Maine the way it used to be. Stay in this comfortable 1800s farmhouse in the village and feel right at home with the warm hospitality, country breakfasts, and cozy guest rooms with oil lamps for added charm. Relax by the wood stove or play the piano. Snowmobiling and cross country skiing from the door, 20 minutes to alpine skiing, including Sunday River. Excellent hunting, fishing, biking, foliage. Lawn games and bikes available. No smoking.

Host: Pat Wyman
Rooms: 4 (1PB; 3SB) $50
Full Breakfast
Credit Cards: A, B, C, D
Notes: 2, 4, 5, 6, 7, 8, 9, 11, 12

BAR HARBOR

Black Friar Inn

10 Summer Street, 04609
(207) 288-5091

Black Friar Inn is a completely rebuilt and restored inn incorporating beautiful woodwork, mantels, windows, and bookcases from old mansions and churches on Mount Desert Island. Gourmet breakfast includes homemade breads, pastry, and muffins, fresh fruit, eggs du jour, waffles, etc. Afternoon refreshments are provided. All rooms have queen beds. Within easy walking distance of the waterfront, restaurants, and shops, with ample parking available. Short drive to Acadia National Park.

Hosts: Barbara and Jim Kelly
Rooms: 6 (PB) $85-105
Full Breakfast
Credit Cards: A, B
Closed winter months
Notes: 2, 7 (over 11), 8, 9, 10

NOTES: Credit cards accepted: A Master Card; B Visa; C American Express; D Discover Card; E Diners Club; F Other; 2 Personal checks accepted; 3 Lunch available; 4 Dinner available; 5 Open all

Hearthside Bed and Breakfast

7 High Street, 04609
(207) 288-4533

Built in 1907 as a private residence, the inn features a blend of country and Victorian furnishings. All rooms have queen beds, some have a private porch or fireplace. We serve a homemade full breakfast, afternoon tea and homemade cookies, and evening refreshments. Located on a quiet side street in town, we are five minutes from Acadia National Park.

Hosts: Susan and Barry Schwartz
Rooms: 9 (PB) $55-70 in winter; $75-110 in-season
Full Breakfast
Credit Cards: A, B
Notes: 2, 5, 8, 9, 10, 11

Wayside Inn

11 Atlantic Ave., 04609
(207) 288-5703; (800) 722-6671

A beautiful English Tudor building decorated in early Victorian offering private and semi-private rooms with fireplaces. Full gourmet breakfast served. Located on a quiet side street in historic district within walking distance to all in-town activities. Open all year. Lower rates off season. 11 Atlantic Avenue, Bar Harbor, Maine 04609.

Hosts: Steve and Sandi Straubel
Rooms: 8 (6PB; 2SB)
Full Breakfast
Credit Cards: A, B
Notes: 2, 5, 7, 8, 9, 10, 11

Wayside Inn

BATH

Fairhaven Inn

Rural Route 2, North Bath Road, Box 85, 04530
(207) 443-4391

A 1790 Colonial nestled on the hillside overlooking the Kennebec River on 20 acres of country sights and sounds. Beaches, golf, and maritime museum nearby, plus cross-country ski trails, wood fires. Gourmet breakfast is served year-round. Candlelight dinners available in winter.

Hosts: Sallie and George Pollard
Rooms: 7 (5PB; 2SB) $50-75
Full Breakfast
Credit Cards: A, B, C
Notes: 2, 3 (box), 4 (weekend package), 5, 6 (by arrangement), 7 (by arrangement), 8, 9, 10, 11

BELFAST

The Jeweled Turret Inn

16 Pearl Street, 04915
(207) 338-2304; (800) 696-2304 (in state)

This grand lady of the Victorian era,

---

year; 6 Pets welcome; 7 Children welcome; 8 Tennis nearby; 9 Swimming nearby; 10 Golf nearby; 11 Skiing nearby; 12 May be booked through travel agent

circa 1898, offers many unique architectural features and is on the National Register of Historic Places. The inn is named for the grand staircase that winds up the turret, lighted by stained- and leaded-glass panels with jewel-like embellishments. Each guest room is filled with Victoriana and has its own bath. A gourmet breakfast is served. Shops, restaurants, and waterfront are a stroll away.

Hosts: Carl and Cathy Heffentrager
Rooms: 7 (PB) $65-85
Full Breakfast
Credit Cards: None
Notes: 2, 5, 8, 9, 10, 11, 12

Northport House Inn Bed and Breakfast

197 Northport Avenue, 04915
(207) 338-1422; (800) 338-1422 U.S., Maine and Canada

The Northport House Inn, a wonderfully restored Victorian house, circa 1873, is in a coastal community near Camden and Searsport. At one time it was an overnight stop on the Portland Bar Harbor Road. In the morning, enjoy our full breakfast of Belgian waffles, pancakes, French toast, eggs, omelets, muffins, biscuits, fresh fruit, and coffee or tea, served in our common room.

Hosts: Peter and Mary Lou Mankevetch
Rooms: 8 (4 PB; 4 SB) $53-85
Full Breakfast
Credit Cards: A, B
Notes: 2, 5, 7, 8, 9, 10, 11

BINGHAM

Mrs. G's Bed and Breakfast

Meadow Street, P.O. Box 389, 04920-0389
(207) 672-4034

An old Victorian home on the picturesque Kennebec River where white water rafting is popular. Hiking on the Appalachian Trail, beautiful waterfalls. Wonderful area for the fall foliage. Open May through November. Good area for fishing and hunting.

Host: Frances Gibson
Rooms: 4 (SB) (loft with 9 beds for groups available) $50
Full Breakfast
Credit Cards: None
Notes: 2, 4, 7, 8, 9, 10, 11, 12

BLUE HILL

Arcady Down East

South St., 04614
(207) 374-5576

Experience yesteryear in the warmth and elegance of our late 1800s Victorian Inn listed on the National Register of Historic Places. Equally suitable for honeymoons, family vacations, or family reunions. Come sit on our porch swing, have pink lemonade or apricot iced tea on our sunporch. We are here to pamper you.

Rooms: 7 (5PB; 2SB) $75-110
Full Breakfast
Credit Cards: A, B, C
Notes: 2, 5, 7, 9, 10, 11, 12

NOTES: Credit cards accepted: A Master Card; B Visa; C American Express; D Discover Card; E Diners Club; F Other; 2 Personal checks accepted; 3 Lunch available; 4 Dinner available; 5 Open all

BOOTHBAY HARBOR

Anchor Watch B&B
3 Eamea Rd., 04538
(207) 633-7565

Our seaside captain's house welcomes you to Boothbay Region. It's a pleasant walk to unique shops, fine dining, and scenic boat trips. A delicious home-made breakfast is served in the sunny breakfast nook looking out to the sea. Quilts, stenciling, and nautical decor make our 4 bedrooms and parlor comfortable and cozy. Your host captains the Monhegan and Squirrel Island ferries from nearby Pier 8.

Hosts: Diane Campbell
Rooms: 4 (PB) $70-75
Full Breakfast
Credit Cards: A, B
Notes: 2, 5, 8, 9, 10, 12

Harbour Towne Inn
71 Townsend Ave., 04543
(800) 722-4240

The First B&B on the waterfront. Harbour Towne Inn on Boothbay harbour, the boating capital of New England. All rooms with private bath and scenic harbor views. Short walk to all activities. Advanced reservations recommended anytime of the year.

Rooms: 12 (PB) $35-175
Continental Breakfast
Credit Cards: A, B, C, D
Notes: 2, 5, 9, 10

BRUNSWICK

Harborgate Bed and Breakfast
Rural Delivery 2, #2260, 04011
(207) 725-5894

This contemporary redwood home is 40 feet from the ocean. Flower gardens and wooded landscape provide gracious relaxation. Two ocean-facing, first-floor bedrooms are separated by a guest living room with patio. Dock for swimming and sunbathing. Close to Bowdoin College, L. L. Bean, and sandy beaches. Wide selection of stores, gift shops, and steak and seafood restaurants. Summer theater, college art museum, Perry McMillan Museum, and historical society buildings and events.

Host: Carolyn Bolles
Rooms: 2 (SB) $60
Continental Breakfast
Credit Cards: None
Closed November - April
Notes: 2, 9

CAMDEN

Blackberry Inn
82 Elm St., 04843
(207) 236-6060; (800) 833-6674

A vintage 1840 Victorian featuring spacious rooms and scrumptious breakfasts, only a stroll from the village's harbor, shops, and restaurants. Rooms with fireplaces, television, and jacuzzis available, and a Carriage House suite with a queen size bed, bunk beds, kitchen and television is perfect for

---

year; 6 Pets welcome; 7 Children welcome; 8 Tennis nearby; 9 Swimming nearby; 10 Golf nearby; 11 Skiing nearby; 12 May be booked through travel agent

families. Relax in the inn's parlors or sunny courtyard. Complimentary social hour and real DownEast hospitality. See why the *Miami Herald* calls us "A delightful B&B." No smoking.

Rooms: 10 (PB) $50-135
Full Breakfast
Credit Cards: A, B
Notes: 2, 5, 7, 8, 9, 10, 11

Blackberry Inn

CLARK ISLAND

Craignair Inn

Clark Island Road, 04859
(207) 594-7644; (800) 524-ROOM

Located on the water, the inn is near great hiking trails along the shore or through the forests. The inn was formerly a boarding house for stonecutters from the nearby quarries that provide great swimming. The annex was once the village chapel. A peaceful and secluded setting.

Host: Terry Smith
Rooms: 22 (8 PB; 14 SB) $57-87
Full Breakfast
Credit Cards: A, B, C
Notes: 2, 4, 6, 7, 8, 9, 10, 11, 12

DAMARISCOTTA

Brannon-Bunker Inn

HCR 64, Box 045B, 04543
(207) 563-5941

Brannon-Bunker Inn is an intimate and relaxed country bed and breakfast situated minutes from sandy beach, lighthouse, and historic fort in Maine's mid-coastal region. Located in a 1920s Cape, converted barn, and carriage house, the guest rooms are furnished in themes reflecting the charm of yesterday and the comforts of today. Antique shops, too!

Hosts: Jeanne and Joe Hovance
Rooms: 7 (4 PB; 3 SB) $55-65
Expanded Continental Breakfast
Credit Cards: A, B, C
Closed Christmas week
Notes: 2, 5, 7, 8, 9, 10, 12

Down Easter Inn at Damariscotta

Bristol Road, Routes 129 and 130, 04543
(207) 563-5332; (201) 540-0500 winter

The Down Easter Inn, one mile from downtown Damariscotta, is in the heart of the rocky coast of Maine. On the National Register of Historic Places, it features a two-story porch framed by Corinthian columns. Minutes from golfing, lakes, and the ocean. Nearby are lobster wharfs for local fare and boat trips around Muscongus Bay and to Monhegan Island. The inn features 22 lovely rooms with TVs.

Hosts: Mary and Robert Colquhoun
Rooms: 22 (PB) $65-75
Continental Breakfast

NOTES: Credit cards accepted: A Master Card; B Visa; C American Express; D Discover Card; E Diners Club; F Other; 2 Personal checks accepted; 3 Lunch available; 4 Dinner available; 5 Open all

Credit Cards: A, B
Notes: 2, 9, 10

EAST BOOTHBAY

Five Gables Inn

Murray Hill Road, 04544
(207) 633-4551; (800) 451-5048

The Five Gables Inn is an elegantly restored 125-year-old bed and breakfast located on Linekin Bay. The inn has 15 rooms, all with a water view and some with working fireplaces. It is located away from the busy Boothbay Harbor area on a quiet street in East Boothbay. Swimming, boating, golfing, or just relaxing on the veranda are available. No smoking.

Hosts: Ellen and Paul Morissette
Rooms: 15 (PB) $80-120
Full Breakfast
Credit Cards: A, B
Closed December-April
Notes: 2, 7

EASTPORT

Todd House

Todd's Head, 04631
(207) 853-2328

Large, center-chimney Cape, circa 1775, overlooking Passamadoddy Bay. Barbecue facilities, deck, library with items of local history. In 1801, men formed a Masonic order in what is now a guest room. Beautiful sunrises and sunsets!

Host: Ruth M. McInnis
Rooms: 5 (2 PB; 3 SB) $45-80
Expanded Continental Breakfast
Notes: 2, 5, 6, 7

ELIOT

The Farmstead

379 Goodwin Rd., 03903
(207) 748-3145; (207) 439-4279

Lovely country inn on 3 acres. Warm friendly atmosphere exemplifies farm life in the late 1800s. Guest rooms are Victorian in style. Each has mini refrigerator and microwave for late evening snacks or special diet. Full breakfast may include blueberry pancakes or french toast, homemade syrup, fruit and juice. Handicap accessible. Minutes from Kittery Factory Outlets, York beaches and Portsmouth, NH, historic sites. 1 hour from Boston.

Hosts: Mel and John Lippincott
Rooms: 6 (PB) $48
Full Breakfast
Credit Cards: A, B, C
Notes: None

FREEPORT

Captain Josiah Mitchell House

188 Main Street, 04032
(207) 865-3289

Two blocks from L. L. Bean, this house is a five-minute walk past centuries-old sea captains' homes and shady trees to all shops in town. After exploring, relax on our beautiful, peaceful veranda with antique wicker furniture and "remember when" porch swing. State inspected and approved. Family owned and operated.

Hosts: Loretta and Alan Bradley

---

year; 6 Pets welcome; 7 Children welcome; 8 Tennis nearby; 9 Swimming nearby; 10 Golf nearby; 11 Skiing nearby; 12 May be booked through travel agent

Rooms: 6 (PB) $75-85 (winter rates are reduced)
Full Breakfast
Credit Cards: A, B
Notes: 2, 5, 9, 10, 11, 12

Country at Heart Bed and Breakfast

37 Bow Street, 04032
(207) 865-0512

Our cozy 1870 home is located off Main Street and only two blocks from L. L. Bean. Park your car and walk to the restaurants and many outlet stores. Stay in one of three country-decorated rooms: the Shaker room, quilt room, or the Teddy bear room. Our rooms have hand-stenciled borders, handmade crafts, and either antique or reproduction furnishings. There is also a gift shop for guests.

Hosts: Roger and Kim Dubay
Rooms: 3 (PB) $65-75
Full Breakfast
Credit Cards: None
Notes: 2, 5, 7, 9, 10, 11, 12

GREAT CRANBERRY ISLAND

The Red House

Great Cranberry Island, 04625
(207) 244-5297

This is a place for total relaxation in a charming shorefront, former saltwater farm on a small island overlooking Mt. Cadillac and Acadia National Park. After a short, scenic passenger ferry ride from Northeast Harbor, you will be met at the dock and transported to an antique Cape with traditionally decorated rooms. There are many opportunities for walks on the shore and bicycle rides. A full home-cooked breakfast is served.

Hosts: Dorothy and John Towns
Rooms: 6 (3 PB; 3 SB) $60-75; $50-60 off-season
Full Breakfast
Credit Cards: A, B
Notes: 2, 4, 8, 9, 10

GREENVILLE

Hillside Gardens

Blairs Hill, Box 1189, 04441
(207) 695-3386

High on a hilltop overlooking miles of beautiful Moorehead Lake is a 100-year-old Victorian mansion with spacious rooms and private baths. The quietness and beauty of the estate makes you think you have slipped back in time to a more peaceful era. Over 70 acres of land and trails for you to explore. Come up with us to Hillside Gardens for your getaway vacation.

Hosts: Mary and Marty Hughes
Rooms: 5 (4PB; 2SB) $65-95
Full Breakfast
Credit Cards: A, B
Notes: 2, 3, 4, 5, 7 (over 12), 8,9, 10, 11, 12

GUILFORD

The Guilford Bed and Breakfast

Elm and Prospect Street, 04443
(207) 876-3477

A lovely 1905 Post-Victorian with a half-wrap porch and situated high on a knoll within walking distance of the town and shops. Enjoy a hearty breakfast of homemade pastries or muffins, hash with poached egg, or buttermilk pancakes. In the winter, enjoy tea by the fireplace in our library. In the summer, have gourmet lunch on our lovely screen porch. Fish Moosehead Lake, hike the Appalachain Trail, ski Squaw Mountain.

Hosts: Pat and John Selicious
Rooms: 5 (2PB; 3SB) $50
Full Breakfast
Credit Cards: A, B
Notes: 2, 5, 9, 10, 11

KENNEBUNK

Sundial Inn

P.O. Box 1147, 48 Beach Ave., 04043
(207) 967-3850

Unique oceanfront inn furnished with turn-of-the-century Victorian antiques. Each of the 34 guest rooms has a private bath, phone, color TV and air conditioning. Several rooms also offer ocean views and whirlpool baths. Visit Kennebunkport's art galleries and studios, museums, and gift shops. Go whale watching, deep-sea fishing, or hiking at the nearby wildlife refuge and estuary. Golf and tennis are nearby. Continental breakfast features muffins and coffee cakes. Wheelchair accessible.

Hosts: Larry and Pat Kenny
Rooms: 34 (PB) $65-151
Continental Breakfast
Credit Cards: A, B, C, E
Notes: 5, 8, 9, 10

KENNEBUNKPORT

The Captain Lord Mansion

P. O. Box 800, 04046
(207) 967-3141; (800) 522-3141

The Captain Lord Mansion is an intimate and stylish Maine coast inn. Built during the War of 1812 as an elegant, private residence, it is now listed on the National Register of Historic Places. The large, luxurious guest rooms are furnished with rich antiques, yet have modern creature comforts. The gracious hosts and innkeepers and their friendly staff are eager to make your visit enjoyable. Family-style breakfasts are served in an atmospheric country kitchen.

Hosts: Bev Davis and Rick Litchfield
Rooms: 16 (PB) $79-159 January-April; $149-199 May to December
Full Breakfast
Credit Cards: A, B, D
Notes: 2, 5, 8, 9, 10

The Green Heron Inn

Ocean Avenue, P.O. Box 2578, 04046
(207) 967-3315

Comfortable, clean, and cozy ten-room bed and breakfast. Each guest room has private bath, air conditioning, and color TV. A full breakfast from a menu is served. "Best breakfast in town."

Hosts: Charles and Elizabeth Reid
Rooms: 10 (PB) $68-120
Full Breakfast
Credit Cards: None
Notes: 2, 5, 6 (in advance), 8, 9, 10

year; 6 Pets welcome; 7 Children welcome; 8 Tennis nearby; 9 Swimming nearby; 10 Golf nearby; 11 Skiing nearby; 12 May be booked through travel agent

Maine Stay Inn and Cottages

34 Maine St., P.O. Box 500-A , 04046
(800) 950-2117; (207) 967-2117

A Grand Victorian Inn that exudes charm from its wrap-around porch to its perennial flower gardens and spacious lawns. The white clapboard house built in 1860 and listed on the National Historic Register and adjoining cottages sit grandly in Kennebunkport's Historic District. A variety of delightful accommodations from inn rooms, suites, and one-bedroom cottages (some with fireplaces), all with private baths and color TVs, await you. A sumptuous full breakfast and afternoon tea are included. The Inn is an easy walk to Harbor, shops, galleries, and restaurants. AAA three diamond, Mobil Guide three star and ABBA excellent rated.

Hosts: Carol and Lindsay Copeland
Rooms: 17 (PB) $75-185
Full Breakfast
Credit Cards: A, B, C
Notes: 2, 5, 7, 8, 9, 10, 11, 12

Maine Stay Inn and Cottages

KENT'S HILL

Home Nest Farm

Box 2350, 04349
(207) 897-4125

Off the beaten track, on a foothill of the Longfellow Mountains of West Central Maine's lake district, Home Nest Farm offers a 60-mile panoramic view to the White Mountains. A place for all seasons, it includes three historic homes, furnished with period antiques: the main house (1784); Lilac Cottage (c. 1800); and the Red Schoolhouse (c. 1830). Local activities include sheep tending, berry picking, Living History Farm Museum, exploring many trails (maintained for snowmobiling and skiing in the winter), swimming, fishing, boating (boats provided).

Hosts: Arn and Leda Sturtevant
Rooms: 4 (PB) $50-95
Closed in March and April
Full Breakfast
Credit Cards: None
Notes: 2, 7, 9, 10, 11

LUBEC

Breakers by the Bay

37 Washington Street, 04652
(207) 733-2487

Enjoy the breathtaking views of the sea from your own private deck in this blue and white New England home located close to the international bridge leading to Campobello and Roosevelt's house. Start your day with a full breakfast in the dining room. Then choose from the beautiful vistas of Quoddy Head State Park and Campobello, or just sit back and enjoy relaxing. All rooms have 19-inch color TV and refrigerator.

Host: E. M. Elg
Rooms: 4 (3 PB (semi-private)); 1 SB) $40-60
Suite: 1

NOTES: Credit cards accepted: A Master Card; B Visa; C American Express; D Discover Card; E Diners Club; F Other; 2 Personal checks accepted; 3 Lunch available; 4 Dinner available; 5 Open all

Full Breakfast
Credit Cards: None
Closed November-April
Notes: 2, 10

MILLINOCKET

Katahdin Area Bed and Breakfast

94-96 Oxford Street, 04462
(207) 723-5220

We are located 17 miles south of the entrance to Baxter State Park, the gateway to Katahdin, Maine's highest peak. With a population fewer than 8,000, Millinocket has small-town charm. The spectacular "Grand Canyon of the East" on Gulf Hagas is a short distance from here off Route 11 South. Appalachian Trail access; 156 miles of groomed trails; walking distance to Main Street, restaurants, shops, houses of worship.

Hosts: Rodney and Mary Lou Corriveau
Rooms: 5 (1 PB; 4 S2B) $40-50
Full Breakfast
Credit Cards: None
Notes: 2, 5, 7, 8, 9, 10

NAPLES

The Augustus Bove House

Rural Route 1, Box 501, 04055
(207) 693-6365

Historic Hotel Naples, recently restored to show off its gracious charm, offers authentic, colonial accommodations in a relaxing atmosphere at affordable prices. Overlooking Long Lake and the Causeway, within easy walking distance of water, restaurants, recreations,

and shops. Air conditioning, color TV, VCR and movies, and phone are provided. Antique and gift shop are on the premises. Off-season specials.

Hosts: David and Arlene Stetson
Rooms: 7 (3 PB; 4 SB) $45-85
Full Breakfast
Credit Cards: A, B, D
Notes: 2, 4 (off-season), 5, 6, 7, 8, 9, 10, 11, 12

NEWPORT

Lake Sebasticook B&B

8 Sebasticook Avenue, P.O. Box 502, 04953
(207) 368-5507

Take a step back in history in our 1903 Victorian home located on a quiet street in Newport, Maine. Relax on the second floor sunporch or comfortable wraparound porch and enjoy the sounds of ducks and loons on Lake Sebasticook. Take a short walk to the lake park or play tennis at the city park a block away. In the morning, savor a full country breakfast including homemade breads and jams.

Rooms: 3 (1PB; 2SB) $50+
Full Breakfast
Credit Cards: C
Notes: 2, 8, 9, 10

SACO

Crown 'n' Anchor Inn

P.O. Box 228, 121 North St., 04072-0228
(207) 282-3829

Located in the Thacher-Goudale House, a National Register Home in the state of

---

year; 6 Pets welcome; 7 Children welcome; 8 Tennis nearby; 9 Swimming nearby; 10 Golf nearby; 11 Skiing nearby; 12 May be booked through travel agent

Maine, the Crown 'n' Anchor Inn is a fully restored federal house in the Adamesque style with Greek Revival temple front and furnished throughout with period and country antiques. After a bountiful breakfast or a busy day, socialize in the parlor or curl up with a good book in the library.

Hosts: John Barclay and Martha Forester
Rooms: 6 (PB) $60-85
Full Breakfast
Credit Cards: A, B
Notes: 2, 5, 7 (by arrangement), 8, 9, 10, 11, 12

SEARSPORT

Homeport Inn

East Main St., Rte. 1, 04974
(207) 548-2259; (800) 742-5814

Enjoy the unusual with a restful stop at this fine example of a New England Sea Captain's mansion. This elegant home, appointed with period antiques, offers a rare opportunity to be an overnight guest or to have a vacation without the customary traveler's commercialism. Truly a warm, homey, hospitable atmosphere. On the sea coast in the quaint village of Searsport. Guests may enjoy restaurants, visits to antique shops, churches, parks, and the "Home Port" for visiting the many neighboring coastal resort towns.

Host: Mrs. Edith Johnson
Rooms: 10 (6PB; 4SB) $55-75
Full Breakfast
Credit Cards: A, B, C, D, F (Enroute)
Notes: 2, 5, 7, 8, 9, 10, 11, 12

Thurston House Bed and Breakfast Inn

8 Elm Street, P. O. Box 686, 04974
(207) 548-2213

This beautiful Colonial home, circa 1830, with ell and carriage house, was built as a parsonage for Stephen Thurston, uncle of Winslow Homer, who visited often. Now you can visit in a casual environment. The quiet village setting is steps away from Penobscot Marine Museum, beach park on Penobscot Bay, restaurants, churches, galleries, antiques, and more. Relax in one of four guest rooms, two with bay views, and enjoy the "forget about lunch" breakfasts.

Hosts: Carl and Beverly Eppig
Rooms: 4 (2 PB; 2 SB) $45-60
Full Breakfast
Credit Cards: A, B
Notes: 2, 5, 7, 8, 9, 10, 11, 12

SOUTHWEST HARBOR

The Island House

P. O. Box 1006, Clark Point Rd., 04679
(207) 244-5180

Relax in a gracious, restful seacoast home on the quiet side of Mount Desert Island. We serve such Island House favorites as blueberry coffee cake and sausage-cheese casserole. A charming private loft apartment is available. Acadia National Park is only a five-minute drive away. Located across the street from the harbor, near swimming, sailing, biking, and hiking.

Host: Ann Gill

NOTES: Credit cards accepted: A Master Card; B Visa; C American Express; D Discover Card; E Diners Club; F Other; 2 Personal checks accepted; 3 Lunch available; 4 Dinner available; 5 Open all

Rooms: 4 (SB) $50-95
Full Breakfast
Credit Cards: None
Closed January-March
Notes: 2, 7 (over 11), 9, 10

THOMASTON

Cap'n Frost
Bed and Breakfast

241 West Main (U.S. Route 1), 04861
(207) 354-8217

Our 1840 Cape is furnished with country antiques, some of which are for sale. If you are visiting our mid-coastal area, we are a comfortable overnight stay, close to Monhegan Island and a two-hour drive to Acadia National Park. Reservations are helpful.

Hosts: Arlene and Harold Frost
Rooms: 3 (1 PB; 2 SB) $40-45
Full Breakfast
Credit Cards: A, B
Notes: 2, 5, 9, 11

VAN BUREN

The Farrell-Michaud
House

231 Main Street 04785
(207) 868-5209

Step back in time to along the scenic St. John River Valley in Northern Maine and enjoy this fully restored 1882 Victorian home. Listed on the National Historic Registry, this home features unique imported hand-carved wooden arches, decorative tin walls and ceilings, and large bedrooms, some with private baths. Activities include cross border shopping, fall foliage, county fairs, local crafts, and harvesting, along with winter sports activities such as downhill and cross country skiing, snowmobiling, ice skating and sled riding. Continental breakfast is served.

Host: Shiela Cyr
Rooms: 5 (2PB; 3SB) $39-49
Continental Breakfast
Credit Cards: A, B
Notes: 2, 4 (reservation), 5, 7, 8, 9, 10, 11

WATERFORD

The Parsonage House
Bed and Breakfast

Rice Road, P.O. Box 116, 04088
(207) 583-4115

Built in 1870 for the Waterford Church, this restored historic home overlooks Waterford Village, Keoka Lake, and Mt. Tirem. It is located in a four-season area providing a variety of opportunities for the outdoor enthusiast. The Parsonage is a haven of peace and quiet. Three double guest rooms are tastefully furnished. Weather permitting, we feature a full breakfast on the screened porch. Guests love our large New England farm kitchen and its glowing wood-burning stove.

Hosts: Joseph and Gail St-Hilaire
Rooms: 3 (1 PB; 2 SB) $40-50
Full Breakfast
Credit Cards: None
Notes: 2, 3, 5, 7, 9, 10, 11

year; 6 Pets welcome; 7 Children welcome; 8 Tennis nearby; 9 Swimming nearby; 10 Golf nearby; 11 Skiing nearby; 12 May be booked through travel agent

YORK BEACH

Homestead Inn B&B

8 South Main St., Rt. 1A, 03910
(207) 363-8952

Friendly, quiet and homey—four rooms in an old (1905) boarding house; connected to our home in 1969. Panoramic view of ocean and shore hills. Walk to beaches (2), shops, and Nubble Lighthouse. Great for small, adult groups. Fireplace in living room. Breakfast served in barn-board dining room and outside on private sun deck.

Hosts: Dan and Danielle Duffy
Rooms: 4 (SB) $59
Continental Breakfast
Credit Cards: None
Notes: 2, 8, 9, 10, 12

YORK HARBOR

Bell Buoy
Bed and Breakfast

570 York Street, 03911
(207) 363-7264

At the Bell Buoy, there are no strangers, only friends who have never met. Located minutes from I-95 and U.S. 1, minutes from Kittery outlet malls and a short walk to the beach, enjoy afternoon tea served either on the large front porch or the living room with fireplace and cable TV. Homemade breads or muffins are served with breakfast in the dining room each morning or on the porch.

Hosts: Wes and Kathie Cook
Rooms: 4 (1 PB; 3 SB) $55-80
Full Breakfast
Credit Cards: None
Notes: 2, 6, 7 (over six), 9, 10

York Harbor Inn

Route 1A, P.O. Box 573, 03911
(207) 363-5119; (800) 343-3869

For more than 100 years, the historic charm and hospitality of York Harbor Inn have welcomed those seeking distinctive lodging and dining experiences. A short walk takes you to a peaceful, protected beach. A stroll along Marginal Way reveals hidden coastal scenes and classic estates. Golf, tennis, biking, deep-sea fishing, and outlet shopping are close by. Air conditioning, antiques, phones, private baths, ocean views, and fireplaces. Full dining room and tavern with entertainment.

Hosts: Joe and Garry Dominguez
Rooms: 32 (28 PB; 4 SB) $45-129
Continental Breakfast
Credit Cards: A, B, C, E, F
Notes: 2, 3, 4, 5, 7, 8, 9, 10, 11, 12

NOTES: Credit cards accepted: A Master Card; B Visa; C American Express; D Discover Card; E Diners Club; F Other; 2 Personal checks accepted; 3 Lunch available; 4 Dinner available; 5 Open all

Maryland

ANNAPOLIS

The Barn on Howard's Cove

500 Wilson Road, 21401
(410) 266-6840

This is a restored 1850s barn on a secluded cove off the Severn River, three miles from historic Annapolis, state capital, and sailing center of the United States. Annapolis is the home of the U.S. Naval Academy and has easy access to Washington, D. C., and Baltimore. Enjoy beautiful gardens and rural setting, country decor with antique quilts and furniture. Guests may dock boats on a private dock.

Hosts: Dr. and Mrs. Graham Gutsche
Rooms: 2 (PB) $60 (plus $7.20 state lodging tax)
Full Breakfast
Credit Cards: None
Notes: 2, 5, 7, 8, 10, 12 (10%)

The Bates House

727 1/2 Rosedale Street, 21401
(410) 263-5559

The Bates House is conveniently located in the City of Annapolis, Maryland's historic capitol. Less than one mile from the United States Naval Academy, State House, the Annapolis Harbor, and the historic area. Built by the owners in 1986, The Bates House is open and casual with country modern decor. Enjoy southern hospitality provided by the Bateses' who are natives of Georgia.

Hosts: Peggy and Bobby Bates
Rooms: 2 (PB) $55 (5% state tax)
Full Breakfast
Credit Cards: None
Notes: 2, 5, 7, 10, 12

Charles Inn

74 Charles St., 21401
(410) 268-1451

The Charles Inn, a charming Civil War era house, is in the heart of Annapolis' historic district with water taxi convenience to restaurants, city dock, etc., or just blocks on foot to Main Street. Guests are pampered with down comforters, featherbeds and cozy antique-filled rooms. A private suite offers a jacuzzi, ceiling fan and water view. A full breakfast each morning features one of the innkeeper's delectable treats such as crepes, dutch apple pancakes, or orange pecan waffles. The inn provides off-street parking for guests' convenience.

Hosts: Paula Ginnetty Hartman and John Hartman
Rooms: 4 (2PB; 2SB) $75-149
Full Breakfast
Credit Cards: A, B, C
Notes: 2, 5, 7, 12

Jonah Williams House, 1830

101 Severn Avenue, 21403
(401) 269-6020

Peach siding and brown trim grace this historic home in a charmingly light and healthy, newly decorated environment featuring 19 windows and Laura Ashley decor. Close to historic town shopping center, Main Street, and city dock; one block from Spa Creek and Severn River; one block from water taxi pick-up to any location in the area, including the U.S. Naval Academy, three minutes

away.

Hosts: Dorothy and Hank Robbins
Rooms: 4 (1 PB; 3 SB) $65-75
Continental Breakfast
Credit Cards: None
Notes: 2, 9, 12

BALTIMORE

Mulberry House

111 West Mulberry Street, 21201
(410) 576-0111

From this historic inn in the downtown area, walk to shopping, restaurants, and attractions. Four deluxe double guest rooms feature antique armoires, four-poster or brass beds, and brass chandeliers. Grand piano, fireplace, and courtyard. Free parking, but a car is not necessary.

Hosts: Charlotte and Curt Jeschke
Rooms: 4 (SB) $75
Full Breakfast
Credit Cards: None
Notes: 2, 5, 7 (over 16), 12

Society Hill Hopkins Hotel

3404 St. Paul St., 21218
(410) 235-8600

Society Hill Hopkins Hotel, built in the 1920s, is part of a cluster of seven buildings. Its 26 guest rooms, parlor and dining room are furnished with antiques from several periods. Original art works decorate the inn, including some thirty paintings and drawings by Marie Pobre, a New York artist commissioned by The Hopkins! Guests may have breakfast served in the dining room or in their own rooms. The Hopkins is convenient to the campus of Johns Hopkins University.

Host: Ken Scherning
Rooms: 26 (PB) $105-125
Continental Breakfast
Credit Cards: A, B, C, E, F (Carte Blanche)
Notes: 2, 5, 7, 10, 12

BERLIN

Merry Sherwood Plantation

8909 Worcester Highway, 21811
(410) 641-2112; (800) 660-0358; FAX (410) 641-3605

This 1859, pre-Civil War mansion allows the visitor to experience a glorious step back in time. Recently restored, this elegant and opulent home is furnished throughout with authentic Victorian antiques. Situated on 19 acres of beautiful 19th-century landscaping. Upon entering the main gates, you definitely begin your very special getaway. Enjoy formal ballroom, stately dining room, warm fireplaces and superb breakfast and loving hospitality.

Host: Kirk Burbage
Rooms: 8 (6PB; 2SB) $95-150
Full Breakfast
Credit Cards: A, B
Notes: 2, 5, 8, 9, 10, 12

CHESTERTOWN

Radcliffe Cross

8046 Quaker Neck Rd., 21620
(410) 778-5540

Quiet rural charm with century-old plantings surround this pre-revolutionary brick manor house (c. 1725) situated on 28 acres 1/2 mile from Historic Chestertown. Antique furnishings, fireplaces and original pine floors add to the authenticity of this lovely home. Breakfast features such specialties as puff pastries, muffins and coffee cakes. Fine dining close by. Area activities include antiquing, biking, hiking and reserves for bird watching.

Hosts: Dan and Marge Brook
Rooms: 2 (PB) $70
Full Breakfast
Credit Cards: None
Notes: 2, 5, 8, 9, 10, 12

The River Inn at Rolph's Wharf

Rd. 1, Box 646, Rolph's Wharf Rd., 21620
(410) 778-6347

The River Inn at Rolph's Wharf is an 1830s Victorian Inn on 5 acres of the scenic Chester River, 3 miles south of Chestertown, Maryland. If you are looking for a quiet getaway, this is it. Enjoy beautiful sunsets on the deck, the beach or the patio of the Sunset grill Restaurant. Come by boat and stay at our marina or the inn. Swimming, crabbing, dining and relaxing...We have it all!

Host: Sandy Strouse
Rooms: 6 (PB) $65-115
Continental Breakfast
Credit Cards: A, B, C, D, E
Notes: 2, 3, 4, 5, 7, 9, 10

---

year; 6 Pets welcome; 7 Children welcome; 8 Tennis nearby; 9 Swimming nearby; 10 Golf nearby; 11 Skiing nearby; 12 May be booked through travel agent

ELKTON

Garden Cottage at Sinking Springs Herb Farm

234 Blair Shore Road, 21921
(410) 398-5566

With an early plantation house, including a 400-year-old sycamore, the garden cottage nestles at the edge of a meadow flanked by herb gardens and a historic barn with a gift shop. It has a sitting room with fireplace, bedroom, bath, air conditioning, and electric heat. Freshly ground coffee and herbal teas are offered with the country breakfast. Longwood Gardens and Winterthur Museum are 50 minutes away. Historic Chesapeake City is nearby with excellent restaurants. Sleeps three in two rooms.

Hosts: Bill and Ann Stubbs
Room: 1 (PB) $85
Full Breakfast
Credit Cards: A, B
Notes: 2, 5, 8, 10, 12

FREDERICK

Middle Plantation Inn

9549 Liberty Road, 21701-3246
(301) 898-7128

From this rustic inn built of stone and log, drive through horse country to the village of Mount Pleasant. The inn is located several miles east of Frederick on 26 acres. Each room is furnished with antiques and has a private bath, air conditioning, and TV. The keeping room, a common room, has stained glass and a stone fireplace. Nearby are antique shops, museums, and many historic attractions. Located within 40 minutes of Gettysburg, Pennsylvania; Antietam Battlefield; and Harper's Ferry.

Hosts: Shirley and Dwight Mullican
Rooms: 4 (PB) $85-95
Continental Breakfast (optional)
Credit Cards: A, B
Notes: 2, 5, 8, 9, 10, 12

Middle Plantation

GAITHERSBURG

Gaithersburg Hospitality Bed and Breakfast

18908 Chimney Place, 20879
(301) 977-7377

This luxury host home just off I-270 with all amenities, including private parking, is located in the beautifully planned community of Montgomery Village, near churches, restaurants and shops and is 5 minutes from DC Metro Station or a convenient drive South to Washington, D.C., and North to historic Gettysburg, PA, and Harper's Ferry. This spacious bed and breakfast has two rooms with private baths; one has a queen bed. Also offered are a large, sunny third room with twin beds, and a fourth room with a single bed. Hosts delight in serving full,

---

NOTES: Credit cards accepted: A Master Card; B Visa; C American Express; D Discover Card; E Diners Club; F Other; 2 Personal checks accepted; 3 Lunch available; 4 Dinner available; 5 Open all

homecooked breakfasts with your pleasure and comfort in mind.

Hosts: Suzanne and Joe Danilowiiz
Rooms: 4 (2 PB; 2 SB) $52
Full Breakfast
Notes: 2, 5, 7, 8, 9, 10, 12

HAGERSTOWN

Lewrene Farm Bed and Breakfast
9738 Downsville Pike, 21740
(301) 582-1735

Enjoy our quiet, Colonial country home on 125 acres near I-70 and I-81, a home away from home for tourists, business people, and families. We have room for family celebrations or seminars for 12 to 16 people. Sit by the fireplace or enjoy the great outdoors. Antietam Battlefield and Harper's Ferry are nearby; Washington, D. C., and Baltimore are one and one-half hours away. Quilts for sale.

Hosts: Irene and Lewis Lehman
Rooms: 6 (3 PB; 3 SB) $50-78
Full Breakfast
Credit Cards: None
Notes: 2, 5, 7, 8, 9

ST. MICHAELS

Parsonage Inn
210 North Talbot Street, 21663
(800) 394-5519

This late Victorian, circa 1883, was lavishly restored in 1985 with seven guest rooms, private baths, and brass beds with Laura Ashley linens. Three rooms have working fireplaces. The parlor and dining room are in the European tradition. Striking architecture! Two blocks to the maritime museum, shops, and restaurants.

Host: Will Workman
Rooms: 7 (PB) $82-114
Full Breakfast
Credit Cards: A, B
Notes: 2, 5, 7, 8

Pasonage Inn

Wades Point Inn on the Bay
P. O. Box 7, 21663
(410) 745-2500

For those seeking the serenity of the country and the splendor of the bay, we invite you to charming Wades Point Inn, just a few miles from St. Michaels. Complemented by the ever-changing view of boats, birds, and water lapping the shoreline, our 120 acres of fields and woodlands, with one-mile walking or jogging trail, provide a peaceful setting for relaxation and recreation on Maryland's eastern shore.

Hosts: Betsy and John Feiler
Rooms: 15 winter, 25 summer (15 PB; 10 SB) $59-169
Continental Breakfast
Credit Cards: A, B
Notes: 2, 5, 7, 8, 10

year; 6 Pets welcome; 7 Children welcome; 8 Tennis nearby; 9 Swimming nearby; 10 Golf nearby; 11 Skiing nearby; 12 May be booked through travel agent

SILVER SPRINGS

Varborg
2620 Briggs Chaney Road, 20905
(301) 384-2842

This suburban Colonial home in the countryside is convenient to Washington, D.C., and Baltimore, just off Route 29 and close to Route 95. Three guest rooms with a shared bath are available. This home has been inspected and given a two-star rating by the American Bed and Breakfast Association. No smoking.

Hosts: Robert and Patricia Johnson
Rooms: 3 (SB) $50
Full Breakfast
Credit Cards: None
Notes: 5, 7, 8

NOTES: Credit cards accepted: A Master Card; B Visa; C American Express; D Discover Card; E Diners Club; F Other; 2 Personal checks accepted; 3 Lunch available; 4 Dinner available; 5 Open all

Massachusetts

AMHERST

Allen House Victorian Bed and Breakfast Inn

599 Main Street, 01002
(413) 253-5000

An authentic 1886 Victorian bed and breakfast inn located on three acres in the heart of Amherst and within walking distance of the area colleges and the Emily Dickenson House. We feature spacious bed chambers, period decor, and a full breakfast. Brochure available. The 1991 Amherst Historic Commission Preservation Award winner. AAA Three Diamond Award.

Hosts: Alan and Ann
Rooms: 5 (PB) $45-95
Full Breakfast
Credit Cards: None
Notes: 2, 5, 7 (over 10), 8, 9, 10, 11

Allen House

BOSTON

A B&B Agency of Boston

47 Commercial Wharf, 02110

Downtown Boston's largest selection of guest rooms in historic bed and breakfast homes including Federal and Victorian townhouses and beautifully restored 1840s waterfront lofts. Available nightly, weekly, monthly. Or choose from the loveliest selection of fully furnished private studios, one and two bedroom condominiums, corporate suites and lofts with all the amenities including fully furnished kitchens, private baths (some with jacuzzis), TV and telephones. Available nightly, weekly, monthly. Exclusive locations include waterfront, Faneuil Hall/Quincy Market, North End, Back Bay, Beacon Hill, Copley Square and Cambridge.

Owner: Ferne Mintz
Rooms: 120 (80PB; 40SB) $65-110
Continental Breakfast
Credit Cards: A, B
Notes: 2, 5, 7, 12

---

year; 6 Pets welcome; 7 Children welcome; 8 Tennis nearby; 9 Swimming nearby; 10 Golf nearby; 11 Skiing nearby; 12 May be booked through travel agent

82 Chandler Street Bed and Breakfast

82 Chandler St., 02116
(617) 482-0408

This 1863 red-brick townhouse is located just off Copley Square in historic residential neighborhood in downtown Boston. Around the corner from John Hancock Tower, Back Bay/South End, Amtrack Station. Short walk to Hynes Convention Center, Freedom Trail, Newbury Street shops. Each well-furnished bedroom has a private bath, kitchenette and telephone. You'll receive a warm welcome, enjoy a tasty American family-style breakfast in our penthouse kitchen, and be within easy walking distance of all the city's sights. Mentioned in *Frommer's Guide* as one of the best. This is a downtown Boston B&B; enjoy the advantages of being in the heart of the city.

Hosts: Denis F. Coté and Dominic C. Beraldi
Rooms: 5 (PB) $95-125
Full Breakfast
Credit Cards: None
Notes: 5, 12

Greater Boston Hospitality

P. O. Box 1142, Brookline, 02146
(617) 277-5430

This bed and breakfast reservation service represents more than 100 homes, unhosted apartments, and inns throughout historic areas of Beacon Hill, Back Bay, and waterfront in Boston, as well as surrounding suburbs and the north and south shore areas of Massachusetts. All have been personally inspected for comfort, cleanliness, and congeniality of hosts. Many include parking and are close to public transportation. Write for free brochure. $70-120. Kelly Simpson, coordinator.

Host Homes of Boston

P.O. Box 117C: Waban Branch, 02168
(617) 244-1308

Marcia Wittington has carefully selected hosts who live in the best areas of Boston and close-to-Boston locations. Whether Historic brownstone, Victorian, Colonials, or contemporary, the feeling is "New England" and welcoming. Since 1982, she has managed all B&B inspections and reservations, giving personalized attention to both hosts and guests. It's a spirit and style that is appreciated by visitors from all over the world. Free brochure describes host homes.

BREWSTER

Captain Freeman Inn

15 Breakwater Road, 02631
(800) 843-4664

A charming Victorian sea captain's mansion located on beautiful historic Cape Cod. Outdoor pool, badminton, croquet, fireplaces, whirlpool spas. Furnished in antiques of the era. A short stroll down beautiful Breakwater Road to the white sand beach on Cape Cod Bay. Full Gourmet breakfast included. Antiquing, whale watching, museums, parks and much more to see and do.

Host: Carol Covitz
Rooms: 12 (9PB; 3SB)
Full Breakfast
Credit Cards: A, B, C
Notes: 2, 5, 7 (over 10), 8, 9, 10, 12

Captain Freeman Inn

CENTERVILLE

Long Dell Inn

436 South Main St., 02632
(508) 775-2750

An historic 1850s sea captain's home in the Greek revival style. Furnished with antiques and oriental rugs. Fireplace living room. Delightfully comfortable and romantic. Full 3 course breakfast served. Everything homemade and home-baked. Five minute walk to famous Craigville Beach. Shelter for bikes. Off-street parking. Shopping nearby. 10 minutes to ferries. Canopied beds and private decks.

Hosts: Roy and Joy Swayze
Rooms: 6 (PB) $70-80 1 efficiency apartment $85/night or $525/week.
Full Breakfast
Credit Cards: None
Notes: 2, 5, 7, 8, 9, 10, 12

CHATHAM—CAPE COD

The Cranberry Inn at Chatham

359 Main Street, 02633
(508) 945-9232; (800) 332-4667 reservations

A historic landmark conveniently located in a quaint seaside village, the Cranberry Inn is Chatham's oldest inn. It is completely restored. All guest rooms are individually appointed with antiques and four-poster and canopy beds. Suites and rooms with fireplaces are available. Some rooms have decks. Air conditioning, TV, phones. Walk to beaches, golf, tennis, shops, and restaurants.

Hosts: Peggy DeHan and Richard Morris
Rooms: 18 (PB) $90-160
Expanded Continental Breakfast
Credit Cards: A, B, C
Notes: 2, 7 (over 12), 8, 9, 10, 12

The Old Harbor Inn

22 Old Harbor Road, 02633
(508) 945-4434; (800) 942-4434

Experience enchantment in this English country-style inn. Guest rooms offer king, queen, or twin beds, decorator fabrics and linens. A home-baked buffet breakfast is served in the sunroom or on the outside deck. Enjoy the gathering room with fireplace. Beaches, art galleries, museums, golf, tennis, fishing, boating, quaint shops, wildlife preserve, theater, outdoor concerts, and fine restaurants are all within easy walk

---

year; 6 Pets welcome; 7 Children welcome; 8 Tennis nearby; 9 Swimming nearby; 10 Golf nearby; 11 Skiing nearby; 12 May be booked through travel agent

ing distance. A warm welcome and pleasurable memory-making await you. AAA-rated three diamonds.

Hosts: Tom and Sharon Ferguson
Rooms: 7 (PB) $95-140
Expanded Continental Breakfast
Credit Cards: A, B, C, D
Notes: 2, 5, 8, 9, 10, 12

CHELMSFORD

Westview Landing

P. O. Box 4141, 01824
(508) 256-0074

This large, contemporary home overlooking Hart's Pond is located three miles from Routes 495 and 3—30 miles north of Boston, and 15 minutes south of Nashua, New Hampshire. It is close to historic Lexington, Concord, and Lowell. Many recreational activities, including swimming, boating, fishing, and bicyling, are nearby; and there is a hot spa on the premises.

Hosts: Robert and Lorraine Pinette
Rooms: 3 (SB) $40-50
Full Breakfast
Credit Cards: None
Notes: 2, 6, 7, 8, 9, 10, 11

DANVERS

Cordwainer Bed and Breakfast at the Samuel Legro House

78 Center Street, 01923
(508) 774-1860

A circa 1854 home on the National Register of Historic Places, featuring beamed ceilings, canopy queen beds, fireplaces in the kitchen and the living room. The swimming pool is open from June to September for your enjoyment. Danvers is located twenty miles north of Boston and five miles west of Salem.

Host: Peggie Blais
Rooms: 3 (1PB; 2SB) $55-65
Full Breakfast
Credit Cards: None
Notes: 5, 7, 8, 9, 10

DEERFIELD-SOUTH

Deerfield's Yellow Gabled House

307 North Main Street, 01373
(413) 665-4922

Located in Deerfield South, this country house is located in the heart of a historical and cultural area and is the site of the Bloody Brook Massacre of 1675. It is furnished with period antiques and promises a comfortable stay with the ambience of yesteryear. One mile from the crossroads of I-91, Route 116 and Routes 5 and 10, and close to historic Deerfield and five-college area.

NOTES: Credit cards accepted: A Master Card; B Visa; C American Express; D Discover Card; E Diners Club; F Other; 2 Personal checks accepted; 3 Lunch available; 4 Dinner available; 5 Open all

Air conditioned.

Host: Edna Julia Stahelek
Rooms: 3 (1 PB; 2 SB) $50-80
Full Breakfast
Credit Cards: None
Notes: 2, 5, 7 (over 10), 8, 9, 10, 11, 12

DENNIS

Isaiah Hall B&B Inn

152 Whig St., 02638
(508) 385-9928; (800) 736-0160

Enjoy country ambience and hospitality in the heart of Cape Cod. Tucked away on a quiet historic side-street, this lovely 1857 farmhouse is within walking distance of the beach, restaurants, shops and playhouse. Delightful gardens surround the Inn with country antiques, orientals and quilts within. Most rooms have private baths and queen size beds. Some have balconies or fireplaces. Near biking, golf and tennis. AAA three diamond rating and ABBA three crown award.

Host: Marie Brophy
Rooms: 11 (10PB; 1SB) $55-98
Expanded Continental Breakfast
Credit Cards: A, B, C
Notes: 2, 7 (7+) 8, 9, 10, 12

DENNISPORT

The Rose Petal B&B

152 Sea St., P.O. Box 974, 02639
(508) 398-8470

Conveniently situated in the heart of Cape Cod and a short walk past century- old homes to a sandy beach. Inviting 1872 home, lovingly restored, beautifully landscaped yard, four attractive guest rooms with queen size or twin beds. Home baked pastries highlight a superb full breakfast. Near all of the cape's attractions: shops, antiques, dining, golf, beaches, bike trails, ferries to the Islands, whale watching.

Hosts: Dan and Gayle Kelly
Rooms: 4 (SB) $40-55
Full Breakfast
Credit Cards: A, B
Notes: 2, 5, 7, 8, 9, 10, 12

DUXBURY

Black Friar Brook Farm

636 Union Street, 02332
(617) 834-8528

Enjoy a restful stay in the historic home of Josiah Soule who, 285 years ago, left the pilgrim shore of Duxbury to farm on a land grant. See the oak gunstock beams, pine floors and antique charm throughout, and enjoy the hearty breakfasts prepared by your host. Blueberry pancakes are a specialty. Make this stop to see historic Plymouth, Boston, and Cape Cod.

Hosts: Anne and Walter Kopke
Rooms: 2 (1 PB; 1 SB) $45
Full Breakfast
Credit Cards: None
Notes: 2, 5, 7, 8, 9, 10

EAST ORLEANS

Nauset House Inn

143 Beach Road, Box 774, 02643
(508) 255-2195

A real old-fashioned country inn farmhouse, circa 1810, is located on three
acres with an apple orchard, one-half
mile from the ocean. No TV, no phones
in the rooms. Large commons room and
dining room have large fireplaces. Cozy,
antiques, eclectic--a true fantasy.

Hosts: Diane and Al Johnson; Cynthia and John
Vessell
Rooms: 14 (8 PB; 6 SB) $45-95
Full or Continental Breakfast
Credit Cards: A, B
Notes: 2, 8, 9, 10

Ship's Knees Inn

186 Beach Road, P. O. Box 756, 02643
(508) 255-1312

This 170-year-old restored sea captain's
home is a three-minute walk to beautiful sand-duned Nauset Beach. Inside
the warm, lantern-lit doorways are 19
rooms individually appointed with special Colonial color schemes and authentic antiques. Some rooms feature
authentic ship's knees, handpainted
trunks, old clipper ship models, braided
rugs, and four-poster beds. Tennis and
swimming are available on the premises. Three miles away overlooking
Orleans Cove, the Cove House property offers three rooms, a one-bedroom
efficiency apartment, and two cottages.

Hosts: Jean and Ken Pitchford
Rooms: 22, 1 apartment, 2 cottages (11 PB; 14
SB) $45-100

Continental Breakfast
Credit Cards: A, B
Notes: 2, 5, 7 (Cove House property), 10, 12

Ship's Knees Inn

EDGARTOWN, MARTHA'S VINE-YARD

The Arbor

222 Upper Main Street, P.O. Box 1228, 02539
(508) 627-8137

This turn-of-the-century Victorian is
delightfully and typically New England
and filled with the fragrance of fresh
flowers. Relax in the garden, have tea in
the parlor, stroll to the enchanting village and bustling harbor of Edgartown.
Come, be our guest at The Arbor.

Host: Peggy Hall
Rooms: 10 (8 PB; 2 SB) $55-95 off-season;
$80-125 in-season
Continental Breakfast
Credit Cards: A, B
Notes: 2, 8, 9, 10

Colonial Inn of Martha's Vineyard

38 North Water Street, 02539
(508) 627-4711; (800) 627-4701; FAX (508)
627-5904

The charm of Martha's Vineyard is
echoed by the history and style of the
Colonial Inn, overlooking the harbor in
the heart of historic Edgartown. Af-

NOTES: Credit cards accepted: A Master Card; B Visa; C American Express; D Discover Card; E
Diners Club; F Other; 2 Personal checks accepted; 3 Lunch available; 4 Dinner available; 5 Open all

fordable luxury awaits you. All rooms have heat, air-conditioning, color cable TV and telephones. Continental breakfast is served in the sunroom with patio seating available.

Host: Linda Malcouronne
Rooms: 42 (PB) $60-175
Continental Breakfast
Credit Cards: A, B, C
Closed January-March
Notes: 2, 3, 4, 7, 8, 9, 10, 12

ESSEX

George Fuller House

148 Main Street, 01929
(508) 768-7766

Built in 1830, this handsome Federalist-style home retains much of its 19th-century charm, including Indian shutters and a captain's staircase. Three of the guest rooms have working fireplaces. Decoration includes handmade quilts, braided rugs, and caned Boston rockers. A full breakfast may include such features as Cindy's French toast drizzled with brandy lemon butter. The inn's 30-foot sailboat is available for day sailing or lessons.

Hosts: Cindy and Bob Cameron
Rooms: 6 (PB) $70-100
Full Breakfast
Credit Cards: A, B, C, D
Notes: 1, 5, 7, 8, 9, 10, 12

FALMOUTH

Captain Tom Lawrence House Bed and Breakfast Inn

75 Locust Street, 02540
(508) 540-1445

1861 whaling Captain's residence in historic village close to beach, bikeway, ferries, bus station, shops, and restaurants. Explore entire Cape, Vineyard and Plymouth by day trips. 6 beautiful guestrooms have private baths, firm beds, some with canopies. Antiques, a Steinway piano and fireplace in sitting room. Homemade delicious breakfasts include specialties from organic grain. German spoken. No Smoking! Closed in January.

Host: Barbara Sabo-Feller
Rooms: 6 (PB) $75-99
Full Breakfast
Credit Cards: A, B
Notes: 2, 7 (over 12), 8, 9, 10

Grafton Inn

261 Grand Ave., So., 02540
(508) 540-8688

Oceanfront Victorian. Miles of beach and breath-taking views of Martha's Vineyard. Sumptuous full breakfast served on enclosed porch overlooking Nantucket Sound. Tastefully decorated rooms with period antiques. Thoughtful amenities. Flowers, homemade chocolates. Complimentary bicycles. Late afternoon wine and cheese. Walk to restaurants, shops and island ferry.

year; 6 Pets welcome; 7 Children welcome; 8 Tennis nearby; 9 Swimming nearby; 10 Golf nearby; 11 Skiing nearby; 12 May be booked through travel agent

Open all year. No Smoking!

Hosts: Liz and Rudy Cvitan
Rooms: 11 (PB) $65-120
Full Breakfast
Credit Cards: A, B, C
Notes: 2, 5, 8, 9, 10

The Palmer House Inn

81 Palmer Avenue, 02540
(508) 548-1230; (800) 472-2632

Located in the historic district, this turn-of-the-century Victorian offers eight rooms, antique furnishings, and a gourmet breakfast. Enjoy *pain perdue* with orange cream or Finnish pancakes with strawberry soup. Walk to beaches, shops, restaurants. Bicycles are available. Reservations suggested.

Hosts: Ken and Joanne Baker
Rooms: 8 (PB) $65-115
Full Breakfast
Credit Cards: A, B, C, D, E, F
Notes: 2, 5, 8, 9, 10, 12

Peacock's Inn on the Sound

P. O. Box 201, 02541
(508) 457-9666

This oceanfront bed and breakfast offers ten spacious guest rooms, fireplaces, country charm, and comfort. Enjoy the breathtaking view, sample our deluxe full breakfast, then spend your day touring year-round attractions. We are within walking distance of the island ferry, shops, and restaurants. Reservations suggested. Two-night minimum stay.
Hosts: Bud and Phyllis Peacock

Rooms: 10 (PB) $65-115
Full Breakfast
Credit Cards: A, B, C, D, E
Notes: 2, 5, 8, 9, 10

FALMOUTH HEIGHTS

The Moorings Lodge

207 Grand Avenue South, 02540
(508) 540-2370

A Victorian sea captain's home is across from a sandy beach with lifeguard safety and within easy walking distance of restaurants and island ferry. The homemade breakfast buffet is served on the large, glassed-in porch overlooking Martha's Vineyard. Comfortable, airy rooms, most with private baths. Call us "home" while you tour Cape Cod.

Hosts: Ernie and Shirley Bernard
Rooms: 8 (6 PB; 2 SB) $50-75
Full Breakfast
Credit Cards: A, B
Notes: 2, 7 (over 6), 8, 9, 10

GLOUCESTER

Williams Guest House

136 Bass Avenue, 01930
(508) 283-4931, (508) 283-5734

Gloucester is a beautiful fishing town located on Cape Ann. Betty's Colonial Revival house borders the finest beach, Good Harbor. Rooms are furnished with comfort in mind, and a light breakfast is served. Boat cruises, sport fishing, whale watching trips, Hammond Castle, shops, and art galleries in both Rockport

---

NOTES: Credit cards accepted: A Master Card; B Visa; C American Express; D Discover Card; E Diners Club; F Other; 2 Personal checks accepted; 3 Lunch available; 4 Dinner available; 5 Open all

and Rocky Neck are nearby.

Hosts: Betty and Ted Williams
Rooms: 7 (5 PB; 2 SB) $50-58 in-season; $40-50 off-season
Continental Breakfast
Credit Cards: None
Closed November-April
Notes: 2, 9, 10

GREAT BARRINGTON

Arrawood Bed and Breakfast
105 Taconic Avenue, 01230
(413) 528-5868

A beautifully restored Victorian in a quaint New England village 100 miles north of New York City, Arrawood is handsomely furnished. Common rooms have fireplaces and guestrooms have four poster and canopy beds. Candlelit breakfasts include homemade muffins and breads, plus entrees like french toast, pancakes, or eggs and biscuits. The Berkshire Mountains' beauty draws visitors year round. In summer Tanglewood, The Berkshire Theatre Festival and Jacob's Pillow. In winter, two ski areas, Butternut Basin and Catamount, are only minutes away. Nearby are shopping outlets, antique shops, craft stores and art galleries.

Hosts: Marilyn and Bill Newmark
Rooms: 4 (2PB; 2SB) $50-85
Full Breakfast
Credit Cards: None
Notes: 2, 5, 7 (not in summer), 8, 9, 10, 11, 12

GREENFIELD

Hitchcock House
15 Congress St., 01301
(413) 774-7452

A Lovely old Victorian house owned by Betty and Peter Gott. It was built in 1881 by Edward Hitchcock and designed by F.C. Currier, renowned Springfield architect. Greenfield was formerly a part of historic Deerfield. Surrounded by well-known colleges and schools, it is a fine place to stop when headed for ski country, leaf peeping, school functions or exploring the many nearby points of historic interest. Our rooms are complemented by antique furnishing, country quilts and accessories. Sit in our homey dining room and savor Betty's homemade muffins, fresh fruits and specialty of the day, after which you can relax on our front porch, sunporch, or patio. You can then embark on your own tour from our conveniently located Inn, a few blocks from a woodland park and minutes from a shopping area. We will be happpy to assist you in tour planning and restaurant selection.

Hosts: Betty and Peter Gott
Rooms: 5 (2PB; 3SB) $55-75
Full Breakfast on weekends, Expanded Continental on weekdays.
Credit Cards: A, B
Notes: 2, 5, 6, 7, 8, 9, 10, 11, 12 (10%)

---

year; 6 Pets welcome; 7 Children welcome; 8 Tennis nearby; 9 Swimming nearby; 10 Golf nearby; 11 Skiing nearby; 12 May be booked through travel agent

HARWICHPORT

Harbor Walk Guest House

6 Freeman Street, 02646
(508) 432-1675

Harbor Walk is in the beautiful Wychmere Harbor area of Harwichport. A few steps from the house will bring you a view of the harbor, and further along is one of the finest beaches on Nantucket Sound. The village of Harwichport is only one-half mile away and contains interesting shops and fine restaurants. We offer queen canopy beds, a good breakfast, private baths and a cool breeze on the porch.

Hosts: Marilyn and Preston Barry
Rooms: 6 (4 PB; 2 SB) $45-70
Expanded Continental Breakfast
Credit Cards: None
Notes: 2, 7 (by arrangement), 8, 9, 10, 12

HYANNIS

The Inn on Sea Street

358 Sea Street, 02601
(508) 775-8030

This elegant 1849 Victorian inn is just steps from the beach and features fireplace, romantic guest rooms, canopy beds, antiques, and Oriental carpets. A gourmet breakfast includes homemade delights, fruit, and cheese. Close to island ferries, entertainment, and Kennedy Compound. Travel writers' choice bed and breakfast. One-night stays welcome.

Hosts: Lois Nelson and J. B. Whitehead
Rooms: 10 (8PB; 2SB) $70-95
Full Breakfast
Credit Cards: A, B, C, D
Notes: 2, 3, 4, 8, 9, 10

Sea Breeze Inn

397 Sea Street, 02601
(508) 771-7213

Sea Breeze is a 14-room quaint bed and breakfast. It is just a three-minute walk to the beach and 20 minutes to the island ferries. Restaurants, night life, shopping, golf, tennis are within a ten-minute drive. Some rooms have ocean views. An expanded continental breakfast is served between 7:30 and 9:30 each morning.

Hosts: Patricia and Martin Battle
Rooms: 14 (PB) $45-85
Expanded Continental Breakfast
Credit Cards: None
Notes: None

LENOX

Garden Gables Inn

141 Main St., P.O. Box 52, 01240
(413) 637-0193

220-year-old charming and quiet inn located in historic Lenox on five wooded acres dotted with gardens. 72 foot swimming pool. Some rooms have fireplaces, and sitting rooms are furnished with antiques and a grand Steinway piano. All rooms have private baths and some also have whirlpool tubs and private porches. Breakfast is included. In-room phones are provided and the famous Tanglewood

---

NOTES: Credit cards accepted: A Master Card; B Visa; C American Express; D Discover Card; E Diners Club; F Other; 2 Personal checks accepted; 3 Lunch available; 4 Dinner available; 5 Open all

Festival is only one mile away. Restaurants are all within walking distance.

Hosts: Mario and Lynn Mekinda
Rooms: 14 (PB) $65-180
Full Breakfast
Credit Cards: A, B, D
Notes: 5, 8, 10, 11

Walker House Inn

74 Walker St., 01240
(413) 637-1271

Situated on three wooded acres near the center of a charming New England village, Walker House, constructed in 1804, offers eight guestrooms named for composers, all with antiques, some with fireplaces. The large parlor has a grand piano, the library, hundreds of books and a seven foot video screen on which guests may watch films, operas and special events. Breakfast and afternoon tea are served in the dining room, and two verandas provide additional space for relaxation. Good restaurants, galleries, an arts center, churches and shops are within walking distance.

Hosts: Richard and Peggy Houdek
Rooms: 8 (PB) $50-160 (seasonal)
Generous Continental Breakfast
Credit Cards: None
Notes: 2, 5, 6 (by approval), 7 (over 12), 8, 9, 10, 11

MARBLEHEAD

Harborside House

23 Gregory Street, 01945
(617) 631-1032

An 1850 Colonial overlooks picturesque Marblehead Harbor, with water views from the paneled livng room with a cozy fireplace, period dining room, sunny breakfast porch, and third-story deck. A generous breakfast includes juice, fresh fruit, home-baked goods, and cereals. Antique shops, gourmet restaurants, historic sites, and beaches are a pleasant stroll away. The owner is a professional dressmaker and a nationally ranked competitive swimmer. No smoking.

Host: Susan Livingston
Rooms: 2 (SB) $60-75
Expanded Continental Breakfast
Credit Cards: None
Notes: 2, 5, 7 (over 10), 8, 9

Spray Cliff on the Ocean

25 Spray Avenue, 01945
(508) 744-8924, (800) 626-1530

Panoramic views stretch out in grand proportions from this English Tudor mansion, circa 1910, set high above the Atlantic. The inn provides a spacious and elegant atmosphere inside. The grounds include a brick terrace surrounded by lush flower gardens where eider ducks, black cormorants, and seagulls abound. Fifteen miles from Boston.

Hosts: Richard and Diane Pabich
Rooms: 7 (PB) $95-200
Continental Breakfast
Credit Cards: A, B, C, D, E
Notes: 5, 8, 9, 12

NANTUCKET

Bed'n Breakfast on Nantucket Island

22 Lovers Lane, 02554
(508) 228-9040

Our accommodations are unique because, for the nightly rate of a room anywhere else, we offer a suite that sleeps four, has a small kitchen, living room, bath, deck, and private entrance. Located two miles from busy Main Street, a beautiful pine forest surrounds our home. Less than one mile down the quiet road brings our guests to a surf beach. Come to the island and let us spoil you! No smoking. Discounts to private pilots!

Hosts: Louise and Jim Ozias
Suite: 1 (PB) $90
Continental Breakfast
Credit Cards: None
Notes: 2, 7, 9

The Woodbox Inn

The Woodbox Inn

29 Fair Street, 02554
(508) 228-0587

The Woodbox is Nantucket's oldest inn, built in 1709. It is one and one-half blocks from the center of town, serves the best breakfast on the island, and offers gourmet dinners by candlelight. There are nine units, queen size beds,

private baths, including 1 and 2 bedroom suites with working fireplaces.

Host: Dexter Tutein
Rooms: 9 (PB) $120-190
Full Breakfast
Credit Cards: None
Notes: 2, 4, 7, 8, 9, 10, 12

NEWBURYPORT

Morrill Place Inn

209 High Street, 01950
(508) 462-2808

Gracious bed and breakfast in an early-19th-century sea captain's mansion. We are within walking distance of Newburyport's restored Federal period downtown. Nearby, Plum Island's pristine dunes and beaches are visited by more than 300 species of birds. Our Old South Church has had the Reverend Whitehead buried under its altar since the 18th century, and The First Religious Society's meeting house has what many consider the finest steeple in New England!

Host: Rose Ann Hunter
Rooms: 9 (6 PB; 3 SB) $66-90
Continental Breakfast
Credit Cards: None
Notes: 2, 5, 6, 7 (over 12), 8, 9, 12

OAK BLUFF

The Beach Rose

Box 2352, Columbian Ave., 02557
(508) 693-6135

This charming home, nestled in an oak and pine woodland on the beautiful island of Martha's Vineyard, is uniquely

NOTES: Credit cards accepted: A Master Card; B Visa; C American Express; D Discover Card; E Diners Club; F Other; 2 Personal checks accepted; 3 Lunch available; 4 Dinner available; 5 Open all

decorated in country antique style. Greet the morning with a continental plus breakfast of fresh fruits, a delicious entree du jour, homemade muffins and jams, and freshly brewed beverages. Your hosts provide warm hospitality and personal attention. They can direct you to such places as the gingerbread cottages of the methodist Campmeeting grounds, the Gay Head Cliffs and the historic whaling homes of Edgartown. The Vineyard has a myriad of sight seeing and other activities including unspoiled beaches, walking trails, sailing, fishing, biking, and much more. Courtesy transportation to and from ferry.

Hosts: Gloria and Rus Everett
Rooms: 3 (SB) (house has two baths) $80-90
Expanded Continental Breakfast
Credit Cards: None
Open May-October
Notes: 2, 7, 8, 9, 10

ONSET

The Onset Pointe Inn
9 Eagleway, P.O. Box 1450, 02558
(508) 295-8442

This elegant, turn-of-the-century restored beachfront mansion, cottage and guesthouse caters to a discerning traveler. All accommodations enjoy a water view. The wide verandas, enclosed sun parlor and beachside gazebo complete a relaxing day on a broad, sandy beach, and the hammock offers itself for a lazy afternoon. A complimentary bay breakfast is served to mansion guests.

Hosts: Toni and Carl Larrabee

Rooms: 14 (12PB; 2SB) $65-135
Both Full and Continental Breakfast (by season)
Credit Cards: A, B, C
Notes: 2, 5, 8, 9, 10, 12

ORLEANS

The Farmhouse at Nauset Beach
163 Beach Rd., 02653
(508) 255-6654

The Farmhouse at Nauset Beach is a delightful blend of a quiet country bed and breakfast and a seaside setting. The rooms in the 1870 Greek revival house are comfortably furnished to reflect their 19th century past filled with quilts, afghans, antiques, and handmade baskets. Some guest rooms have ocean views. Freshly brewed coffee, homemade coffee cake, juice, and fruit greet guests each morning. Guests can fish, golf, bike or play tennis nearby. A charming licensed bed and breakfast.

Host: Dot Standish
Rooms: 8 (4PB; 4SB) $32-95
Continental Plus Breakfast
Credit Cards: A, B
Notes: 2, 5, 7, 8, 9, 10

PLYMOUTH

Be Our Guest Bed and Breakfast, Ltd.
P.O. Box 1333, 02362
(617) 837-9867

Be Our Guest Bed and Breakfast, Ltd. is a network of private bed and breakfast homes. See many attractions within an hour's drive— Boston, Plymouth, Cape Cod and the Islands! Make your next stay away from home a memorable one.

Hosts: Mary Gill and Diane Gillis
Rooms: 20 $60-125
Full and Continental Breakfasts available
Credit Cards: A, B, C
Notes: 7, 8, 9, 10

REHOBOTH

Gilbert's Bed and Breakfast

30 Spring Street, 02769
(508) 252-6416; (800) 828-6821

Our 150-year-old home is special in all seasons. The in-ground pool refreshes weary travelers, and the quiet walks through our 100 acres give food for the soul. Guests also enjoy the horses. We praise God for being allowed to enjoy the beauty of the earth and want to share this beauty with others.

Hosts: Jeanne and Peter Gilbert
Rooms: 3 (SB) $32-50
Full Breakfast
Credit Cards: None
Notes: 2, 5, 6, 7, 8, 9 , 10, 12 (10%)

ROCKPORT

Lantana House

22 Broadway, 01966
(508) 546-3535

An intimate guest house in the heart of historic Rockport, Lantana House is close to Main Street, the T-Wharf, and the beaches. There is a large sun deck

reserved for guests, as well as TV, games, magazines and books, a guest refrigerator, and ice service. Nearby you will find a golf course, tennis courts, picnic areas, rocky bays, and inlets. Boston is one hour away by car.

Host: Cynthia Sewell
Rooms: 7 (5 PB; 2 SB) $60-70
Continental Breakfast
Credit Cards: None
Notes: 2, 7, 8, 9

Linden Tree Inn

26 King Street, 01966
(508) 546-2494

This 1840 Victorian is located in picturesque Rockport. Charm and warm hospitality abound in our guest living and sitting rooms. It is a short walk to restaurants, gift and antique shops, art galleries, beaches, and the train to Boston. Enjoy Penny's famous homebaked breakfast, and lemonade and cookies in the afternoon.

Hosts: Larry and Penny Olson
Rooms: 18 (PB) $80-93 (off season rates available)
Continental Breakfast
Credit Cards: A, B
Notes: 2, 5 (some rooms), 8, 9, 10

SALEM

The Inn at Seven Winter Street

7 Winter St., 01970
(508) 745-9520

The Inn is an impeccably restored, elegant French Second Empire Victorian

---

NOTES: Credit cards accepted: A Master Card; B Visa; C American Express; D Discover Card; E Diners Club; F Other; 2 Personal checks accepted; 3 Lunch available; 4 Dinner available; 5 Open all

Manor. Built in 1870 by a wealthy craftsman and merchant, the Inn is a fine example of Victorian architecture. Every room has been magnificently furnished with period antiques and accompaniments. All rooms have something beautifully unique. Some with fireplaces, canopy bed, victorian bath, jacuzzi, or open into a large sundeck overlooking landscaped gardens. Each room has private bath, cable color TV, telephone and air conditioning for your comfort and enjoyment. Free parking. Absolutely No Smoking please.

Hosts: D.L. and Jill E. Coté and Sally Flint
Rooms: 10 (PB) $75-110
Continental Breakfast
Credit Cards: A, B, C
Notes: 2, 5, 7, 8, 9, 10

The Inn at Seven Winter Street

The Salem Inn

7 Summer Street, 01970
(508) 741-0680; (800) 446-2995

In the midst of the historical and beautifully restored city of Salem is The Salem Inn, originally three townhouses built in 1834 by Captain Nathaniel West. The captain would have approved of the spacious, comfortably appointed guest rooms with a blend of period detail and antique furnishings. Some have working fireplaces. Ideal for families are two-room suites complete with equipped kitchen. All rooms have air conditioning, phones, TV. Complimentary continental breakfast served in our two intimate dining rooms, rose garden, and brick terrace. Rail and bus transportation available to Boston, only 18 miles away.

Hosts: Richard and Diane Pabich
Rooms: 22 (PB) $85-140
Continental Breakfast
Credit Cards: A, B, C, D, E
Notes: 2, 3, 4, 5, 7, 8, 9, 10, 12

SANDWICH

Captain Ezra Nye House

152 Main Street, 02563
(508) 888-6142; (800) 388-2278

Whether you come to enjoy summer on Cape Cod, a fall foliage trip, or a quiet winter vacation, the Captain Ezra Nye House is the perfect place to start. Located 60 miles from Boston, 20 from Hyannis, and within walking distance of many noteworthy attractions, including Heritage Plantation, Sandwich Glass Museum, and the Cape Cod Canal.

Hosts: Elaine and Harry Dickson
Rooms: 6 (4 PB; 2 SB) $55-85
Full Breakfast
Credit Cards: A, B, C, D
Notes: 2, 5, 7 (over six), 8, 9, 10, 12

The Summer House

158 Main Street, 02563
(508) 888-4991

This exquisite 1835 Greek Revival home featured in *Country Living* magazine is located in the heart of historic Sandwich village and features antiques, hand-stitched quilts, flowers, large sunny rooms, and English-style gardens. We are within strolling distance of dining, museums, shops, pond, and the boardwalk to the beach. Bountiful breakfasts and elegant afternoon tea in the garden.

Hosts: David and Kay Merrell
Rooms: 5 (1 PB; 4 SB) $45-75
Full Breakfast
Credit Cards: A, B, C, D
Notes: 2, 5, 7 (over five), 8, 9, 10

SOUTH DARTMOUTH

The Little Red House
631 Elm St., 02748
(508) 996-4554

A charming gambrel colonial home located in the lovely coastal village of Padanaram. This home is beautifully furnished with country accents, antiques, lovely living room with fireplace, luxuriously comfortable fourposter or brass and iron beds. A full homemade breakfast in the romantic candlelit dining room is a delectable treat. Close to the harbor, beaches, historic sites and a short distance to Newport, Plymouth, Boston, Cape Cod. Martha Vineyard's ferry is just 10 minutes away.

Host: Meryl Scully
Rooms: 2 (SB) $60-65
Full Breakfast
Credit Cards: None
Notes: 2, 5, 8, 9, 10, 12 (10%)

STOCKBRIDGE

Arbor Rose B&B
Box 114, 8 Yale Hill Rd., 11262
(413) 298-4744

Lovely old New England mill house with pond, gardens and mountain view. Walk to Berkshire Theater, Norman Rockwell Museum and Stockbridge Center. Beautiful rooms, comfy, good beds, antiques, water colors and sunshine. Fireplace and TV in common room. Home mmm...baked breakfast.

Hosts: Christina M. Alsop and family
Rooms: 4 rooms and 1 apartment (4PB; 2SB)
$55-150
Continental Breakfast on Mon-Sat; Full Breakfast on Sunday
Credit Cards: A, B, C
Notes: 2, 5, 7, 8, 9, 10, 11, 12

The Inn at Stockbridge
P.O. Box 618, (Route 7 north), 01262
(413) 298-3337

This eight room inn is situated on a 12 acre plot one mile north of the village of Stockbridge. This Georgian Colonial, built in the early 20th century as a country estate, has retained its features of elegance and comfort. Located in the heart of the four season Berkshire Hills, it is close to all local attractions including the Norman Rockwell museum, Tanglewood, Berkshire Theater and several ski areas. A memorable full breakfast and gracious hospitality are the highlights.

Hosts: Lee and Don Weitz
Rooms: 8 (PB) $75-225 (vary seasonally)

NOTES: Credit cards accepted: A Master Card; B Visa; C American Express; D Discover Card; E Diners Club; F Other; 2 Personal checks accepted; 3 Lunch available; 4 Dinner available; 5 Open all

Full Breakfast
Credit Cards: A, B, C
Notes: 2, 5, 8, 9, 10, 11, 12

STURBRIDGE

Sturbridge Country Inn

530 Main Street, 01566
(508) 347-5503

At this historic 1840s inn each room has a fireplace and private whirlpool tub. It is close to Old Sturbridge Village and within walking distance of restaurants, shops, antiques. Breakfast available in room.

Host: Mr. MacConnel
Rooms: 9 (PB) $69-149
Continental Breakfast
Credit Cards: A, B, C, D
Notes: 2, 5, 7, 8, 9, 10, 11, 12

STURBRIDGE-WARE

The 1880 Country Bed and Breakfast

14 Pleasant Street, 01082
(413) 967-7847; (413) 967-3773

Built in 1876, this Colonial style house has pumpkin and maple hardwood floors, beamed ceilings, six fireplaces, and antique furnishings. Afternoon tea is served by the fireplace; breakfast is served in the dining room or on the porch, weather permitting. It is a short, pretty country ride to historic Old Sturbridge Village and Old Deerfield Village; hiking and fishing are nearby. Midpoint between Boston and the Berkshires, this is a very comfortable bed

and breakfast.

Host: Margaret Skutnik
Rooms: 5 (2 PB; 3 SB) $40-65
Full Breakfast
Credit Cards: None
Notes: 2, 5, 8, 9, 10, 11, 12

VINEYARD HAVEN

Hanover House

10 Edgartown Road, P. O. Box 2107, 02568
(508) 693-1066

Located on the island of Martha's Vineyard, The Hanover House is a large, old inn that has been brought into the 20th century while still retaining the charm and personalized hospitality of the gracious, old inns of yesteryear. Decorated in a classic country style that typifies a New England inn, Hanover House is just a short walk from town and the ferry.

Hosts: Ron and Kay Nelson
Rooms: 15 (PB) $68-158
Continental Breakfast
Credit Cards: A, B, C
Notes: 2, 7, 8, 9, 10, 12

WELLFLEET

Inn at Duck Creek

P. O. Box 364, 02667
(508) 349-9333

The Inn at Duck Creek on five acres is situated between a salt marsh and its own duck pond. The inn is a short walk to the village and close to bay and ocean beaches, national seashore park, Audubon sanctuary harbor, and marina. The inn is home to two fine restaurants located just across the drive. Enjoy pleasant accommodations in Cape Cod's most charming village.

Hosts: Robert Morrill and Judith Pihl
Rooms: 25 (17 PB; 8 SB) $48-80
Continental Breakfast
Credit Cards: A, B, C
Notes: 4, 7, 8, 9, 10

WEST HARWICH BY THE SEA

Cape Cod Sunny Pines and Claddagh Tavern

P. O. Box 667, 02671
(508) 432-9628; (800) 356-9628

Enjoy Irish hospitality in a Victorian ambience reminiscent of a small Irish manor. A gourmet, family-style Irish breakfast is enjoy by candlelight on bone china and crystal. All suites have private temperature controls. Relax on the Victorian veranda or in the spacious Jacuzzi overlooking the picnic grounds, pool, and garden. TV, air conditioning, and refrigerators. Quality AAA and ABBA approved. The Claddagh Tavern—"Friendship, Love and Loyalty"—an Irish pub with full service restaurant serving home cooked fare at fair prices.

Hosts: Jack and Eileen Connell
Rooms: 6 (PB) $75-100
Cottages: 2 (PB)
Full Breakfast
Credit Cards: A, B, C, D, E
Notes: 2, 3, 4, 7, 8, 9, 10, 12 (10%)

Michigan

ALMA

Saravilla
Bed and Breakfast
633 N. State St., 48801
(517) 463-4078

Great location for travelers, right off highway in the center of the state. Enjoy the charm and original features of this 1894, 10,000-square-foot Dutch colonial home which has Victorian influences. On Michigan's Historical Register, this home has imported woodwork, wood carvings, handpainted wall coverings, lead glass windows. Rooms are spacious and comfortable with private baths, several with fireplaces. A full homemade breakfast is served in the elegant turret dining room on antique china.

Hosts: Linda and John Darrow
Rooms: 6 (5PB; 1SB) $55-75
Full Breakfast
Credit Cards: A, B
Notes: 2, 5, 7, 8, 10

BATTLE CREEK

Greencrest Manor
6174 Halbert Road, 49017
(616) 962-8633

To experience Greencrest is to step back in time to a way of life that is rare today. From the moment you enter the iron gates, you will be mesmerized. This French Normandy mansion situated on the highest elevation of St. Mary's Lake is constructed of sandstone, slate, and copper. Three levels of formal gardens include fountains, stone walls, iron rails, and cut sandstone urns. Air conditioned. Featured "Inn of the Month" in *Country Inns Magazine,* August 1992 edition and chosen as one of their top twelve inns in the nation for 1992.

Hosts: Tom and Kathy Van Daff
Rooms: 5 (3PB; 2SB) $75-150
Expanded Continental Breakfast
Credit Cards: A, B, C
Notes: 2, 5, 7, 8, 10, 11

---

year; 6 Pets welcome; 7 Children welcome; 8 Tennis nearby; 9 Swimming nearby; 10 Golf nearby; 11 Skiing nearby; 12 May be booked through travel agent

BAY CITY

Stonehedge Inn Bed and Breakfast

924 Center Avenue (M25), 48708
(517) 894-4342

With stained-glass windows and nine fireplaces, this 1889 English Tudor home is indeed an elegant journey into the past. The magnificent open foyer and staircase lead to large beautiful bedrooms on the upper floors. Original features include speaking tubes, a warming oven, chandeliers, and a fireplace picturing Bible stories and passages on blue delft tiles. In the historic district, Frankenmuth is 20 miles away. Birth Run Manufacturer's Marketplace is 35 miles away.

Host: Ruth Koerber
Rooms: 7 (S3B) $65-85
Expanded Continental Breakfast
Credit Cards: A, B, C, D
Notes: 2, 5, 8, 9, 10, 11, 12

BIG RAPIDS

Taggart House

321 Maple, 49307
(616) 796-1713

Taggart House is a charming Victorian-style home in the heart of Big Rapids, home of Ferris State University. The warmth, friendliness, and elegant charm of this wonderful home create an ambience that is sure to please you. Relax in the comfortable living room, or catch the news on television. Enjoy a continental breakfast in the formal dining room; or during the warmer months, on the beautiful, enclosed flagstone porch.

Host: Barbara Randle
Rooms: 5 (3PB; 2SB) $45-65
Continental Breakfast
Credit Cards: A, B
Notes: 2, 5, 7 (by arrangement), 8, 9, 10,11

BLANEY PARK

Celibeth House

Route 1, Box 58A, Germfask, 49836
(906) 283-3409

This lovely house was built in 1895. It is situated on 85 acres overlooking Lake Anna Louise. Each room is tastefully furnished. Guests may also use the living room, reading room, and enclosed front porch, as well as a large outside deck and nature trails. Main House is open May 1 to November 1. Winter House is open November 1-May 1. Winter House is located one block from Main House.

Host: Elsa R. Strom
Rooms: 8 (PB) $35-50
Continental Breakfast
Credit Cards: A, B
Notes: 2, 5, 7, 9, 11, 12

BRIGHTON

Log House B&B

2673 Hubert, 48116
(313) 229-2673

Five-year-old custom ranch-style log home. Breakfast in all-glass solarium. Over-size custom log furniture. "Canadian Lodge" decor. Ten acres of 30'

NOTES: Credit cards accepted: A Master Card; B Visa; C American Express; D Discover Card; E Diners Club; F Other; 2 Personal checks accepted; 3 Lunch available; 4 Dinner available; 5 Open all

spruce and pines and wild flower meadows. Great restaurants, golf, ski, horses, antiques, and swimming within three miles. Cat in residence, smokers permitted. 50 miles west of Detroit; 30 miles from Lansing or Ann Arbor.

Hosts: Charlotte and Bill Woods
Rooms: 2 (1PB; 1SB) $50-60
Full Breakfast
Credit Cards: None
Notes: 2, 5, 9, 10, 12

BROOKLYN

Dewey Lake Manor Bed and Breakfast

11811 Laird Road, 49230
(517) 467-7122

Dewey Lake Manor is a century-old house sitting atop a knoll overlooking picturesque Dewey Lake in the Irish Hills of southern Michigan. It was built by A.F Dewey, a prosperous farmer of the area who owned the lake and the land around it. It is a quiet, peaceful place to enjoy the sweet sounds of the summer nights or the quiet stillness of the frozen lake.

Hosts: The Phillips Family
Rooms: 4 (PB) $50-65
Expanded Continental Breakfast
Credit Cards: A, B
Notes: 2, 5, 10, 11, 12

Dewey Lake Manor Bed and Breakfast

CHASSELL

Palosaari's Rolling Acres B&B

Rt. 1, Box 354, North Entry Road, 49916
(906) 523-4947

Operating dairy farm—visit the barn and watch the milking or help feed the baby calves. Three comfortable, cozy rooms with shared bath. Centrally located for day trips to the tip of Keweeenaw or many other local attractions—antique shops and copper mining era sights. Access to Lake Superior fishing, picnic area, swimming. "Home away from home."

Host: Evey Palosaari
Rooms: 3 (SB) $40
Full Breakfast
Credit Cards: None
Notes: 2, 5, 7, 9, 11

CLIO

Chandelier Guest House

1567 Morgan Road, 48420
(313) 687-6061

Relax in our country home. Enjoy bed and breakfast comforts including choice of rooms with twin, full, or queen beds. You may wish to be served full breakfast in bed, or beneath the beautiful crystal chandelier, or on the sun porch with a view of surrounding woods. Located minutes from Clio Amphitheater, Flint Crossroad Village, Birch Run Manufacturer's Marketplace,

year; 6 Pets welcome; 7 Children welcome; 8 Tennis nearby; 9 Swimming nearby; 10 Golf nearby; 11 Skiing nearby; 12 May be booked through travel agent

Frankenmuth, and Chesaning. Senior citizen discount. Call for directions.

Hosts: Alfred and Clara Bielert
Rooms: 2 (1PB; 1SB) $49.95-54.95
Full Breakfast
Credit Cards: None
Notes: 2, 5, 7, 10, 12

COLDWATER

Batavia Inn

1824 West Chicago Road, U.S. 12, 49036
(517) 278-5146

This 1872 Italianate country inn has original massive woodwork, high ceilings, and restful charm. Seasonal decorations are a specialty. Christmas festival of trees. Located near recreation and discount shopping. In-ground pool available in season. Guest pampering is the innkeepers' goal with treats, turn down, homemade breakfasts. Perfect for small retreats.

Hosts: E. Fred and Alma Marquardt
Rooms: 5 (PB) $59-69
Full Breakfast
Credit Cards: None
Notes: 2, 5, 9, 10

Batavia Inn

DAVISON

Oakbrook Inn

7256 East Court Street, 48423
(313) 658-1546

Oakbrook is located on twenty acres of rolling landscape with woods and creek less than five minutes from Flint. Guest rooms are furnished with antiques, handicrafts, and handmade quilts. The indoor pool and hot tub are open year-round. An outdoor deck is available for enjoying the warm summer sun and the cool evening breezes.

Hosts: Jan and Bill Cooke
Rooms: 7 (PB) $46-98
Continental Breakfast
Credit Cards: A, B, C
Notes: 2, 5, 7, 8, 9, 10, 11

EASTPORT

Torch Lake Sunrise Bed and Breakfast

Box 52, 49627
(616) 599-2706

This B&B overlooks what *National Geographic* calls the third-most beautiful lake in the world. All rooms furnished with antiques and have decks and private baths. Close at hand are several golf courses, tennis courts, gourmet restaurants and ski resorts. For summer activities, a canoe, a rowboat and paddleboards are available. In winter, cross-country skiing awaits you just outside. Wake up seeing the sunrise over the lake and smelling the wonderful aroma of fresh muffins baking!

Perhaps you'll be served a frittata, or strawberry pancakes, or eggs Benedict, but always fresh fruit of the season.

Host: Betty A. Collins
Rooms: 3 (PB) $70-80
Full Breakfast
Credit Cards: None
Notes: 2, 5, 8, 9, 10, 11, 12

FENNVILLE

The Kingsley House Bed and Breakfast

626 West Main Street, 49408
(616) 561-6425

This elegant Queen Anne Victorian was built by the prominent Kingsley family in 1886 and selected by *Inn Times* as one of 50 best bed and breakfasts in America. It was featured in *Innsider* magazine. Near Holland, Saugatuck, Allegan State Forest, sandy beaches, cross-country skiing. Bicycles available, whirlpool bath, getaway honeymoon suite. Enjoy the beautiful surroundings, family antiques. Breakfast is served in the formal dining room.

Hosts: David and Shirley Witt
Rooms: 7 (PB) $75-125
Full Breakfast
Credit Cards: A, B, C
Notes: 2, 5, 8, 9, 10, 11, 12

"The Porches" Bed and Breakfast

2297 70th Street (Lakeshore Drive), 49408
(616) 543-4162

Built in 1897, "The Porches" offers five guest rooms each with private bath. Located three miles south of Saugatuck, we have a private beach and hiking trails. The large common room has a TV. We overlook Lake Michigan with beautiful sunsets from the front porch. Open May 1 to November 1.

Hosts: Bob and Ellen Johnson
Rooms: 5 (PB) $59-69
Full or Expanded Continental Breakfast
Credit Cards: A, B
Notes: 2, 7 (Sunday-Thursday) 8, 9, 10

GRAND HAVEN

Boyden House Inn B&B

301 South 5th, 49417
(616) 846-3538

Built in 1874, our charming Victorian inn is decorated with treasures from far away places, antiques and original art. Enjoy the comfort of air conditioned rooms with private baths. Some rooms feature fireplaces or balconies. Relax in our common room and veranda surrounded by a beautiful perennial garden. Full homemade breakfast served in our lovely dining room. Walking distance to boardwalk beaches, shopping and restaurants.

Rooms: 5(PB) $55-85
Full Breakfast
Credit Cards: A, B, C
Notes: 2, 5, 7, 8, 9, 10, 11, 12

year; 6 Pets welcome; 7 Children welcome; 8 Tennis nearby; 9 Swimming nearby; 10 Golf nearby; 11 Skiing nearby; 12 May be booked through travel agent

HARBOR SPRINGS

Mottls Getaway

1021 Birchcrest Ct., 49740
(616) 526-9682

Mottls Getaway B&B apartment includes a kitchenette with stove and refrigerator, large stone fireplace in furnished living room, and a private outside entrance. It is close to the sandy beaches of beautiful Little Traverse Bay and other inland lakes, the ski resorts of Nubs Nob and Boyne Highlands, good golf courses, cross country ski trails, and the art galleries and boutiques of Harbor Springs and Petoskey.

Host: Carol Mottl
Rooms: 2 (PB) $50
Self Serve Full Breakfast
Credit Cards: None
Notes: 2, 3, 4, 5, 7, 8, 9, 10, 11

HOLLAND

Dutch Colonial Inn

560 Central Avenue, 49423
(616) 396-3664

Relax and enjoy a gracious 1928 Dutch Colonial. Your hosts have elegantly decorated their home with family heirloom antiques and furnishings from the 1930s. Guests enjoy the cheery sun porch, honeymoon suites, or rooms with whirlpool tubs for two. Special, festive touches are everywhere during the Christmas holiday season. Nearby are Windmill Island, wooden shoe factory, Delftware factory, tulip festival, Hope College, Michigan's finest beaches, bike paths, and cross-country ski trails.

Corporate rates are available for business travelers.

Hosts: Bob and Pat Elenbaas, Diana Klungel
Rooms: 5 (PB) $65-100
Full Breakfast
Credit Cards: A, B, C, D
Notes: 2, 5, 8, 9, 10, 11

IONIA

Union Hill Inn Bed and Breakfast

306 Union Street, 48846
(616) 527-0955

Elegant 1868 Italiante home noted for its expansive veranda and panoramic view, yet only two blocks from downtown. Home built by Lucius Miles, Captain in the Civil War. He built pontoon bridges during the war. You can see his bridge building capabilities in the porches.

Hosts: Tom and Mar Kay Moular
Rooms: 5 (SB)
Full Breakfast
Credit Cards: None
Notes: 2, 5, 7, 10

LAMONT

The Stagecoach Stop B&B

0-4819 Leonard Road W., P.O. Box 18, 49430
(616) 677-5971

The quaint and charming Grand River Village of Lamont is the setting of this restored 1850s gothic revival home, furnished with antiques and country primitives. Once an overnight stop for

NOTES: Credit cards accepted: A Master Card; B Visa; C American Express; D Discover Card; E Diners Club; F Other; 2 Personal checks accepted; 3 Lunch available; 4 Dinner available; 5 Open all

stagecoaches making the trip between Grand Rapids and Grand Haven, both cities are now only a twenty minute drive. Just three minutes south off of I-96, exit 19. Crib available.

Hosts: Marcia and Gene Ashby
Rooms: 3 (1PB; 2SB) $55-65
Full Breakfast
Credit Cards: A, B
Notes: 2, 5, 6 (by arrangement), 7, 9, 10

LOWELL

McGee Homestead

2534 Alden Nash N.E., 49331
(616) 897-8142

Come join us in the country! 1880 brick farmhouse including a barn full of petting animals. There are five acres surrounded by orchards, right next to golf course. Our guests have a separate entrance to a living room with fireplace, parlor, and small kitchen, all furnished in antiques. We serve a country breakfast with farm fresh eggs.

Hosts: Bill and Ardie Barber
Rooms: 4 (1PB; 3SB) $36-55
Full Breakfast
Credit Cards: A, B
Notes: 2, 7, 9, 10, 11

LUDINGTON

Bed and Breakfast at Ludington

2458 S. Beaune Road, 49431
(616) 843-9768

State land, a horsefarm, and apple orchards surround our 16 acres. We use all for trails, foot or ski. Snowshoes provided, also toboggans—great hill, creek and pond. Golf 1/2 mile; barnloft hideaway, hottub, table tennis. Country Breakfast, crib, fireplaces.

Hosts: Grace Schneider and Robert Schneider
Rooms: 3 (2PB; 1SB) $35-55
Full Breakfast
Credit Cards: None
Notes: 2, 5, 6, 7, 8, 9, 10, 11, 12

The Inn at Ludington

701 E. Ludington Ave., 49431
(616) 845-7055

1889 Queen Anne Victorian located "on the avenue," within walking distance of shops, restaurants, beach and car ferry. Relax in elegance after a summer day at Lake Michigan's finest beach or enjoy one of our four fireplaces after a winter day of cross country skiing. A bountiful breakfast featuring "Michigan Made" products awaits you in the morning.

Host: Diane Shields
Rooms: 6 (4PB; 2SB) $50-85
Full Breakfast
Credit Cards: A, B, C
Notes: 2, 3, 5, 8, 9, 10, 11, 12

MACKINAC ISLAND

Haan's 1830 Inn

Huron Street, P. O. Box 123, 49757
(906) 847-6244; winter (414) 248-9244

The earliest Greek Revival home in the Northwest Territory, this inn is on the Michigan Historic Registry and is completely restored. It is in a quiet neighborhood three blocks around Haldiman Bay from bustling 1800s downtown and Old Fort Mackinac. It is also adjacent to historic St. Anne's Church and gardens. Guest rooms are furnished with antiques. Enjoy the island's 19th-century ambience of horse-drawn buggies and wagons. Winter address: 1134 Geneva Street, Lake Geneva, Wisconsin 53147.

Hosts: Nicholas and Nancy Haan; Vernon and Joy Haan
Rooms: 7 (5PB; 2SB) $75-105
Expanded Continental Breakfast
Credit Cards: None
Closed late October to mid-May
Notes: 2, 7, 8, 9, 10

MAPLE CITY

Leelanau Country Inn

149 E. Harbor Hwy., 49664
(616) 228-5060

For over 100 years, the inn has stood ready to be of service. We feature 8 country appointed guest rooms and a 150-seat award-winning restaurant specializing in fresh seafood flown directly to us from Boston, choice steaks, homemade pasta and a large array of desserts. All items are made from scratch. 8 miles south of Leland on M-22. Surrounded by churches of all faiths.

Hosts: John and Linda Sisson
Rooms: 8 (SB) $30-40
Continental Breakfast
Credit Cards: A, B, C
Notes: 2, 4, 5, 6, 7, 8, 9, 10, 11

MENDON

Mendon Country Inn

440 W. Main, 49072
(616) 496-8132

Overlooking the St. Joseph River, this romantic country inn has antique guestrooms with private baths. Free canoeing, bicycles built for two, fifteen acres of woods and water, restaurants and Amish tour guide. Featured in *Country Living* and *Country Home* magazines. Nine jacuzzi suites with fireplaces. Eighteen rooms total.

Hosts: Dick and Dolly Bueckle
Rooms: 18 (PB) $50-125
Expanded Continental Breakfast
Credit Cards: A, B, C, D
Notes: 2, 5, 7, 8, 9, 10, 11, 12

ONEKAMA

Lake Breeze House

5089 Main Street, 49675-0301
(616) 889-4969

Our two-story frame house on Portage Lake is yours with a shared bath, living room, and breakfast room. Each room has its own special charm with family antiques. Come relax and enjoy our back porch and the sounds of the babbling creek. By reservation only. Boating and charter service available.

Hosts: Bill and Donna Erickson
Rooms: 3 (SB) $55
Full Breakfast
Credit Cards: None
Notes: 2, 5, 8, 9, 10, 11

NOTES: Credit cards accepted: A Master Card; B Visa; C American Express; D Discover Card; E Diners Club; F Other; 2 Personal checks accepted; 3 Lunch available; 4 Dinner available; 5 Open all

OWOSSO

Rossman's R&R Ranch

308 East Hibbard Road, 48867
(517) 723-2553 evening; (517) 723-3232 day

A newly remodeled farmhouse from the early 1900s, the ranch sits on 130 acres overlooking the Maple River valley. A large concrete circle drive with white-board fences leads to stables of horses and cattle. The area's wildlife includes deer, fox, rabbits, pheasant, quail, and song birds. Observe and explore from the farm lane, river walk, or outside deck. Countrylike accents adorn the interior of the farmhouse, and guests are welcome to use the family parlor, garden, game room, and fireplace.

Hosts: Carl and Jeanne Rossman
Rooms: 2 (SB) $40-45
Continental Breakfast
Credit Cards: None
Notes: 2, 5, 6, 7, 10

PENTWATER

Historic Nickerson Inn

P.O. Box 109, 262 Lowell St., 49449
(616) 869-6731

The Historic Nickerson Inn has been serving guests with "special hospitality" since 1914. Our inn was totally renovated in 1991. All our rooms have private baths, with air-conditioning. We have two jacuzzi suites with fireplaces and balconies overlooking Lake Michigan. Two short blocks to Lake Michigan beach and three blocks to shopping district. New ownership. Open all

year. Casual fine dining in our 80 seat restaurant. Excellent for retreats, workshops, year-round recreation.

Hosts: Gretchen and Harry Shiparski
Rooms: 10 rooms, 2 suites - 12 total (PB) $90-70 (rooms), $140(suites)
Full Breakfast
Credit Cards: A, B, C, D
Notes: 2, 3, 4, 5, 8, 9, 10, 11

Historic Nickerson Inn

PETOSKEY

Terrace Inn

P.O. Box 266, 49770
(616) 347-2856; (800) 530-9898

The Victorian Terrace Inn, built in 1911, is located in the center of historic Bay View, a Chautauqua summer community. Guests may participate in the summer religious, recreational or cultural programs, or simply enjoy the peaceful surroundings from the spacious porch. Terrace Inn guests have access to bay View beach and tennis courts. All 44 rooms are furnished in original antiques and have private bathrooms. The dining room serves dinner in season, and a complimentary breakfast each morning. In winter, guests will sit by the fireplace to enjoy conversation and games. Ski resorts are fifteen minutes from the inn.

Hosts: Patrick and May Lou Barbour

year; 6 Pets welcome; 7 Children welcome; 8 Tennis nearby; 9 Swimming nearby; 10 Golf nearby; 11 Skiing nearby; 12 May be booked through travel agent

Rooms: 44 (PB) $42-96
Continental Breakfast
Credit Cards: A, B, C
Notes: 2, 4, 5, 7, 8, 9, 10, 11

PLAINWELL

The 1882 John Crispe House

404 East Bridge Street, 49080
(616) 685-1293

Enjoy museum-quality Victorian elegance on the Kalamazoo River. Situated between Grand Rapids and Kalamazoo just off U.S. 131 on Michigan 89, the John Crispe House is close to some of western Michigan's finest gourmet dining, golf, skiing, and antique shops. Air conditioned. No smoking or alcohol. Gift certificates are available.

Hosts: Ormand J. and Nancy E. Lefever
Rooms: 5 (3PB; 2SB) $55-95
Full Breakfast
Credit Cards: A, B
Notes: 2, 5, 7, 8, 10, 11

PORT HURON

The Victorian Inn

1229 Seventh Street, 48060
(313) 984-1437

The Victorian Inn features fine dining and guest rooms in authentically restored Victorian elegance. One hour north of metropolitan Detroit, it is located in the heart of the church district and one-half block from the museum. All food and beverages are prepared with the utmost attention to detail, which

was the order of the day in a bygone era.

Host: Sheila Marinez
Rooms: 4 (2PB; 2SB) $55-65
Continental Breakfast
Credit Cards: A, B, C, D, E, F
Notes: 2, 3, 4, 5, 7, 8, 9, 10

ROCHESTER HILLS

Paint Creek B&B

971 Dutton Rd., 48306
(313) 651-6785

Our home is a casual, rambling, 5 bedroom ranch in a quiet country setting on 3 1/2 rolling acres. Birds and squirrels abound in the trees surrounding the mostly glass family room which overlooks a pond and a trout stream twenty-five feet below.

Hosts: Loren and Rea Siffring
Rooms: 3 (SB) $40-45
Full Breakfast
Credit Cards: None
Notes: 2, 5, 7, 8, 9, 10, 11, 12

SAUGATUCK

Sherwood Forest Bed and Breakfast

938 Center St., P.O. Box 315, 49406
(616) 857-1246

Surrounded by woods, this beautiful Victorian home was built in the 1890s. Amenities include wraparound porch, traditional furnishings, large guestrooms with private baths, jacuzzi and heated swimming pool. There is also a separate cottage that sleeps seven. The Eastern Shore of Lake Michigan

NOTES: Credit cards accepted: A Master Card; B Visa; C American Express; D Discover Card; E Diners Club; F Other; 2 Personal checks accepted; 3 Lunch available; 4 Dinner available; 5 Open all

and the public beach are 1/2 block away. The area's wide white sandy beaches are the perfect place for strolling, swimming or watching spectacular sunsets. We're also located just minutes from the charming shops of Saugatuck.

Rooms: 5 (PB) $80-120
Expanded Continental Breakfast
Credit Cards: A, B
Notes: 2, 5, 8, 9, 10, 11, 12

Twin Gables Country Inn

P.O. Box 881, 900 Lake Street, 94953
(616) 857-4346

Overlooking Kalamazoo Lake, The State Historic Inn, central airconditioned throughout, features 14 charming guestrooms with private baths furnished in antiques and country. Wintertime cross country skiers relax in indoor hot tub and cozy up to a warm crackling fireplace, whilst summer guests may take a refreshing dip in the outdoor pool and enjoy glorious sunsets on the front veranda overlooking the lake. Three separate two and one bedroom cottages are also available. Open all year.

Hosts: Denise and Michael Simcik
Rooms: 14 (PB) $44-94
Expanded Continental Breakfast
Credit Cards: A, B
Notes: 2, 5, 7 (prior arrangements), 8, 9, 10, 11, 12

SPRING LAKE

Seascape Bed and Breakfast

20009 Breton, 49456
(616) 842-8409

On private Lake Michigan beach. Relaxing lakefront rooms. Enjoy the warm hospitality and cozy "country living" ambience of our nautical lakeshore home. Full homemade breakfast served in gathering room with fieldstone fireplace or on the sun deck. Either offers a panoramic view of Grand Haven Harbor. Open all year. Stroll or cross country ski on Duneland nature trails. Special rates Sunday-Thursday.

Host: Susan Meyer
Rooms: 3 (PB) $65-90
Full Breakfast
Credit Cards: A, B
Notes: 2, 5, 8, 9, 10, 11

WEST BRANCH

The Rose Brick Inn

124 East Houghton Avenue, 48661
(517) 345-3702

A 1906 Queen Anne-style home with a graceful veranda, white picket fence, and cranberry canopy, the Rose Brick Inn is tucked in the center two floors of the Frank Sebastian Smith house listed in Michigan's register of historic sites. It is located on downtown Main Street in Victorian West Branch. Golfing, hiking, biking, cross-country skiing, snowmobiling, hunting, shopping, and special holiday events await you year-round. Jacuzzi.

Host: Leon Swartz
Rooms: 4 (PB) $48-58
Continental Breakfast
Credit Cards: A, B
Notes: 2, 5, 7, 8, 9, 10, 11

year; 6 Pets welcome; 7 Children welcome; 8 Tennis nearby; 9 Swimming nearby; 10 Golf nearby; 11 Skiing nearby; 12 May be booked through travel agent

Minnesota

CHASKA (OF THE MINNEAPOLIS AREA)

Bluff Creek Inn
1161 Bluff Creek Drive, 55318
(612) 445-2735

Named one of the top ten in the Midwest. Enjoy river bluff and country scenery from one of the five porches. Designer coordinated candlelit rooms with special antiques and comfortable sitting areas. Known for gourmet scrumptious breakfasts. Secluded country cottage with double whirlpools, fireplace, balcony and fields/forest views. Minutes from major TC attractions: Mall of America, Chanhassen Dinner Theatre, Minnesota Arboretum, Planes of Fame Air Museum, hiking/skiing paths, 30 minutes to downtown Minneapolis. Mid-week rates available.

Hosts: Anne and Gary Delaney
Rooms: 5 (PB) $75-150
Full Breakfast
Credit Cards: A, B
Notes: 2, 5, 8, 9, 10, 11

CHATFIELD

Lunds' Guest Houses
218 Southeast Winona Street, 55923
(507) 867-4003

These charming 1920s homes are decorated in the 1920s and 1930s style and located only 20 minutes from Rochester, at the gateway to beautiful Bluff country. Personalized service includes use of the kitchens, living and dining rooms, two screened porches, and TV, piano and organ.

Hosts: Shelby and Marion Lund
Rooms: 4 (2PB; 2S1.5B) $50-65
Continental Breakfast
Credit Cards: None
Notes: 2, 6, 7, 8, 9, 10, 11

FARIBAULT

Cherub Hill Victorian Bed and Breakfast
105 NW 1st Ave., 55021
(507) 332-2024

An elegant historic experience awaits you in this lovingly restored Victorian

---

NOTES: Credit cards accepted: A Master Card; B Visa; C American Express; D Discover Card; E Diners Club; F Other; 2 Personal checks accepted; 3 Lunch available; 4 Dinner available; 5 Open all

gem. Sample turn-of-the-century charm and romance; delicious breakfasts and afternoon tea, corner turn-down with locally hand-dipped chocolates on your pillow, private baths, fireplaces, double whirlpool and soaking tubs, smoke-free environment, central air conditioning, antiquing and many other local attractions in historic Faribault.

Bakketop Hus

Hosts: Keith and Kristi LeMieux
Rooms: 3 (PB) $70-88
Full Breakfast
Credit Cards: A, B
Notes: 2, 5, 7 (over 12), 8, 9, 10, 11

FERGUS FALLS

Bakketopp Hus

Rural Route 2, Box 187 A, 56537
(218) 739-2915

Quiet, spacious lake home with vaulted ceilings, fireplace, private spa, flower garden patio and lakeside decks. Antique furnishings, four poster draped French canopy bed, waterbed, private or shared bath. Here you can listen as loons call to each other across the lake in the still of dusk, witness the fall foliage splendor, relax by a crackling fire or sink into the warmth of our spa after a day of hiking or skiing. Near antique shops, Maplewood State Park. Ten minutes off I-94. Gift certificates available. Reservation with deposit.

Hosts: Dennis and Judy Nims
Rooms: 3 (1PB; 2SB) $55-85
Full Breakfast
Credit Cards: None
Notes: 2, 5, 7, 8, 9, 10, 11

HOUSTON

Addie's Attic Bed and Breakfast

P.O. Box 677, 117 S Jackson St., 55943
(507) 896-3010

Beautiful turn-of-the-century home, circa 1903; cozy front parlor with curved glass window. Games, TV, player piano available. Guest rooms decorated and furnished with "attic finds." Shared bath. Hearty country breakfast served in dining room. Near hiking, biking, and cross country skiing trails. Canoeing, antique shops. Weekday rates. No credit cards.

Hosts: Fred and Marilyn Huhn
Rooms: 4 (SB) $45-50
Full Breakfast
Credit Cards: None
Notes: 2, 5, 8, 10, 11

LUTSEN

The Woods Bed and Breakfast

P.O. Box 158, Caribou Trail, 55612
(218) 663-7144

Contemporary A-frame home with

wood interior, large deck with panoramic view of Lake Superior and Superior National Forest. Next to cross country skiing trail; close to downhill ski area, snow mobile trails, golf, hiking. Choose from four lovely bedrooms. Private or shared bath. Full breakfast. Children welcome. No pets. No Smoking. Rates from $60-75 for double occupancy.

Host: Sharon Hendrickson
Rooms: 4 (2PB; 2SB) $60-75
Full Breakfast
Credit Cards: None
Notes: 2, 5, 10, 11

OWATONNA

The Northrop-Oftedahl House

358 East Main Street, 55060
(507) 451-4040

This 1898 Victorian with stained glass is three blocks from downtown. It has pleasant porches, grand piano, six-foot footed bathtub, souvenirs (antiques and collectibles from the estate). Northrop family-owned and operated, it is one of 12 historical homes in the area, rich in local history with an extensive reading library, backgammon, croquet, badminton, bocce, and more. Near hiking, biking trails, golf, tennis, parks, and 35 miles to Mayo Clinic. Special group rates for retreats.

Hosts: Jean and Darrell Stewart
Rooms: 5 (SB) $34-54
Continental Breakfast; Full breakfast on request
Credit Cards: None
Notes: 2, 3 (by arrangement), 4 (by arrangement), 5, 6 (by arrangement, 7, 8, 9, 10, 11

ST. CHARLES

Thoreson's Carriage House Bed and Breakfast

606 Wabasha Avenue, 55972
(507) 932-3479

Located at the edge of beautiful Whitewater State Park with its swimming, trails, and demonstrations by the park naturalist, we are also in Amish territory and minutes from the world-famous Mayo Clinic. Piano and organ are available for added enjoyment. Please write for free brochure.

Host: Moneta Thoreson
Rooms: 2 (SB) $30-35
Full Breakfast
Credit Cards: None
Notes: 2, 5, 7, 8, 9, 10

STILLWATER

Lowell Inn

102 North Second Street, 55082
(612) 439-1100

The Williamsburg-style red-brick building fronts 13 white pillars to represent the 13 original colonies. The inn's remodeled guest rooms create intimate boudoirs with state-of-the-art bathing facilities. The inn is located in the heart of one of Minnesota's earliest settlements on a hillside two blocks from the St. Croix River. We offer American Plan rates that include dinner and breakfast on weekends; European Plan on Sunday through Thursday. Dinner and lunch served daily.

NOTES: Credit cards accepted: A Master Card; B Visa; C American Express; D Discover Card; E Diners Club; F Other; 2 Personal checks accepted; 3 Lunch available; 4 Dinner available; 5 Open all

Hosts: Arthur and Maureen Palmer
Rooms: 21 (PB) $109-189
Full Breakfast
Credit Cards: A, B
Notes: 2, 3, 4, 5

WALKER

Peacecliff
HCR 73, Box 998D, 56484
(218) 547-2832

This contemporary Tudor mansion on the bluff overlooking Leech Lake has rooms charmingly furnished with antiques and old books. It is five minutes by boat to Walker shops; easy access to Itasca State Park, Heartland, and North Country Trails; biking, snowmobiling, cross-country skiing.

Hosts: Dave and Kathy Laursen
Rooms: 5 (1PB; 4SB) $58-92
Full Breakfast
Credit Cards: A, B, C, D
Notes: 2, 5, 8, 9, 10, 11

year; 6 Pets welcome; 7 Children welcome; 8 Tennis nearby; 9 Swimming nearby; 10 Golf nearby; 11 Skiing nearby; 12 May be booked through travel agent

Mississippi

French Camp

FRENCH CAMP

French Camp Bed and Breakfast Inn
Box 120, 39745
(601) 547-6835

The inn is located on the historic Natchez Trace National Parkway halfway between Jackson and Tupelo, Missouri. It has been constructed from two restored, authentic hand-hewn log cabins, each more than 100 years old. Indulge in southern cooking at its finest: sorghum-soaked "scratch" muffins, creamy grits, skillet fried apples, fresh cheese scrambled eggs, crisp slab bacon, and lean sausage, with two kinds of homemade bread and three homemade jellies. Life doesn't get any better!

Hosts: Ed and Sallie Williford
Rooms: 4 (PB) $50
Full Breakfast
Credit Cards: None
Notes: 2, 3, 4, 5, 6, 7, 8, 9, 12

LORMAN

Rosswood Plantation
Route 552, 39096
(601) 437-4215; (800) 533-5889

An authentic 1857 columned mansion stands close to Natchez and Vicksburg, offering luxury, comfort, charm, and hospitality on a serene country estate. Once a cotton plantation, Rosswood now grows Christmas trees. Large bedrooms with canopy beds, antiques, TV, phone, air conditioning. Ideal for honeymoons or anniversaries. A Mississippi landmark, it is also on the National Register of Historic Places. Heated pool and spa.

Hosts: Jean and Walt Hylander
Rooms: 4 (PB) $75-95
Full Breakfast
Credit Cards: A, B
Notes: 2, 7, 9

NATCHEZ TRACE

Natchez Trace Bed and Breakfast Reservation Service

P.O. Box 193, Hampshire, TN, 38461
(800) 377-2770

This reservation service is unusual in that all the homes listed are close to the Natchez Trace, the delightful National Parkway running from Nashville, Tennessee, to Natchez, Mississippi. Kay can help you plan your trip along the Trace, with homestays in interesting and historic homes along the way. Locations of homes include Nashville, Franklin, Hampshire, Lawrenceburg, Tennessee; Florence, Alabama; and Corinth, French Camp, Kosciusko, Vicksburg, Lorman and Natchez, Mississippi. Rates from $50-115.

PORT GIBSON

Oak Square Plantation

1207 Church Street, 39150
(601) 437-4350; (800) 729-0240

This restored antebellum mansion of the Old South is in the town General U. S. Grant said was "too beautiful to burn." On the National Register of Historic Places, it has family heirloom antiques and canopied beds and is air conditioned. Your hosts' families have been in Mississippi for 200 years. Christ is the Lord of this house. "But as for me and my house, we will serve the Lord," Joshua 24:15. On U.S. Highway 61, adjacent to the Natchez Trace Parkway. Four-diamond rated by AAA.

Hosts: Mr. and Mrs. William Lum
Rooms: 10 (PB) $75-85; special family rates
Full Breakfast
Credit Cards: A, B, C, D
Notes: 2, 5, 7

Oak Square Plantation

year; 6 Pets welcome; 7 Children welcome; 8 Tennis nearby; 9 Swimming nearby; 10 Golf nearby; 11 Skiing nearby; 12 May be booked through travel agent

Missouri

BRANSON

Cameron's Crag

P. O. Box 526, Point Lookout, 65726
(417) 335-8134; (800) 933-8529

Located high on a bluff overlooking
Lake Taneycomo and the valley, three
miles south of Branson, enjoy a spectacular view from a three-room private
suite with king bed and Jacuzzi. A second room has a private entrance, queen
bed, view of the lake, private spa on
deck. The third room has twin or king
beds.

Hosts: Glen and Kay Cameron
Rooms: 3 (PB) $50-85
Full Breakfast
Credit Cards: A, B, C
Notes: 2, 4

Country Gardens Bed and Breakfast

HCR 4, Box 2202, Lakeshore Drive. 65616
(417) 334-8564; (800) 727-0723

This bed and breakfast is located along
Lake Taneycomo which provides excellent fishing and a parklike setting,
only ten minutes from the majority of
the music shows. We make reservations for shows on request. Honeymoon-
ers and special occasion guests welcomed. The rose suite has a private spa;
the other two rooms share a spa on a
deck overlooking the lake. All rooms
have private entrances.

Hosts: Bob and Pat Cameron
Rooms: 3 (PB) $70-95
Full Breakfast
Credit Cards: A, B, D
Notes: 2, 9, 12

Ozark Mountain Country Bed and Breakfast Service

Box 295, 65616
(417) 334-4720; (800) 695-1546

Ozark Mountain Country has been ar-
ranging accommodations for guests in
southwest Missouri and northwest Arkansas since 1982. In the current list of
100 homes and small inns, some locations offer private entrances and fantastic views, guest sitting areas, swimming pools, Jacuzzis, or a fireplace.
Most locations are available all year.
Personal checks accepted. Some homes

welcome children; a few welcome pets (even horses). Coordinator: Kay Cameron. $35-95.

CALIFORNIA

Memory Lane Bed and Breakfast

102 S. Oak, 65018
(314) 796-4233

This 1894 home has been carefully renovated to retain its Victorian character. The guest rooms feature antique furnishings while the remainder of the house is decorated with a blend of antique and new furniture. The Lake of the Ozarks, historic Arrow Rock and Hermann, Missouri, are only a few of the many locations within easy driving distance.

Hosts: Joe and Mary Ellen LaPrise
Rooms: 3 (SB) $37
Full Breakfast
Credit Cards: None
Notes: 2, 5, 7

Memory Lane Bed and Breakast

CARTHAGE

Brewer's Maple Lane Farm B&B

Rural Route 1, Box 203, 64836
(417) 358-6312

Listed on the National Register of Historic Places, this Victorian home has 20 rooms furnished mostly with family heirlooms, four guest rooms. Our 240-acre farm is ideal for family vacations and campers. We have a playground, picnic area, hunting, and fishing in our 22-acre lake. Nearby are artist Lowell Davis' farm and Sam Butcher's Precious Moments Chapel.

Hosts: Arch and Renee Brewer
Rooms: 4 (SB) $45
Expanded Continental Breakfast
Credit Cards: None
Notes: 2, 5, 7, 8, 10, 12

HANNIBAL

Fifth Street Mansion Bed and Breakfast Inn

213 South Fifth Street, 63401
(314) 221-0445; for reservations only call
(800) 874-5661

Built in 1858 in Italianate style by friends of Mark Twain, antique furnishings complement the stained glass, ceramic fireplaces, and original gaslight fixtures of the house. Two parlors, dining room, and library with hand-grained walnut paneling, plus wraparound porches provide space for conversation, reading, TV, games. Walk to Mark Twain historic district, shops, restaurants,

year; 6 Pets welcome; 7 Children welcome; 8 Tennis nearby; 9 Swimming nearby; 10 Golf nearby; 11 Skiing nearby; 12 May be booked through travel agent

riverfront. The mansion blends Victorian charm with plenty of old-fashioned hospitality. The whole house is available for reunions and weddings.

Hosts: Mike and Donalene Andreotti
Rooms: 7 (PB) $65-90
Full Breakfast
Credit Cards: A, B, C, D
Notes: 2, 5, 7, 8, 9, 10, 12

HERMANN

Die Gillig Heimat

HCR 62, Box 30, 65041
(314) 943-6942

Capture the beauty of country living on this farm located on beautiful rolling hills. The original Gillig home was built as a log cabin in 1842 and has been enlarged several times. Awake in the morning to beautiful views in every direction, and enjoy a hearty breakfast in the large, country kitchen. Stroll the pastures and hills of the working cattle farm while watching nature at its best. Historic Hermann is nearby.

Hosts: Ann and Armin Gillig
Rooms: 2 (PB) $50-55
Full Breakfast
Credit Cards: None
Notes: 2, 5, 7 (by arrangement)

KAHOKA

Fox Valley Meadows Bed and Breakfast

Rt. 2, Box 71, 63445
(816) 727-3533

Relax in informal, casual style on a

working farm with inviting, modern home conveniently located on state highway but with a country road great for biking or hiking. Make this a hub for a tri-state vacation. Three bedrooms with two baths. Baths shared with host couple. By reservation only, please!

Hosts: Marilyn and Junior Otte
Rooms: 3 (SB) $32-35
Both Full and Continental Breakfasts
Credit Cards: None
Notes: 2, 5, 7, 8, 9

KANSAS CITY

Bed and Breakfast Kansas City

P.O. Box 14781, Lenexa, Kansas, 66285
(913) 888-3636

This reservation service can arrange your accommodations in Kansas City or the St. Louis, Missouri, area. From an 1857 plantation mansion on the river to a geodesic dome in the woods with hot tub, there is a price and style for everyone. Victorian, turn-of-the-century, English Tudor and contemporary are available. Double, queen or king size beds (most with private baths and full breakfast). The service represents 40 inns and homes. $40-125.

Southmoreland on The Plaza

116 E. 46th St., 64112
(816) 531-7979

Two-time winner "Top B&B in the U.S.," "Outstanding Achievement in Preservation" award winner, Associa-

NOTES: Credit cards accepted: A Master Card; B Visa; C American Express; D Discover Card; E Diners Club; F Other; 2 Personal checks accepted; 3 Lunch available; 4 Dinner available; 5 Open all

tion of American Historic Inns; "Most Romantic New Urban Inn" by *Romantic Hideaways Newsletter.* Classic New England Colonial Mansion located between Renowned Country Club Plaza (shopping/entertaining district) and Nelson-Atkins Museum of Art. Elegant B&B ambience with small hotel amenities. Many rooms with private decks or fireplaces. Special services for business travelers. Sport and dining privileges at nearby Historic Private Club.

Hosts: Penni Johnson, Susan Moehl
Rooms: 12 (PB) $105-135
Full Breakfast
Credit Cards: A, B, C
Notes: 2, 5, 8, 9, 10, 12

PLATTE CITY

Basswood Country Inn Resort

15880 Interurban Road, 64079-9185
(816) 431-5556

Come stay where the rich and famous relaxed and played in the 1940s and 1950s! These are the most beautiful, secluded, wooded, lakefront accommodations in the entire Kansas City area. Choose from two-bedroom, full kitchen suites, 1935 cottage, or king suites. Bring your pole--good fishing!

Hosts: Don and Betty Soper
Rooms: 7 (PB) $63-125
Cottage: 1 (PB) $93
Continental Breakfast
Credit Cards: A, B
Notes: 2, 5, 7, 8, 9, 10, 11, 12

ST. JOSEPH

Harding House Bed and Breakfast

219 N 20th St., 64501
(816) 232-7020

Gracious turn-of-the-century home. Elegant oak woodwork and pocket doors. Antiques and beveled leaded glass windows. Historic area near museums, churches, antique shops and restaurants. Four unique guest rooms. Eastlake has romantic woodburning fireplace and queen size bed; Blue Room has antique baby crib. Children welcome. Full Breakfast with homemade pastry. Tea Room across the street serves lunch Tuesday through Saturday, and dinner on Friday and Saturday from 5:30-8:30P.M.

Hosts: Glen and Mary Harding
Rooms: 4 (SB) $40-55
Credit Cards: A, B, C, D
Notes: 2, 3, 4 (Fri-Sat), 5, 7, 12

ST. LOUIS

Lafayette House Bed and Breakfast

2156 Lafayette Avenue, 63104
(314) 772-4429

This 1876 Victorian mansion with modern amenities is in the center of things to do in St. Louis and on a direct bus line to downtown. It is air conditioned and furnished with antiques and traditional furniture. Many collectibles and large varied library to enjoy. Families welcome. Resident cats and dog.

Hosts: Sarah and Jack Milligan
Rooms: 5 (2PB; 3SB) $50-75
Full Breakfast
Credit Cards: A, B
Notes: 2, 5, 7, 8, 9, 10, 12

Stelzer Bed and Breakfast

7106 General Sherman Lane, 63123
(314) 843-5757

Pat and Anita have a corner house with green siding and white awnings. Old family furniture is featured. The sleeping rooms are in the windowed "undercroft." One room has firm twin beds, the other has firm fold-out bed with waffle mattress. Each room has radio and clock with a color TV in the adjacent sitting room. A side driveway and entrance accommodate the guest area. We enjoy sharing the sunroom and living room with guests.

Hosts: Pat and Anita Stelzer
Rooms: 2 (PB or SB) $20-25
Full Breakfast
Credit Cards: None
Notes: 2, 5, 7, 10

The Winter House

3522 Arsenal Street, 63118
(314) 664-4399

This gracious Victorian features a pressed tin ceiling in the lower bedroom and a suite on the second floor.

Freshly squeezed orange juice is always served for breakfast in the dining room, using crystal and antique china. Tea is available and live piano music is included (by reservation only).

Hosts: Sarah and Kendall Winter
Rooms: 3 (PB) $55-70
Expanded Continental Breakfast
Credit Cards: A, B, C, E, F
Notes: 2, 5, 7, 8, 9, 10, 12

SPRINGFIELD

The Mansion at Elfindale Bed and Breakfast

1701 S. Fort, 65807
(417) 831-5400

Welcome to the elegance of the magnificent gray stone structure. Built in the 1800s, The Mansion features ornate fireplaces, stained glass windows and unique architecturally designed rooms. We invite you to choose from 13 private suites. Each is a color essay designed with maximum comfort in mind and each luxuriates in all the splendor of the Victorian era. A hearty breakfast is served in one of our dining areas, featuring foods from around the world.

Host: Jeff Wells
Rooms: 13 (PB) $70-125
Full Breakfast
Credit Cards: A, B, C, D
Notes: 2, 3, 5

Montana

BOZEMAN

Bergfeld
Bed and Breakfast
8515 Sypes Canyon Road, 59715
(406) 586-7778

Bergfeld (German for mountain field) sits on the edge of Bridger Mountain slope and sports 360 degree views. Amenities include hot tub, private bathrooms, queen beds, wildlife watching. Only ten minutes from town and airport. Close to two ski resorts. Quiet and relaxing, country comfortable atmosphere. Built in 1992. Outstanding restaurants are close by.

Hosts: Mark and Laura DeGroot
Rooms: 4 (PB) (one room has kitchenette)
$65-80
Full Breakfast
Credit Cards: A, B
Notes: 5, 7, 8, 9, 10, 11, 12

LAUREL

Riverside
Bed and Breakfast
2231 Theil Rd., 59044
(800) 768-1580

Fly fish the Yellowstone from our back yard. Soak away stress in the hot tub. Enjoy a friendly stay, a restful sleep, a full breakfast. Just minutes off I-90, 15 miles west of Billings on a direct route to the Cooke City entrance to Yellowstone National Park.

Hosts: Lynn and Nancy Perey
Rooms: 2 (PB) $50 (winter)-60 (summer)
Full Breakfast
Credit Cards: B
Notes: 2, 5, 7 (over 10), 10, 11, 12

Riverside Bed and Breakfast

year; 6 Pets welcome; 7 Children welcome; 8 Tennis nearby; 9 Swimming nearby; 10 Golf nearby; 11 Skiing nearby; 12 May be booked through travel agent

Nebraska

GRAND ISLAND

Kirschke House Bed and Breakfast
1124 West 3rd St., 68801
(308) 381-6851

Very comfortable, romantic 1902 Victorian home decorated with period furnishings, lace and stained glass. Rustic wooden hot tub in the wash house. Homemade country gourmet breakfasts.

Hosts: Lois and Hank
Rooms: 4 (SB) $45-55
Full Breakfast
Credit Cards: A, B, C, D
Notes: 2, 5, 7

Kirschke House Bed and Breakfast

HOLDREGE

Century Bed and Breakfast
406 1/2 East Ave, 68949-0013
(308) 995-6750

The Century Bed and Breakfast guest room with private bath is a cozy change from motel rooms, your place to get away from daily stresses or a base for exploring. Walk, jog, run or ride through Holdrege's North Park and arboretum and spend time viewing George Lundeen's magnificent sculpture, "The Promise of the Prairie." Located in small mid-western community, Century Bed and Breakfast is a perfect place to relax and let the world go on by while you rejuvenate.

Host: Kathy Gatewood
Rooms: 1 (PB)
Continental Breakfast
Credit Cards: None
Notes: 2, 5, 8

NOTES: Credit cards accepted: A Master Card; B Visa; C American Express; D Discover Card; E Diners Club; F Other; 2 Personal checks accepted; 3 Lunch available; 4 Dinner available; 5 Open all

OMAHA

The Jones'
1617 South 90th Street, 68124
(402) 397-0721

Large, private residence with large deck and gazebo in the back. Fresh cinnamon rolls are served for breakfast. Your hosts' interests include golf, travel, needlework, and meeting other people. Located five minutes from I-80.

Hosts: Theo and Don Jones
Rooms: 3 (1PB; 2SB) $25
Continental Breakfast
Credit Cards: None
Notes: 2, 5, 6, 7, 8, 10

WILBER

Hotel Wilber
203 South Wilson, P.O. Box 641, 68465
(402) 821-2020

Whether you are in pursuit of business or pleasure, need a room for an intimate social gathering or business meeting, or just desire a romantic peaceful weekend away, Hotel Wilber is an ideal retreat. Upon entering our lobby, you will begin your step back to the old country. Experience old world charm in the dining room, bar, garden, or one of our eleven antique filled rooms.

Host: Frances L. Erb
Rooms: 11 (SB) $39-65
Full Breakfast
Credit Cards: A, B
Notes: 2, 3, 4, 5, 7, 9

---

year; 6 Pets welcome; 7 Children welcome; 8 Tennis nearby; 9 Swimming nearby; 10 Golf nearby; 11 Skiing nearby; 12 May be booked through travel agent

Nevada

INCLINE VILLAGE

Haus Bavaria

593 North Dyer Circle, P. O. Box 3308, 89450
(702) 831-6122

This European-style residence in the heart of the Sierra Nevadas, is within walking distance of Lake Tahoe. Each of the five guest rooms opens onto a balcony, offering lovely views of the mountains. Breakfast, prepared by your host Bick Hewitt, includes a selection of home-baked goods, fresh fruit, juices, freshly ground coffee, and teas. A private beach and swimming pool are available to guests. Ski at Diamond Peak, Mt. Rose, Heavenly Valley, and other nearby areas.

Host: Bick Hewitt
Rooms: 5 (PB) $90
Full Breakfast
Credit Cards: A, B, C
Notes: 2, 5, 8, 9, 10, 11, 12

New Hampshire

ALBANY

Kancamagus Swift River Inn

P.O. Box 1650, 03818
(603) 447-2332

This is a quality inn with that Old World flavor in a stress-free environment. Located in the White Mountains of New Hampshire in the Mt. Washington Valley on the most beautiful highway in the state, the Kancamagus Highway, one and one-half miles off route 16. We are only minutes from all factory outlets, attractions, and fine restaurants.

Hosts: Joseph and Janet Beckenbach
Rooms: 10 (PB) $40-90
Continental Breakfast
Credit Cards: None
Notes: 2, 5, 7, 8, 9, 10, 11, 12

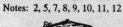
The Bradford Inn

BRADFORD

The Bradford Inn

Rural Route 1, Main Street, Box 40, 03221
(603) 938-5309; (800) 669-5309

The Bradford Inn was built as a small hotel in the 1890s. It has two parlors for guest use, one with a fireplace, one with a TV. J. Albert's Restaurant features turn-of-the-century ragtime and rhapsodies, "grandma gourmet" cuisine, and was the 1991-92 winner Best Apple Pie in New Hampshire, *Yankee* magazine. The area abounds in outdoor activities in all seasons and offers craft and antique shops, auctions, summer theater, local fairs, and festivals. We can accommodate small groups (28-34) for retreats, family parties, or church outings.

Hosts: Tom and Connie Mazol
Rooms: 12 (PB) $59-79
Full Breakfast
Credit Cards: A, B, C, D, E, F
Notes: 2, 4, 5, 6, 7, 8, 9, 10, 11, 12

---

year; 6 Pets welcome; 7 Children welcome; 8 Tennis nearby; 9 Swimming nearby; 10 Golf nearby; 11 Skiing nearby; 12 May be booked through travel agent

CLAREMONT

Goddard Mansion
Bed and Breakfast

25 Hillstead Road, 03743-3399
(603) 543-0603; (800) 736-0603; FAX (603)
543-0657

Located on seven acres with panoramic mountain views, this delightful, restored early-1900s English Manor-style mansion has 18 rooms and expansive porches and tea house. Eight uniquely decorated guest rooms await, including an airy French-country room; step-back-in-time Victorian; whimsical cloud room; and romantic bridal suite. A full, natural breakfast starts each day. Four-season activities are nearby, national historic landmark, antique buff's adventureland, smoke-free inside, clean air outside.

Hosts: Debbie and Frank Albee
Rooms: 8 (2PB; 6SB) $65-95
Expanded Continental Breakfast
Credit Cards: A, B, D, E, F
Notes: 2, 5, 7, 8, 9, 10, 11

COLEBROOK

Monadnock
Bed and Breakfast

One Monadnock Street, 03576
(603) 237-8216

Located one block off Main Street, with easy access to shops and restaurants, in a quiet, picturesque, country community of 2,500 people, this 1916 house has a natural fieldstone porch, chimney, and foundation. Inside it has gorgeous, natural woodwork. Three guest bedrooms upstairs include two with double beds sharing facilities and one with a double and single bed with private half-bath. Common areas are available for relaxing or playing games and watching a large-screen TV. A roomy balcony is good for relaxing and soaking up the sun's rays.

Hosts: Barbara and Wendell Woodard
Rooms: 3 (SB) $43-54
Full Breakfast
Credit Cards: A, B
Notes: 2, 5, 6 (by prior arrangement), 7, 10, 11

EATON CENTER (NEAR CONWAY)

The Inn at Crystal Lake

Route 153, 03832
(603) 447-2120; (800) 343-7336

You deserve pampering! Unwind in our 1884 Victorian inn with balconies in a quiet picture-perfect village. Enjoy our antiques and extraordinary four course, multi-entree, eye-appealing dinner presented on china, crystal, and lace in our metal sculpture-enhanced dining room with fireplace. Begin the day with Irish soda bread and a full country breakfast. We have a Victorian parlor, a comfortable TV den/library, and a cozy lounge (the only room where smoking is permitted).

Hosts: Walter and Jacqueline Spink
Rooms: 11 (PB) $60-116 plus 15% service charge
Full Breakfast
Credit Cards: A, B, C
Notes: 2, 4, 5, 7, 8, 9, 10, 11, 12

NOTES: Credit cards accepted: A Master Card; B Visa; C American Express; D Discover Card; E Diners Club; F Other; 2 Personal checks accepted; 3 Lunch available; 4 Dinner available; 5 Open all

FREEDOM

Freedom House
Bed and Breakfast

1 Maple Street, P.O. Box 478, 03836
(603) 539-4815

This Victorian home with six guest rooms is located 15 minutes from Conway. King Pine ski resort is five minutes away. Lake Ossipee and Loon Lake are great resort areas for enjoying an abundance of recreation. One church is located in the village; others are 15 minutes away. A smoke-free environment.

Hosts: Marjorie and Bob Daly
Rooms: 6 (SB) $60
Full Breakfast
Credit Cards: A, B
Notes: 2, 7, 8, 9, 10, 11

HAMPTON BEACH

The Oceanside

365 Ocean Boulevard, 03842
(603) 926-3542

This boutique hotel on the oceanfront has period furnishings, private baths, and is smoke-free. Within easy walking distance of activities and shops. Intimate breakfast cafe, decks and sidewalk terrace, turndown service. Beach towels and chairs are available.

Hosts: Skip and Debbie Windemiller
Rooms: 10 (PB) $77-105
Expanded Continental Breakfast except July and August
Credit Cards: A, B, C, D
Notes: 8, 10, 12

HOLDERNESS

The Inn on Golden Pond

Route 3, P. O. Box 680, 03245-0680
(603) 968-7269

An 1879 Colonial home is nestled on 50 wooded acres offering guests a traditional New England setting where you can escape and enjoy warm hospitality and personal service of the resident hosts. Rooms are individually decorated with braided rugs and country curtains and bedspreads. Hearty, home-cooked breakfast features farm fresh eggs, muffins, homemade bread, and Bonnie's most requested rhubarb jam.

Hosts: Bonnie and Bill Webb
Rooms: 9 (PB) $85-135
Full Breakfast
Credit Cards: A, B, C
Notes: 2, 5, 8, 9, 10, 11, 12

The Inn on Golden Pond

year; 6 Pets welcome; 7 Children welcome; 8 Tennis nearby; 9 Swimming nearby; 10 Golf nearby; 11 Skiing nearby; 12 May be booked through travel agent

JACKSON

Ellis River House
Route 16, P. O. Box 656, 03846
(603) 383-9339; (800) 233-8309

At this enchanting farmhouse inn, you can enjoy fine lodging and superb country dining, nestled in the heart of the White Mountains of New England overlooking the spectacular Ellis River. Enjoy homemade breads and pick your own farm-fresh eggs. Jackson's world-class cross-country ski trails are at our door. On-premises trout fishing, hiking in our magnificent White Mountains forestry, Jacuzzi in our atrium. Warm and homey.

Hosts: Barry and Barbara Lubao
Rooms: 7 (2PB; 5SB) $40-120
Full Breakfast
Credit Cards: A, B, C
Notes: 2,4, 6, 7, 8, 9, 10, 11

Inn at Thorn Hill
Thorn Hill Road, Box CBB, 03846
(603) 383-4242; (800) 289-8990

Enjoy spectacular mountain views and enticing cuisine at this 1895 Stanford White inn with antique-filled guest rooms in the main inn and a carriage house and three cottages furnished with a country touch--all smoke free. Activities available in every season at the inn and throughout the White Mountains. Air conditioned. Outdoor hot tub. Art, quilting and cooking workshops and seasonal packages available. Ideal for small groups and special occasions. Recommended by *Bon Appetit, Yankee*

Guide, Travel and Leisure, AAA.

Hosts: Jim and Ibby Cooper
Rooms: 19 (PB) $100-182
Full Breakfast
Credit Cards: A, B, C
Closed April
Notes: 2, 4, 8, 9, 10, 11, 12

JEFFERSON

Applebrook
Route 115A, 03583
(603) 586-7713; (800) 545-6504

Taste our mid-summer raspberries while enjoying panoramic mountain views. Applebrook is a comfortable, casual bed and breakfast in a large Victorian farmhouse with a peaceful, rural setting. After a restful night's sleep, you will enjoy a hearty breakfast before venturing out for a day of hiking, fishing, antique hunting, golfing, swimming, or skiing. Near Santa's Village and Six-Gun City. Dormitory available for groups. Brochures available.

Host: Sandra J. Conley
Rooms: 8 plus dormitory (2PB; 6SB) $45-60
Full Breakfast
Credit Cards: A, B, D
Notes: 2, 5, 6, 7, 8, 9, 10, 11

The Jefferson Inn
Route 2, 03583
(603) 586-7998; (800) 729-7908

This charming 1896 Victorian near Mt. Washington has a 360-degree mountain view. Summer activities include hiking from our door, a swimming pond, six golf courses nearby, summer the-

---

NOTES: Credit cards accepted: A Master Card; B Visa; C American Express; D Discover Card; E Diners Club; F Other; 2 Personal checks accepted; 3 Lunch available; 4 Dinner available; 5 Open all

ater, and excellent cycling. In the winter, enjoy Bretton Woods, cross-country skiing, and skating across the street. Afternoon tea is served daiy. Three family suites are available.

Hosts: Greg Brown and Bertie Koelewijn
Rooms: 13 (PB) $52-77
Full Breakfast
Credit Cards: A, B, C
Notes: 2, 7, 8, 9, 10, 11, 12

NEW IPSWICH

The Inn at New Ipswich
Porter Hill Road, P. O. Box 208, 03071
(603) 878-3711

The inn is situated at the heart of New England in New Hampshire's Monadnock region. The 1790 Colonial, with classic red barn, set amid stone walls and fruit trees, heartily welcomes guests. Guest rooms feature firm beds and country antiques. Also featured are widepine floors and six original fireplaces. Downhill and cross-country skiing, hiking, antique shops, concerts, auctions are all nearby.

Hosts: Ginny and Steve Bankuti
Rooms: 6 (PB) $60
Full Breakfast
Credit Cards: A, B
Notes: 2, 5, 10, 11, 12

NEW LONDON

Pleasant Lake Inn
125 Pleasant Street, P. O. Box 1030, 03257
(603) 526-6271; (800) 626-4907

Our 1790 lakeside country inn is nestled on the shore of Pleasant Lake with Mt. Kearsarge as its backdrop. The panoramic location is only one of the many reasons to visit. All four seasons offer activities from our doorway: lake swimming, fishing, hiking, skiing, or just plain relaxing. Dinner is available. Call or write for a brochure.

Hosts: Margaret and Grant Rich
Rooms: 11 (PB) $75-90
Full Breakfast
Credit Cards: A, B
Notes: 2, 4, 5, 7 (over seven), 8, 9, 10, 11, 12

NEWPORT

The Inn at Coit Mountain
HCR 63, Box 3, 03773
(603) 863-3583; (800) 367-2364

All four seasons provide nature's backdrop to this gracious, historic Georgian home. Whether you prefer the greening spring, languid summer afternoons, colorful autumn foiliage, or winter-white mornings, you will delight in a stay at the inn. Available for small retreats of ten to fifteen people.

Hosts: Dick and Judi Tatem
Rooms: 5 (2PB; 3SB) $85-125
Full Breakfast
Credit Cards: A, B, C
Notes: 2, 4 (by arrangement), 6, 7,8, 9, 10, 11

NORTH CONWAY

The Buttonwood Inn
Mt. Surprise Road, P. O. Box 1817, 03860
(603) 356-2625; (800) 258-2625 outside New Hampshire

---

year; 6 Pets welcome; 7 Children welcome; 8 Tennis nearby; 9 Swimming nearby; 10 Golf nearby; 11 Skiing nearby; 12 May be booked through travel agent

The Buttonwood is tucked away on Mt. Surprise in the heart of the White Mountains. It is secluded and quiet, yet only two miles from excellent town restaurants and factory outlet shopping. Built in 1820, this New England-style Cape Cod has antique-furnished guest rooms with wide-plank floors, a large outdoor pool, hiking, and cross-country skiing from the door. Alpine skiing is one mile away.

Hosts: Hugh, Ann, and Walter Begley
Rooms: 9 (3PB; 6S3B) $40-100
Full Breakfast
Credit Cards: A, B, C
Notes: 2, 5, 7, 8, 9, 10, 11, 12

The Center Chimney—1787

River Road, P.O. Box 1220, 03860
(603) 356-6788

Cozy, affordable Cape in a quiet location just off Saco River with swimming, canoeing, and fishing. Near Main Street and North Conway village with summer theater, free cross-country skiing, ice skating, shops and restaurants. Package plans available.

Host: Farley Whitley
Rooms: 4 (SB) $44-55
Continental Breakfast
Credit Cards: None
Notes: 2, 5, 7, 8, 9, 10, 11

Nereledge Inn

River Road, 03860
(603) 356-2831

Enjoy the charm, hospitality, and relaxation of a small 1787 bed and breakfast inn overlooking Cathedral Ledge. Walk to river or village. Close to all activities. Comfortable, casual atmosphere. Rates include delicious breakfast with warm apple pie.

Hosts: Valerie and Dave Halpin
Rooms: 9 (4PB; 5SB) $59-85
Full Breakfast
Credit Cards: A, B, C
Notes: 2, 5, 7, 8, 9, 10, 11

The 1785 Inn

3582 White Mtn Hwy, P.O. Box 1785, 03860-1785
(603) 356-9025; (800) 421-1785 reservations for U.S. and Canada

A lovely inn with lots of charm and history, the 1785 Inn offers romantic lodging with spectacular views of the White Mountains and the finest food in New England. Each of the 17 bedrooms is individually decorated and the 200-year-old fireplaces in the guest living rooms will warm and relax you. Elegant dining and gracious service complement the fine food, and be sure to save room for one of Becky's famous desserts or morning pastries.

Hosts: Beckie and Charlie Mallar
Rooms: 17 (12PB; 5SB) $69-129
Full Breakfast
Credit Cards: A, B, C, D, E
Notes: 2, 4, 5, 7, 8, 9, 10, 11, 12

The 1785 Inn

The Victorian Harvest Inn

P.O. Box 1763, Locust Lane, 03680
(603) 356-3548; (800) 642-0749

Non-smokers delight in our comfortably elegant B&B home at the edge of quaint North Conway Village. Explore unique shops, outlets and the AMC trails. Our 1850s multi-gabled Victorian find comes with six large comfy rooms, all with mountain views. Start your romantic adventure with a bounteous dining experience and classic New England hospitality. Relax by the fireplace or snuggle with a literary treasure in our elegant library. Private baths, lovely in-ground pool and full A/C add to your comfort. AAA 3 diamond award. American Bed and Breakfast Association: rated "A" 3 crowns. Cross country skiing from the door and 3-10 minutes to downhill skiing.

Hosts: Linda and Robert Dahlberg
Rooms: 6 (4PB; 2SB) $55-90
Full Breakfast
Credit Cards: A, B, C, D
Notes: 2, 5, 7 (over 6), 8, 9, 10, 11, 12

PLYMOUTH

Northway House

Rural Free Delivery 1, 03264
(603) 536-2838

Located in the heart of New Hampshire in the beautiful Pemigewasset River Valley, the Northway House is near Newfound, Squam, and Winnepesaukee lakes, as well as the ski areas of Tenney, Waterville Valley, Loon, and Cannon. Hospitality-plus awaits the traveler in this charming Colonial house that is

homey, comfortable, and reasonably priced.

Hosts: Micheline and Norman McWilliams
Rooms: 3 (SB) $27-41
Full Breakfast
Credit Cards: None
Notes: 2, 5, 6, 7, 9, 10, 11

RYE

Rock Ledge Manor Bed and Breakfast

1413 Ocean Boulevard, Route 1-A, 03870
(603) 431-1413

A gracious, traditional, seaside manor home with an excellent location offers an ocean view from all rooms. It is central to all New Hampshire and southern Maine seacoast activities; six minutes to historic Portsmouth and Hampton; 20 minutes to the University of New Hampshire; 15 minutes to Exeter Academy. Reservations are advised.

Hosts: Norman and Janice Marineau
Rooms: 4 (2PB; 2SB) $70-85
Full Breakfast
Credit Cards: None
Notes: 2, 5, 7 (over 10), 8, 9, 10, 11

SUTTON MILLS

The Village House at Sutton Mills

Box 151, Grist Mill Road, 03221
(603) 927-4765

This Village House is an 1857 country Victorian overlooking the quaint New England village of Sutton Mills. The location is quiet, yet convenient to New London, shopping, antiquing, and all summer and winter activities. The house is situated on four acres, and hikers, cross-country skiers, and snowmobilers enjoy starting out through our property. Guests enjoy the privacy of the guest house, tastefully decorated with antiques and old quilts. No smoking.

Hosts: Peggy and Norm Forand
Rooms: 3 (S2.5B) $50
Full Breakfast
Credit Cards: None
Notes: 2, 5, 8, 9, 10, 11, 12

WARNER

Jacob's Ladder Bed and Breakfast

Main Street, Rural Free Delivery 1, Box 11, 03278
(603) 456-3494

Situated in the quaint village of Warner, Jacob's Ladder is conveniently located between I-89, Exits 8 and 9. The early-1800s home is furnished predominantly with antiques, creating a tasteful country atmosphere. Cross-country ski and

snowmobile trail on site with three ski areas within 20 miles. Lakes, mountains, covered bridges, arts and crafts, and more nearby. No smoking.

Hosts: Deb and Marlon Baese
Rooms: 4 (S2B) $40
Full Breakfast
Credit Cards: D
Notes: 2, 5, 7, 8, 10, 11

WILTON CENTER

Stepping Stones Bed and Breakfast

Bennington Battle Trail, 03086
(603) 654-9048

Stepping Stone is owned by a garden designer and weaver. Display gardens surround the 19th-century house set in the quiet, rural Monadnock region. A scrumptious breakfast is served on the porch or terrace in summer, and in the solar garden room year-round. Enjoy good reading, stereo, TV in the cozy living room, or watch active weaver and gardener at work in a serene and civilized atmosphere.

Host: Ann Carlsmith
Rooms: 3 (1PB; 2SB) $35-50
Full Breakfast
Credit Cards: None
Notes: 2, 5, 6, 7, 10, 11, 12

NOTES: Credit cards accepted: A Master Card; B Visa; C American Express; D Discover Card; E Diners Club; F Other; 2 Personal checks accepted; 3 Lunch available; 4 Dinner available; 5 Open all

New Jersey

AVON-BY-THE-SEA

The Avon Manor Inn

109 Sylvania Avenue, 07717
(908) 774-0110

The Avon Manor Inn is a gracious turn-of-the-century home (circa 1907) built in the Colonial Revival style. Enjoy breakfast in our sunny dining room, ocean breezes on our full wrap-around veranda and the charm of this small seaside town. Eight air conditioned bedrooms and only one block to beach and boardwalk. The large living room has a cozy fireplace for winter nights. Many antiques, period pieces and family heirlooms make this a special retreat to savor the serenity of yesteryear.

Hosts: Kathleen and Jim Curley
Rooms: 8(4PB; 4SB) $60-100
Full Breakfast
Credit Cards: A, B, C
Notes: 7, 8, 9, 10, 12

Cashelmara Inn

22 Lakeside Avenue, 07717
(908) 776-8727; (800) 821-2976

A tastefully restored turn-of-the-century inn rests on the bank of a swan lake and the Atlantic Ocean. This desirable beachfront location offers a unique opportunity to smell the fresh salt air, to feel the ocean breeze, and to hear the sounds of the surf and sea gulls from the privacy of your seaside room. Hearty breakfasts are a tradition at Cashelmara Inn.

Host: Martin Mulligan
Rooms: 14 (PB) $60-157
Full Breakfast
Credit Cards: A, B, C, D
Notes: 2, 5, 7, 8, 9, 10

The Avon Manor Inn

CAPE MAY

The Albert Stevens Inn

127 Myrtle Avenue, 08204
(609) 884-4717; (609) 884-2627

Built in 1890 by Dr. Albert G. Stevens as a wedding gift for his bride, Bessie, the inn is just a ten-minute walk to the beach and two blocks from Victorian shopping. The guest rooms are furnished with genuine antiques, and the two parlors have the original parlor furniture. A 102-degree, six-person Jacuzzi in the stress-reduction room is privately scheduled for guests' comfort. Dinner is included off-season.

Hosts: Curt and Diane Rangen
Rooms: 8 (PB) $85-135
Full Breakfast
Credit Cards: A, B, D
Notes: 2, 4, 5, 8, 9, 10, 12

Bedford Inn

805 Stockton Avenue, 08204
(609) 884-4158

The Bedford Inn is centrally located in Cape May, 300 feet from the ocean. Fully heated with a cozy fireplace in the parlor, the inn is completely Victorian and furnished with antiques. All rooms have air conditioning. On-site parking; mid-week discounts September to June. Many activitites nearby.

Hosts: Cindy and Al Schmucker
Rooms: 11 (PB) $85-145
Full Breakfast
Credit Cards: A, B, C
Notes: 2, 7, 8, 9, 10

The Chalfonte Hotel

301 Howard Street, 08204
(609) 884-8409

Come home to gracious Southern hospitality. The Chalfonte hotel, built in 1876, offers traditional Southern cooking, delightful architecture, breezy rooms and long porches for rocking. Dinner and breakfast are included in the room rates. Families are always welcome, and children enjoy their own supervised children's dining room. Ideal location for retreats, reunions, rest and relaxation.

Hosts: Anne LeDuc and Judy Bartella
Rooms: 72 (11PB; 61SB) $53-154
Full Breakfast & Dinner
Credit Cards: A, B
Notes: 2, 4, 7, 8, 9, 10, 12

Duke of Windsor Inn

817 Washington Street, 08204
(609) 884-1355

This grande 1890 Victorian home offers gracious, relaxing accommodations furnished with period antiques, high-backed beds, and marble-topped tables and dressers. Two octagon rooms in our 40-foot turret are particularly fun and romantic. The dining room has five chandeliers and an elaborate plaster ceiling. We are within walking distance of the beach, historical attractions, tennis, and shopping. Open February to December.

Hosts: Bruce and Fran Prichard
Rooms: 9 (8PB; 1SB) $65-125
Full Breakfast
Credit Cards: A, B (for deposit only)
Notes: 2, 8, 9, 10

NOTES: Credit cards accepted: A Master Card; B Visa; C American Express; D Discover Card; E Diners Club; F Other; 2 Personal checks accepted; 3 Lunch available; 4 Dinner available; 5 Open all

The Mason Cottage

625 Columbia Avenue, 08204
(609) 884-3358

Built in 1871 for a wealthy Philadelphia businessman, the inn is in the French Empire style. The Mason family purchased the house in 1945 and started welcoming guests in 1946. The curved, wood-shingle mansard roof was built by local shipyard carpenters, and restored original furniture remains in the house. The house endured the 1878 Cape May fire and several hurricanes. Honeymoon packages and gift certificates available.

Host: Joan E. Mason
Rooms: 9 $85-165
Full Breakfast
Credit Cards: A, B
Notes: 2, 7 (over 12), 8, 9, 10, 12

The Queen Victoria

102 Ocean Street, 08204
(609) 884-8702

The Queen Victoria includes three 1800s homes that have been restored and furnished with antiques. There are two parlors, one with fireplace and one with TV and games. Two dining rooms serve a hearty country breakfast and afternoon tea. Special services include free bicycles, beach showers and towels, and turned-down beds with a special chocolate on your pillow. All rooms are air conditioned.

Hosts: Dane and Joan Wells
Rooms: 22 (PB) $65-235
Full Breakfast
Credit Cards: A, B
Notes: 2, 5, 7, 8, 9, 10

Windward House

24 Jackson Street, 08204
(609) 884-3368

An elegant, Edwardian seaside inn has an entry room and staircase that are perhaps the prettiest in town. Spacious, antique-filled guest rooms have queen beds and air conditioners. With three sun-and-shade porches, cozy parlor fireplace, and Christmas finery, the inn is located in the historic district, one-half block from the beach and shopping mall. Rates include homemade breakfast, beach passes, parking, and bicycles. Midweek discounts September to June; off season weekend packages.

Hosts: Owen and Sandy Miller
Rooms: 8 (PB) $75-140
Full Breakfast
Credit Cards: A, B (deposit only)
Notes: 2, 5, 7 (over 12), 8, 9, 10

Windward House

CRANFORD

Innovations, Inc.

118 South Ave., 07016
800-962-INNS (4667)

National reservation service for B&Bs

---

year; 6 Pets welcome; 7 Children welcome; 8 Tennis nearby; 9 Swimming nearby; 10 Golf nearby; 11 Skiing nearby; 12 May be booked through travel agent

and country inns nationwide. All properties are inspected and rated. Directory and video available by mail order.

GLENWOOD

Apple Valley Inn

Corner of Rt 517 and Rt 565, P.O. Box 302, 07418
(210) 764-3735

Elegantly appointed B&B in the early American tradition. Colonial mansion circa 1831. Pool, trout stream, apple orchard, antique shop, Old Grist Mill, skiing, water park, Appalachian Trail, West Point, N.J., Botanical Gardens, two state parks, and Hudson Valley attractions a short drive. Holidays. 2 night minimum. Reduced rates for 6+ day stay. Special events weekends.

Hosts: Mitzi and John Durham
Rooms: 6 (2PB; 4SB) $55-65
Full Breakfast
Credit Cards: None
Notes: 2, 5, 8, 9, 10, 11

OCEAN CITY

BarnaGate Bed and Breakfast Inn

637 Wesley Avenue, 08226
(609) 291-9366

Enjoy the small, intimate accommodations of our 1895 seashore Victorian. The cozy rooms are decorated in country style with quilts on the antique beds and paddle fans to keep you cool. All rooms are named for flowers. Guests use our common area or front porch

under burgundy awnings with white wicker rockers. Near Cape May, Atlantic City, county zoo, and antique shops. We've got everything--beach, boardwalk, and ocean. Hospitality is our specialty.

Hosts: Frank and Lois Barna
Rooms: 5 (1PB; 4SB) $50-70
Full Breakfast; Continental in sumnmer
Credit Cards: A, B
Notes: 2, 5, 7, 8, 9, 10

New Brighton Inn

519 Fifth Street, 08226
(609) 399-2829

This charming 1880 Queen Anne Victorian has been magnificently restored to its original beauty. All rooms and common areas (living room, library, sun porch) are elegantly and comfortably furnished with antiques. The front veranda is furnished with rockers and a large swing. Rates include beach tags and use of bicycles.

Hosts: Daniel and Donna Hand
Rooms: 6 (4PB; 2SB) $75-85
Full Breakfast
Credit Cards: A, B, C
Notes: 2, 5

Northwood Inn

401 Wesley Avenue, 08226
(609) 399-6071

Winner of the Cape May county beautification award, this elegantly restored 1894 Queen Anne Victorian has 19th-century charm and 20th-century comfort. It features eight distinctive guest rooms, central air conditioning, fully stocked library/game room, two porches, and roof-top deck. It is three blocks from the beach, boardwalk, shops, and restaurants. Complimentary beach tags and off-street parking.

Hosts: Marj and John Loeper
Rooms: 8 (6PB; 2SB) $80-140
Full Breakfast; Continental weekdays
Credit Cards: A, B
Notes: 2, 5, 7 (10 and older), 8, 9, 10

OCEAN GROVE

The Cordova

26 Webb Avenue, 07756
(908) 774-3084 in season; (212) 751-9577 winter

Ocean Grove was founded as a religious retreat center at the turn of the century. This flavor has lasted in the quiet, peaceful atmosphere. Constant religious programs for the family are arranged in the 7,000-seat Great Auditorium. The Cordova rooms are uniquely charming and Victorian. Friendliness, hospitality, cleanliness, and quiet one block from the magnificent white sand beach and boardwalk. The porches have a splendid ocean view. Midweek specials; also, seven nights for the price of five. Saturday night refreshments.

Host: Doris Chernik
Rooms: 14 (1PB; 13SB) $32-65
Cottages: 2 (PB) $85-105
Continental Breakfast
Credit Cards: None
Notes: 2, 7, 8, 9, 12

Keswick Inn

32 Embury Avenue, 07756
(908) 775-7506

Built in 1875, the inn is near beach and shopping and is located in a Victorian village incorporated in 1969 as a camp meeting ground and seaside summer resort. The Great Auditorium seats 7,000, is a national historic monument, and houses a summer program of religious, cultural, and entertainment events.

Host: Robert Centorino
Rooms: 20 (18PB; 2SB) $24-70
Continental Breakfast
Credit Cards: A, B, C, D
Notes: 2, 8, 9, 10

PRINCETON

Bed and Breakfast of Princeton

P.O. Box 751, 08542
(609) 924-3189; FAX (609) 921-6271

Bed and Breakfast of Princeton is a reservation service offering a pleasant alternative to local hotel/motel lodging. The service represents several private residences and provides a variety of "homestay" accommodations. Rates reflect the accommodations and facilities provided. Availability and content of the complimentary breakfast varies from host to host but is usually continental style. Bathrooms may be shared. Some hosts do not permit smoking. Homes are recommended based on availability and information provided by the guest. A listing of host homes is **not** available.

---

year; 6 Pets welcome; 7 Children welcome; 8 Tennis nearby; 9 Swimming nearby; 10 Golf nearby; 11 Skiing nearby; 12 May be booked through travel agent

SPRING LAKE

The Hewitt Wellington Hotel

200 Monmouth Avenue, 07762
(908) 974-1212

"Spring Lake's landmark in luxury." AAA four-diamond award winner. Twelve beautifully appointed single rooms and 17 two-room suites on the lake overlooking the ocean have private balconies, wraparound porches, air conditioning, ceiling fans, private marble baths, remote cable TVs, and phones. Heated pool and free beach passes. Refined dining in our intimate restaurant. Free brochure.

Rooms: 29 (PB) $70-210
Continental Breakfast
Credit Cards: A, B, C
Notes: 3, 4, 7, 8, 10

New Mexico

ALBUQUERQUE

Bottger Mansion Bed and Breakfast
110 San Felipe N.W., 87104
(505) 243-3639

A historic landmark, built before New Mexico was granted statehood. Its Victorian style is unusual as compared to most of Old Town's architecture. The gracious tin ceilings, hand painted wall murals, marble fireplaces, floor and courtyards add elegance to the comfortable accommodations awaiting our guests. King and queen size beds, private baths, jet tub, full breakfast and afternoon tea and bizcichitos right in historic Old Town, just footsteps to museums, shops and restaurants.

Hosts: Patsy Garcia and Frances Maldonado
Rooms: 3 (PB) $79-99
Full Breakfast
Credit Cards: A, B, C
Notes: 2, 5, 7, 8, 9, 10, 11, 12

D'Lightful Haven
915 Warm Sands SE, 87123
(505) 294-3842

Welcome to D'Lightful Haven nestled in the foothills of the Manzano Mountains. Behold mountain views, city lights and spectaculr sunsets. Choose from two master suites. Enjoy the luxury and romance of a Victorian decorated suite on the upper level or an English country suite with a fireplace, private patio and a choice to dine in your own setting. Easy access to expressways makes it convenient to all Albuquerque offers, such as military base, State Fair, Indian festivals, Sandia Peak Ski Area, Aerial Tram and International Balloon Festival.

Hosts: Paul and JoAnn Collins
Rooms: 2 (PB) $50-70
Full Breakfast
Credit Cards: None
Notes: 2, 5, 8, 10, 11

---

year; 6 Pets welcome; 7 Children welcome; 8 Tennis nearby; 9 Swimming nearby; 10 Golf nearby; 11 Skiing nearby; 12 May be booked through travel agent

CEDAR CREST (ALBUQUERQUE)

The Apple Tree
12050 Highway 14 North, Box 287, 87008
(505) 281-3092; (800) 648-4262

Rustic adobe Casita with brick floors, log beamed ceiling and a kiva fireplace; or two other suites (Hummingbird Suite and El Nido). Each can sleep up to four persons with private bath, cable TV, fireplace, kitchenette, phone, private deck. Breakfast (served in suite) might include: blue corn waffles, whole wheat cinnamon rolls, muffins, quiche, omelettes, or eggs New Mexican. On the scenic Turquoise Trail, 1 and 1/2 miles north of I-40, seven miles from Albuquerque.

Hosts: Garland and Norma Curry
Rooms: 3 (PB) $55-105
Full Breakfast
Credit Cards: None
Notes: 2, 5, 6, 7, 8, 9, 10, 11, 12

Adobe Abode

SANTA FE

Adobe Abode
202 Chapelle, 87501
(505) 983-3133

This charming bed and breakfast just three blocks from Santa Fe's plaza is a sophisticated mix of authentic Santa Fe style and European touches, featuring an eclectic art collection, fine antiques, and native New Mexican furniture. It offers two guest rooms (queen and double beds) in the main house and a guest house with twin beds and a walled patio.

Host: Pat Harbour
Rooms: 3 (PB) $85-120
Full Gourmet Breakfast
Credit Cards: A, B, D
Notes: 2, 5, 7, 8, 10, 11, 12

Canyon Road Casitas
652 Canyon Road, 87501
(505) 988-5888; (800) 279-0755

Luxury accommodations are featured in this 100-year-old historic Territorial adobe within walking distance of distinctive art galleries, numerous museums, unique shops, and historic landmarks. Both guest rooms have kitchenettes, down quilts and pillows, feather beds, separate entrances, and private patios. This is truly a four-season retreat.

Host: Trisha Ambrose
Rooms: 2 (PB) $85-165
Continental Breakfast
Credit Cards: A, B, C, D
Notes: 2, 5, 7, 11, 12

El Paradero
220 West Manhattan, 87501
(505) 988-1177

El Paradero is located on a quiet, downtown side street, ideal for exploring the

NOTES: Credit cards accepted: A Master Card; B Visa; C American Express; D Discover Card; E Diners Club; F Other; 2 Personal checks accepted; 3 Lunch available; 4 Dinner available; 5 Open all

heart of historic Santa Fe. The owners have turned the old adobe Spanish farmhouse into a warm and relaxing experience of true southwestern camaraderie and hospitality. The inn is furnished in the southwestern tradition with folk art and has an eccentric, rambling character typical of old adobes. Breakfasts are huge and special.

Hosts: Ouida MacGregor and Thom Allen
Rooms: 12 (8 PB; 4 SB) $50-130
Suites: 2
Full Breakfast
Credit Cards: None
Notes: 2, 5, 6, 7(4 and older), 8, 9, 10, 11, 12

El Paradero

TAOS

Stewart House

P. O. Box 2326, 87571
(505) 776-2913

This Taos landmark was built over a 15-year period from what the artist/builder called reclaimed parts of history. The inn is an extraordinary mix of styles and textures, combining elements from Moorish to Mayan, Spanish to Scandinavian. The innkeepers have been in the fine art business for more than 20 years, so each room is filled with art and antiques. Gallery artists are frequent visitors. Enjoy mountain views, sunsets, outdoor hot tub, and hearty breakfasts only five minutes from Taos Plaza in a quiet, country setting.

Hosts: Mildred and Don Cheek
Rooms: 5 (PB) $75-120
Full Breakfast
Credit Cards: A, B
Notes: 2, 5, 7 (12+ years), 8, 9, 10, 11, 12

New York

ALBANY

American Country Collection of Bed and Breakfasts and Country Inns Reservation Service

4 Greenwood Lane, Delmar, 12054-1606
(518) 439-7001 information; (800) 800-5908,
ext. 21 reservations

This reservation service provides reservations for eastern New York, western Massachusetts, all of Vermont, Northern New Hampshire, and St. Thomas, U.S.V.I. Just one call does it all. Relax and unwind at any of our 115 immaculate, personally inspected bed and breakfasts and country inns. Many include fireplace, Jacuzzi, and/or Modified American Plan. We cater to the budget-minded, yet also offer luxurious accommodations in older Colonial homes and inns. Urban, suburban, and rural locations available. $35-180. Arthur R. Copeland, coordinator.

AVERILL PARK

Ananas Hus Bed and Breakfast

Route 3, Box 301, 12018
(518) 766-5035

The Tomlinsons invite you to share the beauty, tranquility, smoke-free, and pet-free environment of their hillside home on 30 acres with a panoramic view of the Hudson River valley. Ananas Hus lies just off Route 43 on South Road in West Stephentown, convenient to western Massachusetts and the state capital district of New York, which abounds with cultural, natural, historic, and sports attractions. Great ski country.

Hosts: Clyde and Thelma Olsen Tomlinson
Rooms: 3 (SB) $55
Full Breakfast
Credit Cards: C
Notes: 2, 5, 7 (over 12), 9, 10, 11

BAINBRIDGE

Berry Hill Farm
Bed and Breakfast

Rural Delivery 1, Box 128, 13733
(607) 967-8745

This restored 1820s farmhouse on a hilltop is surrounded by vegetable and flower gardens and 180 acres where you can hike, swim, bird-watch, pick berries, skate, cross-country ski, or sit on the wraparound porch and watch the natural parade. Our rooms are furnished with comfortable antiques. A ten-minute drive takes you to restaurants, golf, tennis, auctions, and antique centers. Cooperstown and most local colleges are only 45 minutes away.

Hosts: Jean Fowler and Cecilio Rios
Rooms: 3 (SB) $55-65
Full Breakfast
Credit Cards: A, B, C
Notes: 2, 5, 7, 8, 9, 10, 11, 12

Berry Hill Farm Bed and Breakfast

BOLTON LANDING

Hilltop Cottage
Bed and Breakfast

Box 186, Lakeshore Drive, 12814
(518) 644-2492

A clean, comfortable, renovated farmhouse is near Lake George in the beau-tiful eastern Adirondack Mountains. Walk to beaches, restaurants, and marinas. Enjoy a quiet, home atmosphere with hearty breakfasts. In the summer, this is a busy resort area. Autumn offers fall foliage, hiking, skiing. There is a wood-burning stove for use in winter. A brochure is available.

Hosts: Anita and Charlie Richards
Rooms: 4 (2PB; 2SB) $45-65
Full Breakfast
Credit Cards: A, B
Notes: 2, 5

BURDETT

The Red House
Country Inn

4586 Picnic Area Road, 14818
(607) 546-8566

The inn is located in the beautiful 13,000-acre Finger Lakes National Forest with 28 miles of maintained hiking and cross-country ski trails. Six award-winning wineries are within ten minutes from the completely restored 1840s farmstead on five acres of groomed lawns and flower gardens. Enjoy beautifully appointed rooms, country breakfasts, in-ground pool, fully equipped kitchen. Twelve minutes north of Watkins Glen, 20 minutes from Ithaca, 30 minutes from Corning.

Hosts: Sandy Schmanke and Joan Martin
Rooms: 5 (S4B) $60-85
Full Breakfast
Credit Cards: A, B, C, D
Notes: 2, 5, 9, 11, 12

year; 6 Pets welcome; 7 Children welcome; 8 Tennis nearby; 9 Swimming nearby; 10 Golf nearby; 11 Skiing nearby; 12 May be booked through travel agent

CAMBRIDGE

Battenkill Bed and Breakfast

Route 313, Rural Delivery 1, Box 143, 12816-9717
(518) 677-8868; (800) 676-8768

Relax in the beautiful Annaquassicoke Valley and enjoy our post-and-beam home. Veronica delights in creative cooking, and Walt is a jazz musician. In the winter, our bed and breakfast offers snow-shoeing on site and cross-country skiing nearby. Spring, summer, and fall offer you fishing, canoeing, tubing the beautiful Battenkill River, or biking through the valley. Equipment for all these activities is available at our rental office.

Hosts: Veronica and Walter Piekarz
Rooms: 2 (SB) $60
Full Breakfast
Credit Cards: A, B, C, D
Notes: 2, 3 & 4 (by arrangement), 5, 10, 11

CAMILLUS

The Re Family Bed and Breakfast

4166 Split Rock Rd, 13031
(315) 468-2039

100-year-old early American farm house featuring lodge style den, country kitchen, side deck utilized for fair weather breakfasts, 40' pool, lawns, 2 guest rooms with queen size brass beds and orthopedic mattresses, pedestal sink in each room. Next to garden style bathroom with walk in tile shower, vanity with double sinks and full mirrored backwall. Also one room with full bed and captain's bed for two singles or for children. Stress free environment close to Syracuse.

Hosts: Joseph and Terry Re
Rooms: 3 (SB) $55-75
Full or Continental Breakfast
Credit Cards: None
Notes: 2, 5, 7, 8, 9, 10, 11, 12

CAMPBELL HALL

Point of View Bed and Breakfast

RR 2, Box 766H, Ridge Rd, 10916
(914) 294-6259

Enjoy peace and tranquility in a country setting with splendid views of rolling hills and farmland. Adjoins 250 acre horse farm with full equine facility. One hour from New York City, 20 minutes from the Stewart Airport and three miles from historic village of Goshen. Spacious rooms, private baths and guest-only sitting room.

Hosts: Rev Bill Frankle and Elaine Frankle
Rooms: 2 (PB) $60
Full Breakfast
Credit Cards: A, B
Notes: 2, 5, 10, 11

CAZENOVIA

Lincklaen House

79 Albany Street, Box 36, 13035
(315) 655-3461

To visit Lincklaen House is to return to

an era of elegant hospitality. Lincklaen House is an extraordinary four-season country inn built in 1835 as a luxurious stopover for colonial travelers. Carefully renovated, the hotel provides the amenities that 20th-century travelers demand, while retaining a charm preserved since the 19th century. Afternoon tea is served.

Host: Howard M. Kaler
Rooms: 21 (PB) $70-130
Continental Breakfast
Credit Cards: A, B
Notes: 2, 3, 4, 5, 6, 7, 8, 9, 10, 11, 12

COOPERSTOWN

The Inn at Brook Willow

Rural Delivery 2, Box 514, 13326
(607) 547-9700

A pastoral retreat nestled in willows and pines, the Victorian house sits among meadows and hills and is furnished with antiques in the house and a "reborn" barn. A common room overlooks the gardens. Jack's famous muffins are served each morning. Chosen as one of the 100 best bed and breakfast homes in North America.

Hosts: Joan and Jack Grimes
Rooms: 4 (PB) $64-84
Full Breakfast
Credit Cards: None
Notes: 2,5, 7, 8, 9, 10, 11

CORNING

Delevan House

188 Delevan Avenue, 14830
(607) 962-2347

This southern Colonial house sits on a hill overlooking Corning. It is charming, graceful, and warm in quiet surroundings. Delicious breakfast. Check in time 3P.M., check out time 10:30 A.M.. Breakfast served from 8:00-9:00P.M. Free transportation to airport.

Host: Mary De Pumpo
Rooms: 3 (1PB; 2SB) $55-85
Full Breakfast
Notes: 2, 5, 7 (over 10), 10, 11, 12

1865 White Birch Bed and Breakfast

69 East First Street, 14830
(607) 962-6355

The White Birch, Victorian in structure but decorated in country, has been refurbished to show off its winding staircase, hardwood floors, and wall window in the dining room that overlooks the back yard. We are located in a residential area two blocks from restored historic Market Street and six blocks from the Corning Museum of Glass. A warm fire during the colder months welcomes guests in the common room where TV and great conversation are available. A full gourmet breakfast is served each morning.

Hosts: Kathy and Joe Donahue
Rooms: 4 (2PB; 2SB) $50-70
Full Breakfast
Credit Cards: A, B, C
Notes: 2, 5, 7, 8, 9, 10, 11

---

year; 6 Pets welcome; 7 Children welcome; 8 Tennis nearby; 9 Swimming nearby; 10 Golf nearby; 11 Skiing nearby; 12 May be booked through travel agent

CUBA

Helen's Tourist Home
7 Maple Street, 14727
(716) 968-2200

Your hostess has been welcoming tourists in her turn-of-the-century home for 39 years. Guests have full use of the house, including the living room with TV. Coffee, a toaster, and a refrigerator are always available. Visit the Cuba Cheese Shop and historic Seneca Springs. Restaurants are nearby. Less than five minutes from Exit 28, Route 17. Reservations are appreciated. Rates are very reasonable.

Host: Dora Wittmann
Rooms: 5 (1PB; 4SB) $20-35
Credit Cards: None
Notes: 5, 7, 10, 11

DRYDEN

Margaret Thacher's Spruce Haven Bed and Breakfast
9 James Street, 13053
(607) 844-8052

This 1976 log home is warm and friendly and is surrounded by spruce trees that give the feeling of being in the woods, even though we are located in the village. Within 12 miles of Ithaca, Courtland, lakes, golf, skiing, colleges, museums, and restaurants.

Host: Margaret Thacher Brownell
Rooms: 2 (SB) Call for rates
Full Breakfast

Credit Cards: None
Notes: 2, 5, 6, 8, 9, 10, 11

DUNDEE

The Old Manse
9 Harpending Ave., 14837
(607) 243-5618

1869 Victorian home used as a parsonage for around 100 years. On a quiet residential street, near restaurants, Watkins Glen, Seneca, and Keuka lakes. Just off routes #14 and #14a. No smoking, no pets. We accept Mastercard and Visa. Two bedrooms, each with private bath. Hot tub enclosed on porch.

Hosts: Bruce and Gwen Allen
Rooms: 2 (PB) $55
Expanded Continental
Credit Cards: A, B
Notes: 2, 5

EAST HAMPTON

Mill House
33 North Main Street, 11937
(516) 324-9766

This 1790 Colonial is located in "America's most beautiful village." Enjoy lemonade while overlooking the old Hook windmill, or take a restful nap in our back-yard hammock. In the off-season, enjoy hot cider by the fireplace or a brisk walk to the ocean beach. Antiquing, golf, tennis, Long Island wineries, and whale watching are nearby.

Hosts: Barbara and Kevin Flynn
Rooms: 8 (6PB; 2SB) $95-165

NOTES: Credit cards accepted: A Master Card; B Visa; C American Express; D Discover Card; E Diners Club; F Other; 2 Personal checks accepted; 3 Lunch available; 4 Dinner available; 5 Open all

Full Breakfast
Credit Cards: A, B, C
Notes: 2, 5, 7, (over 11), 8, 9, 10

FORESTBURGH

The Inn at Lake Joseph

400 St. Joseph's Road, 12777
(914) 791-9506

The inn, previously owned by the Dominican sisters, was once the vacation estate used by Cardinals Hayes and Spellman of New York. Its 125-year-old Queen Anne Victorian-style mansion is surrounded by 2,000 acres of wildlife preserve and hardwood forest on a 250-acre, unspoiled private lake. Rates include dinner.

Host: Ivan Weinger
Rooms: 9 (8PB; 1SB) $138-218
Full Breakfast
Credit Cards: A, B, C
Notes: 2, 4, 8, 9, 10, 11

FOSTERDALE

Fosterdale Heights House

205 Mueller Road, 12726
(914) 482-3369

This historic 1840 European-style country estate in the Catskill Mountains is less than two hours from New York City. It is gentle and quiet, with a bountiful breakfast. Enjoy the mountain view overlooking the pond, acres of Christmas trees (cut your own in season), and natural forest. Informal evenings of chamber music and parlor games break out frequently.

Host: Roy Singer
Rooms: 12 (3PB; 9SB) $56-115
Full Breakfast
Credit Cards: A, B
Notes: 4, 5, 8, 9, 10, 11

FULTON

Battle Island Inn

RR 1, Box 176, 13069
(315) 593-3699

Battle Island Inn is a pre-Civil War farm estate that has been restored and furnished with period antiques. The inn is across the road from a golf course that also provides cross-country skiing. Guest rooms are elegantly furnished with imposing high-back beds, TVs, phones, and private baths. Breakfast is always special in the 1840s dining room.

Hosts: Joyce and Richard Rice
Rooms: 5 (PB) $60-85
Full Breakfast
Credit Cards: A, B, C, D
Notes: 2, 5, 7, 10, 11

HAMMONDSPORT

Gone with the Wind on Keuka Lake

453 West Lake Road, 14418
(607) 868-4603

The name paints the picture of this 1887 stone Victorian on 14 acres on a slight rise overlooking a quiet lake cove that is adorned by an inviting gazebo. Feel the magic of total relaxation and peace of mind in the solarium hot tub, nature trails, three fireplaces, delectable breakfasts, private beach, and dock. One hour

---

year; 6 Pets welcome; 7 Children welcome; 8 Tennis nearby; 9 Swimming nearby; 10 Golf nearby; 11 Skiing nearby; 12 May be booked through travel agent

south of Rochester in the Finger Lakes area of New York.

Hosts: Linda and Robert Lewis
Rooms: 6 $65-95
Full Breakfast
Credit Cards: None
Notes: 2, 5, 8, 9, 10, 11

HERKIMER

Bellinger Woods Bed and Breakfast

611 West German Street, 13350
(315) 866-2770

This Victorian bed and breakfast, circa 1860, is located one mile from I-90, New York State Thruway, Exit 30 in the village of Herkimer. It offers comfortable elegance in the heart of central leatherstocking country, complete with marble fireplaces and crown plaster moldings. Area attractions include the Herkimer diamond mines, Remington Arms Museum, and antique shops. The Cooperstown area is just a 40-minute scenic ride away.

Hosts: Barbara and Paul Mielcarski
Rooms: 3 (2PB; 1SB) $35-55
Full Breakfast
Credit Cards: A, B
Notes: 2, 5, 8, 9, 10, 11, 12

Bellinger Woods Bed and Breakfast

ITHACA

A Slice of Home

178 N. Main St., Spencer, 14883
(607) 589-6073

Newly remodeled 150-year-old farmhouse with 4 bedrooms and two baths. Country cooking with hearty weekend breakfasts and continental weekday breakfasts. Acreage to ski, hike, fish. 20 minutes to Ithaca, Elmira and Watkins Glen. No smoking, outside pets.

Host: Beatrice Brownell
Rooms: 4 (1PB; 2SB) $35-75
Both Full and Continental Breakfasts
Credit Cards: None
Notes: 2, 5, 7 (over 12), 12

Log Country Inn B&B of Ithaca

P.O. Box 581, 14851
(607) 589-4771; (800) 274-4771

Rustic charm of a log house at the edge of 7,000 acres of state forest; 11 miles south from Ithaca, off 96B. Modern accommodations provided in the spirit of international hospitality. Home atmosphere. Sauna and afternoon tea. Full eastern European breakfast. Convenient to Cornell, Ithaca College, Corning Glass Center, Watkins Glen, wineries and antique stores. Open year round.

Host: Wanda Grunberg
Rooms: 3 (1PB; 2SB) $45-65
Full Breakfast
Credit Cards: A, B
Notes: 2, 5, 6, 7, 10, 11

NOTES: Credit cards accepted: A Master Card; B Visa; C American Express; D Discover Card; E Diners Club; F Other; 2 Personal checks accepted; 3 Lunch available; 4 Dinner available; 5 Open all

JAMESVILLE

High Meadows Bed-N-Breakfast

3740 Eager Road, 13078
(315) 492-3517

You are invited to enjoy country hospitality nestled in the tranquil hills just 12 miles south of Syracuse. High Meadows offers two guest rooms, a shared bath, air conditioning, fireplace, plant-filled solarium, and a wraparound deck with magnificent 40-mile view. One queen and one double room are available. Syracuse area offers restaurants, museums, theaters, concerts, and collegiate and professional sporting events. Corporate and weekly rates and seniors' discounts available.

Hosts: Alexander and Nancy Mentz
Rooms: 2 (SB) $35-55
Continental Breakfast
Credit Cards: None
Notes: 2, 5, 7, 10, 11

JEFFERSON

Open Door B&B

Box 227, Enid Rd, 12043
(607) 652-7626

Open Door is located at Jefferson in historic Schoharie County on 200 acres nestled in the rural hills, woodlands and valleys whose boarders and divisions are still marked by stonewalls of yesteryear. An 1800s farm house, on an operating beef farm, creates an atmosphere where the past meets the present with comfortable accommodations,

decorated rooms, and hearty meals available. Hiking, skiing, hunting, fishing, golfing, horseback riding, swimming on premises or nearby. 8 miles from I-88.

Host: Ruth Enderson
Rooms: 3 (SB) 1 room has sink and toilet $40-50
Full Breakfast
Credit Cards: None
Notes: 2, 3, 4, 5, 7, 8, 9, 10, 11

LAKE PLACID

Highland House Inn

3 Highland Place, 12946
(518) 523-2377

The Highland House Inn is centrally located in a lovely residential setting just above Main Street in the village of Lake Placid. Seven tastefully decorated rooms are available, along with a darling, fully efficient country cottage. A full breakfast is served, with blueberry pancakes a renowned specialty served in our year round garden dining room. New additions include outdoor hot tub spa and televisions in all rooms.

Hosts: Teddy and Cathy Blazer
Rooms: 7 plus cottage (PB) $47-85
Full Breakfast
Credit Cards: A, B
Notes: 2, 5, 7, 8, 9, 10, 11, 12

LEWISTON

The Cameo Inn

4710 Lower River Rd. (Rte 18F), 14092
(716) 745-3034

Just five miles north of Niagara Falls,

this stately Victorian commands a majestic view of the Lower Niagara River and Canadian shoreline. Lovingly furnished with period antiques and family heirlooms, the Cameo will charm you with its quiet elegance. Three guestrooms with private or shared bath are available as well as three-room suite overlooking the river. A full breakfast buffet is served daily.

Hosts: Greg and Carolyn Fisher
Rooms: 4 (2PB; 2SB) $65-99
Full Breakfast
Credit Cards: None
Notes: None

LIMA

The Fonda House Bed and Breakfast

1612 Rochester Street, 14485
(716) 582-1040

National Register listed Italiante Village home circa 1853 situated on 2 acre wooded lot. All rooms tastefully decorated with antiques. Be pampered in the Victorian style. Within walking distance to village services and Elim Bible Institute.

Host: Millie Fonda
Rooms: 3 (1PB; 2SB) $45-65
Full Breakfast
Credit Cards: A, B, D, E
Notes: 2, 5, 6, 7, 8, 10, 11, 12

NEWPORT

What Cheer Hall

N. Main Street, P.O. Box 417, 13416
(315) 845-8312

What Cheer Hall was built in 1812 for Benjamin Bowen, pioneer, miller, distiller of the Kuyahoora Valley. The stone home is of Georgian Federal foursquare architecture, comfortably furnished with antiques, some of which may be purchased. Area attractions include premier golf course, fishing in renowned West Canada Creek, antique shopping, skiing, hiking, biking, restaurants, and theater.

Hosts: Phyllis and James Fisher
Rooms: 2 (PB) $50-55
Full Breakfast
Credit Cards: A, B
Notes: 2, 5, 10, 11

NEW YORK

Off Park B&B

C. McPherson, 61 Irving Place #4D, 10003
(212) 228-4645

A home of your own in midtown Manhattan! Several private studio and one bedroom B&B apartments in eastside, lower, and midtown Manhattan. From the simple to the sublime are available for stays of 3-30 nights. All apartments offer stocked kitchens, answering machines, cable TV and all the comforts of home. Most apartments are on E 35th Street off Park Avenue in the Murray Hill neighborhood.

Host: C. McPherson
Rooms: 8 apartments (PB) $75-130
Continental Breakfast
Credit Cards: None
Notes: 5, 7

NOTES: Credit cards accepted: A Master Card; B Visa; C American Express; D Discover Card; E Diners Club; F Other; 2 Personal checks accepted; 3 Lunch available; 4 Dinner available; 5 Open all

ONTARIO

The Tummonds House
5392 Walworth/Ontario Rd., 14519
(315) 524-5381

1897 Victorian home in a quiet, country setting. Guests enjoy private entrance, dining room, living room with TV and piano. Home is completely restored to original elegance, chestnut wood trim. Modern bath conveniences and full sprinkler fixtures for fire safety. Located 20 miles east of Rochester, N.Y.

Hosts: James and Judith Steensma
Rooms: 4 (2PB; 2SB) $40-50
Full Breakfast
Credit Cards: None
Notes: 2, 5, 10, 11

The Tummonds House

PALENVILLE

The Kenmore Country B&B
HCR1, Box 102 (Malden Ave), 12463
(518) 678-3494

A charming 1890s boarding house nestled at the foot of Hunter Mountain. Full country breakfast. Near major ski areas and many summer attractions. Four bedroom efficiency cottage also available, which is perfect for families.

Stay with us and "rediscover" Greene County.

Hosts: John and Lauren Hanzl
Rooms: 3 (1PB; 2SB) $45-55
Full Breakfast
Credit Cards: A, B, D, E
Notes: 5, 7, 9, 10, 11

QUEENSBURY

Crislip's Bed and Breakfast
Rural Delivery 1, Ridge Road, Box 57, 12804
(518) 793-6869

Located in the Adirondack area just minutes from Saratoga Springs and Lake George, this landmark Federal home provides spacious accommodations complete with period antiques, four-poster beds, and down comforters. The country breakfast menu features buttermilk pancakes, scrambled eggs, and sausages. Your hosts invite you to relax on the porches and enjoy the mountain view of Vermont.

Hosts: Ned and Joyce Crislip
Rooms: 3 (PB) $55-75
Full Breakfast
Credit Cards: A, B, C
Notes: 2, 5, 7

RICHFIELD SPRINGS

Country Spread Bed and Breakfast
23 Prospect Street, Route 28, P. O. Box 1863, 13439
(315) 858-1870

From our guest book. . . . "A refreshing

night and fun conversation." Enjoy genuine hospitality in our 1893 country-decorated home. Located in the heart of central New York, we are close to the National Baseball Hall of Fame in Cooperstown, opera, antiquing, and four-season recreation. Delicious breakfasts (your choice) await. Member of local and national associations. Families welcome. Rated and approved by the American Bed and Breakfast Association.

Hosts: Karen and Bruce Watson
Rooms: 2 (PB) $45-65
Full Breakfast
Credit Cards: A, B
Notes: 2, 5, 7, 8, 9, 10, 11, 12

ROCHESTER

Dartmouth House Bed and Breakfast

215 Dartmouth St., 14607
(716) 271-7872; (716) 473-0778

Enjoy 1905 Edwardian charm, warm hospitality, antiques, cozy window seats, grand piano, fireplace and private baths. Stroll through this quiet architecturally fascinating neighborhood to visit George Eastman Mansion and Museum of Photography. Walk to Rochester's largest collection of antique shops, bookstores and trendy restaurants. Breakfast? Full, gourmet and served by candlelight. Dress code? "Be comfy!" Children over 12 welcome. No pets. Smoking outside please. Cable TV, in-room phones. Beverages.

Hosts: Ellie and Bill Klein
Rooms: 4 (2PB; 2SB) $65-80

Full Breakfast
Credit Cards: C
Notes: 2, 5, 8, 9, 10

SARATOGA SPRINGS

Six Sisters Bed and Breakfast

149 Union Ave., 12866
(518) 583-1173

A uniquely styled 1880s Victorian beckons you with its relaxing veranda. Conveniently situated within walking distance of museums, city park, downtown specialty shops, antiques and restaurants. Spacious rooms, each with private bath and luxurious bed, prepare you for a full home-cooked breakfast. Mineral bath and massage package available November-March.

Hosts: Kate Benton and Steve Ramirez
Rooms: 4 (PB) $65-100 (except racing and special weekends)
Full Breakfast
Credit Cards: None
Notes: 2, 5, 8, 9, 10, 11

SENECA FALLS

Locustwood Inn

3563 Route 89, 13148
(315) 549-7132

Locustwood Inn is a charming, old country inn built in 1820. Located in the heart of the Finger Lakes, the inn is one of the oldest in Seneca County. Constructed of early brick, it still has the huge beams, wide-plank floors, and five fireplaces that were familiar to an era long past. Our guests are welcome to stroll the grounds, view the herbs and flowers, visit with our animal friends, or while away the hours in our hammock for two under the pines.

Hosts: Bob and Nancy Hill
Rooms: 3 (S2B) $60-80
Full Breakfast
Notes: 2

SOUTHOLD

Goose Creek Guesthouse

1475 Waterview Drive, 11971
(516) 765-3356

Goose Creek Guesthouse is a Civil War-era farmhouse secluded on a creek by the woods. We are in a resort area with many beaches, golf, charter boat fishing, antique shops, and museums. Near ferries to Connecticut or Montauk and the south shore via Shelter Island.

Host: Mary Mooney-Getoff
Rooms: 4 (SB) $50-75
Full Breakfast
Notes: 2 (for deposit), 7, 8, 9, 10, 12

STONE RIDGE

Hasbrouck House B&B

P.O. Box 76, 12484
(914) 687-0151

This is a 25 room stone house built in 1757 and 1835. 35 acre estate-large outdoor swimming pool. Close to hiking and biking areas. Large liviong room for lounging. Period antiques in rooms.

Hosts: Staff of the Hasbrouck House
Rooms: 8 (SB) $85-100

Full Breakfast
Credit Cards: A, B, D
Notes: 2, 5, 8, 9, 10, 11

SYRACUSE--SEE ALSO JAMESVILLE

Elaine's Bed and Breakfast Reservation Service

4987 Kingston Rd., 13060
(315) 689-2082 (after 10 A.M.)

This is a reservation service in Central New York handling Finger Lakes, the metro Syracuse area, including: Apulia, Auburn, Baldwinsville, Cazenovia, Clay, Cleveland and Constantia (on Oneida Lake), Conquest, DeWitt, Durhamville, Elbridge, Edmeston (near Cooperstown), Fayetteville, Geneva, Glen Haven, Homer, Jamesville, Lafayette, Liverpool, Manlius, Owasco Lake, Phoenix, Pompey, Rome, Saranac Lake, Skaneateles, Syracuse, Tully, Vernon, Vesper, and Watertown. Also in the Berkshires in Western Massachusetts: Alford, Great Barrington, Lenox, New Lebanon, NY, North Egremont, Otis, Sheffield, Stockbridge and South Egremont. Elaine can match you up with just what you want.

UTICA

The Iris Stonehouse Bed and Breakfast

16 Derbyshire Place, 13501-4706
(315) 732-6720; (800) 446-1456

Enjoy city charm close to everything, three miles south of I-90, Exit 31. This

year; 6 Pets welcome; 7 Children welcome; 8 Tennis nearby; 9 Swimming nearby; 10 Golf nearby; 11 Skiing nearby; 12 May be booked through travel agent

stone Tudor house has leaded-glass windows that add charm to the eclectic decor of the three guest rooms. A guest sitting room offers a comfortable area for relaxing, reading, watching TV, or socializing in a smoke-free atmosphere. Air conditioned.

Hosts: Shirley and Roy Kilgore
Rooms: 3 (1PB; 2SB) $35-60
Full Breakfast
Credit Cards: A, B, C
Notes: 2, 5, 7 (over seven), 10, 11, 12

WARRENSBURG

White House Lodge
53 Main Street, 12885
(518) 623-3640

An 1847 Victorian home in the heart of the queen village of the Adirondacks, an antiquer's paradise. The home is furnished with many Victorian antiques which send you back in time. Five minutes to Lake George, Fort William Henry, Great Escape. Walk to restaurants and shopping. Enjoy Air conditioned TV lounge for guests only. Wicker rockers and chairs on front porch. Window and Casablanca fans.

Hosts: Jim and Ruth Gibson
Rooms: 3 (SB 3 rooms two baths) $55
Continental Breakfast
Credit Cards: A, B
Notes: 5, 7 (over 8 years), 9, 10, 11

WESTHAMPTON BEACH

1880 Seafield House Bed and Breakfast
2 Seafield Lane, P. O. Box 648, 11978
(800) 346-3290

The Seafield House is a hidden, 100-year-old country retreat perfect for a romantic hideaway, a weekend of privacy, or just a change of pace from city life. Only 90 minutes from Manhattan, Seafield House is ideally situated on Westhampton Beach's exclusive Seafield Lane. The estate includes a swimming pool and tennis court and is a short, brisk walk to the ocean beach. The area offers outstanding restaurants, shops, and opportunities for antique hunting. Indoor tennis, Guerney's International Health Spa, and Montauk Point are nearby.

Host: Elsie Collins
Rooms: 3 (PB) $100-200 Suites
Full Breakfast
Credit Cards: A, B, C
Notes: 2, 5, 8, 9, 10, 12

WINDSOR

Country Haven
66 Garrett Rd., 13865
(607) 655-1204

A restored 1800s farmhouse in a quiet country setting on 350 acres. A haven for today's weary traveler and a weekend hideaway where warm hospitality awaits you. Craft shops with 70 artisans. Located 1 mile from Rt. 17 East, Exit 78, 12 miles east of Binghamton and 7 miles from Rt. 81.

Host: Rita Saunders
Rooms: 4 (1PB; 2SB) $45-55
Full Breakfast
Credit Cards: None
Notes: 2, 5, 8, 9, 10

Country Haven

YOUNGSTOWN

The Cameo Manor North
3881 Lower River Road, 14174
(716) 745-3034

Located just seven miles north of Niagara Falls, our English manor house is the perfect spot for that quiet getaway you have been dreaming about. Situated on three secluded acres, the manor offers a great room with fireplaces, solarium, library, and an outdoor terrace for your enjoyment. Our beautifully appointed guest rooms include suites with private sunrooms, cable TV, and phones. A breakfast buffet is served daily.

Hosts: Greg and Carolyn Fisher
Rooms: 9 (5PB; 4SB) $60-125
Full Breakfast
Credit Cards: A, B
Notes: 2, 5, 7, 8, 9, 10, 11, 12

year; 6 Pets welcome; 7 Children welcome; 8 Tennis nearby; 9 Swimming nearby; 10 Golf nearby; 11 Skiing nearby; 12 May be booked through travel agent

North Carolina

Cairn Brae

217 Patton Mountain Road, 28804
(704) 252-9219

A mountain retreat on three secluded acres above Asheville features beautiful views, walking trails, and a large terrace overlooking Beaver Dam Valley. Homemade full breakfast. Quiet, away from traffic, only minutes from downtown.

Hosts: Edward and Millicent Adams
Rooms: 3 (PB) $80-95
Full Breakfast
Credit Cards: A, B
Open April-November
Notes: 2, 3, 7 (over 8), 8, 9, 10

Dry Ridge Inn

26 Brown Street, Weaverville, 28787
(704) 658-3899

Part of this country-style inn was built in 1849 as a parsonage and was used as a hospital during the Civil War. The rest of the house was built in 1889. Large guest rooms have antiques and hand-made quilts. In a small town setting, it is ten minutes north of Asheville and all of its attractions.

Hosts: Paul and Mary Lou Gibson
Rooms: 7 (PB) $50-65
Full Breakfast
Credit Cards: A, B
Notes: 2, 5, 7, 10, 11, 12

Reed House

119 Dodge Street, 28803
(704) 274-1604

This comfortable Queen Anne Victorian with rocking chairs and swings on the porch has a rocking chair and fireplace in every room. Breakfast features homemade muffins, rolls, and jams and is served on the porch. Listed on the National Register of Historic Places; near Biltmore Estate. Open May 1 through November 1.

Host: Marge Turcot
Rooms: 2 (SB) $50, 2BR Family Cottage $95
Suite: 1 (PB) $75
Continental Breakfast
Credit Cards: A, B
Notes: 2, 7, 8, 9, 10, 11

NOTES: Credit cards accepted: A Master Card; B Visa; C American Express; D Discover Card; E Diners Club; F Other; 2 Personal checks accepted; 3 Lunch available; 4 Dinner available; 5 Open all

BAT CAVE

Stonehearth Inn

P.O. Box 242, 28710
(704) 625-4027; (800) 535-6647

Welcome to Stonehearth Inn, nestled
on the banks of the Rocky Broad River
in Hickory Nut Gorge, a short distance
from the "Bat Cave." A gentle reminder of days and nights at Grandma's
House while enjoying Grandma's cooking or napping in the swing by the river.
An easy drive to surrounding areas of
Chimney Rock Park, Biltmore House,
Lake Lure, Downtown Hendersonville,
the Blue Ridge Parkway and various
other attractions. Dining room open to
the public during lunch and dinner. Daily
and weekly rates available.

Hosts: John and Susi Simmons
Rooms: 4 (PB) $45
Continental Breakfast
Credit Cards: A, B
Notes: 2, 3, 4, 5, 7, 8, 9, 10

BELHAVEN

Pungo River Inn

105 River View St., 27810
(919) 943-2117

A comfortable southern inn with a river
view. Located in friendly, quiet
Belhaven. TV lounge for guests. Drinks
are served in courtyard. Bicycles available. Nearby tennis courts, antique
shops and Dutch flower farm. 25 miles
from Swanquarter ferry to North Carolina Outer Banks. A delicious southern
breakfast served.

Host: Fran Johnson
Rooms: 3 (1PB; 2SB) $50
Full Breakfast
Credit Cards: A, B
Notes: 5, 7, 8, 9, 10

BREVARD

The Red House Inn

412 West Probart Street, 28712
(704) 884-9349

The Red House was built in 1851 and
has served as a trading post, a railroad
station, the county's first courthouse,
and the first post office. It has been
lovingly restored and is now open to the
public. Charmingly furnished with
turn-of-the-century antiques. Convenient to the Blue Ridge Parkway,
Brevard Music Center, and Asheville's
Biltmore Estate.

Host: Mary Lynne MacGillycuddy
Rooms: 6 (3PB; 4SB) and one cottage $43-69
Full Breakfast
Credit Cards: A, B, C
Closed January-March
Notes: 2, 7, 8, 9, 10, 12

CHARLOTTE

McElhinney House

10533 Fairway Ridge Road, 28277
(704) 846-0738

A two story traditional home located in
popular southeast Charlotte, 25 minutes from Charlotte-Douglas Airport.
Close to fine restaurants, museums,

Carowinds Park and many golf courses. A lounge area with cable TV, a hot tub, laundry facilities and barbeque are available. Families are welcome. A continental breakfast is served in the lounge or on the deck.

Hosts: Mary and Jim McElhinney
Rooms: 2 (PB) $55-65
Continental Breakfast
Credit Cards: A, B
Notes: 2, 5, 7, 8, 9, 10

The Morehead Inn

1122 East Morehead Street, 28204
(704) 376-3357; (800) 322-3965;
FAX (704) 335-1110

A designated historic property, this inn is central to the downtown area and all other Charlotte-Mecklenburg suburbs. It is close to fine restaurants, shopping, buses, and airport. A southern estate, it is endowed with quiet elegance and spacious public areas. It is an excellent site for corporate and other executive conferences. Full catering service.

Rooms: 12 (PB) $79-115
Expanded Continental Breakfast
Credit Cards: A, B, C, E
Notes: 5, 7, 8, 10, 12

CHIMNEY ROCK

The Gingerbread Inn

P.O. Box 187, 28720
(704) 625-4038

The Gingerbread Inn is located on the Rocky Broad River. The rooms are decorated with country furnishings. It is wonderful to sit on the decks in rocking chairs and enjoy the beautiful views. Tubing is also available on the river.

Hosts: Tom and Janet Sherman
Rooms: 5 (2PB; 2SB)
Continental Breakfast
Credit Cards: None
Notes: 2, 5, 8, 9, 10

CLINTON

The Shield House

216 Sampson Street, 28328
(919) 592-2634; (800) 462-9817(reservation only)

Reminiscent of *Gone with the Wind* and listed on the National Register of Historic Places, the Shield House has many dramatic features, including soaring Corinthian columns, wraparound porches, coffer ceilings with beading, and a large foyer with enclosed columns outlining a grand central-flight staircase. The red carpeted stairs twist up to a landing and then back to the front of the house. A large guest lounge is naturally lighted through glass doors that open only onto a balcony. Private phones, cable TV. Victorian street lights.

Hosts: Anita Green and Juanita G. McLamb
Rooms: 6 plus bungalow (PB) $45.95-74.95
Continental Breakfast
Credit Cards: A, B, D
Notes: 2, 4, 7, 8, 10

NOTES: Credit cards accepted: A Master Card; B Visa; C American Express; D Discover Card; E Diners Club; F Other; 2 Personal checks accepted; 3 Lunch available; 4 Dinner available; 5 Open all

DURHAM

Arrowhead Inn

106 Mason Road, 27712
(919) 477-8430

The 1775 Colonial manor house is filled with antiques, quilts, samplers, and warmth. Located on four rural acres, Arrowhead features fireplaces, original architectural details, air conditioning, and homemade breakfasts. A two-room log cabin is also available. Easy access to restaurants, Duke University, University of North Carolina-Chapel Hill, Raleigh, and historic sites, including Duke Homestead Tobacco Museum, Bennett Place. Near I-85.

Hosts: Jerry, Barbara, and Cathy Ryan
Rooms: 8 (6PB; 2SB) $65-135
Full Breakfast
Credit Cards: A, B, C, E
Notes: 2, 5, 7, 8, 9, 10, 12

FRANKLIN

Lullwater Retreat

950 Old Highlands Road, 28734
(704) 524-6532

The 120-year-old farmhouse and cabins are located on a river and creek in a peaceful mountain cove. Hiking trails, river swimming, tubing, and other outdoor activities are on the premises. It serves as a retreat center for church groups and family reunions. Guests cook their own meals or visit nearby restaurants. Chapel, rocking chairs, wonderful views, indoor and outdoor games. Christian videos, and reading materials are supplied.

Hosts: Robert and Virginia Smith
Rooms: 11 (5PB; 6SB) $32-46
Self-serve Breakfast
Credit Cards: None
Notes: 2, 5, 7, 8, 9, 10, 11

HENDERSONVILLE

Claddagh Inn at Hendersonville

755 North Main Street, 28792
(704) 697-7778; (800) 225-4700 reservations

The Claddagh Inn at Hendersonville is a recently renovated, meticulously clean bed and breakfast that is eclectically furnished with antiques and a variety of collectibles. The inn is located two blocks from the main shopping promenade of beautiful, historic downtown Hendersonville. The friendly, home-like atmosphere is complemented by a safe and secure feeling guests experience while at this lovely inn. The Claddagh Inn is listed on the National Register of Historic Places.

Hosts: Vicki and Dennis Pacilio
Rooms: 15 (PB) $63-89
Full Breakfast
Credit Cards: A, B, C, D
Notes: 2, 5, 7, 8, 9, 10, 12

---

year; 6 Pets welcome; 7 Children welcome; 8 Tennis nearby; 9 Swimming nearby; 10 Golf nearby; 11 Skiing nearby; 12 May be booked through travel agent

Echo Mountain Inn

2849 Laurel Park Hwy, 28739
(704) 693-9626

Built in 1896 on top of Echo Mountain overlooking the city of Hendersonville 1000' below and 180 degree panoramic view of the Appalachian Mountain Range. 25 rooms, 3 efficiencies, 6 one bedroom and 2 two bedroom suites, all with private baths. Many have fireplace. Cable TV and continental breakfast included. Excellent food in our air conditioned dining room, serving lunch from 11:30-2:00 P.M. and dinner from 5:30 to 8:00 P.M. Tuesday thru Sunday evening. Dining room closed Monday. Our friendly staff welcomes you.

Hosts: Cooper and Elizabeth Smith
Rooms: 36 units (PB) $50-100
Continental Breakfast
Credit Cards: A, B
Notes: 2, 3, 4, 7, 9, 10

KILL DEVIL HILL

Ye Olde Cherokee Inn B&B

500 N. Virginia Dare Trail, 27948
(919) 441-6127

Our beach house, located at Nags Head beach on the outer banks of North Carolina, is 600 feet from the ocean. Fine food, history, sports and adventure galore. We welcome you for a restful, active or romantic getaway. Enjoy the cypress walls, white ruffled curtains and wrap-around porch. Oh Yes! Reserve the featherbed!

Host: Phyllis Comh
Rooms: 6 (PB) $55-85
Continental Breakfast
Credit Cards: A, B, C
Notes: 2, 8, 9, 10, 12

LAKE JUNALUSKA

Providence Lodge

207 Atkins Loop, 28745
(704) 456-6486

Providence Lodge is located on the assembly grounds of the United Methodist Church and near the Great Smoky Mountain National Park, Biltmore Estate, and the Cherokee Indian Reservation. The lodge is old, rustic, clean, and comfortable. Meals are especially good—bountiful, delicious food served family style in our large dining room.

Hosts: Ben and Wilma Cato
Rooms: 16 (10PB; 6SB) $45-80
Full Breakfast
Credit Cards: None
Closed September 15-June 1
Notes: 2, 4, 7, 8, 9, 10, 11, 12

MEBANE

The Old Place

1600 Saddle Club Rd., 27302
(919) 563-1733

The perfect place for a honeymoon,

anniversary or just to get away. Some of the old and some of the new with a whirlpool bath, central air and heat, and a fireplace in the bedroom. Begin your day with an authentic southern breakfast. Take a hike on a trail through the woods or just relax on the spacious front porch or screened-in back porch. Minutes away from Duke University, The University of North Carolina, or shopping outlets.

Hosts: Joe and Avis Rice
Rooms: 2 (1PB; 2SB) $60
Full Breakfast
Credit Cards: None
Notes: 2, 5, 10

NAGS HEAD

First Colony Inn

6720 South Virginia Dare Trail, 27959
(919) 441-2343; (800) 368-9390 reservations

Enjoy southern hospitality in our completely renovated historic inn with a boardwalk directly to our private ocean beach. We are the only historic bed and breakfast inn on North Carolina's outer banks. The Wright Brothers Memorial, lighthouses, Fort Raleigh (site of the first English colony in the New World) are nearby, or just rock on our two stories of wraparound verandas.

Hosts: The Lawrences
Rooms: 26 (PB) $50-100 winter; $60-110 spring/fall; $100-200 summer
Continental Breakfast
Credit Cards: A, B, D
Notes: 2 (30 days in advance), 4, 5, 7, 8, 9, 10, 12

NEW BERN

Harmony House Inn

215 Pollock Street, 28560
(919) 636-3810

Enjoy comfortable elegance in an unusually spacious Greek Revival inn built circa 1850 with final additions circa 1900. Guests enjoy a parlor, front porch with rocking chairs and swings, antiques and reproductions, plus a full breakfast in the dining room. Located in the historic district near Tryon Palace, shops, and restaurants. No smoking!

Hosts: A. E. and Diane Hansen
Rooms: 9 (PB) $55-80
Full Breakfast
Credit Cards: A, B, C
Notes: 2, 5, 8, 10, 12

OLD FORT

The Inn at Old Fort

P.O. Box 1116, W. Main St., 28762
(704) 668-9834

Two story frame house built in Gothic Revival Style on 3.75 acres with terraced lawn and gardens. Located near Asheville, Blue Ridge Parkway and Ridge Crest. Built in 1870s, the Inn at Old Fort features rooms furnished in antiques, warm and friendly conversation, front porch rocking and extended continental breakfasts featuring fresh baked bread.

Hosts: Chuck and Debbie Aldridge
Rooms: 4 (PB) $40-50
Expanded Continental Breakfast
Notes: 2, 5, 7, 8, 9, 10, 11, 12

year; 6 Pets welcome; 7 Children welcome; 8 Tennis nearby; 9 Swimming nearby; 10 Golf nearby; 11 Skiing nearby; 12 May be booked through travel agent

ORIENTAL

The Tar Heel Inn

205 Church Street, P. O. Box 176, 28571
(919) 249-1078

The Tar Heel Inn is over 100 years old and has been restored to capture the atmosphere of an English country inn. Guest rooms have four-poster or canopy king and queen beds. Patios and bicycles are for guest use. Five churches are within walking distance. Tennis, fishing, and golf are nearby. This quiet fishing village is known as the sailing capital of the Carolinas. Sailing cruises can be arranged, and there are great restaurants. No Smoking!

Hosts: David and Patti Nelson
Rooms: 8 (PB) $60-80
Full Breakfast
Credit Cards: A, B
Notes: 2, 7 (by arrangement), 8, 9, 10, 12

SALISBURY

The 1868 Stewart-Marsh House

220 South Ellis Street, 28144
(704) 633-6841

This Federal-style 1868 home is on a quiet, tree-lined street in the historic district. Spacious guest rooms have antiques, heart-of-pine floors, and air conditioning. Enjoy the cozy library and screened porch with wicker furniture. Homemade breads and muffins and a breakfast entree are served in the sunny dining room. Historic sites, churches, shopping, and restaurants are all within walking distance. One and one-half miles off I-85, Exit 76B.

Hosts: Gerry and Chuck Webster
Rooms: 2 (PB) $50-55
Expanded Continental Breakfast
Notes: 2, 5, 7, 8, 10

Rowan Oak House

208 S. Fulton, 28144
(704) 633-2086; (800) 786-0437 (reservation only)

An elegant high Victorian with stained and leaded glass, seven fireplaces, porches and gardens. Each of four bedrooms is lavishly furnished with antiques, sitting area, desk, duvet with down comforters, reading lights, fruit and flowers. Two have private baths (one with double jacuzzi tub). Air conditioning, central heat and phone jacks. Color cable TV, books, magazines, puzzles are in upstairs common area. Designated smoking areas. Gourmet breakfast includes coffee, juice, seasonal fresh fruit, entree and homemade breads served in our gracious dining room on china with silver, crystal and Queen Louise.

Hosts: Ruth Ann and Bill Coffey
Rooms: 4 (2PB; 2SB) $65-95
Full Breakfast
Credit Cards: A, B, D
Notes: 2, 12

Rowan Oak House

NOTES: Credit cards accepted: A Master Card; B Visa; C American Express; D Discover Card; E Diners Club; F Other; 2 Personal checks accepted; 3 Lunch available; 4 Dinner available; 5 Open all

TRYON

Fox Trot Inn

P. O. Box 1561, 28782
(704) 859-9706

This lovingly restored residence, circa 1915, is situated on six wooded acres within the city limits. It is convenient to everything, yet secluded with a quietly elegant atmosphere. Full gourmet breakfast, afternoon refreshments, heated swimming pool, fully furnished guest house with two bedrooms, kitchen, living room, deck with mountain views. Two guest rooms have sitting rooms.

Hosts: Betty Daugherty and Mimi Colby
Rooms: 4 (PB) $60-110
Guest House: $450 weekly
Full Breakfast
Credit Cards: None
Notes: 2, 8, 10

WAYNESVILLE

Palmer House
Bed and Breakfast

108 Pigeon Street, 28786
(704) 456-7521

Built in the 1880s, the Palmer House is the last of Waynesville's once numerous 19th-century hotels. Located less than one block from Main Street, the Palmer House is also near the Blue Ridge Parkway, the Great Smoky Mountains, Cherokee, and Biltmore Estate. Guests are entitled to a ten-percent discount off any purchase at the Palmer House Bookshop on Main Street.

Hosts: Jeff Minick and Kris Gillet
Rooms: 7 (PB) $50
Full Breakfast
Credit Cards: A, B, C, D
Notes: 2, 5, 7

WILSON

Miss Betty's
Bed and Breakfast Inn

600 West Nash Street, 27893-3045
(919) 243-4447; (800) 258-2058 reservations

Selected in 1992 as one of the best places to stay in the South. 3-diamond rated by AAA, the highest rating to date accorded B&B inns. Located on a gracious lot in the downtown historic section, "Miss Betty's," comprised of two beautifully restored homes; the National Registered Davis-Whitehead-Harriss House (circa 1858) and the adjacent Riley House (circa 1900), is recaptured elegance and style of days gone by. Quiet Victorian charm abounds in an atmosphere of all modern day conveniences. Guests can browse for antiques in the Inn or visit any of the numerous antique shops that have given Wilson the title "Antique capital of North Carolina." Wilson, with its four beautiful golf courses and numerous tennis courts, is ideally located midway between Maine and Florida along the main North-South route I-95.

Host: Elizabeth A. Spitz
Rooms: 8 (PB) $60-80
Full Breakfast
Credit Cards: A, B, C, D, E
Notes: 2, 5, 8, 9, 10

---

year; 6 Pets welcome; 7 Children welcome; 8 Tennis nearby; 9 Swimming nearby; 10 Golf nearby; 11 Skiing nearby; 12 May be booked through travel agent

North Dakota

LIDGERWOOD

Kaler's Bed and Breakfast

9650 Highway 18, 58053
(701) 538-4848

Enjoy country living on this 640-acre small grain farm situated in pheasant heartland. This older home has four beautiful bedrooms upstairs. A delicious full breakfast is served, and children are most welcome.

Host: Dorothy Kaler
Rooms: 4 (SB) $30
Full Breakfast
Credit Cards: None
Notes: 2, 5, 7, 8, 9, 10

MCCLUSKY

Midstate Bed and Breakfast

Route 3, Box 28, 58463
(701) 363-2520

In the center of North Dakota, this country home built in 1980 operates under the banner "The beauty of the house is order, the blessing of the house is contentment, and the glory of the house is hospitality." The guest entrance opens the way to a complete and private lower level with your bedroom, bath, large TV lounge with fireplace, and kitchenette. Three upstairs bedrooms have a bath. Breakfast in your choice of locations: your room, formal dining room, the plant-filled atrium or on the patio. Midstate is an adult only household located on a third generation working farm raising small grains and livestock. Very easy to locate: mile marker 232 on ND200. In an area of great hunting of deer, water fowl, and upland game. Our guests are allowed hunting privileges on over 4000 acres. Special rates and provisions for hunting parties. Air conditioned.

Hosts: Allen and Grace Faul
Rooms: 4 (1PB; 3SB) $25-30
Full Breakfast
Credit Cards: None
Notes: 2, 3, 4, 5, 6, 7, 8, 9

Midstate Bed and Breakfast

NOTES: Credit cards accepted: A Master Card; B Visa; C American Express; D Discover Card; E Diners Club; F Other; 2 Personal checks accepted; 3 Lunch available; 4 Dinner available; 5 Open all

Ohio

CIRCLEVILLE

Castle Inn
Bed and Breakfast
610 S. Court St., 43113
(614) 477-3986

A medieval "castle" in the heart of Ohio features towers, battlements, arches, flying buttresses, stained glass and a suit of armor named Sir Reginald. Furnished in Victorian antiques, private baths, bedroom fireplaces; full breakfast is served in museum-quality dining room overlooking two walled Shakespeare garden, featuring plants mentioned in Shakespeare's plays. Guests enjoy playing the antique grand piano and the collection of "castle" books, games and puzzles. Books and magazines available on a wide variety of subjects.

Hosts: Sue and Jim Maxwell
Rooms: 4 (PB) $55-85
Full Breakfast
Credit Cards: A, B
Notes: 2, 7 (over 6), 8, 9, 10, 12

COSHOCTON

1890 Bed and Breakfast
663 N. Whitewoman St., Roscoe Village, 43812
(614) 622-1890

Spend a romantic getaway in a Victorian Bed and Breakfast nestled in the heart of historic Roscoe Village. The home is furnished with antiques and features an exquisite touch of hand sponge painted walls. Restaurants, museums and exclusive shops are within walking distance of the B&B. Just 1 and a half hours east of Columbus and 2 and a half hours south of Cleveland.

Hosts: Curt and Debbi Crouso
Rooms: 4 (PB) $60-70
Expanded Continental Breakfast
Credit Cards: A, B, C, D
Notes: 2, 5, 9, 10

Castle Inn Bed and Breakfast

year; 6 Pets welcome; 7 Children welcome; 8 Tennis nearby; 9 Swimming nearby; 10 Golf nearby; 11 Skiing nearby; 12 May be booked through travel agent

DANVILLE

The White Oak Inn

29683 Walhonding Road, 43014
(614) 599-6107

This turn-of-the-century farmhouse on 14 acres in the rolling hills of north central Ohio features rooms with antiques and quilts or comforters. Three rooms have fireplaces; four have queen beds. With a large fireplace, the common room is comfortable for reading, playing board games, or socializing. The grounds and adjacent conservation land are ideal for hiking, canoeing, and other outdoor activities. Area attractions include the largest Amish population in the world, antiquing, and a restored, historic canal town, Roscoe Village. Facilities are available for meetings, retreats, weddings, and receptions.

Hosts: Ian and Yvonne Martin
Rooms: 10 (PB) $75-135
Full Breakfast
Credit Cards: A, B
Notes: 2, 4, 5, 8, 10, 12

The White Oak Inn

EAST FULTONHAM

Hill View Acres Bed and Breakfast

7320 Old Town Road, 43735
(614) 849-2728

Old World hospitality and comfort await each of our guests. During your visit, wander over the 21 acres, relax on the deck or patio, use the pool or year-round spa, or cuddle up by the fireplace in the cooler months. A hearty, country breakfast with homemade breads, jams, and jellies is served. We are located ten miles southwest of Zanesville.

Hosts: Jim and Dawn Graham
Rooms: 2 (SB) $35-40
Full Breakfast weekends; Continental on weekdays.
Credit Cards: A, B
Notes: 2, 3, 4 (by arrangement), 5, 7, 9, 10

GENEVA-ON-THE-LAKE

Otto Court Bed and Breakfast

5653 Lake Road, 44041
(216) 466-8668

Otto Court Bed and Breakfast is a family-run business situated on two acres of lakefront property. There are eight cottages and a 19-room hotel overlooking Lake Erie. Besides a small game room, there is a horseshoe pit, a volleyball court, picnic tables, and plenty of beach with area for a bonfire. Within walking distance is the Geneva State Park and Marina. The Old Firehouse winery, Geneva-on-the-Lake Amuse-

---

NOTES: Credit cards accepted: A Master Card; B Visa; C American Express; D Discover Card; E Diners Club; F Other; 2 Personal checks accepted; 3 Lunch available; 4 Dinner available; 5 Open all

ment Center, and the Jennie Munger Museum are nearby.

Hosts: Joyce Otto and family
Rooms: 12 (8PB; 4SB) $50
Full Breakfast
Credit Cards: A, B, F
Notes: 2, 4, 5, 7, 9, 10, 12

LAURELVILLE

Hocking House B&B

18597 Laurel Street, 43113
(800) 477-1541

A large turn-of-the-century house tucked into a friendly small village on the edge of Hocking Hills. Guest rooms offer private baths and are furnished in "country Victorian" with antiques and handcrafted pieces, many made locally. Quilts—old, new, and some made by our Amish neighbors— are featured in every room. Two good restaurants are within one block. A new herb garden is being established. Guests are near all Hocking Hills attractions and the studios and shops of many artisans. You can also visit our Amish neighbors for quilts, rugs, baskets and produce. Spectacular caves, waterfalls, scenery nearby.

Hosts: Max & Evelyn England, Jim & Sue Maxwell
Rooms: 4 (PB) $45-65 (seasonal discount)
Full Breakfast
Credit Cards: A, B
Notes: 2, 5, 12

LEXINGTON

The White Fence Inn

8842 Denman Road, 44904
(419) 884-2356; (800) 628-5793

The White Fence Inn is a beautiful country retreat situated among 73 acres. The 100-year-old farmhouse is decorated in a warm, country style. Common rooms include a large dining room with French doors, a parlor with fireplace and piano, a spacious sitting room with fireplace and TV. Breakfast is served indoors or outdoors. Guest rooms are decorated in individual themes--primitive, baskets and bottles, Victorian, Southwest, Amish, and country. One room has a fireplace and cathedral ceiling.

Hosts: Bill and Ellen Hiser
Rooms: 6 (4PB; 2SB) $49-90
Full Breakfast
Credit Cards: None
Notes: 2, 5, 6, 7, 8, 10, 11

MARIETTA

The Buckley House Bed and Breakfast

332 Front Street, 45750
(614) 373-3080

The Buckley House is the most ideally located B&B in the city. It is located across the street from Muskingam Park which is on the banks of the beautiful Muskingam River. We are within walking distance of the city's museums, restaurants and shopping. Built in 1879, this historically registered beautiful old home is of the Victorian period with its two-tier porch showing its Southern influence. Well heated in winter and air conditioned in summer for our guests'

year; 6 Pets welcome; 7 Children welcome; 8 Tennis nearby; 9 Swimming nearby; 10 Golf nearby; 11 Skiing nearby; 12 May be booked through travel agent

comfort.

Hosts: Alf and Dell Nicholas
Rooms: 3 (PB) $50-70
Full Breakfast
Credit Cards: None
Notes: 2, 5, 10

MARION

Olde Towne Manor

245 St. James St., 43302
(614) 382-2402

Elegant stone home nestles on a beautiful acre of land on a quiet street in Marion's historic district. Enjoy a quiet setting in the gazebo or the soothing sauna, or relax reading one of the more than 1000 books available in the library. A pool table is also available for your enjoyment. A leisurely stroll will take you to the home of President Warren G. Harding and the Harding Memorial. Awarded the 1990 Marion's Beautifications Most Attractive Building.

Host: Mary Louisa Rimbach
Rooms: 4 (PB) $55-65
Full Breakfast
Credit Cards: A, B
Notes: 2, 5, 8, 9, 10

MARTINS FERRY

Mulberry Inn Bed and Breakfast

53 North 4th Street, 43935
(614) 633-6058

Victorian frame home built in 1868 by Dr. Ong, the thirteen room home was also used as his office. In 1911 Dr. Blackford bought the house and also used three rooms for his practice. The Probsts purchased the home in 1971. It became a bed and breakfast in 1987. The guest rooms are done in different periods. The Roosevelt Room (1930s) Victorian, Country, Lucinda has twin beds. All others have double beds. Guests have a beautiful parlor to relax and a private dining room. There is a wood burning fireplace for cold winter nights in the parlor. Homemade quilts, up-down lights, pocket doors, antiques, 3 stairways. 5 minutes from Wheeling, WV.

Hosts: Charles and Shirley Probst
Rooms: 4 (2PB; 2SB) $45
Full Breakfast
Credit Cards: D, E
Notes: 2, 5, 8, 9, 10, 11, 12

TIPP CITY

The Willow Tree Inn

1900 West State Route 571, 45371
(513) 667-2957

This restored pre-Civil War (1830) Federal manor home has a pond and combination springhouse and smokehouse. The original 1830 barn is also on the premises. Four working fireplaces, porches on which to swing and relax, and TV and air conditioning in all rooms; all but one room are suites. Easily located off Exit 68W from N75, just minutes north of Dayton.

Hosts: Tom and Peggy Nordquist
Rooms: 4 (1PB; 3SB) $45-65
Full Breakfast

NOTES: Credit cards accepted: A Master Card; B Visa; C American Express; D Discover Card; E Diners Club; F Other; 2 Personal checks accepted; 3 Lunch available; 4 Dinner available; 5 Open all

Credit Cards: A, B
Notes: 1, 7 (over 8) , 8, 9, 10

URBANA

At Home in Urbana

301 Scioto St., 43078
(800) 800-0970

Restored 1842 home in historic district. Furnished in Victorian period pieces and family antiques. Two blocks away from downtown shops and restaurants. At the center of the Simon Kenton Historic Corridor. Non-smoking guests only.

Hosts: Grant and Shirley Ingersoll
Rooms: 3 (1PB; 2SB) $50-60
Full Breakfast
Credit Cards: A, B, C
Notes: 2, 4, 5, 10

At Home in Urbana

WALNUT CREEK

Troyer's Country View B&B

P.O. Box 91, 4859 Olde Pump St., 44687
(216) 893-3284

The house is over 100 years old, newly remodeled into self-contained suites, each with private bath, country decor, cable TV, air conditioning. Breakfast stocked in your private kitchenette (with oak table and chairs in kitchen area). Couch or bentwood rockers in sitting area. Private deck entrances from beautiful viewing deck, fenced animals to watch in the summer. Honeymoon and anniversary suite has heart shaped jacuzzi, microwave and other extras, plus all the amenities mentioned above. Comfortable Amish crafted beds.

Hosts: Owen and Sue Troyer
Rooms: 4 (PB) $65 (slightly less in winter)
Full Self Serve Breakfast
Credit Cards: A, B
Notes: 2 (from Ohio), 5

WAVERLY

Governor's Lodge

171 Gregg Road, 45690
(614) 947-2266

Governor's Lodge is a place like no other. Imagine a beautiful, shimmering lake and an iridescent sunset. A quiet calm in the friendly atmosphere of an eight-room bed and breakfast open all year and situated on a peninsula in Lake White. Every room has a magnificent view. An affiliate of Bristol Village Retirement Community, we offer a meeting room and group rates for gatherings using the whole lodge.

Hosts: David and Jeannie James
Rooms: 8 (PB) $37-62
Expanded Continental Breakfast
Credit Cards: A, B
Notes: 2, 7, 9, 11

year; 6 Pets welcome; 7 Children welcome; 8 Tennis nearby; 9 Swimming nearby; 10 Golf nearby; 11 Skiing nearby; 12 May be booked through travel agent

WEST MILTON

Locust Lane Farm Bed and Breakfast

5590 Kessler Cowlesville Road, 45383
(513) 698-4743

Delightful, old Cape Cod home in a rural setting 20 minutes north of Dayton and seven miles southwest of Troy. Browse through local antique shops, enjoy the nature center, golf course, and canoeing. Choose from queen or double guest rooms with private or shared bath. Relax in the library or in front of the fireplace. Full breakfast is served on the screened porch in the summer. I-75, Exit 69.

Hosts: Don and Ruth Shoup
Rooms: 3 (1PB; 2SB) $40-50
Full Breakfast
Credit Cards: None
Notes: 2, 5, 7, 10

NOTES: Credit cards accepted: A Master Card; B Visa; C American Express; D Discover Card; E Diners Club; F Other; 2 Personal checks accepted; 3 Lunch available; 4 Dinner available; 5 Open all

Oklahoma

EDMOND

The Arcadian Inn Bed and Breakfast

328 East First, 73034
(405) 348-6347

With angels watching over you, you are ministered peace and relaxation. The Arcadian Inn is a step back in time to the era of Christian love and hospitality, and family values. The historical home of Dr. Ruhl, the inn has five luxurious Victorian guest rooms with tubs and fireplaces and canopy beds and sunrooms. Sumptuous homemade breakfast served in the sunny dining room beneath cherub paintings. Perfect for romantic getaways, business travelers, or old-fashioned family gatherings.

Host: Martha Hall
Rooms: 5 (PB) $45
Full Breakfast
Credit Cards: A, B, C
Notes: 2, 4 (by reservation), 5, 7, 8, 9, 10

The Arcadian Inn Bed and Breakfast

year; 6 Pets welcome; 7 Children welcome; 8 Tennis nearby; 9 Swimming nearby; 10 Golf nearby; 11 Skiing nearby; 12 May be booked through travel agent

Oregon

ASHLAND

Mt. Ashland Inn

550 Mt. Ashland Road, 97520
(503) 482-8707

Enjoy mountain serenity and warm hospitality in this beautifully hand-crafted log inn 16 miles from Ashland. The craftsmanship and attention to detail is evident throughout in the hand carvings, finely-crafted furniture, stained glass, rock fireplace, and comfortable yet elegant decor. The inn's five guest rooms, including three romantic suites, all have spectacular views. Hike, bike, or cross-country ski from the inn's door or downhill ski nearby.

Hosts: Jerry and Elaine Shanafelt
Rooms: 5 (PB) $75-125
Full Breakfast
Credit Cards: A, B
Notes: 2, 5, 10, 11, 12

Pinehurst Inn at Jenny Creek

17250 Hwy. 66, 97520
(503) 488-1002

Nestled in beautiful Southern Oregon Cascades, this 1920s roadhouse has been lovingly restored as a bed and breakfast/dinner house. The rooms are all individually decorated, embracing our guests in warm country elegance. The food is the finest in "American Fresh" cuisine, prepared by our classically trained chef and served in our beautiful dining room. Located on historic Highway 66, the Pinehurst Inn is a lovely half hour drive from Ashland and forty-five minutes west from Klamath Falls. Discover the unforgettable haven and charming reminder of a less hurried time!

Rooms: 6 (PB) $75-95
Full Breakfast
Credit Cards: A, B
Notes: 2, 4, 5, 6, 7, 11

NOTES: Credit cards accepted: A Master Card; B Visa; C American Express; D Discover Card; E Diners Club; F Other; 2 Personal checks accepted; 3 Lunch available; 4 Dinner available; 5 Open all

The Woods House B&B Inn

333 N. Main St., 97520
(503) 488-1598; (800) 435-8260; FAX (503) 482-7912

Peaceful, English-style gardens with roses, herbs, majestic trees and places to pause surround this 1908 Craftsman, just four blocks from theatres, restaurants and shops. Six sunny rooms filled with flowers and laces, great books and fine amenities, watercolors and antiques. Delightful breakfasts served in the garden and homemade cookies to savor anytime. The fireplace in the sitting room warms the weary and encourages conviviality. "Where you feel like a personal friend, not just a paying guest." Private baths, air conditioning, king, queen, and twin beds. Winter rates available.

Hosts: Francoise and Lester Roddy
Rooms: 6 (PB) $65-105
Full Breakfast
Credit Cards: A, B
Notes: 2, 5, 8, 9, 10, 11, 12

ASTORIA

Columbia River Inn Bed and Breakfast

1681 Franklin Ave., 97103
(503) 325-5044

Beautiful Victorian 1870 "Painted Lady," one of Astoria's finest B&Bs with all private baths and queen beds. Three rooms have views of Columbia River. Located on a quiet street.

Warmly decorated with many antiques and of course a homecooked breakfast every morning. You'll discover memories that last forever. You'll enjoy our beautiful gardens with the "Stairway to the Stars." Private off-street parking. "My speciality is hospitality."

Host: Karen N. Nelson
Rooms: 5 (PB) $65-80
Full Breakfast
Credit Cards: A, B
Notes: 2, 5, 7, 10

BROOKINGS

Chetco River Inn

21202 High Prairie Road, 97415
(503) 469-8128; (800) 327-2688

Old World hospitality with "New World comfort" is achieved while using alternative energy sources. The inn is small; guest numbers are limited to give you peaceful tranquility on the 35 wooded acres right along the river. Beds are comfortable, and the food is good. Seventeen miles from a small seacoast town with beautiful beaches and shopping.

Host: Sandra Brugger
Rooms: 4 (3PB; 1SB) $75-85
Full Breakfast
Credit Cards: A, B
Notes: 2, 4, 9

CANNON BEACH

Tern Inn

3663 South Hemlock, P. O. Box 952, 97110
(503) 436-1528

A personal touch in an impersonal world. Home-baked goods and home-

year; 6 Pets welcome; 7 Children welcome; 8 Tennis nearby; 9 Swimming nearby; 10 Golf nearby; 11 Skiing nearby; 12 May be booked through travel agent

made jams and jellies are part of the complete, hot breakfast or brunch cooked from scratch and served in your room anytime between 8:30 and 11:30 A.M. We are located on the north coast of Oregon, in the arts resort of Cannon Beach. We offer light goose-down quilts for year-round comfort, private bath, and color TV. Choose between a fireplace or a sunroom to warm your heart. Both rooms have an ocean view.

Hosts: Gunter-Chris and Enken Friedrichsen
Rooms: 2 (PB) $75-95
Full Breakfast
Credit Cards: None
Closed January
Notes: 1, 8, 10

Sandlake Country Inn

CLOVERDALE

Sandlake Country Inn

8505 Galloway Road, 97112
(503) 965-6745

This 1894 farmhouse on the Oregon historic register is the perfect hideaway for making marriage memories. The honeymoon suite offers a four-room sanctuary with private luxury bath, deck, view of Cape Lookout, parlor, and vintage movies. One mile from the beach; private garden spa; bikes and picnic lunches available; forest setting. Honeymoon cottage. Wheelchair accessible.

Hosts: Margo and Charles Underwood
Rooms: 4 (PB) $65-100
Full Breakfast
Credit Cards: A, B
Notes: 2, 3, 4, 5, 12

CORVALLIS

Shady Maple Farm Bed and Breakfast

27183 Bundy Rd., 97333
(503) 847-5992; (800) 821-4129

Shady Maple Farm offers a peaceful, relaxed atmosphere on 48 park-like acres along the banks of the Willamette River. You'll find a charming 1912 farmhouse, bunkhouse, flower gardens, rolling lawns and a tennis court. A hearty breakfast of orchard fruits, farm-fresh eggs and homemade specialties is served fireside in the library/dining room with a view of grazing cattle and sheep. Guests are offered a variety of indoor and outdoor games, stereo, VCR, piano, guest refrigerator, picnic area and barbeque.

Host: Carol May
Rooms: 3 (1PB; 2SB) $55-75
Full Breakfast
Credit Cards: A, B
Notes: 2, 5, 6, 7, 8, 9, 10, 12

ELMIRA

McGillivray's Log Home Bed and Breakfast

88680 Evers Road, 97437
(503) 935-3564

Fourteen miles west of Eugene, on the

NOTES: Credit cards accepted: A Master Card; B Visa; C American Express; D Discover Card; E Diners Club; F Other; 2 Personal checks accepted; 3 Lunch available; 4 Dinner available; 5 Open all

way to the coast, you will find the best of yesterday and the comforts of today. King beds, air conditioning, and quiet. Old-fashioned breakfasts are usually prepared on an antique wood-burning cookstove. This built-from-scratch new log home is near Fern Ridge.

Host: Evelyn R. McGillivray
Rooms: 2 (PB) $50-70
Full Breakfast
Credit Cards: A, B
Notes: 2, 5

GARIBALDI

Gracy Manor

119 E. Driftwood, P.O. Box 220, 97118
(503) 322-3369

Gracy Manor is a quiet, smoke free, homey, cheery atmosphere facing hillsides and view of the bay. Three rooms are immaculate, beautifully decorated in ruffled curtains, matching spreads and shams, cushiony carpeting throughout. All have comfortable brass queen size beds. Color TV in each room. Guests share bathroom and are served a full breakfast.

Host: Dorothy Gracy
Rooms: 3 (SB) $45-65
Full Breakfast
Credit Cards: None
Notes: 2, 5, 10, 12

GOVERNMENT CAMP

Falcon's Crest Inn

P.O. Box 185, 87287 Government Camp Loop Highway, 97028
(503) 272-3403; (800) 624-7384

Falcon's Crest Inn is a beautiful mountain lodge/chalet-style house, architecturally designed to fit into the quiet natural forest and majestic setting of the Cascades. Conveniently located at the intersection of Highway 66 and The Government Camp Loop Highway, it is within walking distance to Ski Bowl, a year round playground, featuring downhill skiing in the winter and the Alpine Slide in the summer! The Inn has five suites, all with private baths. Each guest room is individually decorated with interesting and unique collectibles and views of mountains and forest are a feature of each. Telephones are available for guest use in each suite.

Hosts: BJ and Melody Johnson
Rooms: 5 (PB) $85-139
Full Breakfast
Credit Cards: A, B, C, D
Notes: 2, 4, 5, 9, 10, 11, 12

GRANTS PASS

Clemens House Bed and Breakfast

612 N.W. Third St., 97526
(503) 476-5564; (800) 344-2820 for reservation

Delightful 1905 Craftsman style home with antique furnishings, nestled in a beautiful flower garden setting and listed on the National Register of Historic Places. It is only five minutes from I-5 and walking distance to old town shops and restaurants. Comfortable queen beds, private baths, air conditioning and no smoking. The two-bedroom family suite has a queen and two twins.

year; 6 Pets welcome; 7 Children welcome; 8 Tennis nearby; 9 Swimming nearby; 10 Golf nearby; 11 Skiing nearby; 12 May be booked through travel agent

Hosts: Gerry and Maureen Clark
Rooms: 3 (PB) $60-80
Full Breakfast
Credit Cards: A, B
Notes: 2, 5, 7, 8, 10, 11, 12

LAGRANDE

Pitcher Inn
Bed and Breakfast

608 N Avenue, 97850
(503) 963-9152

The hosts have redecorated their 1925 home to maintain its original flavor. The homey dining room with oak floor and table welcomes you for a full breakfast. The unique, open staircase will lead you to your room. Each of four guest rooms has a touch of romance featuring a different color theme with accents of roses, bows, and pitchers. The honeymoon suite is a spacious room of lace and roses done in pink and black.

Hosts: Carl and Deanna Pitcher
Rooms: 4 (1PB; 3S2B) $55-95
Full Breakfast
Credit Cards: A, B
Closed January 2-15
Notes: 2, 8, 10, 11

Stange Manor Inn

1612 Walnut, 97850
(503) 963-2400

Stange Manor is an impressive 1922 lumber baron's Georgian Colonial mansion. The spacious 10,000 square foot structure features extraordinary architectural detail, including a basement ballroom and stage. The Manor sits on spacious grounds with a rose garden

and magnificent trees. Guest rooms have queen beds and private baths. One room has balcony overlooking the rose garden—the suite features a sitting room with fireplace. Full breakfast in the formal dining room sparkles with silver, crystal and candles.

Hosts: Marjorie and Pat McClure
Rooms: 4 (PB) $65-85
Full Breakfast
Credit Cards: A, B
Notes: 2, 5, 10, 11, 12

LINCOLN CITY

The Rustic Inn

2313 Northeast Holmes Road, 97367
(503) 994-5111

This log cabin-style home has a comfortable, homey atmosphere in a garden setting within walking distance of the ocean. Rooms are decorated with antiques and have color TV. One room has a Jacuzzi for two, one room is handicapped accessible, and two rooms have a private entrance. We are near antique shops and a large outlet mall. We have a large front porch and rear deck for your relaxation.

Hosts: Evelyn and Lloyd Bloomberg
Rooms: 3 (PB) $40-65 Sunday through Thursday, $55-70 Friday and Saturday
Full Breakfast
Credit Cards: A, B
Notes: 2

NEWBERG

Secluded
Bed and Breakfast

19719 Northeast Williamson Road, 97132
(503) 538-2635

This secluded, beautiful, country home on ten acres is an ideal retreat in a wooded setting for hiking, walking in the country, and observing wildlife. Located near Newberg behind the beautiful Red Hills of Dundee, it is convenient to George Fox College. McMinnville is a 20-minute drive, and the Oregon coast is one hour away. A delectable breakfast varies for your pleasure, tempting you with succulent French farm fruit from the famous Willamette Valley of Oregon. The home has many antiques and collectibles and stained glass in each room.

Hosts: Del and Durell Belanger
Rooms: 2 (1PB; 1SB) $40-50
Full Breakfast
Credit Cards: None
Notes: 2, 5, 7, 8, 9, 10

PORTLAND

John Palmer House
4314 N. Mississippi Ave., 97217
(503) 284-5893

This Victorian inn is run by three generations of the same family and you become one of the family the moment you enter the door. We are told we serve the best breakfast in town. Close to the ocean and the mountains. Make this your home away from home whether on business or vacation.

Rooms: 7 (2PB; 6SB) $40-125
Full Breakfast
Credit Cards: A, B, C, D
Notes: 2, 5, 7, 8, 12 (with restrictions)

STAYTON

Horncroft
42156 Kingston-Lyons Drive, 97383
(503) 769-6287

This private home in a quiet, rural area southeast of Stayton, is 12 miles east of Salem, the center of the Willamette Valley, a rich and scenic agricultural area. Mt. Jefferson Wilderness Area is one hour east; ocean beaches are one and one-half hours west.

Hosts: Dr. and Mrs. K. H. Horn
Rooms: 3 (1PB; 2SB) $35-45
Full Breakfast
Credit Cards: None
Closed Holidays
Notes: 2, 8, 9, 10, 11

YACHATS

Serenity B&B
5985 Yachats River Road, 97498
(503) 547-3813

"Serenity" is centrally located between Newport and Florence near Pacific beauty. Gentle place to relax after countryside, forest and tidepool explorations. Retreat nestled in Yachats Valley of Coast Range. Minutes from Cape Perpetua, Sea Lion Caves, Heceta Lighthouse and covered bridges. Four rooms with private baths. Some rooms with two person jacuzzi.

Hosts: Sam and Baerbel Morgan
Rooms: 4 (PB) $65-145
Full Breakfast
Credit Cards: A, B
Notes: 2, 5, 8, 9, 10

---

year; 6 Pets welcome; 7 Children welcome; 8 Tennis nearby; 9 Swimming nearby; 10 Golf nearby; 11 Skiing nearby; 12 May be booked through travel agent

Pennsylvania

ADAMSTOWN

Adamstown Inn
62 West Main Street, 19501-0938
(215) 484-0800; (800) 594-4808

Experience simple elegance in a Victorian home resplendent with leaded-glass windows and door, magnificent chestnut woodwork, and Oriental rugs. All four guest rooms are decorated with family heirlooms, handmade quilts, lace curtains, fresh flowers, and many distinctive touches. Accommodations range from antique to king beds. Two rooms have Jacuzzis for two. The inn is located in a small town brimming with antique dealers and only minutes from Reading and Lancaster.

Hosts: Tom and Wanda Berman
Rooms: 4 (PB) $65-95
Expanded Continental Breakfast
Credit Cards: A, B
Notes: 2, 5, 8, 9, 10, 12

AIRVILLE

Spring House
Muddy Creek Forks, 17302
(717) 927-6906

Built in 1798 of warm fieldstone, Spring House is a fine example of colonial architecture with original stenciling. Overlooking a river valley, the house has welcomed guests from around the world who seek a historic setting, tranquility, and access to Amish country and Gettysburg. Regional breakfast specialties and Amish cheeses welcome the traveler.

Host: Ray Constance Hearne
Rooms: 5 (3PB; 2SB) $60-85
Full Breakfast
Notes: 2, 5, 7, 8, 9, 10, 12

ATGLEN

Glen Run Valley View Farm
Rural Delivery 1, Box 69, 19310
(215) 593-5656

In Chester County in southeastern Pennsylvania, this 50-acre farm is owned and operated by a Mennonite family. Guests can watch milking at a nearby farm. Wholesome, country-style, home-cooked meals are eaten with the family. Nearby attractions include Gettysburg, Hershey Chocolate Plant,

---

NOTES: Credit cards accepted: A Master Card; B Visa; C American Express; D Discover Card; E Diners Club; F Other; 2 Personal checks accepted; 3 Lunch available; 4 Dinner available; 5 Open all

cloisters, Longwood Gardens, Wheatland, Lancaster County, Amish folk, Dutch Wonderland. Can go along to a Mennonite church if you want. Mrs. Stoltzfus also makes quilts for sale.

Hosts: Harold and Hanna Stoltzfus
Rooms: 3 (1PB; 2SB) $40-55
Full Breakfast
Notes: 2, 4, 5, 6, 7, 10, 12

AVONDALE

Bed and Breakfast at Walnut Hill

214 Chandler's Mill Road, 19311
(215) 444-3703

An 1844 Pennsylvania mill house, located near Kennett Square and convenient to Longwood Gardens, Winterhur and other major area attractions. Located on a crooked little road, across from a horse filled meadow, where guests can watch for deer, Canadian geese and an occasional red fox and blue heron. Warmly decorated with antiques and crafts. Tips on best routes for hiking, biking and touring. Reservations at local restaurants. Full (gourmet) breakfasts.

Hosts: Sandy and Tom Mills
Rooms: 2 (SB) $75
Full Breakfast
Credit Cards: None
Notes: 2, 5, 7, 8, 10

Bed and Breakfast at Walnut Hill

BIRD-IN-HAND

Greystone Manor

P. O. Box 270, 17505
(717) 393-4233

Greystone Manor is a lovely, old French Victorian mansion and carriage house with Victorian furnishings and decorative windows and doors. It sits on two acres of shaded lawn with flowering trees and plants. Surrounded by Amish farms, we are minutes from Lancaster, Lititz, Intercourse, and Strasburg. Near the farmers' market, outlet malls, and local craft shops.

Host: Sally Davis
Rooms: 13 (PB) $55-90
Continental Breakfast
Credit Cards: A, B
Notes: 2, 5, 7, 8, 9, 12

BOYERTOWN

The Enchanted Cottage

Box 337 Rd 4, South Benfield Rd., 19512
(215) 845-8845

Complete privacy awaits you in this romantic and secluded cotswold-like cottage nestled in acres of woods. Large living room with Franklin fireplace and kitchenette. Double bedroom and Laura Ashley bathroom. Gourmet breakfast served in main house. Complimentary beverages and cheese. Fresh flowers, antiques. Near historic sites, cultural activities, Reading outlets, Amish country, churches. You—our only guests— will find our life-style informal but gracious.

year; 6 Pets welcome; 7 Children welcome; 8 Tennis nearby; 9 Swimming nearby; 10 Golf nearby; 11 Skiing nearby; 12 May be booked through travel agent

Hosts: Richard and Peg Groff
Rooms: One cottage (PB) $75-80
Full Breakfast
Credit Cards: None
Notes: 2, 4, 5, 8, 10, 11, 12

CAMBRIDGE SPRINGS

Bethany Guest House

325 South Main Street, 16403
(814) 398-2046; (800) 777-2046

Relax in the luxury of an 1876 Italianate home built in a Victorian resort community by one of the area's pioneering Christian families. This home on the National Register of Historic Places has been restored and is decorated with period furnishings. It has a parlor, drawing room, Greek Revival dining room, and library. The Covenant Room, with a double-wide whirlpool tub, is ideal for special occasions. Visit nearby Lake Erie, wildlife refuges, bicycle trails, and amusement parks. Christian missionaries stay at no charge Sunday through Thursday, and clergy discounts are available.

Hosts: David and Katie White
Rooms: 4 (PB) $35-55
Full Breakfast
Credit Cards: A, B, D
Notes: 2, 5, 7, 8, 9, 10, 11, 12

CANADENSIS

Brookview Manor

Route 447, R.R. #1, Box 365, 18325
(717) 595-2451

Situated on four picturesque acres, the Inn offers the traveler an ideal retreat from workaday world. Enjoy the simple pleasures of a cozy porch glider on a spacious wrap around porch and hiking trails. Each room offers a panoramic view of the forest, mountains and stream, and all have private baths. Breakfast is served in our cheery dining room and includes fruits, juices, fresh muffins and a hearty main entree.

Hosts: Nancie and Lee Cabana
Rooms: 6 (PB) $65-145
Full Breakfast
Credit Cards: A, B, C, D
Notes: 2, 5, 8, 9, 10, 11, 12

Dreamy Acres

Route 447 and Seese Hill Road, 18325-0007
(717) 595-7115

Esther and Bill Pickett started Dreamy Acres as a bed and breakfast inn in 1959, doing bed and breakfast before it was in style. Situated on three acres with a stream and a pond, Dreamy Acres is in the heart of the Pocono Mountains vacationland, close to stores, churches, gift shops, and recreational facilities. Guest rooms have air conditioning, color cable TV, and some have VCRs. Continental breakfast served May 1 through October 31. Open year-round.

Hosts: Esther and Bill Pickett
Rooms: 6 (4PB; 2SB) $36-50
Expanded Continental Breakfast
Credit Cards: None
Notes: 2, 5, 8, 9, 10, 11

The Pine Knob Inn

Rt. 447, P.O. Box 295, 18325
(717) 595-2532

An historic Civil War period inn of distinction nestled in a picturesque setting in the heart of the Pocono Mountains creates a perfect year round resort. The inn offers simple hospitality with a friendly and informal atmosphere with antique furnished guest rooms. Continental cuisine, rack of lamb, roast duckling are featured in the five course gourmet dinner served in the candlelit dining room with classical music. We are on six and a half acres along Brodhead Creek. Ideal for small conferences and wedding receptions.

Hosts: Dick and Charlotte Dornich
Rooms: 22 (18PB; 4SB)
Full Breakfast
Credit Cards: A, B
Notes: 2, 4, 5, 7 (over 8), 8, 9, 10, 11, 12

CARLISLE

Line Limousin Farm House

2070 Ritner Highway, 17013
(717) 243-1281

Relax and unwind in an 1864 brick and stone farmhouse on 100 acres, two miles off I-81, Exit 12. French Limousin cattle are raised here. Enjoy antiques, including a player piano, the use of a golf driving range. Join us for worship at our historic First Presbyterian Church. One suite and two rooms with king/twin extra-long beds. No smoking is permitted.

Hosts: Bob and Joan Line
Rooms: 3 (2PB; 1SB) $45-60
Full Breakfast

Notes: 2, 5, 7, 10

CHAMBERSBURG

Falling Spring Inn

1838 Falling Spring Road, 17201
(717) 267-3654

Enjoy country living only two miles from I-81, Exit 6 and Route 30, on a working farm with animals and Falling Spring, a nationally renowned freshwater trout stream. A large pond, lawns, meadows, ducks, and birds all make a pleasant story. Historic Gettysburg is only 25 miles away. Relax in our air-conditioned rooms with queen beds.

Hosts: Adin and Janet Frey
Rooms: 5 (PB) $49-69
Full Breakfast
Credit Cards: A, B
Notes: 2, 7, 5, 8, 9, 10, 11, 12

CLEARFIELD

Victorian Loft

216 S. Front St., 16830
(814) 765-4805; (814) 765-1712; FAX (814) 765-9596

Elegant 1894 Victorian home on the river in historic district. Lots of gingerbread, original stained glass, magnificnet cherry and oak woodwork. Air conditioned rooms with skylights, private kitchen and dining area, grand piano, billiards and whirlpool bath. Design studio featured in *Threads* Magazine—weaving and spinning demonstrations. Perfect stop for I-80 travelers—just three miles off exit 19 in rural west-central Pennsylvania. Also off-premises completely equipped 3 bedroom cabin on 8 acres adjacent to state forest available for one party only.

Hosts: Tim and Peggy Durant
Rooms: 5 (2PB; 3SB) $45-80
Full Breakfast
Credit Cards: A, B
Notes: 2, 5, 6, 7, 8, 9, 10, 11, 12

CLEARVILLE

Conifer Ridge Farm

Rural Delivery 2, Box 202A, 15535
(814) 784-3342

Conifer Ridge Farm has 126 acres of woodland, pasture, Christmas trees, and crops. There is a one-acre pond with a pier for swimming, fishing, and boating. The home's rustic exterior opens to a spacious contemporary design. You'll feel its country character in the old barn beams and brick walls that collect the sun's warmth for solar heat. Near Bedford Village and Raystown Dam.

Hosts: Dan and Myrtle Haldeman
Rooms: 2 (1PB; 1SB) $40-55
Cabin: $30
Full Breakfast
Credit Cards: None
Notes: 2, 4, 5, 7, 9, 10, 11

Conifer Ridge Farm

CRANESVILLE

Carriage Hill Farm

9023 Miller Rd., 16410
(814) 774-2971

Bed and breakfast at historic Zion's Hill, an 1830 Colonial style home situated on a knoll surrounded by majestic maples. Beautiful farm setting providing security, privacy, nostalgia. Cross country skiing and hiking trails, bird sanctuary, sleigh and carriage rides, children's petting farm. Convenient to Erie area universities, Presque Isle, Pymatuming State Parks. Excellent fishing, swimming and boating area as well as cross country and downhill skiing and snow mobile areas.

Hosts: John and Kathy Byrne
Rooms: 5 (3PB; 2SB) $40-70
Continental Breakfast
Credit Cards: None
Notes: 7, 8, 9, 10, 11, 12

CRESCO

LaAnna Guest House

Rural Route 2, Box 1051, 18326
(717) 676-4225

The 111-year-old Victorian is furnished with Victorian and Empire antiques and has spacious rooms, quiet surroundings, and a trout pond. Walk to waterfalls, mountain views, and wildlife.

Hosts: Julie Wilson and Kay Swingle
Rooms: 3 (SB) $25-30
Continental Breakfast
Credit Cards: None
Notes: 2, 5, 7, 8, 9, 10,11

NOTES: Credit cards accepted: A Master Card; B Visa; C American Express; D Discover Card; E Diners Club; F Other; 2 Personal checks accepted; 3 Lunch available; 4 Dinner available; 5 Open all

EAGLES MERE

Shady Lane
Bed and Breakfast

Allegheny Ave., P.O. Box 314, 17731
(717) 525-3394

Surrounded by tall trees on a mountain
top with a mesmerizing view of the
endless mountains. A five minute walk
to swimming, boating, canoeing and
fishing on the gorgeous mile-long
spring-fed lake (with groomed path
around the perimeter). Minutes' walk
to craft and gift shops in small village.
All in a Victorian "town that time for-
got," a resort town since the late 1800s,
with summer theater and winter cross
country skiing, ice skating and famous
toboggan slide.

Hosts: Pat and Dennis Dougherty
Rooms: 7 (PB) $65
Full Breakfast
Notes: 2, 5, 8, 9, 10, 11, 12

EAST BERLIN

Bechtel Mansion Inn

400 West King Street, 17316
(717) 259-7760

This charming Victorian mansion has
been tastefully restored and furnished
with antiques. Located on the western
frontier of the Pennsylvania Dutch country, amid the East Berlin national historic district, the inn is a perfect location for a honeymoon, relaxing getaway, or visiting historic churches and
sites in Gettysburg, York, or Lancaster.
Gift certificates are available.

Hosts: Ruth Spangler, Charles and Mariam
Bechtel
Rooms: 9 (7PB; 2SB) $72.50-130
Expanded Continental Breakfast
Credit Cards: A, B, C, D
Notes: 2, 7, 8, 9, 10

ELIZABETHTOWN

West Ridge Guest House

1285 West Ridge Road, 17022
(717) 367-7783

Tucked midway between Harrisburg
and Lancaster, this European manor
can be found four miles off Route 283 at
Rheems-Elizabethtown Exit. Eight
guest rooms are each decorated to reflect a different historical style. All
nine rooms have private baths. The
exercise room, with hot tub, and large
social room are in an adjacent guest
house. Twenty to 40 minutes to local
attractions, including Hershey Park,
Lancaster County Amish community,
outlet shopping malls, masonic homes,
Harrisburg state capital.

Host: Alice P. Heisey
Rooms: 9 (PB) $50-80
Full Breakfast
Credit Cards: A, B
Notes: 2, 7, 8, 10, 12

EMLENTON

Whippletree Inn
and Farm

Rural Delivery 3, Box 285, 16373
(412) 867-9543

The inn is a restored, turn-of-the-century
home on a cattle farm. The house, barns,
and 100 acres of pasture sit on a hill
above the Allegheny River. A pleasant

---

year; 6 Pets welcome; 7 Children welcome; 8 Tennis nearby; 9 Swimming nearby; 10 Golf nearby; 11
Skiing nearby; 12 May be booked through travel agent

trail leads down to the river. Guests are welcome to use the one-half-mile race track for horses and carriages. Hiking, biking, cross-country skiing, canoeing, hunting, and fishing are nearby. Emlenton offers antique and craft shopping in the restored Old Mill.

Hosts: Warren and Joey Simmons
Rooms: 4 (2PB; 2SB) $47.20-53
Full Breakfast
Credit Cards: None
Notes: 2, 5, 7, 9, 10

EPHRATA

Clearview Farm Bed and Breakfast

355 Clearview Road, 17522
(717) 733-6333

This restored 1814 limestone farmhouse is surrounded by 200 acres of peaceful farmland that overlook a pond graced by a pair of swans. Although in the country, we are very easy to find and are just minutes from several major highways. Located in the heart of Pennsylvania Dutch Lancaster County, excellent restaurants, antique malls, and outlet shopping are nearby. Featured in *Country Decorating Ideas*; a touch of elegance in a country setting. Three diamond AAA rating.

Host: Mildred Wissler
Rooms: 5 (3PB; 2SB) $59-79
Full Breakfast
Credit Cards: A, B
Notes: 2, 5, 9, 10

Clearview Farm Bed and Breakfast

The Guesthouse at Doneckers

318-324 North State and 301 West Main, 17522
(717) 733-9502

Indulge in country elegance in a turn-of-the-century guest house with suites, fireplaces, and Jacuzzis. Rooms are appointed with fine antiques and hand stenciling. There is exceptional shopping at our 18-department specialty store and fine dining at our renowned French restaurant. Artists and craftpersons are at work in 40 studios at the Artworks and a farmer's market that offers the freshest produce, meats, gourmet items and Lancaster specialties, all within walking distance of the Doneckers community. Nearby are major antique and collectibles markets. Call or write for prices.

Host: Jan Grobengieser
Rooms: 36 (34PB; 2SB)
Continental Breakfast
Credit Cards: A, B, C, D, E
Notes: 2, 3, 4, 5, 7, 8, 9, 10

FRANKLIN

Quo Vadis Bed and Breakfast "Whither Goest Thou?"

1501 Liberty St., 16323
(814) 432-4208

A stately looking home, accented with terracotta tile, Quo Vadis is an eclectic Queen Anne house built in 1867, in an historic district. The high ceilinged

---

NOTES: Credit cards accepted: A Master Card; B Visa; C American Express; D Discover Card; E Diners Club; F Other; 2 Personal checks accepted; 3 Lunch available; 4 Dinner available; 5 Open all

spacious rooms, parquet floors, detailed woodworking, mouldings and friezes are from a time of caring craftsmanship and Victorian elegance. The furniture is mahogany, rosewood, oak, walnut and wicker and has been acquired by the same family for four generations. The quilts, embroidery and lacework are the handiwork of two beloved ladies.

Hosts: Kristal and Stanton Bowmer-Vath
Rooms: 6 (PB) $50-70
Continental Breakfast
Credit Cards: A, B, C
Notes: 2, 5, 7 (12 and over), 8, 9, 10, 11, 12

GAP

Ben Mar Tourist Farm B&B

5721 Old Phila Pike, 17527
(717) 768-3309

Come stay with us on our working dairy farm two-guest home. We are located in the heart of famous "Amish Country." Experience quiet country life while staying in the large, pleasantly decorated rooms of our 200-year-old farmhouse. Our efficiency apartment is a favorite including a full kitchen, queen and double bed with private bath. Enjoy a fresh continental breakfast brought to your room.

Hosts: Herb and Melanie Benner
Rooms: 2 (PB) $35-40
Continental Breakfast
Notes: 2, 5, 7

GETTYSBURG--SEE ALSO HANOVER

The Brafferton Inn

44 York Street, 17325
(717) 337-3423

Stay in the first house built in Gettysburg's historic district. The inn offers 18th-century antiques and hospitality. One of Pennsylvania's finest restorations, it includes a wonderful mural of Gettysburg's historic buildings and is within walking distance of all the town's historic sites, the college, and entertainment.

Hosts: Mimi and Jim Agard
Rooms: 10 (6PB; 4SB) $65-95
Full Breakfast
Credit Cards: A, B
Notes: 2, 7 (over 7), 8, 9, 10, 11

The Doubleday Inn

104 Doubleday Avenue, 17325
(717) 334-9119

The only B&B directly on the Gettysburg Battlefield, the Inn is beautifully restored, combining a special ambience featuring Civil War furnishings with modern amenities including central air conditioning. Enjoy afternoon tea with hors d'oevres and a candlelight country breakfast. On selected evenings, participate in "Civil War Nights" where a historian brings the battle to life with displays of authentic memorabilia. 50% discount off the second night Sundays through Thursdays completes a gracious combination of History and Hospitality.

Hosts: Olga Krossick (Joan and Sal Chandon)
Rooms: 9 (5PB; 4SB) $75-100
Full Breakfast
Credit Cards: A, B
Notes: 2, 5, 8, 10, 11, 12

Keystone Inn

231 Hanover Street, 17325
(717) 337-3888

The Keystone Inn is a large, brick Victorian home built in 1913. The high-ceilinged rooms are decorated with lace and flowers, and a handsome chestnut staircase rises to the third floor. The guest rooms are bright, cheerful, and air conditioned. Each has a reading nook and writing desk. Choose your own breakfast from our full breakfast menu. One suite available.

Hosts: Wilmer and Doris Martin
Rooms: 4 plus suite (3PB; 2SB) $59-100
Full Breakfast
Credit Cards: A, B
Notes: 2, 5, 7, 8, 9, 10, 11

HANOVER

Beechmont Inn

315 Broadway, 17331
(717) 632- 3012; (800) 553-7009

Near Gettysburg, this elegant 1834 Federal inn is furnished with antiques and fireplaces and is air conditioned. Enjoy antiquing, outlet shopping, Codorus State Park's large lake, and nearby Amish countryside. Breakfast is a special event served outdoors, in your room, or in the dining room. Weekend packages available.

Hosts: Terry and Monna Hormel
Rooms: 7 (PB) $70-125
Full Breakfast
Credit Cards: A, B
Notes: 2, 5, 8, 9, 10

HERSHEY

Pinehurst Bed and Breakfast

50 Northeast Dr., 17033
(717) 533-2603

Spacious brick home surrounded by lawns and countryside. There is a warm welcoming, many-windowed living room or, for outdoor relaxing, a large porch with an old-fashioned porch swing. All this within walking distance of all Hershey attractions: Hershey Museum, Rose Gardens, Hershey Park and Chocolate World. Less than one hour's drive to Gettysburg and Lancaster County. Each room welcomes you with a queensize bed and a Hershey Kiss on each pillow.

Host: Phyllis Long
Rooms: 14 (2PB; 12SB) $45-59
Full Breakfast
Credit Cards: A, B
Notes: 2, 5, 7, 8, 9, 10, 12

HESSTON

Aunt Susie's Country Vacations

Rural Delivery 1, Box 225, 16647
(814) 658-3638

Experience country living in a warm, friendly atmosphere with antiques and oil paintings. Nearby attractions include

---

NOTES: Credit cards accepted: A Master Card; B Visa; C American Express; D Discover Card; E Diners Club; F Other; 2 Personal checks accepted; 3 Lunch available; 4 Dinner available; 5 Open all

28-mile-long Raystown Lake, historic houses, and a restored general store.

Hosts: John and Susan
Rooms: 8 (2PB; 6SB) $45-50
Expanded Continental Breakfast
Credit Cards: None
Notes: 2, 5, 7, 8, 9, 10, 11, 12

INTERCOURSE

Carriage Corner Bed and Breakfast

3705 E. Newport Road, 17534-0371
(717) 768-3059

"A comfortable bed, a hearty breakfast, a charming village and friendly hosts" has been used to describe our B&B. We have 4 comfortable rooms, two with private baths and two with a shared bath. Our home offers a relaxing country atmosphere with handcrafted touches of folk-art and country. Rooms are air conditioned. We are centered in the heart of beautiful farms and a culture which draws many to nearby villages of Intercourse, Bird-in-Hand and Paradise.

Hosts: Gordon and Gwen Schuit
Rooms: 4 (2PB; 2SB) $55-65
Full Breakfast
Credit Cards: A, B
Notes: 2, 5, 7

JIM THORPE

The Inn at Jim Thorpe

24 Broadway, 18229
(717) 325-2599

The Inn rests in a unique and picturesque setting in the heart of historic Jim Thorpe. Our elegant, restored guestrooms are complete with private baths, remote controlled color TVs and air conditioning. While in town, take historic walking tours, shop in over 50 quaint shops and galleries, go mountain biking on the northeast's best trails, or raft the turbulent Lehigh River. It's all right outside our door!

Host: David Drury
Rooms: 22 (PB) $65-100
Continental Breakfast
Credit Cards: A, B, C, D, E
Notes: 3, 4, 5, 7, 8, 9, 10, 11, 12

KINZERS

Sycamore Haven Farm

35 South Kinzer Road, 17535
(717) 442-4901

We have approximately 40 milking cows and many young cattle and cats for children to enjoy. Our farmhouse has three guest rooms, all with double beds and one single. We also have cots and a playpen. Located 15 miles east of Lancaster on Route 30.

Hosts: Charles and Janet Groff
Rooms: 3 (SB) $30-40
Continental Breakfast
Credit Cards: None
Notes: 2, 5, 6, 7, 8, 10

LAMPETER

Bed and Breakfast—The Manor

830 Village Rd., Box 416, 17537
(717) 464-9564

This cozy farmhouse is minutes away from Lancaster's historical sites and

---

year; 6 Pets welcome; 7 Children welcome; 8 Tennis nearby; 9 Swimming nearby; 10 Golf nearby; 11 Skiing nearby; 12 May be booked through travel agent

attractions. Guests delight in Mary Lou's homemade breakfasts featuring Eggs Mornay, crepes, stratas, fruit cobblers and homemade breads and jams. A swim in the pool and a nap under a shade tree is the perfect way to cap your day of touring. Dinner, an overnight stay and a buggy ride with an old order Amish family can be arranged. Children welcome. We cater to groups/ meeting room.

Hosts: Mary Lou Paolini and Jackie Curtis
Rooms: 5 (2PB; 3SB) $65-75
Full Breakfast
Credit Cards: A, B
Notes: 2, 3, 4, 5, 7, 8, 9, 10

Bed and Breakfast—The Manor and Reservation Service

830 Village Rd., Box 416, 17537
(717) 464-9564

This reservation service covers Lancaster County/Philadelphia area. An example inn — cozy farmhouse in the heart of Amish country minutes away from Lancaster's attractions. Full gourmet breakfast, deluxe in-ground pool. A dinner, overnight stay and a buggy ride with an old order Amish family can be arranged. In nearby Philadelphia enjoy your stay at a B&B in the historic district as well as the famous Phila art museum area. Children welcome. We cater to groups. Meeting room available.

LANCASTER

Buona Notte Bed and Breakfast

2020 Marietta Avenue, 17603
(717) 295-2597

This turn-of-the-century home has comfortable rooms, wraparound porch, and a large back yard. Hershey Park and Gettysburg are nearby. Pennsylvania Dutch country is only ten minutes away. Franklin and Marshall College is two miles away. Breakfast includes homemade breads, muffins, and jams. French and Italian are spoken here.

Hosts: Joe and Anna Kuhns Predoti
Rooms: 3 (1PB; 2SB) $40-50
Continental Breakfast
Credit Cards: None
Notes: 5, 7, 8

The King's Cottage, A Bed and Breakfast Inn

1049 East King St., 17602
(717) 397-1017

Traditionally styled elegance, modern comfort, and warm hospitality in Amish country. King and queen beds, private baths, gourmet breakfasts and personal service create a gracious friendly atmosphere at this award-winning Spanish-style mansion. Relax by the fire and enjoy afternoon tea in the library while chatting with innkeepers about directions to restaurants and attractions. Special Amish dinners or personal bus tours arranged. Near farmers' markets, Gettysburg and Hershey. On National Register, AAA and Mobil listed EXCELLENT!

NOTES: Credit cards accepted: A Master Card; B Visa; C American Express; D Discover Card; E Diners Club; F Other; 2 Personal checks accepted; 3 Lunch available; 4 Dinner available; 5 Open all

Hosts: Karen and Jim Owens
Rooms: 8 (PB) $75-120
Full Breakfast
Credit Cards: A, B, D
Notes: 2, 4, 5, 6, 8, 9, 10, 12

Lincoln Haus Inn Bed and Breakfast

1687 Lincoln Highway East, 17602
(717) 392-9412

Lincoln Haus Inn is the only inn in Lancaster County with a distinctive hip roof. It is furnished with antiques and rugs on gleaming, hardwood floors, and it has natural oak woodwork. I am a member of the Old Order Amish Church, serving family-style breakfast with a homey atmosphere. Convenient location, close to Amish farmlands, malls, historic Lancaster; five minutes from Route 30 and Pennsylvania Dutch Visitors Bureau.

Host: Mary K. Zook
Rooms: 6 (PB) $45-65
Apartments: 2 (PB)
Full Breakfast
Credit Cards: None
Notes: 2, 5, 7, 8, 9, 10, 12

New Life Homestead Bed and Breakfast

1400 East King Street (Route 462), 17602
(717) 396-8928

In the heart of the Amish area is a stately, brick Victorian close to all attractions, markets, farms, and outlets. Each room is decorated with family heirlooms and antiques. Full breakfast and evening refreshments are served. Tours and meals are arranged with lo-

cal families. Worship with us in our Mennonite church. Private baths and air conditioning.

Hosts: Carol and Bill Giersch
Rooms: (PB) $40-65
Full Breakfast
Credit Cards: None
Notes: 2, 5, 7, 8, 9, 10, 12

O'Flaherty's Dingeldein House

1105 East King St., 17602
(717) 293-1723; 800-779-7765

Enjoy genuine warmth and hospitality in the friendly atmosphere of our home. The Dutch Colonial house is traditionally appointed for your comfort, two fireplaces in the fall and winter, AC when needed to provide a restful, relaxing stay in beautiful Lancaster County. Conveniently located near downtown Lancaster attractions and just a short, scenic ride to the Amish farmland, outlet shopping and antique area. Personalized maps prepared. Our breakfast guarantees you won't go away hungry.

Hosts: Jack and Sue Flatley
Rooms: 4 (2PB; 2SB) $60-70
Full Breakfast
Credit Cards: A, B, D
Notes: 2, 5, 7, 10

Penn's Valley Farm and Inn

6182 Metzler Rd., Manheim, 17545
(717) 898-7386

A private efficiency guest house. Sleeps up to seven people. A full breakfast is served in adjacent farmhouse dining room. 64-acre farm. Air conditioned,

---

year; 6 Pets welcome; 7 Children welcome; 8 Tennis nearby; 9 Swimming nearby; 10 Golf nearby; 11 Skiing nearby; 12 May be booked through travel agent

TV, colonial decor.

Hosts: Melvin and Gladys Metzler
Rooms: 1 guest house (PB) $55-65
Choice of Full or Continental Breakfast
Credit Cards: A, B, C
Notes: 2, 5, 7, 8, 10

Walkabout Inn

837 Village Road, 17537
(717) 464-0707

This 1925 brick Mennonite farmhouse features large wraparound porches, balconies, English gardens, and antique furnishings. The inn takes its name from the Australian word, which means to go out and discover new places. Australian-born host Richard will help you explore the Amish country surrounding the home. An elegant, full breakfast is served by candlelight. The honeymoon and anniversary suites are beautiful.

Hosts: Richard and Margaret Mason
Rooms: 4 (PB) $79-99
Suite: 1 (PB) $159 for five adults
Full Breakfast
Credit Cards: A, B, C
Notes: 2, 3, 4, 5, 7, 8, 9, 10, 12

Witmer's Tavern— Historic 1725 Inn

2014 Old Philadelphia Pike, 17602
(717) 299-5305

This three-story, all stone inn, originally built in 1725 and later added to, rests just off the nation's first turnpike. It is the sole still functioning survivor of some 62 pre-Revolutionary War inns and is listed on the local, state, and national registers of historic places and landmarks. Restored to the original, simple pioneer state, each romantic room has its own working fireplace, antique quilts, and fresh flowers. Pandora's antique and quilt shop is in the east end. Add your names to the guest list that includes John Adams, Marquis de Lafayette, and others. Villages of Bird-in-Hand and Intercourse are just beyond.

Hosts: Brant Hartung and family
Rooms: 7 (2PB; 5SB) $60-100
Continental Breakfast
Credit Cards: None
Notes: 2, 5, 7, 8, 9, 10, 11, 12

LIMA

Hamanassett

P.O. Box 129, 19037
(215) 459-3000

This early 19th-century country manor house is on 36 secluded acres of woodlands, gardens, and trails near Pennsylvania and Delaware's Brandywine Valley. Near Winterthur, Hagley, Nemours Brandywine (Wyeth) museums, and Longwood Gardens. Well-appointed, large rooms prevail: queen, doubles, twins, canopied king beds, TVs, private baths and amenities. Beautiful Federalist living room and extensive library. Full country breakfast, sophisticated cuisine. Near tennis, golf, and excellent dining opportunities. Great for quiet weekend escape. Two-night minimum stay.

Host: Evelene H. Dohan
Rooms: 6 (PB) $85-120
Full Breakfast
Credit Cards: None
Notes: 2, 5, 8, 10, 12

NOTES: Credit cards accepted: A Master Card; B Visa; C American Express; D Discover Card; E Diners Club; F Other; 2 Personal checks accepted; 3 Lunch available; 4 Dinner available; 5 Open all

LITITZ

The Alden House
62 East Main Street, 17543
(717) 627-3363; (800) 584-0753

Fully restored townhouse in the heart of the town's historic district. Al local attractions within walking distance. Relax on one of three spacious porches and watch Amish buggies or experience a whiff of fresh chocolate from the local candy factory. Home of the nation's oldest pretzel factory. Family suites, Amish dining, bicycle storage available, and only 10 minutes north of Lancaster. Enjoy our "OLD FASHIONED HOSPITALITY."

Host: Leanne Schweitzer
Rooms: 7 (5PB; 2SB) $65-95
Expanded Continental Breakfast
Credit Cards: A, B, C
Notes: 2, 5, 7 (over 6), 8, 9, 10

The Alden House

Swiss Woods Bed and Breakfast
500 Blantz Road, 17543
(717) 627-3358; (800) 594-8018; FAX (717)627-3483

A visit to Swiss Woods is reminiscent of a trip to one of Switzerland's quaint, charming guest houses. Located in beautiful Lancaster County, this inn was designed with comfort in mind. Breakfast is a memorable experience of inn specialties. The gardens are a unique variety of flowering perennials and annuals. A massive sandstone fireplace dominates the sunny common room. Rooms feature natural woodwork and queen beds with down comforters, some with Jacuzzis, patios, and balconies. Enjoy our spectacular view and special touches. German spoken.

Hosts: Debrah and Werner Mosimann
Rooms: 7 (PB) $66-110
Full Breakfast
Credit Cards: A, B
Notes: 2, 7, 9, 12

MANHEIM

Herr Farmhouse
2256 Huber Drive, 17545
(717) 653-9852

Historic circa 1750 stone farmhouse nestled on 11.5 acres of scenic farmland. The Inn has been fully restored and retains all original trim, flooring and doors. Of the six working fireplaces, two are located in guest rooms. Take a step into yesteryear amidst the colonial furnishings. Breakfast served in country kitchen with walk-in fireplace. Amish dining, family suite and indoor bicycle storage available. Nine miles west of Lancaster, outside of Mount Joy. Excellent dining nearby.

Host: Berry Herr
Rooms: 4 (2PB; 2SB) $70-95
Expanded Continental Breakfast
Credit Cards: A, B
Notes: 2, 5, 8, 9, 10

year; 6 Pets welcome; 7 Children welcome; 8 Tennis nearby; 9 Swimming nearby; 10 Golf nearby; 11 Skiing nearby; 12 May be booked through travel agent

MILFORD

Cliff Park Inn and Golf Course

RR 4, Box 7200, 18337
(800) 225-6535

Historic country inn on secluded 600-acre estate. Spacious rooms with private bath, telephone and climate control. Victorian style furnishings. Fireplaces. Golf at the door on one of America's oldest golf courses (1913). Hike or cross country ski on seven miles of marked trails. Golf and ski equipment rentals. Golf school. Full service restaurant rated 3-stars by Mobil Guide. MAP or B&B plans available. Specialists in business conferences and country weddings.

Host: Harry W. Buchanan III
Rooms: 18 (PB) $90-145
Full Breakfast
Credit Cards: A, B, C, D, E
Notes: 2, 3, 4, 5, 7, 8, 9, 10, 11, 12

MONTOURSVILLE

The Carriage House at Stonegate

Road 1, Box 11A, 17754
(717) 433-4340

The Carriage House at Stonegate is the original carriage house for one of the oldest farms in the beautiful Loyalsock Valley. It offers 1,400 square feet of space on two levels and is totally self-contained and separate from the main house. It is located within easy access to I-80, I-180, and U.S. 15 and on the edge of extensive forests offering a wide range of outdoor activities in all seasons.

Hosts: Harold and Dena Mesaris
Rooms: 2 (SB) $50
Continental Breakfast
Credit Cards: None
Notes: 2, 5, 6, 7, 8, 9, 10, 11

MOUNT JOY

Cedar Hill Farm

305 Longenecker Road, 17552
(717) 653-4655

This 1817 stone farmhouse overlooks a peaceful stream. Each comfortable, charming guest room is centrally air conditioned. The honeymoon suite offers a private balcony. The host was born on this working farm located near Lancaster and Hershey. Farmers' markets, antique shops, and well-known restaurants abound. Gift certificates are available for anniversary or holiday giving.

Hosts: Russel and Gladys Swarr
Rooms: 5 (PB) $60-65
Expanded Continental Breakfast
Credit Cards: A, B, C, D
Notes: 2, 5, 7, 8, 10

Green Acres Farm Bed and Breakfast

1382 Pinkerton Road, 17552
(717) 653-4028; Fax (717) 653-2840

Our 1830 farmhouse is furnished with antiques and offers a peaceful haven for your getaway. The rooster, chickens, wild turkey, Pigmy goats, lots of kittens, pony, and 1,000 hogs give a real

---

NOTES: Credit cards accepted: A Master Card; B Visa; C American Express; D Discover Card; E Diners Club; F Other; 2 Personal checks accepted; 3 Lunch available; 4 Dinner available; 5 Open all

farm atmosphere on this 160-acre grain farm. Children love the pony car rides, and everyone enjoys the trampoline and swings. We offer tour information in the Amish country.

Hosts: Wayne and Yvonne Miller
Rooms: 7 (5PB; 2SB) $45-55
Full Breakfast
Credit Cards: A, B
Notes: 2, 5, 6, 7, 8, 9, 10, 12

Hillside Farm Bed and Breakfast

607 Eby Chiques Road
(717) 653-6697

Quiet, secluded, two-acre 1863 farm homestead overlooking Chickies Creek. Comfortable, cozy country furnishings and antiques. Private and semi-private baths, children 10 and over welcome, full country all-you-can-eat breakfast, strictly non-smoking, air conditioned. First floor and second floor porches for guests' use. Second floor refrigerator for guests' use. All rooms decorated differently. No TV or phone in guest rooms. Phone for guests' use in foyer. TV, VCR, movies, tapes, baby grand piano for guests' use in living room. Small library on second floor. Large barn to explore. On biking trail.

Hosts: Gary and Deb Lintner/Bob and Wilma Lintner
Rooms: 5 (3PB; 2SB) $53-66.25
Full Breakfast
Credit Cards: None
Notes: 2, 5, 7 (Over 10), 8, 9, 10, 12

MUNCY

The Bodine House

307 South Main Street, 17756
(717) 546-8949

The Bodine House, featured in the December 1991 issue of *Colonial Homes* magazine, is located on tree-lined Main Street in the historic district. Built in 1805, the house has been authentically restored and is listed on the National Register of Historic Places. Most of the furnishings are antiques. The center of Muncy, with its shops, restaurants, library, and churches, is a short walk down the street. No smoking.

Hosts: David and Marie Louise Smith
Rooms: 4 (PB) $50-65
Full Breakfast
Credit Cards: A, B, C
Notes: 2, 5, 7 (over six)

NEWFOUNDLAND

Buena Vista

Rt. 447 (Panther Rd), Box 195, 18445
(717) 676-3800

Come and relax with us in rural northeastern Pennsylvania. High above the valley floor, we overlook the village of Newfoundland. Our buildings began as a Moravian farm in the 1800s and have been converted to a country inn. Our location in the Lake Wallenpaupack Watershed region offers natural beauty and ample opportunities for recreation, shopping and dining. A pool is located on our property. Breakfast is served, other meals may be available. Reservations required.

Hosts: Dave and Denise Keevil
Rooms: 15 (9PB; 6SB) $30-45
Full Breakfast
Credit Cards: A, B
Notes: 2, 5, 7, 9, 10, 11

year; 6 Pets welcome; 7 Children welcome; 8 Tennis nearby; 9 Swimming nearby; 10 Golf nearby; 11 Skiing nearby; 12 May be booked through travel agent

NEWVILLE

Nature's Nook Farm

740 Shed Rd., 17241
(717) 776-5619

Nature's Nook Farm is located in a quiet, peaceful setting along the Blue Mountains. Warm Mennonite hospitality and clean, comfortable lodging await you. Enjoy freshly brewed garden tea in season. Homemade cinnamon rolls, muffins or coffee cake a speciality. Stroll along the flower gardens. Close to Colonel Denning State Park with hiking trails, fishing, and swimming. Two hours to Lancaster, one hour to Harrisburg, one and a half hours to Gettysburg and Hershey. Wheelchair accessible.

Hosts: Don and Lois Leatherman
Rooms: 1 (PB) $40
Continental Breakfast
Credit Cards: None
Notes: 2, 5, 7, 8, 9, 10

ORRTANNA

Hickory Bridge Farm

96 Hickory Bridge Road, 17353
(717) 642-5261

Only eight miles west of historical Gettysburg. Unique country dining and Bed and Breakfast. Cozy cottages with woodstoves and private baths located in secluded wooded settings along a stream. Full farm breakfast served at the farmhouse which was built in the late 1700s. Country dining offered on Fridays, Saturdays and Sundays in a 130-year-old barn decorated with many antiques. Family owned and operated for 15 years.

Hosts: Dr. and Nancy Jean Hammett
Rooms: 7 (6PB; 1SB) $79-89
Full Breakfast
Credit Cards: A, B
Notes: 2, 4 (on weekends), 5, 7, 8, 9, 10, 11

OXFORD

Log House Bed and Breakfast

15225 Limestone Road, 19363
(215) 932-9257

Clean, quiet, country Chester County log home, away from city and traffic noises. Midway between Lancaster (Amish country), Philadelphia, Wilmington. AC rooms, private baths. Family room available. Picnic area, hiking, biking, no smoking, full breakfast, no limit to your stay. Open Year round.

Hosts: E. E. and Arlene E. Hershey
Rooms: 3 (PB) $45
Full Breakfast
Credit Cards: None
Notes: 2, 5, 7, 8, 9, 10, 11

PARADISE

Maple Lane Farm Bed and Breakfast

505 Paradise Lane, 17562
(717) 687-7479

Clean, comfortable, air-conditioned rooms have antiques, quilts, poster and canopy beds. This working dairy farm has a winding stream, woodland, and a 40-mile view. Real Amish country, near museums, craft shops, antique shops, and farmers' markets.

NOTES: Credit cards accepted: A Master Card; B Visa; C American Express; D Discover Card; E Diners Club; F Other; 2 Personal checks accepted; 3 Lunch available; 4 Dinner available; 5 Open all

Hosts: Edwin and Marion Rohrer
Rooms: 4 (2PB; 2SB) $45-55
Expanded Continental Breakfast
Credit Cards: None
Notes: 2, 5, 7, 8, 9, 10, 12

PEACH BOTTOM

Pleasant Grove Farm

368 Pilottown Road, 17563
(717) 548-3100

Located in beautiful, historic Lancaster County, this 160-acre dairy farm has been a family-run operation for 110 years, earning the title of Century Farm by the Pennsylvania Department of Agriculture. As a working farm, it provides guests the opportunity to experience daily life in a rural setting. Built in 1814, 1818, and 1820, the house once served as a country store and post office.

Hosts: Charles and Labertha Tindall
Rooms: 4 (SB) $45-50
Full Breakfast
Notes: 2, 5, 7, 9

PHILADELPHIA

B&B Accommodations in Downtown Philadelphia

728 Manning St., 19106
(215) 923-7349

Unattached, 3-story, renovated townhouse with nine-cornered patio is on a quiet little street in Society Hill. Just two blocks to Independence Hall, you can walk to the historical area, restaurants, movies and theatres. Beautifully furnished in Colonial Style with oriental carpets, Franklin Stove and library. First story dining room and second story living room overlook the patio. Central air. Bedrooms have clock radios, TVs, and ceiling fans. Smoking on the patio. Close to all transportation.

Host: Margaret Poxon
Rooms: 2 (SB) $60-65
Full Breakfast
Notes: 2, 5, 12

Germantown B&B

5925 Wayne Ave., 19144-3334
(215) 848-1375

This 100-year-old farm features an oak bedroom and private, tiled bath. A historic neighborhood and Philadelphia sites are close by. This unitarian household has four children and a dog, very gentle. No smoking except on the big porch. Children welcome. Sitting possible. One night surcharge, one night free with 6 paid. Double bed and single bed. Crib available. Maximum: 3 adults. $15 for 3rd adult, $10 for children 3-17. Babies are free.

Hosts: Molly and Jeff Smith
Rooms: 1 (PB) $40-45
Continental Breakfast
Notes: 2, 5, 7, 12

POINT PLEASANT (NEW HOPE)

Tattersall Inn

Cafferty and River Road, Box 569, 18950
(215) 297-8233

This 18th-century plastered fieldstone home with its broad porches and manicured lawns resembles the unhurried atmosphere of a bygone era. Enjoy the richly wainscoted entry hall and formal dining room with marble fireplace and a collection of vintage phonographs.

year; 6 Pets welcome; 7 Children welcome; 8 Tennis nearby; 9 Swimming nearby; 10 Golf nearby; 11 Skiing nearby; 12 May be booked through travel agent

Step back in time when you enter the colonial common room with beamed ceiling and walk-in fireplace. The spacious, antique-furnished guest rooms are a joy. Air conditioned. Private baths.

Hosts: Gerry and Herb Moss
Rooms: 6 (PB) $75-95
Continental Breakfast
Credit Cards: A, B
Notes: 2, 5, 7, 8, 9, 12

QUARRYVILLE

Runnymede Farm Guest House Bed and Breakfast

1030 Robert Fulton Highway, 17566
(717) 786-3625

Enjoy our comfortable farmhouse in south Lancaster County. The rooms are clean and air conditioned, and the lounge has a TV. Close to tourist attractions, but not in the main stream. Biking, hiking, picnicking. Country breakfast is optional.

Hosts: Herbert and Sara Hess
Rooms: 3 (SB) $35-40
Full Breakfast
Credit Cards: None
Notes: 2, 5, 7, 8, 9, 10

SCOTTDALE

Pine Wood Acres Bed and Breakfast

Rural Route 1, Box 634, 15683-9567
(412) 887-5404

A country home surrounded by four acres of woods, wildflowers, and herb and flower gardens. Ten miles from the Pennsylvania Turnpike and I-70, New Stanton exits; 25 miles from Frank Lloyd Wright's Fallingwater. Full breakfasts and warm hospitality are yours to enjoy at Pine Wood Acres. Hosts are members of the Mennonite Church.

Hosts: Ruth and James Horsch
Rooms: 3 (SB) $45-50
Full Breakfast
Credit Cards: A, B
Notes: 2, 5, 6, 7, 8, 9, 10, 11, 12

SMOKETOWN

Homestead Lodging

184 East Brook Road, 17576
(717) 393-6927

Welcome to Homestead Lodging where quiet, country living and a homey atmosphere await you. After a leisurely morning coffee and danish, enjoy a walk down the lane to the scenic farmland around us. You can tour the countryside or go on a shopping spree in one of our many markets, quilt, antique shops, and craft shops. Restaurants are within walking distance.

Hosts: Robert and Lori Kepiro
Rooms: 4 (PB) $28-49
Continental Breakfast
Credit Cards: A, B
Notes: 2 (deposit only), 5, 7, 8, 9, 10, 11

Old Road Guest Home

2501 Old Phila Pike, 17576
(717) 393-8182

Old Road Guest Home is nestled in the rolling farmlands in the heart of PA Dutch country. Comfortable air conditioned rooms with TV. Ground floor rooms available. Spacious shaded lawn to enjoy picnics. Easy parking. Private and shared baths. Near fine restaurants. Alcoholic beverages and indoor smoking prohibited.

Host: Marian Buckwalter
Rooms: 6 (3PB; 3SB) $25-35
No Breakfast
Notes: 2, 5, 7, 9, 10

SPRUCE CREEK

Cedar Hill Farm of Spruce Creek Valley

HC-01, Box 26, Rte 45 east, 16683
(814) 632-8319

This early 1800s farmhouse is located in Huntington County on an active livestock farm. Individual and family activities are available at Old Bedford Village, Horse Shoe Curve, Lakemont Amusement Park, Raystown Lake and Resort, Lincoln and Indian Caverns and Pennsylvania State University. Fishing and hunting available on private and state game lands during stated seasons; proper licenses required.

Host: Sharon M. Dell
Rooms: 4 (SB) $35-50
Full Breakfast
Credit Cards: A, B
Notes: 2, 5, 7, 11

STAHLSTOWN

Thorn's Cottage Bed and Breakfast

R.D. #1, Box 254, 15687
(412) 593-6429

Located in the natural, cultural and historic Ligonier Valley area of Pennsylvania's scenic Laurel Mountains, PA turnpike eight miles away, fifty miles east of Pittsburgh, the secluded three room cottage offers guests a homey woodland privacy. In addition, the hosts offer one bedroom, shared bath in their cozy arts and crafts bungalow. Porches and herb garden complement the European country inspired ambience. Breakfast includes homebaked muffins and scones to complement country gourmet style dishes.

Hosts: Larry and Beth Thorn
Rooms: 1 cottage (PB), 1 room (SB) $40-55
Full Breakfast
Notes: 2, 5, 7, 9, 10, 11

STRASBURG (LANCASTER COUNTY)

The Decoy Bed and Breakfast

958 Eisenberger Road, 17579
(717) 687-8585

This former Amish home is set in farmland with spectacular views and an informal atmosphere. Craft shops and attractions are nearby, and bicycle tours can be arranged. Two cats in residence.

Hosts: Debby and Hap Joy
Rooms: 4 (PB) $50-60; $40-50 December 1-April 30
Full Breakfast
Notes: 2, 5, 7, 8, 10

---

year; 6 Pets welcome; 7 Children welcome; 8 Tennis nearby; 9 Swimming nearby; 10 Golf nearby; 11 Skiing nearby; 12 May be booked through travel agent

THOMPSON

Jefferson Inn

Route 171, Rural Delivery 2, Box 36, 18465
(717) 727-2625

Built in 1871, the inn offers reasonably priced accommodations and a full-service restaurant. Situated in the rolling hills of northeast Pennsylvania, there are thousands of acres available nearby for fishing, boating, and some of the best deer and turkey hunting around. Other seasonal activities include skiing, snowmobiling, horseback riding, and golf. Good, Gospel-preaching churches are nearby.

Hosts: Douglas and Margie Stark
Rooms: 6 (3PB; 3SB) $25-50
Full Breakfast
Credit Cards: A, B
Notes: 2, 3, 4, 5, 6, 7, 8, 9, 10, 11 (XC), 12

TOWANDA

The Victorian Guest House

118 York Avenue, 18848
(717) 265-6972

Considered one of the grandest homes in Bradford County, this elegant 1897 structure is classic Victorian, with porches, arches, tower rooms, and a host of period architectural splendors. Bedrooms and open areas of the home are furnished with 19th-century antiques. Warm, cozy, Christian atmosphere.

Hosts: Tom and Nancy Taylor
Rooms: 11 (6PB; 5SB) $40-60
Continental Breakfast

Credit Cards: A, B, C, E
Notes: 2, 7, 8, 9, 10, 11 (XC)

VALLEY FORGE--SEE ALSO MALVERN

Valley Forge Mountain Bed and Breakfast

Box 562, 19481
(215) 783-7783; (800) 344-0123;
FAX (215) 783-7783

George Washington headquartered here! Centrally located between Philadelphia, Lancaster County, Reading outlets, and the Brandywine Valley, this French Colonial is on three wooded acres adjacent to Valley Forge Park. Air conditioning, phones, TV/VCR, computer, printer, FAX, fireplaces, and bridle and hiking trail. Near fine shopping, antiquing, restaurants, cross-country skiing, horseback riding, golf. Two guest suites--one double Victorian, one California king.

Hosts: Dick and Carolyn Williams
Suites: 2 (PB) $50-65
Full or Continental Breakfast
Credit Cards: A, B, C, E
Notes: 2, 5, 7, 8, 9, 10, 11, 12

WELLSBORO

Kaltenbach's Bed and Breakfast

Stony Fork Road, Rural Delivery 6, Box 106A, 16901
(717) 724-4954; (800) 722-4954

This sprawling, country home with room for 32 guests offers visitors comfortable lodging, home-style breakfasts, and

---

NOTES: Credit cards accepted: A Master Card; B Visa; C American Express; D Discover Card; E Diners Club; F Other; 2 Personal checks accepted; 3 Lunch available; 4 Dinner available; 5 Open all

warm hospitality. Set on a 72-acre farm, Kaltenbach's provides ample opportunity for walks through meadows, pastures, and forests, picnicking, and watching the sheep, pigs, rabbits, and wildlife. All-you-can-eat country-style breakfasts are served. Honeymoon suites have tubs for two, and hunting and golf packages are available. Pennsylvania Grand Canyon.

Host: Lee Kaltenbach
Rooms: 11 (9PB; 2SB) $60-125
Full Breakfast
Credit Cards: A, B
Notes: 2, 3, 4, 5, 7, 8, 9, 10, 11

The Easler's Bed and Breakfast

WHITE OAK

The Easler's Bed and Breakfast

3401 Foster Road, 15131
(412) 673-1133

Encircled by silver maples on the highest hill in Allegheny County, this 1929 English Tudor mansion welcomes family travelers with four restful guest rooms. White Oak is located about 17 miles southeast of Pittsburgh and seven miles from the Pennsylvania Turnpike (Exits 6 and 7). Gourmet breakfasts are a specialty. Children under ten stay free in parents' room. New solarium with hot tub.

Host: Kathleen Easler
Rooms: 4 (2PB; 2SB) $40-60
Full Breakfast
Notes: 2, 7, 8, 9

WILKES-BARRE

Ponda-Rowland Bed and Breakfast Inn and Farm Vacations

Rural Route 1, Box 348, Dallas, 18612
(717) 639-3245

On this large, scenic farm in the endless mountain region of Pennsylvania, guests can see and touch pigs, goats, sheep, cows, rabbits and a horse. They also can enjoy 34 acres of a private wildlife refuge, including six ponds, walking and skiing trails, canoeing, swimming and ice skating. Nearby are horseback riding, air tours, state parks, trout fishing, hunting, restaurants, county fairs, downhill skiing. The farmhouse, circa 1850, features large stone fireplace, beamed ceilings and museum-quality country antiques.

Hosts: Jeanette and Cliff Rowland
Rooms: 5 (PB) $55-85
Full Breakfast
Credit Cards: A, B
Notes: 2, 5, 7, 9, 10, 11, 12

year; 6 Pets welcome; 7 Children welcome; 8 Tennis nearby; 9 Swimming nearby; 10 Golf nearby; 11 Skiing nearby; 12 May be booked through travel agent

WRIGHTSVILLE

Roundtop Bed and Breakfast

6995 Roundtop Lane, 17368
(717) 252-3169

Roundtop is situated high above the Susquehanna River on more than 100 acres of woodland. Built in 1880, this German stone house has been renovated to take full advantage of the spectacular views. Its many porches and fireplaces, as well as its spacious, attractive rooms, make it a romantic weekend getaway anytime of the year. It is halfway between York and Lancaster.

Hosts: Jodi and Tyler Sloen
Rooms: 6 (1PB; 4SB) $50-75
Full Breakfast
Credit Cards: A, B
Notes: 2, 5, 7

YORK

Smyser-Bair House Bed and Breakfast

30 South Beaver Street, 17401
(717) 854-3411

A magnificent Italianate townhouse in the historic district. Rich in history and architectural details with crystal chandeliers and stained glass windows. Enjoy our antiques, warm hospitality and player piano. Near Lancaster, Gettysburg and Baltimore. Walk to farmers' markets, convenient parking.

Hosts: The King Family
Rooms: 4 (1PB; 3SB) $60-80
Full Breakfast
Credit Cards: A, B
Notes: 2, 5, 7, 10, 12

Roundtop Bed and Breakfast

NOTES: Credit cards accepted: A Master Card; B Visa; C American Express; D Discover Card; E Diners Club; F Other; 2 Personal checks accepted; 3 Lunch available; 4 Dinner available; 5 Open all

Rhode Island

BLOCK ISLAND

Hotel Manisses

1 Spring Street, 02807
(401) 466-2421

Restored Victorian hotel with authentic turn-of-the-century furnishings and today's comforts. All rooms with private bath and telephone, some have jacuzzis. Fine dining in our dining room overlooking the fountains and gardens. After-dinner drinks and flaming coffees served in upstairs parlor.

Hosts: Justin and Joan Abrams; Steve and Rita Draper
Rooms: 17 (PB) $55-225
Full Breakfast
Credit Cards: A, B, C
Notes: 2, 4, 7 (over 10), 8, 9, 12

CHARLESTOWN

General Stanton Inn

P. O. Box 222, 02813
(401) 364-8888

The inn stands on the old Boston Post Road (U.S. 1-A), about halfway between Narragansett and Watch Hill. It features old, original low ceilings, flaring fireplaces, brick ovens, and hand-hewn timbers. The inn serves breakfast, lunch, and dinner. On the premises is a large flea market open each Sunday and Monday holidays from April to October.

Hosts: Angelo and Janice Falcone
Rooms: 15 (13PB; 2SB) $65-105
Full Breakfast
Credit Cards: A, B, C
Notes: 2, 4, 8, 9, 10

GREEN HILL

Fairfield-By-The-Sea Bed and Breakfast

527 Green Hill Beach Road, 02879-6215
(401) 789-4717

An artist's contemporary home in an intimate, country setting offers beauty and seclusion. Stress reduction is the order of the day at this comfortable, airy house with an eclectic collection of art and an interesting library. Day trips are possible to Block Island, Martha's Vineyard, Cape Cod, Boston, Newport, Plymouth, and Mystic Seaport. Golf, bird

year; 6 Pets welcome; 7 Children welcome; 8 Tennis nearby; 9 Swimming nearby; 10 Golf nearby; 11 Skiing nearby; 12 May be booked through travel agent

watching, tennis, sailing, nature trails, fine shops, museums, historical sights, antiques, restaurants are all nearby.

Host: Jeanne A. Lewis
Rooms: 2 (SB) $40-55
Expanded Continental Breakfast
Credit Cards: C
Notes: 2, 5, 8, 9, 10, 11, 12

KINGSTON

Hedgerow
Bed and Breakfast

1747 Mooresfield Road, P.O. Box 1586, 02881
(401) 783-2671; (800) 486-4587

A lovely Colonial built in 1933 on two and one-quarter acres with tennis courts and formal gardens. Conveniently located 15 miles from Newport, 30 miles south of Providence, and next to the University of Rhode Island. The ferry to Block Island, beaches, and Mystic, Connecticut's seaport are within easy reach. Call for price information.

Hosts: Ann and Jim Ross
Rooms: 4 (S2B)
Full Breakfast
Credit Cards: D
Notes: 2, 5, 7, 8, 9, 10

NARRAGANSETT

Peace of the Rock
Bed and Breakfast

54 Ocean Spray Avenue, Pt. Judith, 02882
(401) 789-8899

Oceanfront cottage situated on private cove. Charming seaside getaway with panoramic views of the Atlantic. Offers lovely front-row seat on warm summer evenings facing Pt. Judith Lighthouse or for wintery nights warmed by our cobblestone fireside. Minutes to public/private beaches, Block Island ferry, restaurants, unique shops and wildlife sanctuary. Enjoy quiet, restful days, bicycling, birding, nature walking, sight seeing or just relaxing by the seashore. Peace of the Rock welcomes you!

Host: Reverend Debra S. Lynn
Rooms: 1 (SB) $50
Continental Breakfast (served at 8:30 A.M.)
Notes: 5, 7, 8, 9, 10

Stone Lea

40 Newton Avenue, 12882-1368
(401) 783-9546

An oceanfront Victorian estate built in 1884 and on the National Historic Register. Situated on over 2 acres of land at the end of a dead-end street. Enjoy magnificent views, ocean traffic, billiards, library, games or just relaxing on our sunporch or patio. House is full of antiques and collectibles. Rooms with twin, double, and queen beds. Children over 10 welcome.

Hosts: Carol and Ernie Cormier
Rooms: 4 (PB) $60-100 (off season), $80-125 (in season)
Full Breakfast
Credit Cards: A, B
Notes: 2, 5, 8, 9, 10, 12

NEWPORT

Admiral Farragut Inn

31 Clarke Street
Mailing address: 8 Fair Street, 02840
(401) 846-4256; (800) 343-2863

NOTES: Credit cards accepted: A Master Card; B Visa; C American Express; D Discover Card; E Diners Club; F Other; 2 Personal checks accepted; 3 Lunch available; 4 Dinner available; 5 Open all

The Admiral Farragut Inn, circa 1702, is a most unique colonial inn. Everywhere, in our guest rooms, great room, foyer, and halls, there are fresh interpretations of colonial themes, and even a bit of whimsy, to make anyone's stay a delight. Our personal favorites are the Shaker-style four-poster beds made by our in-house carpenter. There are painted armoires, gaily colored stencils, imported English antiques, faux-marble mantels with real Delft tiles. Located in one of Newport's historic areas and central to attractions. Afternoon tea is served.

Host: Deanna Shinnick
Rooms: 10 (PB) $50-110
Full Breakfast
Credit Cards: A, B, C, E
Closed January
Notes: 7 (over 12), 8, 9, 10, 12

Bed and Breakfast Rhode Island, Inc.

P.O. Box 3291, 38 Bellvue Avenue, 02840
(401) 849-1298; (800) 828-0000

This is a professional full-time, reservation service representing historic inns, guest houses and home stays throughout Rhode Island and southeastern Massachusetts. Quality accommodations are offered at elegant Victorian and historic Colonial inns and homes located in towns, villages, on the ocean and in great rural settings. All are closely quality controlled and personally inspected for cleanliness and desirability. Barbara and Rodney Wakefield, owners.

Halidon Hill Guest House

Halidon Avenue, 02840
(401) 847-8318

Location is everything in Newport, and we are a ten-minute walk from Hammersmith Farm, minutes from the beach, convenient to shopping areas, restaurants, and mansions. Our rooms are modern and spacious, and we have a deck and in-ground pool for your enjoyment.

Hosts: Helen and Ginger Burke
Rooms: 4 (2PB; 2SB) $55-125
Continental Breakfast
Credit Cards: C
Notes: 2, 5, 7, 8, 9, 10, 12

PROVIDENCE

The Old Court B&B

144 Benefit Street, 02903
(401) 751-2002

The Old Court is filled with antique furniture, chandeliers and memorabilia from the nineteenth century, with each room designed to reflect period tastes. All rooms have private baths, and the antique Victorian beds are comfortable and spacious. Just a three-minute walk from the center of downtown Providence, near Brown University and Rhode Island School of Design.

Host: Christa Collins
Rooms: 11 (PB) $110-160
Continental Breakfast
Credit Cards: A, B, C, D
Notes: 8

State House Inn

43 Jewett Street, 02908
(401) 785-1235

A country inn usually means peace and quiet, friendly hosts, comfort and simplicity, with beautiful furnishings. The State House Inn has all of these qualifications, but just happens to be located in the city of Providence. Our inn has fireplaces, hardwood floors, Shaker or colonial furnishings, canopy beds, and modern conveniences such as FAX, TV, and phone. Located near downtown and local colleges and universities.

Hosts: Frank and Monica Hopton
Rooms: 10 (PB) $59-99
Full Breakfast
Credit Cards: A, B, C
Notes: 5, 7, 12

WAKEFIELD

Larchwood Inn

521 Main St., 02879
(401) 783-5454; FAX (401) 783-1800

Watching over the main street of this quaint New England town for over 160 years, this grand old house, surrounded by lawns and shaded by stately trees, dispenses hospitality and good food and spirits from early morning to late at night. Historic Newport, picturesque Mystic Seaport, and salty Block Island are a short ride away.

Hosts: Francis and Diann Browning
Rooms: 19 (12PB; 7SB) $30-90
Full Breakfast
Credit Cards: A, B, C, D, E
Notes: 2, 3, 4, 5, 6, 7, 8, 9, 10, 12

WYOMING

The Cookie Jar Bed and Breakfast

64 Kingstown Road (Rte. 138 off I-95), 02898
(401) 539-2680

The heart of our home, the living room, was built in 1732 as a blacksmith's shop. Later, the forge was removed and a large granite fireplace was built by an American-Indian stonemason. The original wood ceiling, hand-hewn beams, and granite walls remain today. The property was called the Perry Plantation, and yes, they had two slaves who lived above the blacksmith's shop. We offer friendly, home-style living in a comfortable, country setting. On Route 138 just off I-95.

Hosts: Dick and Madelein Sohl
Rooms: 3 (1PB; 2SB) $55-60
Full Breakfast
Credit Cards: None
Notes: 2, 5, 8, 9, 10, 12

NOTES: Credit cards accepted: A Master Card; B Visa; C American Express; D Discover Card; E Diners Club; F Other; 2 Personal checks accepted; 3 Lunch available; 4 Dinner available; 5 Open all

South Carolina

BENNETTSVILLE

The Breeden House Inn
404 East Main Street, 29512
(803) 479-3665

Built in 1886, the romantic Breeden House is a beautifully restored southern mansion on 2 acres. Provides very comfortable and livable surroundings which will capture your interest and inspire your imaginations. Listed on the National Register of Historic Places, the Inn is located 20 minutes off I-95. A great half-way point between Florida and New York. Both houses have inviting porches with wicker, rockers, swings and ceiling fans. Beautiful antique decor, pool, cable TV in each room, phone in most rooms. Great country kitchen in Carriage House. A haven for antique lovers, runners and walkers. Owned and operated by a Christian family. No smoking. Retreats and reunions welcome.

Hosts: Wesley and Bonnie Park
Rooms: 7 (PB) $50-55
Full Breakfast
Credit Cards: A, B, D
Notes: 2, 5, 9, 10, 12

The Breeden House Inn

CHARLESTON

The Belvedere
40 Rutledge Avenue, 19401
(803) 722-0973

A late 1800s Colonial mansion in the downtown historic district on Colonial Lake has an 1800 Georgian interior with mantels and woodwork. Three large bedrooms have antiques, Oriental rugs, and family collections. Easy access to everything in the area.

Hosts: David Spell and Rick Zender
Rooms: 3 (PB) $95
Continental Breakfast
Credit Cards: None
Closed December 1-February 15
Notes: 2, 7 (over 8), 8, 9, 10

---

year; 6 Pets welcome; 7 Children welcome; 8 Tennis nearby; 9 Swimming nearby; 10 Golf nearby; 11 Skiing nearby; 12 May be booked through travel agent

Country Victorian Bed and Breakfast

105 Tradd Street, 29401-2422
(803) 577-0682

Come, relive the charm of the past. Relax in a rocker on the piazza of this historic home and watch the carriages go by. Walk to antique shops, churches, restaurants, art galleries, museums, and all historic points of interest. The house, built in 1820, is located in the historic district south of Broad. Rooms have private entrances and contain antique iron and brass beds, old quilts, antique oak and wicker furniture, and braided rugs over heart-of-pine floors. Home-made cookies will be waiting. Many extras!

Host: Diane Deardurff Weed
Rooms: 2 (PB) $65-90
Expanded Continental Breakfast
Credit Cards: None
Notes: 2, 5, 7, 8, 9, 10, 12

Country Victorian Bed and Breakfast

1837 Bed and Breakfast

126 Wentworth Street, 29401
(803) 723-7166

Enjoy accommodations in a wealthy cotton planter's home and brick carriage house centrally located in Charleston's historic district. Walk to boat tours, the old market, antique shops, restaurants, and main attractions. Near the Omni and College of Charleston. Full gourmet breakfast is served in the formal dining room and includes sausage pie, Eggs Benedict, ham omelets, and home-baked breads. The 1837 Tea Room serves afternoon tea to our guests and the public. Off-street parking.

Hosts: Sherri and Richard Dunn
Rooms: 8 (PB) $59-99
Full Breakfast
Credit Cards: A, B, C
Notes: 2, 5, 8, 9, 10

King George IV Inn and Guests

32 George Street, 29401
(803) 723-9339

A 200-year-old, circa 1790, Charleston Historic House located in the heart of historic district. The inn is Federal style with three levels of Charleston side porches. All rooms have fireplaces, 10-12 foot ceilings, wide-planked hardwood floors, old furnishings and antiques. Private baths, parking, AC, TVs. One-minute walk to historic King Street, five-minute walk to historic market. A step back in time!

Hosts: Jean, Lynn, Sara, BJ, and Mike
Rooms: 8 (PB) $55-80
Continental Breakfast
Credit Cards: A, B
Notes: 2, 5, 6 (by arrangement), 7, 8, 9, 10, 12

NOTES: Credit cards accepted: A Master Card; B Visa; C American Express; D Discover Card; E Diners Club; F Other; 2 Personal checks accepted; 3 Lunch available; 4 Dinner available; 5 Open all

The Kitchen House, Circa 1732

126 Tradd Street, 29401
(803) 577-6362

Nestled in the heart of the historic district, the Kitchen House is a completely restored 18th-century kitchen dwelling. Southern hospitality, absolute privacy, cozy fireplaces, antiques, patio, and colonial herb garden await you. The refrigerator and pantry are stocked for breakfast. The pre-Revolutionary War house was featured in *Colonial Homes* magazine and written up in the *New York Times*.

Host: Lois Evans
Rooms: 3 (PB) $75-150
Full Breakfast
Credit Cards: A, B
Notes: 2, 5, 7, 8, 9, 10, 12

Rutledge Victorian Inn and Guest House

114 Rutledge Avenue, 29401
(803) 722-7551

Welcome to the past! This century-old Victorian house in Charleston's downtown historic district is quaint but elegant, with large, decorative porches, columns, and antique gingerbread. The authentic Old Charleston house has decorative fireplaces, hardwood floors, 12-foot ceilings, ten-foot doors and windows, old furnishings, and antiques. Modern amenities include air conditioning, TV, private or shared baths, ice machine, and refrigerator. Walking distance to all historic attractions. Homemade goodies served in continental breakfast.

Hosts: Jean, Sara, BJ, Lynn, and Mike
Rooms: 11 (6PB; 5SB) $45-85
Continental Breakfast
Credit Cards: A, B
Notes: 2, 5, 6 (some), 7, 8, 9, 10, 12

Two Meeting Street Inn

2 Meeting Street, 29401
(803) 723-7322

Acclaimed as the belle of Charleston's bed and breakfasts, this 1890 Victorian mansion offers southern elegance. Located in the historic district at Battery Park, the inn is filled with antiques, Oriental rugs, and Tiffany windows. Your continental breakfast is served in the side garden or formal dining room, while the afternoons are enjoyed on the front porch rocking chairs. Within six blocks of most historic sites, restaurants, and shops.

Host: Karen M. Spell
Rooms: 9 (PB) $90-155
Continental Breakfast
Credit Cards: None
Notes: 2, 5, 7 (over 8), 9, 10

CLIO

The Henry Bennett House

301 Red Bluff Street, 29525

The Henry Bennett House is a turn-of-the century Queen Anne Victorian and is located in the historic district of Clio. Built in 1903 by Mr. Bennett, who was a cotton farmer. The exterior is most striking with the enormous wrap around

---

year; 6 Pets welcome; 7 Children welcome; 8 Tennis nearby; 9 Swimming nearby; 10 Golf nearby; 11 Skiing nearby; 12 May be booked through travel agent

veranda and pillars. The interior has wide board paneled wainscoting and paneled-beaded board ceilings. There are fireplaces throughout the house. The walls are plaster and the floors are heart pine. Must be seen to appreciate.

Hosts: Connie and Dennis Hodgkinson
Rooms: 2 $50
Full Breakfast
Credit Cards: A, B
Notes: 2, 5, 7, 9, 10

DILLON

Magnolia Inn Bed and Breakfast

601 E. Main St. — Hwy 9, 29536
(803) 774-0679

Located 2.5 miles from I-95. Southern hospitality and decor grace this century old Southern Colonial home. Watch TV or relax in the Duck Library or Victorian Parlor. Full Breakfasts. Azalea Room-Southern Rice Canopy bed; Caellia Room-white iron bed with heart-shaped head and foot boards; Dogwood Room-Oak Victorian Mansion bed; Wisteria Room-Victorian Roll-top bed; Beds are queen size. Rooms have decorative fireplaces. Private baths except Wisteria Room. Within driving distance of Myrtle Beach.

Hosts: Jim and Pam Lannoo
Rooms: 4 (3PB; 1SB) $30-50
Full Breakfast
Credit Cards: A, B
Notes: 2, 5, 6, 7, 9, 10

GEORGETOWN

1790 House

630 Highmarket Street, 29440
(803) 546-4821

Meticulously restored 200-year-old plantation style inn located in the heart of historic Georgetown. Spacious, luxurious rooms, fireplaces, central air and heat. Lovely gardens to enjoy. Stay in the "slave quarters," "rice planters" rooms, our beautiful honeymoon cottage with jacuzzi tub, or one of our other lovely rooms. Walk to shops, restaurants and historic sites. Short drive to Myrtle Beach and the Grandstrand, Brokgreen Gardens, Pawley's Island and Charleston. A golfer's paradise!

Hosts: Patricia and John Wiley
Rooms: 6 (PB) $65-115
Full Breakfast
Credit Cards: A, B, C
Notes: 2, 5, 8, 10, 12

The Shaw House

613 Cypress Court, 29440
(803) 546-9663

After eight years, we are still excited about everyone who visits. We have a wonderful location overlooking a beautiful marsh, seen from a spacious den with an all-glass view. Large bedrooms; many antiques; well-stocked with books and magazines; wonderful nooks to relax and read; piano. Only five blocks from downtown and great restaurants. Our guests always leave with a recipe or prayer tied with a ribbon. Great birdwatching and bikes available.

NOTES: Credit cards accepted: A Master Card; B Visa; C American Express; D Discover Card; E Diners Club; F Other; 2 Personal checks accepted; 3 Lunch available; 4 Dinner available; 5 Open all

Host: Mary Shaw
Rooms: 3 (PB) $50
Full Breakfast
Credit Cards: None
Notes: 2, 5, 7, 8, 9, 10

HONEA PATH

Sugarfoot Castle

211 S. Main St., 29654
(803) 369-6565

Enormous trees umbrella this 19th century brick Victorian home. Fresh flowers grace the 14-inch-thick walled rooms furnished with family heirlooms. Enjoy the living room's interesting collections or the library's comfy chairs, TV, VCR, books, fireplace, desk and game table. Upon arising, guests find coffee and juice outside their doors, followed by breakfast of hot breads, cereal, fresh fruit and beverages served by candlelight in the dining room. Rock away the world's cares on a screened porch overlooking peaceful grounds.

Hosts: Gale and Cecil Evans
Rooms: 3 (SB) $44-48
Continental Breakfast
Credit Cards: A, B
Notes: 2, 5, 8, 9, 10

MCCLELLANVILLE

Laurel Hill Plantation

8913 North Highway 17, P. O. Box 190, 29458
(803) 887-3708

Laurel Hill faces the Atlantic Ocean and Intercoastal Waterway. Wrap-around porches provide a spectacular view of creeks and marshes. The reconstructed house is furnished with country and primitive antiques that reflect the Low Country life-style. Boating on the waterway depends on the tide, weather, and availability of the captain. Thirty minutes north of Charleston. 45 minutes north of Charleston, 1 1/2 hours south of Myrtle Beach.

Host: Jackie and Lee Morrison
Rooms: 4 (PB) $65-75
Credit Cards: None
Notes: 2, 5, 7 (over six), 9, 10, 12

MYRTLE BEACH

Serendipity, an Inn

407 North 71st Avenue, 29577
(803) 449-5268

An award-winning, mission-style inn is just 300 yards from the ocean beach and has a heated pool and Jacuzzi. All rooms have air conditioning, color TV, private baths and refrigerators. Secluded patio, Ping-Pong, and shuffleboard. Over 70 golf courses nearby, as well as fishing, tennis, restaurants, theaters, and shopping. Ninety miles to historic Charleston.

Hosts: Cos and Ellen Ficarra
Rooms: 12 (PB) $62-85
Expanded Continental Breakfast
Credit Cards: A, B, C, D
Notes: 7, 8, 9, 10, 12

year; 6 Pets welcome; 7 Children welcome; 8 Tennis nearby; 9 Swimming nearby; 10 Golf nearby; 11 Skiing nearby; 12 May be booked through travel agent

ROCK HILL

East Main Guest House
600 E. Main St., 29730
(803) 366-1161

Built by the Douglas family just after
the turn of the century, this craftsman
style home had an unfinished second
floor until the Petersons acquired the
property in 1990. After extensive construction, renovation and remodeling,
the upstairs now contains three beautifully decorated guestrooms, modern
baths and a comfortable sitting room.
Our dining room is ideal for luncheons
and small receptions. Cozy sitting room/
game room contains seating, a game
table and television. Games and books
are also available for your enjoyment.
Close to many attractions in both Carolinas.

Hosts: Jerry and Melba Peterson
Rooms: 3 (PB) $59-79
Expanded Continental Breakfast
Credit Cards: A, B, C
Notes: 2, 5, 8, 9, 10, 11, 12

SUMTER

Sumter Bed and Breakfast
6 Park Avenue, 29150
(803) 773-2903

Charming 1896 home with large, front
porch facing lush green, quiet park in
the historic district with tennis courts.
Private entrance. HBO. Spacious guest
rooms upstairs with fireplaces and antiques. Library with extensive collection of artifacts. 15 area golf courses.
Formal breakfast.

Hosts: Bob and Merilyn Carnes
Rooms: 4 (2PB; 2SB) $45-55
Continental Breakfast
Credit Cards: A, B
Notes: 2, 5, 7, 8, 10

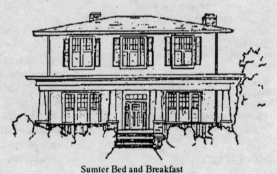

Sumter Bed and Breakfast

NOTES: Credit cards accepted: A Master Card; B Visa; C American Express; D Discover Card; E
Diners Club; F Other; 2 Personal checks accepted; 3 Lunch available; 4 Dinner available; 5 Open all

South Dakota

BRYANT

The Big Brown Country Inn Bed-n-Breakfast

RR 1, Box 186, 57221-9793
(605) 628-2049

This 100-year-old Victorian style home is decorated in country crafts and early American style furniture. It sits on a tree-lined street in a small town. It is close to a Laura Wilder Museum and several small lakes for fishing. Laundry facilities are available and you may play the piano or ride bikes. Breakfast consists of homemade breads, jams and jellies.

Hosts: Floyd and Myrta Rossel
Rooms: 3 (SB) $25
Both Full and Continental Breakfast
Credit Cards: None
Notes: 2, 5, 6, 7, 8, 9, 10

CANOVA

Skoglund Farm

Route 1, Box 45, 57321
(605) 247-3445

Skoglund Farm brings back memories of Grandpa and Grandma's home. It is furnished with antiques and collectibles. A full, home-cooked evening meal and breakfast are served. You can sight-see in the surrounding area, visit Little House on the Prairie Village, hike, or horseback ride, or just relax. Several country churches are located nearby.

Hosts: Alden and Delores
Rooms: 5 (SB) $30 each adult; $20 each teen; $15 each child; children 5 and under free
Full Breakfast
Credit Cards: None
Notes: 2, 3, 4 (included), 5, 6, 7, 8, 9, 10, 12

---

year; 6 Pets welcome; 7 Children welcome; 8 Tennis nearby; 9 Swimming nearby; 10 Golf nearby; 11 Skiing nearby; 12 May be booked through travel agent

CHAMBERLAIN

Riverview Ridge

HC69, Box 82A, 57325
(605) 734-6084

Modern home with queen and king beds. Beautiful view of the Missouri River. Lots of country peace and quiet with angle parking for your recreational vehicles. Full breakfasts with homemade breads and jellies. Enjoy fishing and golfing nearby. Make our home your home. Just 3 1/2 miles north of Chamberlain on Highway 50.

Hosts: Frank and Alta Cable
Rooms: 3 (1PB; 2SB) $45-55
Full Breakfast
Credit Cards: None
Notes: 2, 5, 7, 9, 10, 12

CUSTER

Custer Mansion Bed and Breakfast

35 Centennial Drive, 57730
(605) 673-3333

This historic 1891 Victorian Gothic mansion is on one acre and has a lovely patio and willow trees. Charmingly restored and beautifully decorated, it offers western hospitality and delicious home cooking in the unique setting of the beautiful Black Hills. Near Custer State Park, Mount Rushmore, and Crazy Horse Monument. Nearby restaurants. Recommended by *Bon Appètit* and *GMC Friends* magazines and *Mobil Travel Guide.*

Hosts: Mill and Carole Seaman
Rooms: 6 (2PB; 4S2B) $45-75
Full Breakfast
Credit Cards: None
Notes: 2, 5, 7, 8, 9 , 10, 11

Custer Mansion Bed and Breakfast

RAPID CITY

Audrie's Cranbury Corner Bed and Breakfast

Rural Route 8, Box 2400, 57702
(605) 342-7788

The ultimate in charm and Old World hospitality, our country home and five-acre estate is surrounded by thousands of acres of national forest in a secluded Black Hills setting. Each quiet, comfortable suite and cottage has private entrance, hot tub, patio, cable TV, and refrigerator. Free trout fishing, hiking, biking available on property.

Hosts: Hank and Audry Kuhnhauser
Rooms: 6 (PB) $85
Full Breakfast
Credit Cards: None
Notes: 2, 5, 8, 9, 10, 11

NOTES: Credit cards accepted: A Master Card; B Visa; C American Express; D Discover Card; E Diners Club; F Other; 2 Personal checks accepted; 3 Lunch available; 4 Dinner available; 5 Open all

The Carriage House
721 West Boulevard, 57701
(605) 343-6415

The stately, three-story, pillared Colonial house is on a historic, tree-lined boulevard of Rapid City. The English country decor creates an ambience of elegance, refinement, and relaxing charm. Gourmet breakfasts are served in the formal dining room. The famous Black Hills and Badlands are minutes away, offering attractions like Mount Rushmore, Crazy Horse Monument, boating, and skiing.

Hosts: Betty and Joel King
Rooms: 5 (2PB; 3SB) $59-89
Full Breakfast
Credit Cards: A, B
Notes: 2, 5, 8, 9, 10, 11

SENECA

Rainbow Lodge
HC 78, Box 81, 57473
(605) 436-6795

Spend a quiet, relaxing day or evening by the lake on the prairie. Beautiful landscaping and trees, meditation areas, and chapel. You will enjoy country charm and hospitality on this oasis of the prairie; handicapped accessible; full, country-style breakfast; four miles off Highway 212. Reservations required.

Hosts: Ralph and Ann Wheeler
Rooms: 3 (SB) $30-45
Full Breakfast
Credit Cards: None
Notes: 2, 4, 5, 7

YANKTON

Mulberry Inn
512 Mulberry Street, 57078
(605) 665-7116

The beautiful Mulberry Inn offers the ultimate in comfort and charm in a traditional setting. Built in 1873, the inn features parquet floors, six guest rooms furnished with antiques, two parlors with marble fireplaces, and a large porch. Minutes from Lewis and Clark Lake and within walking distance of the Missouri River, fine restaurants, and downtown, the inn is listed on the National Register of Historic Places.

Host: Millie Cameron
Rooms: 6 (2PB; 4SB) $30-48 May-September; $25-43 October-April
Continental Breakfast; Full breakfast available with extra charge
Credit Cards: A, B, C
Notes: 2, 5, 7, 8, 9, 10

---

year; 6 Pets welcome; 7 Children welcome; 8 Tennis nearby; 9 Swimming nearby; 10 Golf nearby; 11 Skiing nearby; 12 May be booked through travel agent

Tennessee

CHATTANOOGA

Alford House

Alford Hill Dr., Rt. 4, 37419
(615) 821-7625

Seventeen room Traditional style home, antique decor, located on site of Lookout Mountain. Surrounded by forest on three sides with hiking trails. Ten minutes to downtown, and just minutes to local attractions. Coffee is served at wake-up and breads, muffins, fresh fruits, cheeses and juice start your day off right. Relax on the porch or gazebo while enjoying the mountain scenery.

Host: Rhoda Alford
Rooms: 3 (1PB; 2SB) $50-75
Expanded Continental Breakfast
Credit Cards: B
Notes: None

KODAK

Grandma's House

734 Pollard Road, 37764
(615) 933-3512; (800) 676-3512

Colonial style home on 3 acres at the base of the Great Smokey Mountains. Only 2 miles off I-40 at the 407 exit. Owners live on premises and are both native East Tennesseans. Country decor with handmade quilts and crafts. Farm style "loosen your belt" breakfast begins when guests gather around the big oak table and Hilda says the blessing.

Hosts: Charlie and Hilda Hickman
Rooms: 3 (PB) $65
Full Breakfast
Credit Cards: None
Notes: None

LIMESTONE

Snap Inn
Bed and Breakfast

Route 3, Box 102, 37681
(615) 257-2482

Your hosts will welcome you into this gracious 1815 Federal home furnished with antiques and set in farm country. Enjoy the peaceful mountain view from the full back porch, or play a game of pool. Located close to Davy Crockett State Park; 15 minutes to historic

Jonesborough or Greenville.

Hosts: Dan and Ruth Dorgan
Rooms: 2 (PB) $50
Full Breakfast
Credit Cards: None
Notes: 2, 5, 6, 7 (1 only), 8, 9, 10, 12

MEMPHIS

Sassafras Inn Bed and Breakfast

785 Highway 51, Hernando, Mississippi. 38632
(601) 429-5864; (800) 882-1897

Relax, unwind in a cozy inn where hospitality has not gone out of style. A clean, secure, friendly haven for travelers. A destination for guests who want to enjoy a "private" indoor heated pool, spa, waterfall, tropical gardens. Queen size beds, private baths. Recreation room with billiards, ping pong, treadmill. Delicious Southern Cuisine. Our goal is to make your stay as memorable as possible. Just minutes from Memphis.

Host: Frances R. McClanahan
Rooms: 3 (PB)
Full Breakfast
Credit Cards: A, B
Notes: 2, 5, 8, 9, 10, 12

MONTEAGLE

Adams Edgeworth Inn

Monteagle Assembly, 37356
(615) 924-2669; FAX (615) 924-3236

Circa 1896, Adams Edgeworth Inn has provided fine lodging for almost 100 years and is still the region's leader in elegance and quality. Recently refur-

bished in English Manor decor, the inn is a showcase for fine antiques, important original paintings and sculptures and a prize-winning rose garden. Stroll through the 96-acre Victorian Village which surrounds the inn or drive 6 miles to the gothic campus of Sewanee, University of the South. Cultural activities are year round; 150 miles of hiking trails, scenic vistas, waterfalls. Tennis, swimming, golf, riding nearby. *New York Times* available. Gourmet meals by special arrangement. " One of the best inns I've ever visited anywhere..." (Sara Pitzer, *Recommended Country Inns* in *Country Inns Magazine*).

Hosts: Wendy and David Adams
Rooms: 12 (PB) $55-95
Expanded Continental Breakfast
Credit Cards: A, B
Notes: 2, 4, 5 (by special arrangement), 8, 9, 10, 12 (by special arrangement)

Adams Edgeworth Inn

MURFREESBORO

Clardy's Guest House

435 East Main Street, 37130
(615) 893-6030

This large Victorian home was built in 1898 and is located in Murfreesboro's historic district. You will marvel at the ornate woodwork, beautiful fireplaces, and magnificent stained glass overlooking the staircase. The house is filled with antiques, as are local shops and malls. The hosts will help you with dining, shopping, and touring plans.

Hosts: Robert and Barbara Deaton
Rooms: 4 (2PB; 2SB) $35-45
Continental Breakfast
Credit Cards: None
Notes: 2, 5, 8, 9, 10

NATCHEZ TRACE (SEE NATCHEZ TRACE MISSISSIPPI)

PIGEON FORGE

Hilton's Bluff Bed and Breakfast

2654 Valley Heights Dr., 37863
(615) 428-9765

Truly elegant country living. Secluded hilltop setting only 1/2 mile from heart of Pigeon Forge. Minutes from outlet shopping, Dollywood and Smoky Mountain National Park. Ten honeymoon, executive and deluxe rooms, all with private baths, 5 with two-person jacuzzis, king beds and waterbeds. Tastefully decorated in romantic mingling of the old and new. Private balconies, covered decks with rockers and checkerboard tables. Den with mountain stone fireplace, gameroom/conference room. Southern gourmet breakfast. Group rates for corporate seminars and church groups.

Hosts: Jack and Norma Hilton
Rooms: 10 (PB) $69-104
Full Breakfast
Credit Cards: A, B, C
Notes: 2, 3&4 (to groups reserving entire inn), 5, 7 (by arrangement), 8, 9, 10, 11, 12 (certain restrictions apply)

RUGBY

Grey Gables Bed 'N Breakfast

Highway 52, P.O. Box 5252, 37733
(615) 628-5252

Grey Gables, located one mile from the 1880s historic village of Rugby, offers visitors the best of its Victorian English heritage. The house is decorated with country and Victorian antiques and has porches with white wicker and rustic rockers. Enjoy an elegant evening meal and a hearty country breakfast. Access to golf, swimming, hiking, and bicycling; canoe rental and shuttle available. Private luncheons, teas, dinners, receptions, conferences, retreats, and group functions are accommodated by reservation. Horses boarded; no smoking.

Hosts: Bill and Linda Brooks Jones
Rooms: 8 (4PB; 4SB) $90
Full Breakfast
Credit Cards: A, B
Notes: 2, 3, 4, 5, 9, 10

SEVIERVILLE

Blue Mountain Mist Country Inn

1811 Pullen Rd., 37862
(615) 428-2335

Our inn is a new Victorian style farmhouse with a big wrap-around porch overlooking rolling hills with the Smokey Mountains as a backdrop. Country antique furnishings, grandmother's quilts and old photos of

---

NOTES: Credit cards accepted: A Master Card; B Visa; C American Express; D Discover Card; E Diners Club; F Other; 2 Personal checks accepted; 3 Lunch available; 4 Dinner available; 5 Open all

our inn provide a very homey atmosphere. We have two sitting rooms with fireplaces, a TV room, outdoor jacuzzi and other relaxing surprises. Nestled in the woods behind the inn are 5 new country cottages designed for romantic getaways. We are minutes from the Great Smokey Mountains National Park, Gatlinburg and Dollywood.

Hosts: Norman and Sarah Ball
Rooms: 12 rooms and 5 cottages (PB) $79-125
Full Breakfast
Credit Cards: A, B
Notes: 5, 7, 10, 11

SHELBYVILLE

Bottle Hollow Lodge

Mailing: P.O. Box 92, Shelbyville, 37160/
Actual: 111 Gobbler Ridge Road, Flat Creek
(615) 695-5253

Nestled high in the rolling hills of middle Tennessee with breathtaking views of the valley below, this all new B&B offers quiet seclusion with all the comforts of true Southern hospitality. Its four spacious guest rooms and 600-square-foot master suite with its own large stone fireplace, offer a most welcome respite from the frenzied pace of our work-a-day world. Be our guest

and enjoy quiet luxury in a tranquil rustic setting.

Hosts: Pat and Jim Whiteside
Rooms: 4 rooms and 1 suite (PB) $75-150
Full Breakfast
Credit Cards: A, B
Notes: 2, 3, 4, 5, 10, 12

TOWNSEND

Richmont Inn

220 Winterberry Lane, 37882
(615) 448-6751

A Bed and Breakfast in an Appalachian Cantilever Barn on the "peaceful side of the Smokies." Beautifully furnished with 18th-century English antiques and French paintings in the living and dining rooms. Guest rooms capture the history, culture and nature of the Smokies in their furnishings and offer private baths with spa tubs for two, fireplaces, king beds, balconies and "breathtaking mountain views." A full breakfast and evening candlelight dessert are served looking into the majestic meadows of Laurel Valley and towering Rich Mountain.

Hosts: Susan and Jim Hind
Rooms: 10 (PB) $85-110
Full Breakfast
Credit Cards: None
Notes: 2, 5, 9, 10, 12

Smoky Bear Lodge

160 Bear Lodge Drive, 37882
(615) 448-6442; (800) 48-SMOKY

The Smoky Bear Lodge has a 1,500-square-foot conference room complementing the ideal Christian oriented retreat site for youth, choirs, leadership, Sunday school classes, and pastors. The lodge is also perfect for that special family vacation. Situated in the foothills of the Great Smoky Mountains, the view from the rocker-lined front porch is incredible. Enjoy the activities, pool, hot tub, and beautiful sunrises and sunsets while you learn or relax. Call for brochure.

Hosts: Cary and Sandy Plummer
Rooms: 12 (10PB; 2SB) $65-85
Full Breakfast
Credit Cards: A, B, C
Notes: 2, 3, 4, 5, 7, 9, 10, 11

NOTES: Credit cards accepted: A Master Card; B Visa; C American Express; D Discover Card; E Diners Club; F Other; 2 Personal checks accepted; 3 Lunch available; 4 Dinner available; 5 Open all

Texas

ABILENE

Bolin's Prairie House Bed and Breakfast

508 Mulberry, 79601
(915) 675-5855

Nestled in the heart of Abilene is a 1902 home furnished with antiques and modern luxuries combined to create a homelike, warm atmosphere. Downstairs are high ceilings, hardwood floors, and a wood-burning stove. Upstairs are four unique bedrooms—Love, Joy, Peace, and Patience—each beautifully decorated. Breakfast is a special baked egg dish, fruit, and homemade bread served in the dining room on blue and white china.

Hosts: Sam and Ginny Bolin
Rooms: 4 (SB) $40-50
Full Breakfast
Credit Cards: A, B, C, D, E
Notes: 2, 5

AUSTIN

Peaceful Hill Bed and Breakfast

10817 Ranch Road 2222, 78730-1102
(512) 338-1817

Country inn on ranch land high in rolling hills west of Austin, 15 minutes to city, 5 minutes to Lake Travis. Great porch—rocking chairs, porch swing, big breakfast table, soak up countryside and view of city skyline. Hammock for two; hiking and bicycling; 2 miles to golf, tennis and swimming. Huge living room looks out to countryside and city view. Grand stone fireplace—crackling fire. Full home cooked breakfast. Peaceful is the name, Peaceful is the game.

Host: Mrs. Peninnah Thurmond
Rooms: 2 (PB) $60+
Full Breakfast
Credit Cards: A, B, C (executive)
Notes: 2, 5, 6 (in cage), 7, 8, 9, 10

---

year; 6 Pets welcome; 7 Children welcome; 8 Tennis nearby; 9 Swimming nearby; 10 Golf nearby; 11 Skiing nearby; 12 May be booked through travel agent

BRENHAM

Heartland Country Inn and Retreat

Rt. 2, Box 446, 77883
(409) 836-1864

Perched on a hilltop overlooking a spectacular panoramic view of country church, rolling hills, cows, trees, lakes, 158 acres, peaceful stress-free getaway to promote R&R. Two two-story inns offer 14 bedrooms tastefully furnished with antiques in country, traditional, Victorian, French, Primitive decor. Comfortable king, queen and twin beds. Conference room for $40, large building for $125. Experience a delightful step back in time—more gentle lifestyle with a touch of the past and luxuries of the present.

Host: Shirley Sacks
Rooms: 14 (5PB; 9SB) $65
Full Breakfast
Credit Cards: None
Notes: 2, 3 & 4 (by arrangement), 5, 7, 12

CANYON LAKE

Aunt Nora's Bed and Breakfast

RR 9, Box 814, 78133
(210) 899-3989

In the Texas hill country, minutes from New Braunfels Guadelupe River at Canyon Lake is a country house with a touch of Victorian, nestled on a hillside amid oak and cedar trees. Breathe fresh country air from the front porch swing, enjoy patio hot tub and handmade furnishings. Tastefully decorated queen rooms in main house and a separate king's cottage all in a delightful scenic setting.

Hosts: Alton and Iralee Hale
Rooms: 3 (1PB; 2SB) $65-125
Full Breakfast on weekends, Continental Breakfast on weekdays
Credit Cards: None
Notes: 2, 5, 7, 9, 10, 12

COMFORT

Idlewilde Lodge

115 Highway 473, 78013
(210) 995-3844

Customized service is the motto at Idlewilde Lodge. The main house was built in 1902, has a Texas historical marker and has been completely restored, renovated and modernized. A Christian camp for over 60 years, Idlewilde is owned and operated by a Christian family who really enjoy sharing God's beauty with their guests. Also has two cabins, tennis courts, pool, large pavilion with barbeque pit, children's playground, access to river and a wonderful, large homestyle breakfast. Forty-five miles west of San Antonio. Unconditional guarantee you'll enjoy your visit.

Hosts: Hank and Connie Engel
Rooms: 6 (3PB; 3SB) $72-87
Full Breakfast
Credit Cards: A, B
Notes: 2, 3, 4, 5, 6, 7, 8, 9, 10, 12

NOTES: Credit cards accepted: A Master Card; B Visa; C American Express; D Discover Card; E Diners Club; F Other; 2 Personal checks accepted; 3 Lunch available; 4 Dinner available; 5 Open all

ENNIS

Raphael House

500 W. Ennis Avenue, 75119
(214) 875-1555

This elegant 1906 Neoclassic Revival mansion is on the National Register and for the last two years was voted one of the top B&Bs in the USA. The 19-room mansion is a showcase of quality antiques, rich wall coverings and luxurious fabrics. Amenities include large baths with antique clawfoot tubs, down comforters and pillows, scented soaps and toiletries, afternoon refreshments and turn down service. Swedish massage, honeymoon packages and corporate deals available. Very Romantic!

Hosts: Danna K. Cody
Rooms: 6 (PB) $55-95
Full Breakfast
Credit Cards: A, B, C, E, F
Notes: 2, 3, 4, 5, 8, 9, 10

FREDERICKSBURG

Baron's Creek Inn

110 East Creek Street, 78624
(210) 997-9398; (800) 800-4082

This turn-of-the-century home provides guests with unique accommodations: four complete suites, plus a Sunday house, each with private bath. A continental breakfast may be enjoyed on the front porch or veranda, or in the privacy of your suite. Located two blocks from the downtown area.

Hosts: Kenneth and Brooke Schweers
Rooms: 5 (PB) $85-95

Expanded Continental Braekfast
Credit Cards: A, B, D
Notes: 2, 5, 12

J Bar K Ranch Bed and Breakfast

HC 10, Box 53 A, 78624
(210) 669-2471

A large German rock home with a historic marker on a Texas hill country ranch is furnished with antiques. We offer a full country breakfast, Texas hospitality, and convenience to Fredericksburg, with its German heritage and architecture. Many quaint shops, antique stores, excellent restaurants, Nimitz Naval Museum, Enchanted Rock, and tours of Lyndon Johnson's ranch are nearby.

Hosts: Kermit and Naomi Kothe
Rooms: 4 (3PB; 1SB) $65-75
Full Breakfast
Credit Cards: None
Notes: 2, 7, 8, 9, 10

Magnolia House

101 East Hackberry, 78624
(210) 997-0306

Circa 1925; restored 1991. Enjoy southern hospitality in a grand and gracious manner. Outside, lovely magnolias and a bubbling fish pond and waterfall set a soothing mood. Inside, beautiful living room, game room, and formal dining room provide areas for guests to mingle. Four romantic rooms and two suites have been thoughtfully planned, appointed with antiques and original paint-

year; 6 Pets welcome; 7 Children welcome; 8 Tennis nearby; 9 Swimming nearby; 10 Golf nearby; 11 Skiing nearby; 12 May be booked through travel agent

ings by the owner. A southern-style, seven-course breakfast completes a memorable experience.

Host: Geri Lilley
Rooms: 4 (2PB; 2SB) $68-98
Suites: 2 (PB)
Full Breakfast
Credit Cards: None
Notes: 2, 5, 8, 9, 10, 12

Schmidt Barn

Route 2, Box 112A3, 78624
(210) 997-5612 — Ask for Schmidt Barn

The Schmidt Barn is located one and one-half miles outside historic Fredericksburg. This 130-year-old limestone structure has been turned into a charming guest house with loft bedroom, living room, bath, and kitchen. The hosts live next door. German-style breakfast is left in the guest house for you. The house has been featured in national magazines and is decorated with antiques.

Hosts: Dr. Charles and Loretta Schmidt
Guest House: 1 (PB) $70-100
Continental Breakfast
Credit Cards: A, B
Notes: 2, 6, 7, 8, 9, 10

GALVESTON

The Gilded Thistle

1805 Broadway, 77550
(409) 763-0894; (800) 654-9380

An oasis on Galveston Island. Enter a wonderland of Victorian collectibles, superb service, and bountiful amenities. Take tea with Blanche, Black Bart, and the other bears, and see their pretties. Be pampered by hosts who endeavor to share a feeling of history and that special sense of graciousness of times gone by. Featured in the *New York Times* and *Country Inns, Southern Living, House Beautiful* and other magazines. Call or write for brochure. Teddy bears are free.

Host: Helen Hanemann
Rooms: 3 (1PB: 2SB) $135-145
Full Breakfast
Credit Cards: A, B
Notes: 2, 3, 4, 5, 7, 8, 9, 10

The Victorian Bed and Breakfast Inn

511 17th Street, 77550
(409) 762-3235

Galveston's first bed and breakfast, this 1899 home exudes Victorian romantic charm. A wraparound veranda, bird's eye maple floors, tiled fireplaces, and unique built-in benches welcome guests once they pass by 90-year-old palm and magnolia trees. Extremely large bedrooms offer guests king beds, porches, antiques, and warm, personal touches. Located in a historic district, the home is less than one mile from the gulf beach and an easy walk to museums, shopping, restaurants, and theaters.

Hosts: Janice and Bob Hellbusch
Rooms: 6 (2PB; 4SB) $55-125
Continental Breakfast
Credit Cards: A, B, C
Notes: 2, 5, 8, 9, 10, 12

NOTES: Credit cards accepted: A Master Card; B Visa; C American Express; D Discover Card; E Diners Club; F Other; 2 Personal checks accepted; 3 Lunch available; 4 Dinner available; 5 Open all

GRANBURY

Dabney House
Bed and Breakfast

106 South Jones, 76048
(817) 579-1260; evenings (817) 823-6867

Craftsman style one story home built in
1907 by local banker. Furnished with
antiques, hard wood floors and original
woodwork. Long term business rates
available per request and romantic dinner by reservation only. We offer custom special occasion baskets in room
upon arrival by advance order only.
Book whole house for family occasions, staff retreats or Bible retreats at
discount rate.

Hosts: John and Gwen Hurley
Rooms: 4 (2PB; 2SB) $60-90
Full Breakfast
Credit Cards: A, B, C
Notes: 2, 5, 9, 10, 12

Dabney House

Nutt House Hotel and
Bed and Breakfast Inn

Town Square, 76048
(817) 573-5612

The Nutt House Hotel, located on the
square, was built in 1893. Furnishings
are from the 1880s with air conditioning and ceiling fans. The inn, a log
cabin, is located one block from the
square on a beautiful wooded lot on the
water. The buffet-style restaurant specializes in country cooking, serving
specialties of chicken and dumplings,
bite-size cornbread, and homemade
cobblers. After the ringing of the dinner
bell, period-costumed young ladies are
there to serve you dinner.

Host: Sylvia "Sam" Overpeck
Rooms: 17 (8PB; 9SB) $39-75
Full or Continental Breakfast
Credit Cards: A, B, C
Notes: 3, 4, 5, 7, 9, 10

HOUSTON

Robin's Nest

4104 Greeley, 77006
(713) 528-5821; (800) 622-8343

This white two-story Victorian, circa
1894, started life as the main house for
a dairy farm. The Holsteins and Jerseys
are gone now, and somewhat astound-
ing, it stands today in a vibrant, urban
neighborhood nestled between downtown, universities, the theater district,
and the Texas Medical Center. We have
casual eateries as well as quality restaurants. Interesting attractions are too
numerous to list. We also conduct indi-

year; 6 Pets welcome; 7 Children welcome; 8 Tennis nearby; 9 Swimming nearby; 10 Golf nearby; 11
Skiing nearby; 12 May be booked through travel agent

vidualized tours for our registered guests.

Host: Robin Smith
Rooms: 2 (1PB; 1SB) $45-75
Full Breakfast
Credit Cards: A,B
Notes: 2, 5, 8, 9, 10, 12

JEFFERSON

McKay House Bed and Breakfast Inn

306 East Delta, 75657
(903) 665-7322; (214) 348-1929

Jefferson is a town where one can relax, rather than get tired. The McKay House, an 1851 Greek Revival cottage, features a pillared front porch and many fireplaces, offering genuine hospitality in a Christian atmosphere. Heart-of-pine floors, 14-foot ceilings, and documented wallpapers complement antique furnishings. Guests enjoy a full "gentleman's" breakfast. Victorian nightshirts and gowns await pampered guests in each bed chamber.

Hosts: Alma Ann Parker
Rooms: 4 plus 3 suites (PB) $75-125
Full Breakfast
Credit Cards: A, B
Notes: 2, 5, 10, 12

NEW BRAUNFELS

Historic Danville School and Waldrip House

1620 Hueco Springs Loop, 78132
(210) 625-8372

A restored pioneer German home and original schoolhouse on 43 acres just five minutes from historic Gruene and New Braunfels, museums, river and water park activities, bicycling and horse stables. Watch a variety of wildlife or play croquet. Maggy Waldrip and son Darrell Waldrip will create a "downhome" welcome. Eight private rooms and private baths (one wheelchair accessible and 2 jacuzzis) sleep 14-25 people and includes a full breakfast. Meeting rooms also available and seat 45-50 people. Plan romantic getaways, weddings, honeymoons, reunions, conferences, etc. Children are welcome.

Hosts: Margaret Kuebler-Waldrip and son, Darrel Waldrip
Rooms: 8 (PB) $79-105
Full Breakfast
Credit Cards: A, B, C, D
Notes: 2, 5, 7, 8, 9, 10

SAN ANTONIO

Beckman Inn and Carriage House

222 E. Guenther Street, 78024
(210) 229-1449

Charming Victorian inn located in the heart of San Antonio and the King William Historic District. The beautiful wrap-around porch warmly welcomes guests to the cozy home. Guestrooms are colorfully decorated featuring antique Victorian queen size beds, with private baths. The Inn's location is perfect. Guests can stroll leisurely on the scenic river walk or ride the trolley to enjoy all the festivities...the best of

San Antonio.

Hosts: Betty Jo and Don Schwartz
Rooms: 4 (PB) $80-120 1 Carriage House
Full Gourmet Continental Breakfast
Credit Cards: A, B
Notes: 2, 5

The Belle of Monte Vista

505 Belknap Place, 78212
(210) 732-4006

J. Riely Gordon designed this 1890
Queen Anne Victorian home located
conveniently in this famous Monte Vista
historic district, one mile from downtown San Antonio. The house has eight
fireplaces, stained-glass windows,
hand-carved oak interior, and Victorian
furnishings. Near zoo, churches, river
walk, El Mercardo, arts, and universities. Transportation to and from airport,
bus, and train station upon request. Easy
access from all major highways.

Hosts: Mary Lou and Jim Davis
Rooms: 8 (4PB; 4SB) $60
Full Breakfast
Credit Cards: None
Notes: 2, 5, 7, 8, 9, 10

UVALDE

Casa de Leona

1149 Pearsall, P. O. Box 1829, 78802
(512) 278-8550

The Spanish hacienda sits in the center
of 17 acres along the Leona River on the
old Fort Inge historic site. Enjoy flow-
ing fountains, sun deck, gazebo on the
river, hiking trails, bird watching, access to markets in Mexico, art and antique collections, and unique shopping
boutiques. Four rooms plus guest cottage. Dinner by reservation.

Hosts: Carolyn and Ben Durr
Rooms: 4 (3PB; 1SB) $55-76
Cottage: 1 (PB)
Full or Continental Breakfast
Credit Cards: A, B, C
Notes: 2, 4, 5, 12

Beckman Inn and Carriage House

Utah

SAINT GEORGE

Seven Wives Inn

217 North 100 West, 84770
(801) 628-3737; (800) 484-1048 code 0165

The inn consists of two adjacent pioneer adobe homes with massive hand-grained moldings framing windows and doors. Bedrooms are furnished with period antiques and handmade quilts. Some rooms have fireplaces; two have a whirlpool tub. Swimming pool on premises.

Hosts: Donna and Jay Curtis; Alison and Jon Bowcutt
Rooms: 13 (PB) $50-70, suites $100
Full Breakfast
Credit Cards: A, B, C, E
Notes: 2, 5, 7, 8, 9, 10, 11, 12

Vermont

ALBURG

Thomas Mott Homestead Bed and Breakfast

Blue Rock Road on Lake Champlain
Route 2, Box 149-B, 05440
(802) 796-3736; (800) 348-0843

Hosted by a criminology/American history major who enjoys gourmet cooking, this completely restored 1838 farmhouse has a guest living room with TV and fireplace overlooking the lake; game room with bumper pool and darts; quilt decor. Full view of Mt. Mansfield and Jay Peak. One hour to Montreal/Burlington; one and one-half hour to Lake Placid, New York, and Stowe. Lake activities winter and summer. Amenities include Ben and Jerry's ice cream, lawn games, and horseshoes.

Host: Patrick J. Schallert, Sr., M.A., B.A.
Rooms: 4 (PB) $50-70
Full Breakfast
Credit Cards: A, B, D
Notes: 2, 4 (gourmet dinners w/advance notice), 5, 7 (over 6), 9, 10, 11, 12

ARLINGTON

Arlington Inn

Historic Rt. 7A, 05250
(802) 375-6532; (800) 443-9442

Step back into time to the bygone days of the Victorian era. Enjoy our antique-filled guest rooms. Sample our award-winning cuisine by romantic candle-light. Spend a leisurely evening in front of a roaring fire or rocking away the hours on the front porch. Simply enjoy yourself.

Hosts: Sandee and Bob Ellis
Rooms: 13 (PB) $75-160
Expanded Continental Breakfast
Credit Cards: A, B, C, D, E
Notes: 2, 4, 5, 6, 7, 8, 9, 10, 11, 12

Hill Farm Inn

Rural Route 2, Box 2015, 05250
(802) 375-2269; (800) 882-2545

Hill Farm is one of Vermont's original farmsteads. The property was owned by the Hill family for more than 200 years after they received a land grant from King George III in 1775. It has been an inn since 1905 and still retains much of the character of an old farm vacation inn with hearty home cooking, home-grown vegetables, and rooms decorated to capture the spirit and charm of New England farmhouses. Home-made jam is a complimentary take-home gift. Families welcome.

Hosts: George and Joanne Hardy
Rooms: 13 (8PB; 5SB) $60-95
Full Breakfast
Credit Cards: A, B, C, D
Notes: 2, 4, 5, 6 (limited), 7, 8, 9, 10, 11, 12

Shennandoah Farm

05250
(802) 375-6372

Experience New England in this lovingly restored 1820 Colonial overlooking the Battenkill River. Wonderful "Americana" year-round. Full "farm fresh" breakfast is served daily and is included.

Host: Woody Masterson
Rooms: 5 (1PB; 4SB) $60-75
Credit Cards: 1, 2
Notes: 2, 5, 8, 10, 11, 12

BENNINGTON

Bennington Hus B&B

208 Washington Ave., 05201
(802) 447-7972

Rates are $50 for double or $35 for singles. Comfortable fifty-year-old Colonial B&B with fireplace. Scandinavian hospitality, quiet street in historic area. No smoking.

Host: Lias Sparta
Rooms: 4 (2PB; 2SB) $50

Full Breakfast
Credit Cards: None
Notes: 2, 5, 7, 8, 9, 10, 11

BRANDON

Rosebelle's Victorian Inn

31 Franklin St., Route 7, 05733
(802) 247-0098

Elegantly restored non-smoking 1830s Victorian Mansard is listed on the National Register of Historic Places. Six spacious rooms, with private and semi-private baths, full gourmet breakfast, afternoon tea and candlelight dining available to our guests. Only minutes to Killington, Pico and Sugarbush downhill and cross country skiing. A true four season inn to enjoy the foliage, winter activities, hiking, biking or visit museums, antique shops or read a good book. Not suggested for children under twelve. Sorry, no pets allowed. Cash preferred, Visa and Mastercard accepted. Ici on parle Francais. Summer and winter packages available.

Hosts: Ginette and Norm Milot
Rooms: 6 (4PB; 2SB) $50-85
Full Breakfast
Credit Cards: A, B
Notes: 4, 5, 7 (over 12), 8, 9, 10, 11

CALAIS

Evergreen's Chalet

HC 32, Box 41, 05648
(802) 223-5156

Charming "Nature Lover's Paradise." Located on 140 private acres. Furnished in colonial Maple. Dining/liv-

---

NOTES: Credit cards accepted: A Master Card; B Visa; C American Express; D Discover Card; E Diners Club; F Other; 2 Personal checks accepted; 3 Lunch available; 4 Dinner available; 5 Open all

ing room, all electric kitchen, 3 bedrooms with posturpedic beds, 2 baths, large deck with grill, private tika, carport. Miles of nature trails provide hours of pleasure, nature pond, hiking, cross country skiing, snowmobiling. Many lakes and ponds nearby. No smoking or pets. Free guided tours available. Rates by day, weekend or weekly. Brochure available.

Hosts: Elizabeth and Wayne Morse
Rooms: 3 (1PB; 2SB) $35.75
Continental Breakfast
Credit Cards: A, B
Notes: 2, 5, 7, 9, 10, 11

CHELSEA

Shire Inn

8 Main Street, P. O. Box 37, 05038
(802) 685-3031; (800) 441-6908

The Shire Inn was built in 1832, and the Federal brick facade is an architectural gem of the period. The inn still operates five of the original fireplaces, four of which are in guest bedrooms. At the inn, guests enjoy cycling, cross-country skiing, and hiking. Nearby they can swim, canoe, fish, hunt antiques, downhill ski, and go sleigh riding. Chelsea is within 30 to 34 miles of Woodstock/ Quechee, Montpelier, or Hanover, New Hampshire, home of Dartmouth College.

Hosts: Jay and Karen Keller
Rooms: 6 (PB) $80-165
Full Breakfast
Credit Cards: A, B
Notes: 2, 4, 5, 7 (over 8), 8, 9, 10, 11

CHESTER

The Hugging Bear Inn and Shoppe

Main Street, 05143
(802) 875-2412

Teddy bears peek out the windows and are tucked in all the corners of this beautiful Victorian house built in 1850. If you love Teddy bears, you'll love the Hugging Bear. There are six guest rooms with private shower baths and a Teddy bear in every bed. Full breakfast and afternoon snack are served.

Hosts: Georgette, Paul, and Diane Thomas
Rooms: 6 (PB) $55-90
Full Breakfast
Credit Cards: A, B, C, D
Notes: 2, 5, 6 (limited), 7, 8, 9, 10, 11

CUTTINGSVILLE

Buckmaster Inn

Lincoln Hill Road, Rural Route 1, Box 118, Shrewsbury, 05738
(802) 492-3485

The Buckmaster Inn (1801) was an early stagecoach stop in Shrewsbury. Standing on a knoll overlooking a picturesque barn scene and rolling hills, it is situated in the Green Mountains. A center hall, grand staircase, and wide-pine floors grace the home, which is decorated with family antiques and crewel handiwork done by your hostess. Extremely large, airy rooms, wood-burning stove, four fireplaces, two large porches.

Hosts: Sam and Grace Husselman

Rooms: 4 (2PB; 2SB) $45-60
Full Breakfast
Credit Cards: None
Notes: 5, 7, 8, 9, 10, 11

Maple Crest Farm

Lincoln Hill, Box 120, 05738
(802) 492-3367

This 27-room 1808 farmhouse has been preserved for five generations and is located in the heart of the Green Mountains in Shrewsbury. It has been a bed and breakfast for 21 years. Ten miles north of Ludlow and ten miles south of Rutland, an area that offers much to visitors. Pico, Killington, and Okemo are nearby for downhill skiing. Cross-country skiing and hiking are offered on the premises.

Hosts: William and Donna Russell
Rooms: 4 (SB) $25-35 per person
Full Breakfast
Credit Cards: None
Notes: 2, 5, 7, 8, 9, 10, 11, 12

DANBY

Silas Griffith Inn

South Main Street, Rural Route 1, Box 66F, 05739
(802) 293-5567

Built by Vermont's first millionaire, this Victorian inn was built in 1891 in the heart of the Green Mountains, with spectacular mountain views. It features 17 delightful, antique-furnished rooms and a fireplace in the living and dining room. Hiking, skiing, antiquing nearby. Come and enjoy our elegant meals and New England hospitality.

Hosts: Paul and Lois Dansereau
Rooms: 17 (11PB; 6SB) $69-86
Full Breakfast
Credit Cards: A, B, C
Notes: 2, 4, 5, 7, 9, 10, 11, 12

Derby Village Inn

DERBY LINE

Derby Village Inn

46 Main St., 05830
(802) 873-3604

Enjoy this charming old Victorian mansion situated in the quiet village of Derby Line, within walking distance of the Canadian border and the world's only international library and opera house. The nearby countryside offers year-round recreation—downhill and cross country skiing, water sports, cycling, fishing, hiking, golf, snowmobiling, sleigh rides, antiquing and most of all peace and tranquility. We are a non-smoking facility.

Hosts: Tom and Phyllis Moreau
Rooms: 8 (5PB; 3SB) $50-60
Full Breakfast
Credit Cards: A, B, D
Notes: None

NOTES: Credit cards accepted: A Master Card; B Visa; C American Express; D Discover Card; E Diners Club; F Other; 2 Personal checks accepted; 3 Lunch available; 4 Dinner available; 5 Open all

ENOSBURG FALLS

Berkson Farms

RR1, Box 850, 05450
(802) 933-2522

Relax in our 150-year-old farmhouse on a working dairy farm. Located on 600 acres of meadowland surrounded by a variety of animals, nature and warm hospitality. Picnic, hike, bike in the warmer months; cross country ski and sled in the winter. Enjoy our hearty homestyle meals using our maple syrup and farm fresh dairy products. Close to Canada and major ski areas. Children and pets welcome. Reservations suggested.

Hosts: Susan and Terry Spoonire
Rooms: 4 (1PB; 3SB) $50-60
Full Breakfast
Credit Cards: None
Notes: 2, 3, 4, 5, 6, 7, 9, 10, 11

FAIR HAVEN

Maplewood Inn

Route 22A South, 05743
(802) 265-8039; (800) 253-7729

Exquisite 1843 Greek Revival on the Vermont Register of Historic Places and a romantic, antique-filled haven! Keeping room with fireplace, gathering room with books and games, parlor with complimentary cordials. Elegant rooms and suites are air conditioned, have color cable TV, radios and in-room phone available. Near everything! Bikes, canoe and antique shop on-site. Lakes Region. Pet boarding arranged. A true four-season experi-

ence! Guidebook and Mobil recommended.

Hosts: Doug and Cindy Baird
Rooms: 5 (PB) $70-100
Continental Buffet Breakfast
Credit Cards: A, B, D
Notes: 2, 5, 7 (over 5), 8, 9, 10, 11, 12

FAIRLEE

Rutledge Inn and Cottages

Lake Morey Drive, 05045
(802) 333-9722

An outstanding lakeside resort offers genuine hospitality and excellent New England dining. It is located in the lovely Connecticut Valley on a spring-fed lake with a sandy beach and 1,000 feet of waterfront. No phones or TV! We have all kinds of activities for adults and young people that you can take part in, or just plain ignore. A place to step back in time to enjoy summer the way it was meant to be enjoyed.

Hosts: Bob and Nancy Stone
Rooms: 38 (33PB; 5SB) $75-160
Continental or Full Breakfast
Credit Cards: None
Open June to Labor Day
Notes: 2, 3, 4, 7, 8, 9, 10, 12

Silver Maple Lodge and Cottages

Rural Route 1, Box 8, 05045
(802) 333-4326; (800) 666-1946

A historic bed and breakfast country inn is located in a four-season recreational area. Enjoy canoeing, fishing, golf, tennis, and skiing within a few miles of the lodge. Visit nearby flea markets and country auctions. Choose a newly renovated room in our antique farmhouse or a handsome, pine-paneled cottage room. Many fine restaurants are nearby. Dartmouth College is 17 miles away. Also offered are hot air balloon packages, inn-to-inn bicycling, canoeing, and walking tours. Brochure available.

Hosts: Scott and Sharon Wright
Rooms: 14 (12PB; 2SB) $42-64
Continental Breakfast
Credit Cards: A, B, C, D
Notes: 2, 5, 7, 8, 9, 10, 11, 12

GREENSBORO

Highland Lodge

Caspian Lake, 05841
(802) 533-2647

Secluded 1860s inn on Caspian Lake set in Vermont's most rural region. Spectacular lake and mountain views. Private beach with rowboats, paddleboats and canoes. Tennis, golfing, hiking and biking from our doorstep. During summer, a free play program for guests' kids 4 to 9. Country gourmet dining and a friendly staff. During winter, lots of snow and 40 miles of groomed nordic trails for all levels. Surrounded by the peace and beauty of nature. Children always welcome. A rare find.

Hosts: David and Wilhelmina Smith
Rooms: 11 rooms and 11 cottages (All PB) $140-185
Full Breakfast and Dinner Included
Credit Cards: A, B
Notes: 2, 3, 4, 7, 8, 9, 10, 11, 12

LOWER WATERFORD

Rabbit Hill Inn

Pucker Street and Route 18, 05848
(802) 748-5168; (800) 76-BUNNY

Full of whimsical and charming surprises, this Federal-period inn, established in 1795, has been lavished with love and attention. Many guest rooms have fireplaces and canopied beds. Chamber music, candlelit gourmet dining, and turn-down service make this an enchanting and romantic hideaway in a tiny, restored village overlooking the mountains. Award-winning, nationally acclaimed inn. Our service is inspired by Philippians 2:7.

Hosts: John and Maureen Magee
Rooms: 18 (PB) $78-159
Full Breakfast
Credit Cards: A, B
Closed first two weeks of November and all of April
Notes: 2, 4, 8, 9, 10, 11, 12

MIDDLEBURY

A Point of View

Rural Delivery 3, Box 2675, 05753
(802) 388-7205

Only three and one-half miles from the village, this country bed and breakfast has a view of the Green Mountains (hence its name) in a quiet setting in an exclusive neighborhood perfect for walking. Excellent beds in comfortable rooms with access to living room with large TV; game room with regulation pool table; bike. The atmosphere is warm and friendly; each guest is special.

NOTES: Credit cards accepted: A Master Card; B Visa; C American Express; D Discover Card; E Diners Club; F Other; 2 Personal checks accepted; 3 Lunch available; 4 Dinner available; 5 Open all

Host: Marie Highter
Rooms: 2 (SB) $40-50
Full Breakfast
Credit Cards: None
Notes: 2, 5, 7 (by arrangement), 8, 9, 10, 11

MORETOWN

Camel's Hump View

Box 720, 05660
(802) 496-3614

Camel's Hump View is an 1831 farmhouse complete with white-faced Hereford cows, chickens, and Lassie, a sheltie dog. The inn accommodates sixteen guests. You can sleep in an antique rope bed with handmade quilts and braided rugs. Meals prepared with fruits and vegetables from our garden to give you country cooking at its best. Skiing, hiking, biking, golf, canoeing or horseback riding either on premises or nearby.

Hosts: Jerry and Wilma Maynard
Rooms: 8 (1PB; 7SB) $25-30
Full Breakfast
Credit Cards: F
Notes: 2, 4, 5, 7, 8, 9, 10, 11

NORTH TROY

The 1893 House
Bed and Breakfast

30A Highland Ave, Rt. 105, 05859
(802) 988-9614

Come visit us in our 1893 Victorian home in North Troy, Vermont, a quaint valley town surrounded by beautiful mountains. We are eight miles from Jay Peak, and one and one-half miles

from Montreal. Lots of hiking trails, biking routes, skiing, antiquing or just relaxing in the quiet country.

Hosts: Rick and Pat Shover
Rooms: 3 (1PB; 2SB) $50
Full Breakfast
Credit Cards: None
Notes: 2, 5, 7, 9, 11

PITTSFIELD

Swiss Farm Lodge

P.O. Box 630, Rt. 100 North, 05762
(802) 746-8341

Working Hereford beef farm. Enjoy the casual, family-type atmosphere in our living room with fireplace and TV or in the game room. Home cooked meals and baking served family style. Our own maple syrup, jams and jellies. Walk in cooler available for guests' use. Cross country trails on-site. B&B available all year. M.A.P. November to April only. Mountain bike trails close by. Owned and operated by the same family for 45 years. Lower rates for children in same room as parents.

Rooms: 17 (14PB; 3SB) $40-50
Full Breakfast
Notes: 2, 5, 7, 8, 9, 10, 11

RANDOLPH

Placidia Farm
Bed and Breakfast

R.D. 1, Box 275, 05060
(802) 728-9883

Beautiful log home on 81 tranquil acres

---

year; 6 Pets welcome; 7 Children welcome; 8 Tennis nearby; 9 Swimming nearby; 10 Golf nearby; 11 Skiing nearby; 12 May be booked through travel agent

with brook, pond, hiking, cross country skiing on property. Four season sports nearby. Private apartment includes bedroom, living room, equipped kitchen, bath, private entrance and deck. Comfortable country furnishings. Linens provided. Hearty breakfast.

Host: Viola Frost-Laitinen
Rooms: 1 apartment (PB) $75-85
Full Breakfast
Notes: 2, 5, 7, 8, 9, 10, 11

SAINT JOHNSBURY, EAST

Echo Lodge Farm Inn
P.O. Box 77, 05838
(802) 748-4750; FAX (802) 748-1640

A charming colonial farmhouse, settled in 1793 with six bedrooms and private baths. Afternoon teas, old books and magazines, classic films on TV/VCR. Convenient to summer and winter activities. Recommended by National Geographic Traveler. No smoking, pets, or small children. On route 2, five miles east of St. Johnsbury. On state historical society list.

Hosts: Fred and Dorothy Herman
Rooms: 6 (5PB; 1SB) $47-67
Full Breakfast
Credit Cards: A, B, E
Notes: 2 (three weeks in advance), 5, 7 (over 10), 9, 10, 11

STOWE

Inn at the Brass Lantern
717 Maple Street, 05672
(802) 253-2229; (800) 729-2980

This traditional Vermont bed and break-
fast country inn in the heart of Stowe is an award-winning restoration of an 1810 farmhouse and carriage barn overlooking Mt. Mansfield, Vermont's most prominent mountain. The inn features period antiques, quilts, and planked floors. The entire inn is air conditioned. Most rooms have views, and some have fireplaces. Special packages include honeymoon, skiing, golf, sleigh and surrey rides, and more. No smoking.

Host: Andy Aldrich
Rooms: 9 (PB) $65-120
Full Breakfast
Credit Cards: A, B, C
Notes: 2, 5, 8, 9, 10, 11, 12

The Siebeness Inn
3681 Mountain Rd., 05672
(800) 426-9001; (802) 253-8942

A warm welcome awaits you at our charming country inn nestled in the foothills of Mt. Mansfield. Romantic rooms have country antiques, private baths, air conditioning. Awake to the aroma of freshly baked muffins, which accompany your hearty New England breakfast. Relax in our outdoor hot tub in winter, or our pool with mountain views in summer. Fireplace in lounge. Bike, walk, or cross country ski from inn on recreation path. Near ski slopes. Honeymoon, golf and ski packages.

Hosts: Sue and Nils Anderson
Rooms: 11 (PB) $60-100
Full Breakfast
Credit Cards: A, B, C, D, E
Notes: 2, 4 (winter), 5, 7, 8, 9, 10, 11, 12

NOTES: Credit cards accepted: A Master Card; B Visa; C American Express; D Discover Card; E Diners Club; F Other; 2 Personal checks accepted; 3 Lunch available; 4 Dinner available; 5 Open all

The Siebeness Inn

Ski Inn

Route 108, 05672
(802) 253-4050

Back in the 1940s, Larry and Harriet Heyer, the only original owners left in Stowe, designed their ski lodge along New England architectural lines. The result is a lovely, white Vermont country inn with fieldstone fireplace on a sloping hillside in a setting of green hemlocks and fir trees. In appearance, it is a traditional Old New England inn, but in comfort it is modern. Located back from the highway among the evergreens, this is a quiet, restful place to relax. Flat hiking, trout stream, cookouts, cross-country ski trails, close to downhill ski area.

Host: Harriet Heyer
Rooms: 10 (5PB; 5SB) $40-50
Continental Breakfast; Full Breakfast and Dinner in ski season
Credit Cards: None
Notes: 2, 4 (in winter), 5, 6 (by arrangement), 7, 8, 9, 10, 11

Timberhölm Inn

452 Cottage Club Road, 05672
(802) 253-7603; (800) 753-7603

This delightful country inn in a quiet, wooded setting serves afternoon tea and cookies in the summer and après ski soup in the winter. We have ten individually decorated rooms with quilts and antiques and a spacious, sunny great room with a large fieldstone fireplace. Game room with shuffleboard; deck overlooking the Worchester Mountains; outdoor hot tub; cable TV.

Hosts: The Hildebrand family
Rooms: 10 (PB) $60-100
Full Breakfast
Credit Cards: A, B
Notes: 2, 5, 7, 8, 9, 10, 11, 12

WAITSFIELD

Mad River Barn

Route 17, 05673
(802) 496-3310

This classic Vermont lodge has spacious rooms, some with TVs and kitchenettes. There are three meeting rooms on the premises. Dinner is served by reservation. We are near skiing, hiking, and biking and have an outdoor pool, white perennial garden, and grand stone fireplace in the pub.

Host: Betsy Pratt
Rooms: 15 (PB) $24-48 per person
Full Breakfast
Credit Cards: A, B, C
Notes: 2, 4, 5, 7, 8, 9, 10, 11, 12

Mountain View Inn

Rural Free Delivery Box 69, Route 17, 05673
(802) 496-2426

The Mountain View Inn is an old farmhouse, circa 1826, that was made into a lodge in 1948 to accommodate skiers at nearby Mad River Glen. Today it is a country inn with seven rooms. Meals are served family style around the antique harvest table where good fellow-

---

year; 6 Pets welcome; 7 Children welcome; 8 Tennis nearby; 9 Swimming nearby; 10 Golf nearby; 11 Skiing nearby; 12 May be booked through travel agent

ship prevails. Sip mulled cider around a crackling fire in our living room when the weather turns chilly.

Hosts: Fred and Suzy Spencer
Rooms: 7 (PB) $45-65 per person
Full Breakfast
Credit Cards: None
Notes: 2, 4, 5, 7, 8, 9, 10, 11, 12

Newtons' 1824 House Inn

Route 100, Box 159, 05673
(802) 496-7555

Enjoy relaxed elegance in one of six beautiful guest rooms at this quintessential farmhouse on 52 acres. The inn features antiques, chandeliers, fireplaces, and classical music. Breakfast by the fire includes such whimsical gourmet delights as soufflés, crepes, blueberry buttermilk pancakes, and freshly squeezed orange juice. Cross-country skiing and swimming hole are nearby. AAA Three-diamond rated.

Hosts: Nick and Joyce Newton
Rooms: 6 (PB) $75-115
Full Breakfast
Credit Cards: A, B, C
Notes: 2, 5, 8, 9, 10, 11, 12

WARREN

Beaver Pond Farm Inn

Golf Course Road, RD Box 306, 05674
(802) 583-2861

Beaver Pond Farm Inn, a small, gracious country inn near the Sugarbush ski area, is located 100 yards from the first tee of the Sugarbush Golf Course, transformed into 40 kilometers of cross-country ski trails in the winter. *Bed & Breakfast in New England* calls it "The best of the best." Rooms have down comforters and beautiful views. Hearty breakfasts are served, and snacks are enjoyed by the fireplace. Continental dinners are offered three times a week during the winter. Hiking, biking, soaring, and fishing nearby. Ski and golf packages are available.

Hosts: Bob and Betty Hansen
Rooms: 6 (4PB; 2SB) $64-90
Full Breakfast
Credit Cards: A, B, C
Notes: 2, 4, 7 (over 5), 8, 9, 10, 11, 12

WATERBURY

Grünberg Haus Bed and Breakfast

Route 100 South, Rural Route 2, Box 1595, 05676
(802) 244-7726; Reservations —(800) 800-7760

Spontaneous, personal attention in a hand-built Austrian mountain chalet with a huge fieldstone fireplace, sauna, Jacuzzi, grand piano, trails, tennis court, and imaginative full breakfasts. Cozy Old World chalet guest rooms feature balconies and antiques. Innkeeper and professional musician Chris plays the piano regularly. Innkeeper Mark takes care of the chickens, cats, and guineas. "Like visiting a pal," *Hudson Dispatch*. "Quiet, romantic," *Vermont* magazine. Central to Stowe, Waitsfield, Sugarbush, Burlington, Montpelier. Home of Ben & Jerry's! Adventure packages.

Hosts: Christopher Sellers and Mark Frohman
Rooms: 10 (5PB; 5SB) $55-90
Full Breakfast
Credit Cards: A, B, C, D, F
Notes: 2, 4 (for 10+), 5, 7, 8, 9, 10, 11, 12

NOTES: Credit cards accepted: A Master Card; B Visa; C American Express; D Discover Card; E Diners Club; F Other; 2 Personal checks accepted; 3 Lunch available; 4 Dinner available; 5 Open all

Inn at Blush Hill

Blush Hill Road, Rural Route 1, Box 1266,
05676
(802) 244-7529; (800) 736-7522

This Cape Cod bed and breakfast, circa
1790, sits on five acres with spectacular
mountain views. The inn has a large
common room, library, antiques, and
four fireplaces, one in a guest room.
Enjoy a breakfast of Vermont products
at a ten-foot farmhand's table in front of
a bay window overlooking the Worcester Mountains. Afternoon refreshments
are served. We are adjacent to Ben and
Jerry's ice cream factory, and skiing at
Stowe and Sugarbush are only minutes
away.

Hosts: Gary and Pamela Gosselin
Rooms: 6 (4PB; 2SB) $55-110 seasonal
Full Breakfast
Credit Cards: A, B, C, D, F
Notes: 2, 5, 8, 9, 10, 11, 12

WEST DOVER

Deerhill Inn and Restaurant

Box 136 Valleyview Rd., 05356-0136
(802) 464-3100; (800) 626-5624

A gracious English country house with
mountain views, candlelight dining,
superb cuisine, spacious sitting rooms,
fine English and American antiques,
afternoon tea, licensed lounge, private
baths, some rooms with canopy beds,
lovely grounds, swimming pool, tennis
court. Located in Mount Snow area.
Alpine and Nordic skiing, mountain
biking, two champion golf courses, golf
school, walking, fishing, boating,
antiquing, shopping, craft fairs,

Marlboro Music Festival, and just plain
relaxing.

Hosts: Robert and Joan Ritchiz
Rooms: 17 (15PB; 2SB) $99-119
Full Breakfast
Credit Cards: A, B, C, D, E
Notes: 2, 4, 7 (over 8), 8, 9, 10, 11, 12

WESTON

The Inn at Weston

P.O. Box 56, 05161
(802) 824-5804

A full service country inn nestled in a
picture book Vermont village in the
heart of the Green Mountains. Enjoy
gourmet dining in an award-winning
dining room. A pleasant walk to lovely
shops, galleries and the Weston Playhouse, the oldest professional summer
theater in Vermont. The Weston Priory,
a Benedictine Monastery, is just north
of the village. Walking trails abound.
Winter brings excellent alpine and
nordic skiing.

Hosts: Robert and Jeanne Wilder
Rooms: 19 (12PB; 2SB) $66-108
Full Breakfast
Credit Cards: A, B, D
Notes: 2, 4, 5, 7, 8, 9, 10, 11

The Inn at Weston

The Wilder Homestead Inn

Lawrence Hill Road, Rural Route 1, Box 106D, 05161
(802) 824-8172

Built in 1827 with Rumford fireplaces and original Moses Eaton stenciling, the inn has been carefully restored by us and has quiet surroundings and antique furnishings. Walk to village shops, museums, summer theater. Nearby are Weston Priory, fine restaurants, skiing. Weston is a village that takes you back in time. Craft Shoppe on premises. No smoking.

Hosts: Peggy and Roy Varner
Rooms: 7 (5PB; 2SB) $60-95
Full Breakfast
Credit Cards: A, B (deposit only)
Notes: 2, 7 (over 6), 8, 9, 10, 11

Virginia

ABINGDON

Maplewood Farm Bed and Breakfast

Route 7, Box 461, 24210
(703) 628-2640

Maplewood's home, built circa 1880, is a comfortable and beautifully reno-vated farmhouse, surrounded by maples. Bountiful breakfasts are served in the Garden Room or on an outside deck overlooking the property. The 66-acre farm has wooded land with hiking trails and a lake stocked for bass fishing. Thousands of daffodils bloom on the hill in April. Horses graze contentedly in the pasture. Overnight stabling for horses is available.

Host: Doris Placak
Rooms: 4 (PB) $73.15
Full Breakfast
Credit Cards: None
Notes: 2, 3, 4, 5, 10, 12

ALEXANDRIA--DISTRICT OF COLUMBIA

Morrison House

116 South Alfred Street, 22314
(703) 838-8000

Awarded 1990 "Best Inn of the Year," Morrison House is an 18th-century-style manor house in historic Old Town Alexandria, just minutes from Wash-ington, D.C. Elegant Federal-period reproductions, including mahogany four-poster beds, marble baths, crystal chandeliers, and decorative fireplaces.

Hosts: Robert and Rosemary Morrison
Rooms: 45 (PB) $135-400
Full Breakfast Available
Credit Cards: A, B, C, D
Notes: 2, 3, 4, 5, 9, 10

AMHERST

Dulwich Manor Bed and Breakfast

Rte. 5, Box 173A, 24021
(804) 946-7207

Elegant English-style manor house in

---

year; 6 Pets welcome; 7 Children welcome: 8 Tennis nearby: 9 Swimming nearby; 10 Golf nearby; 11 Skiing nearby; 12 May be booked through travel agent

beautiful countryside setting. Blue Ridge Mountains views. Large distinguished bed chambers with fireplaces or whirlpool. Luxurious outdoor hot tub in Victorian gazebo. Full country breakfasts and arrival refreshments are served. Stroll the expansive grounds or relax on the columned veranda, in our hammock or swing under a three hundred-year-old oak. Visit historic Monticello or Appomattox. Hike Crabtree Fall. Horseback riding, golf, skiing.

Hosts: Bob and Judy Reilly
Rooms: 6 (4PB; 2SB) $65-85
Full Breakfast
Credit Cards: None
Notes: 2, 5, 7, 8, 10, 11, 12

ARLINGTON

Memory House

6406 North Washington Boulevard, 22205
(703) 534-4607

In a prime location is this charming, ornate, restored 1899 Victorian with period antiques, wall stenciling, prize-winning handicrafts, and collectibles. The subway, one block away, quickly takes you to the mall area of Washington, D.C. By car, it is ten minutes to the White House, museums, and monuments. Two guest rooms; air conditioning; TV; antique clawfoot tubs. Relax on wicker furniture on the porch or in double parlors. Share in old-fashioned comfort and friendship.

Hosts: John and Marlys McGrath
Rooms: 2 (1PB; 1SB) $70
Expanded Continental Breakfast
Credit Cards: None
Notes: 2, 5, 7, 8, 9, 12

BOSTON

Thistle Hill Bed and Breakfast

Rte. 1, Box 291, 27713
(703) 987-9142

Lovely, spacious rooms, private baths, cottages, great room with balcony and wide inviting decks, A/C and fireplaces. Sunny breakfasts that beg you to indulge. Acres of flowers and trees on a beautiful hillside just east of Skyline Drive and the Blue Ridge Mountains. Enjoy tea in the gazebo, relax in our hot tub or stroll to our little stream. Fine dining by reservation.

Hosts: Charles and Marianne Wilson
Rooms: 4 (PB) $95-135
Full Breakfast
Credit Cards: A, B, C, D
Notes: 2, 3, 4, 5, 7, 12

CASTLETON

Blue Knoll Farm Bed and Breakfast

Rt. 1, Box 141, 22716
(703) 937-5234

Blue Knoll Farm is a lovingly restored 19th-century farmhouse located 65 miles west of Washington, D.C., and 15 minutes from the renowned 5-star restaurant at the Inn at Little Washington. Surrounded by rolling foothills of the Blue Ridge Mountains, the setting is peaceful and charming. Enjoy a hearty breakfast, then explore Shenandoah National park, local antique shops and vineyards, hike Old Rag or just rock and relax on one of our three lovely porches.

Hosts: Mary and Gil Carlson
Rooms: 4 (PB) $95-125
Full Breakfast
Credit Cards: A, B
Notes: 2, 5

CHARLOTTESVILLE

The Clifton Country Inn

Route 13, Box 26, 22901
(804) 971-1800; FAX (804) 971-7098

Built in the 1800s, this nationally recognized inn was originally owned by Thomas Mann Randolph, an early governor of Virginia. Only five miles from Charlottesville, Clifton is nestled on 48 acres and offer 14 luxurious rooms and suites all having working fireplaces and private baths. Room rates of $138 to $188 per night include both afternoon tea and breakfast.

Hosts: Craig Hartman, Chef and Innkeeper
Rooms: 14 (PB) $138-188
Full Breakfast
Credit Cards: A, B
Notes: 2, 4 (Wednesday thru Sunday), 8

CULPEPER

Fountain Hall

609 South East Street, 22701
(703) 825-8200; (800) 476-2944

Fountain Hall is a charming 1859 Colonial Revival Bed and Breakfast. All of our rooms are tastefully restored and most are furnished with antiques. Three guest rooms have private porches overlooking the grounds. Fireplaces can be found in the common rooms along with books, local literature, board games, music, TV/VCR. Fountain Hall is within walking distance to Amtrak. Charlottesville and Dulles airports are nearby.

Hosts: Steve, Kathi and Leah-Marie Walker
Rooms: 5 (PB) $50-115
Expanded Continental Breakfast
Credit Cards: A, B, C, D
Notes: 2, 5, 7, 8, 9, 10

Fountain Hall

FREDRICKSBURG

La Vista Plantation

4420 Guinea Station Rd., 22408
(703) 898-8444

This Classical revival-style manor house, circa 1838, is situated on ten quiet, country acres and is surrounded by farm fields and mature trees. Stocked pond, six fireplaces, antiques, rich Civil War past, radio, phone, TV, bicycles. Fresh eggs and homemade jams are served for breakfast; air conditioned; close to historic attractions.

Hosts: Edward and Michele Schiesser
Rooms: 1 (PB); 1 suite (PB) $85
Full Breakfast
Credit Cards: A, B
Notes: 2, 5, 7, 9, 10, 12

year; 6 Pets welcome; 7 Children welcome; 8 Tennis nearby; 9 Swimming nearby; 10 Golf nearby; 11 Skiing nearby; 12 May be booked through travel agent

HARRISONBURG

Kingsway Bed and Breakfast

3581 Singers Glen Road, 22801
(703) 867-9696

Enjoy the warm hospitality of your hosts who make your comfort their priority. This private home is in a quiet rural area with a view of the mountains in the beautiful Shenandoah Valley. Carpentry and homemaking skills, many house plants and outdoor flowers, a large lawn and the in-ground pool help to make your stay restful and refreshing. Just 4 and 1/2 miles from downtown; nearby is Skyline Drive, caverns, historic sites, antique shops and flea markets.

Hosts: Chester and Verna Leaman
Rooms: 2 (PB) $45-55
Expanded Continental Breakfast
Credit Cards: D
Notes: 2, 5, 6, 9, 10, 12

HILLSVILLE

Bray's Manor B&B

Route 3, Box 210, 24343
(703) 728-7901

The early 20th-century home is surrounded by a rambling porch perfect for rocking, visiting and relaxing in the cool breezes spring through fall. The parlor and sitting rooms provide TV, VCR and books before a warm fire in season. Croquet and badminton lawn games. Golf, tennis, Blue Ridge Parkway and New River Trail nearby.

Hosts: Dick and Helen Bray

Rooms: 4 (2PB; 2SB) $42.60-53.25
Full Breakfast
Credit Cards: A, B, D
Notes: 2, 5, 7, 8, 10, 12

LEXINGTON

Historic Country Inns of Lexington

11 N. Main Street, 24450
(703) 463-2044

Historic Country Inns of Lexington, 3 beautifully restored homes, Alexander-Withrow house, McCampbell Inn in historic district and Maple Hall 6 miles north of Lexington, offering elegant lodging, intimate dining, fireplaces, fishing, swimming, tennis, historic touring, hiking, shopping, relaxing. Wedding parties, honeymoons, small conferences, family reunions as well as travelers enjoy our facilities. Come visit us and discover Lexington, W&L and VMI.

Hosts: Don Fredenburg, Innkeeper; Peter M. Meredith family, owners
Rooms: 43 (PB) $95-140
Expanded Continental Breakfast
Credit Cards: A, B, D
Notes: 2, 4, 5, 7, 8, 9, 12

LURAY

Shenandoah River Roost

Route 3, Box 566, 22835
(703) 743-3467

Sit on the front porch of this two-story log home and enjoy beautiful views of the mountains and the Shenandoah River. Located three miles west of Luray Caverns, ten miles west of Skyline Drive

---

NOTES: Credit cards accepted: A Master Card; B Visa; C American Express; D Discover Card; E Diners Club; F Other; 2 Personal checks accepted; 3 Lunch available; 4 Dinner available; 5 Open all

and Shenandoah National Park. Swimming, tubing, canoeing, and golf are all nearby. No smoking.

Hosts: Rubin and Gerry McNab
Rooms: 2 (SB) $60
Full Breakfast
Credit Cards: None
Closed November 1-May 1
Notes: 2, 7 (over 12), 9, 10

MEADOWS OF DAN

Spangler Bed and Breakfast

Route 2, Box 108, 24120
(703) 952-2454

The Spangler Bed and Breakfast borders the National Parkway at milepost 180, four miles south of Mabry Mill, elevation 3,000 feet. The farmhouse dates from 1904 with four large bedrooms, living room with piano, dining room, and kitchen. There is an old log cabin for one couple, and a new log cabin for two couples with shared bath. These face a three and one-half-acre lake with fishing, boating, and swimming. No smoking. Groups welcome.

Hosts: Trudy and Harold Spangler
Rooms: 7 (1PB; 6SB) $50-60
Full Breakfast
Credit Cards: None
Notes: 2, 5, 7, 8, 9, 10, 11

NATURAL BRIDGE

Burger's Country Inn

Route 2, Box 564, 24578
(703) 291-2464

Historic inn furnished in antiques and collectibles is on corner of ten wooded acres. Has three baths and four guest rooms, large deck, porches and yard with croquet ready to set up. Special continental breakfast is included. We are one mile from Natural Bridge and near the new golf course, and Lexington is only 12 miles north. Write or call for brochure or reservations.

Host: Frances B. Burger
Rooms: 4 (2PB; 2SB) $45-50
Expanded Continental Breakfast
Credit Cards: None
Notes: 2, 5, 6, 7, 10, 12

NELLYSFORD

Trillium House

P.O. Box 280, 22958
(804) 325-9126

Designed and built in 1983 to meet today's standards while retaining the charm of yesteryear. Outstanding library and sunroom. In the heart of Wintergreen's Devil's Knob Village, a year round 11,000 acre resort, an assortment of activities and recreation available to guests. Mountain country with trees and birds and a golf course can be seen from the breakfast table.

Hosts: Ed and Betty Dinwiddie
Rooms: 12 (PB) $85-150
Full Breakfast
Credit Cards: A, B
Notes: 2, 4 (on Friday and Saturday), 5, 7, 8, 9, 10, 11, 12

year; 6 Pets welcome; 7 Children welcome; 8 Tennis nearby; 9 Swimming nearby; 10 Golf nearby; 11 Skiing nearby; 12 May be booked through travel agent

Upland Manor

Upland Manor

Route 1, Box 375, 22958
(804) 361-1101

Restored historic country manor situated on 14 acres between Charlottesville and the Blue Ridge Parkway. Choose from ten guest rooms or suites, all with private baths and period furnishings. Several rooms offer whirlpool tubs or clawfoot tub with shower. Area attractions include University of Virginia, Blue Ridge Parkway, historic sites, skiing, fishing, hiking, golf, horseback riding. Hearty breakfast each morning.

Hosts: Debbie and Gary
Rooms: 10 (PB) $85-115
Full Breakfast
Credit Cards: A, B
Notes: 2, 5, 7, 8, 9, 10, 11, 12

NEW CHURCH

The Garden and the Sea Inn

Route 710, P. O. Box 275, 23415
(804) 824-0672

This elegant, European-style country inn with French-style gourmet restaurant is near Chincoteague and Assateague Islands. Large, luxurious rooms, beautifully designed; spacious private baths; Victorian detail; stained glass; Oriental rugs; antiques; bay windows. Beautiful beach and wildlife refuge are nearby; afternoon tea; romantic escape package; chamber music dinner-concerts. Three more guest rooms are under renovation.

Hosts: Jack Betz and Victorian Olian
Rooms: 5 (PB) $85-125
Expanded Continental Breakfast
Credit Cards: A, B, C, D, E
Notes: 2, 4, 8, 9, 10, 12

RAPHINE (LEXINGTON-STAUNTON)

Oak Spring Farm and Vineyard

Rt. 1, Box 356, 24472
(703) 377-2398

Located midway between Lexington and Staunton. A circa 1826 plantation house on 40 acres recently restored with modern conveniences. Filled with antiques of the period, family memorabilia and items gathered from 26 years of military service around the world. We offer peace and quiet in rural and beautiful surroundings. We enjoy sharing our home with others and are well acquainted with the many things to do in our area. There are also many lovely churches nearby.

Hosts: Pat and Jim Tichenar
Rooms: 3 (PB) $63-73
Expanded Continental Breakfast
Credit Cards: A, B
Notes: 2 (preferred), 5, 8, 9, 10

NOTES: Credit cards accepted: A Master Card; B Visa; C American Express; D Discover Card; E Diners Club; F Other; 2 Personal checks accepted; 3 Lunch available; 4 Dinner available; 5 Open all

RICHMOND

The Emmanuel Hutzler House

2036 Monument, 23220
(804) 353-6900

Designed in the Italian Renaissance style, the interior of this house has a classical, early Renaissance appearance, with natural mahogany paneling, leaded-glass windows, and coffered ceilings with dropped beams. The large living room where guests can relax has a marble fireplace flanked by mahogany bookcases. Centrally located, the inn is convenient for a mid-week business trip or a lovely setting for a weekend getaway.

Host: Lyn M. Benson
Rooms: 4 (PB) $85-125
Full Breakfast
Credit Cards: A, B, C, D
Notes: 2, 5, 7 (over 12), 12

The William Catlin House

2304 East Broad Street, 23223
(804) 780-3746

Richmond's first and oldest bed and breakfast features antique, canopy poster beds, and working fireplaces. A delicious full breakfast is served in the elegant dining room. Built in 1845, this richly appointed home is in the Church Hill historic district and was featured in *Colonial Homes* and *Southern Living* magazines. Directly across from St. John's Church, where Patrick Henry gave his famous Liberty or Death speech. Just two minutes from I-95 and Route 64.

Hosts: Robert and Josie Martin
Rooms: 5 (3PB; 2SB) $89.50 (price includes all taxes)
Full Breakfast
Credit Cards: A, B, D
Notes: 2, 5, 7, 12

SMITH MOUNTAIN LAKE

The Manor at Taylor's Store

Route 1, Box 533, 24184
(703) 721-3951

This historic 120-acre estate with an elegant manor house provides romantic accommodations in guest suites with fireplaces, antiques, canopied beds, private porches, and use of hot tub, billiards, exercise room, guest kitchen, and many other amenities. A separate three-bedroom, two-bath cottage is ideal for a family. Enjoy six private, spring-fed ponds for swimming, canoeing, fishing, hiking. Full heart-healthy, gourmet breakfast is served in the dining room with panoramic views of the countryside.

Hosts: Lee and Mary Lynn Tucker
Rooms: 6 (4PB; 2SB) $75-100
Full Breakfast
Credit Cards: A, B
Notes: 2, 3, 5, 7, 8, 9, 10, 11, 12

STAFFORD

Renaissance Manor B&B and Art Gallery

2247 Courthouse Road, 22554
(703) 659-8999

---

year; 6 Pets welcome; 7 Children welcome; 8 Tennis nearby; 9 Swimming nearby; 10 Golf nearby; 11 Skiing nearby; 12 May be booked through travel agent

Designed to resemble Mt. Vernon (25 miles away) in architecture, decor and charm. Ten foot ceilings, clawfoot tubs, hardwood floors, canopied king size bed, fireplaces and unlimited hospitality. Formal courtyard and gardens with gazebo and windmill. Local artists' works reasonably priced. Afternoon tea and homemade expanded breakfast. Located on a winding country road four miles off I-95 between Fredricksburg and Washington, D.C. Near Potomac and Rappahannock Rivers, historic battlefields, antique shops, vineyards, and other local attractions.

Rooms: 4 (3PB; 2SB) $55-85
Continental breakfast
Credit Cards: None
Notes: 2, 3 (baskets), 5, 7, 9, 12

STAUNTON

Ashton Country Home

1205 Middlebrook Avenue, 24401
(800) 296-7819

Ashton is a delightful blend of town and country. This 1860 Greek revival home is located on 24 acres, yet one mile from the center of Staunton. There are four comfortable and attractive bedrooms, each with a private bath. A graduate of the New York Restaurant School, Innkeeper Shiela Kennedy greets guests each morning with a hearty breakfast of eggs, bacon, homefries, muffins, fruit, juice and coffee. Innkeeper Stanley Polanski provides the music of Gershwin and Porter on the grand piano.

Hosts: Shiela Kennedy and Stanley Polanski
Rooms: 4 (PB) $65-80
Full Breakfast
Credit Cards: None
Notes: 2, 5, 8, 9, 10

Frederick House

Frederick and New Streets, 24401
(703) 885-4220; (800) 334-5575

An historic townhouse hotel in the European tradition, Frederick House is located downtown in the oldest city in the Shenandoah Valley. It is convenient to shops and restaurants; across the street from Mary Baldwin College; two blocks from Woodrow Wilson's birthplace. All rooms are furnished with TV, phone, air conditioning, and private entrance and private bath.

Hosts: Joe and Evy Harman
Rooms: 14 (PB) $45-95
Full Breakfast
Credit Cards: A, B, C, D, E
Notes: 2, 3, 4, 5, 7, 8, 9, 10, 11, 12

Thornrose House at Gypsy Hill

531 Thornrose Avenue, 24401
(703) 885-7026

Outside, this turn-of-the-century Georgian residence has a wraparound veranda and Greek colonnades. Inside, a fireplace and grand piano create a formal but comfortable atmosphere. Five attractive bedrooms with private baths are on the second floor. Your hosts offer afternoon tea, refreshments, and conversation. Adjacent to a 300-acre park that is great for walking, with tennis, golf, and ponds. Other nearby attractions include the Blue Ridge National Park, natural chimneys, Skyline Drive, Woodrow Wilson's birthplace, and the Museum of American Frontier Culture.

Hosts: Suzanne and Otis Huston, owners
Rooms: 5 (PB) $55-70
Full Breakfast
Credit Cards: None
Notes: 2, 5, 7, 8, 9, 10

STEELE'S TAVERN

The Osceola Mill Country Inn

24476
Fax and Phone (703) 377-6455; reservations (800) 242-7352

The Osceola Mill Country Inn is a unique and gracious, yet unpretentious inn, consisting of a restored grist mill, the miller house, and the mill store (now a honeymoon cottage). Located in the heart of the Shenandoah Valley/ Blue Ridge area, "The Mill" is easily accessible from both the Blue Ridge parkway (M.P. 27) and I-81/64 (exit 205). With at least fourteen colleges and universities and all major attractions of the Shenandoah Valley and Blue Ridge Mountains within an hour or so, the inn is less than three hours from D.C., yet can keep vacationers busy for as long as they like. Members PAII, BBAV, VTC, SVTC, etc. AAA 3-diamond; Mobil 2-star.

Host: Paul Newcomb
Rooms: 12 (PB) $69-139
Full Breakfast
Credit Cards: None

Notes: 2, 4, 5, 7, 9, 10, 11, 12

TANGIER ISLAND

Sunset Inn

Box 156, 23440
(804) 891-2535

Enjoy accommodations one-half block from the beach with a view of the bay. Deck, air conditioning, bike riding, nice restaurants.

Host: Grace Brown
Rooms: 9 (PB) $50 winter; $60 summer
Continental Breakfast
Notes: 2, 5, 7, 9

WASHINGTON

Caledonia Farm Bed and Breakfast

Route 1, Box 2080, Flint Hill, 22627
(703) 675-3693

Enjoy ultimate hospitality, comfort, scenery, and recreation adjacent to Virginia's Shenandoah National Park. This romantic getaway to history and nature includes outstanding full breakfast, fireplaces, air conditioning, hayride, bicycles, lawn games, VCR, and piano. World's finest dining, caves, Skyline Drive, battlefields, stables, antiquing, hiking, and climbing are all nearby. Washington, D.C., is 68 miles away; Washington, Virginia, just four miles. A Virginia historic landmark, the farm is listed on the National Register of Historic Places.

Host: Phil Irwin
Rooms: 3 (1PB; 2SB) $70-100

year; 6 Pets welcome; 7 Children welcome; 8 Tennis nearby; 9 Swimming nearby; 10 Golf nearby; 11 Skiing nearby; 12 May be booked through travel agent

Full Breakfast
Credit Cards: A, B, D
Notes: 2, 3, 4, 5, 7 (over 12), 8, 9, 10, 11, 12

WILLIAMSBURG

Applewood Colonial Bed and Breakfast

605 Richmond Road, 23185
(804) 229-0205; (800) 899-2753

The owner's unique apple collection is evidenced throughout this restored colonial home. Four elegant guest rooms (one suite with fireplace) are conveniently located four short blocks from Colonial Williamsburg and very close to the College of William and Mary campus. Antiques complement the romantic atmosphere. The dining room has a beautiful built-in corner cupboard and a crystal chandelier above the pedestal table where homemade breakfast is served. Afternoon tea; no smoking.

Host: Fred Strout
Rooms: 4 (PB) $70-100
Expanded Continental Breakfast
Credit Cards: A, B
Notes: 2, 5, 7, 8, 10, 12

Fox Grape

701 Monumental Avenue, 23185
(804) 229-6914; (800) 292-3699

Genteel accommodations just five blocks north of Virginia's restored colonial capital. Furnishings include canopied beds, antiques, counted cross stitch, a duck decoy collection and a cup plate collection. Points of interest include Colonial Williamsburg, Cart-ers Grove Plantation, Jamestown, Yorktown and the College of William and Mary.

Hosts: Pat and Bob Orendorff
Rooms: 4 (PB) $78-88
Continental Breakfast
Credit Cards: A, B, D
Notes: 2, 5, 7, 8, 9, 10, 12

Newport House Bed and Breakfast

710 South Henry Street, 23185-4113
(804) 229-1775

A reproduction of an important 1756 home, Newport House has museum-standard period furnishings, including canopy beds. A five-minute walk to historic area. Full breakfast with Colonial recipes; Colonial dancing in the ballroom every Tuesday evening (beginners welcome). The host is a historian/author (including a book on Christ) and former museum director. The hostess is a gardener, beekeeper, 18th-century seamstress, and former nurse. A pet rabbit entertains at breakfast. No smoking.

Hosts: John and Cathy Millar
Rooms: 2 (PB) $90-110
Full Breakfast
Credit Cards: None
Notes: 2, 5, 7, 10, 12

The Travel Tree

P.O. Box 838, 23187
(800) 989-1571

The Travel Tree, Williamsburg's Bed and Breakfast Reservation Service, offers a variety of choices among charming inns and gracious homes of Williamsburg. Rates range from $50-

NOTES: Credit cards accepted: A Master Card; B Visa; C American Express; D Discover Card; E Diners Club; F Other; 2 Personal checks accepted; 3 Lunch available; 4 Dinner available; 5 Open all

125, double occupancy. A brochure is available upon request. Office hours are 6 P.M. to 9 P.M., Monday thru Friday. Please call during those times only. Joann Proper, owner.

WOODSTOCK

Azalea House Bed and Breakfast

551 South Main Street, 22664
(703) 459-3500

A large Victorian house built in 1892 features family antiques and stenciled ceilings. Located in the historic Shenandoah Valley, it is close to Skyline Drive and mountains. Many Civil War and Revolutionary War historic sites are within a short driving distance. This home was used as the parsonage for the church two blocks away for about 75 years.

Hosts: Price and Margaret McDonald
Rooms: 3 (1PB; 2SB) $45-65
Full Breakfast
Credit Cards: A, B, C
Closed January 1-February 1
Notes: 2, 7 (over 5), 9, 10, 11

The Country Fare

402 North Main Street, 22664
(703) 459-4828

A warm, Shenandoah-country welcome awaits you in historic Woodstock. Built in 1772, this charming bed and breakfast was the site of one of the valley's many field hospitals during the Civil War. The house is furnished with Grandmother's antiques and area pieces. Stenciled designs and country collectibles abound in the three guest rooms. Home-baked breads, fruits in season, and some of Grandmother's surprises are breakfast features. A stay will surprise and delight you.

Host: Bette Hallgren
Rooms: 3 (1PB; 2SB) $45-65
Continental Breakfast
Credit Cards: B
Notes: 2, 5

year; 6 Pets welcome; 7 Children welcome; 8 Tennis nearby; 9 Swimming nearby; 10 Golf nearby; 11 Skiing nearby; 12 May be booked through travel agent

Washington

ANACORTES

Albatross
Bed and Breakfast
5708 Kingsway West, 98221
(206) 293-0677

Our 1927 Cape Cod-style home offers
king and queen beds and private baths
in all guest rooms. The quiet, relaxing
living room, patio and deck areas view
waterfront, islands and mountains. You
can walk to Washington Park, Skyline
marina, fine dining and inspirational
beaches. We also offer sight-seeing
cruises aboard a 46-foot sailboat and
have 21-speed cross bikes available.
We are close to the State Ferry Boat
terminal for access to the San Juan
Islands and Victoria, B.C. We are also
close to over 25 churches.

Hosts: Ken and Barbie
Rooms: 4 (PB) $75-85
Full Breakfast
Credit Cards: A, B
Notes: 2, 5, 7, 8, 9, 10, 11, 12

ANDERSON ISLAND

The Inn at Burg's Landing
8808 Villa Beach Road, 98303
(206) 884-9185; (206) 488-8682

Catch the ferry from Steilacoom to stay
at this contemporary log homestead
built in 1987. It offers spectacular views
of Mt. Rainier, Puget Sound, and Cascade Mountains and is south of Tacoma
off I-5. Choose from three guest rooms.
The inn has a private beach. Collect
seashells and agates, swim on two freshwater lakes nearby, tennis or golf. Tour
the island by bicycle or on foot and
watch for sailboats and deer. Hot tub.
Full breakfast. Families welcome. No
smoking.

Hosts: Ken and Annie Burg
Rooms: 3 (2PB; 1SB) $65-90
Full Breakfast
Credit Cards: None
Notes: 2, 5, 7, 8, 9, 10, 11

NOTES: Credit cards accepted: A Master Card; B Visa; C American Express; D Discover Card; E
Diners Club; F Other; 2 Personal checks accepted; 3 Lunch available; 4 Dinner available; 5 Open all

ASHFORD

Mountain Meadows Inn B&B

28912 S.R. 706 E, 98304
(206) 569-2788

Built in 1910, as a mill superintendent's house, Mountain Meadows Inn Bed and Breakfast has made a graceful transition to quiet country elegance. An era of Northwest logging passed by and was seen in vivid detail from the vantage point of spring board and misery whip. Old growth stumps scattered around the house and pond still wear spring board notches as witness to a time when trees, men, and the stories of both were tall. The innkeeper says guests tell him its the best B&B they have ever stayed in.

Host: Chad Darrah
Rooms: 5 (PB) $55-85
Full Breakfast
Credit Cards: A, B
Notes: 2, 5, 7, 9, 10, 11

BELLEVUE

Bellevue Bed and Breakfast

830 100th Avenue, Southeast, 98004
(206) 453-1048

Hilltop, mountain, and city views are enjoyed from our private suite or single rooms, which feature private baths and entrance. We serve a full breakfast, gourmet coffee, and complimentary extras at reasonable rates.

Hosts: Cy and Carol Garnett
Rooms: 2 (PB) $55
Full Breakfast
Credit Cards: A, B
Notes: 2, 3, 4, 5, 7 (over 12), 8, 9, 10, 11

Petersen Bed and Breakfast

10228 Southeast Eighth Street, 98004
(206) 454-9334

We offer two rooms five minutes from Bellevue Square with wonderful shopping and one-half block from the bus line to Seattle. Rooms have down comforters, and we have a hot tub on the deck. Children are welcome. No smoking.

Hosts: Eunice and Carl Peterson
Rooms: 2 (SB) $50-55
Full Breakfast
Credit Cards: None
Notes: 5, 7, 12

BELLINGHAM

Bed and Breakfast Service

P.O. Box 5025, 98226
(206) 733-8642

We are a reservation service with host homes all over the United States. Call and let us set up your next stay at a bed and breakfast. Hosts: Dolores and George.

---

year; 6 Pets welcome; 7 Children welcome; 8 Tennis nearby; 9 Swimming nearby; 10 Golf nearby; 11 Skiing nearby; 12 May be booked through travel agent

Circle F Bed and Breakfast

2399 Mt. Baker Highway, 98226
(206) 733-2509

Circle F Bed and Breakfast is a home away from home for all our guests. The Victorian-style ranch house was built in 1892 and is located on 330 acres of pasture and woodlands. We are a working farm, and you can enjoy hiking trails and visits with the farm animals. A hearty breakfast is served by a friendly farm family who enjoy the company of all visitors.

Host: Guy J. Foster
Rooms: 4 (1PB; 3SB) $45-55
Full Breakfast
Credit Cards: None
Notes: 2, 5, 7

CAMANO ISLAND

Willcox House Bed and Breakfast

1462 Larkspur Lane, 98292
(206) 629-4746

This island retreat, a short drive from Seattle, is designed for relaxing! Enjoy the panoramic view of the Cascade Mountains. Named for the owner's great-aunt, early 1900s illustrator, Jesse Willcox Smith, and decorated with her works. It's a step back in time to a less stressful pace. Leisurely, country breakfast of Willcox House blended coffee, assorted omelettes, Swedish pancakes, muffins and fresh fruits in season, with sun streaming into a cozy breakfast room.

Hosts: Esther Harmon, Madelyn and Joe Braun
Rooms: 4 (1PB; 3SB) $55-60
Full Breakfast
Credit Cards: A, B
Notes: 2, 5, 8, 9, 10, 11

CATHLAMET

The Gallery Bed and Breakfast

Little Cape Horn, 98612-9544
(206) 425-7395; FAX (206) 425-1351

The Gallery is a contemporary elegant country home with sweeping views of the majestic Columbia River ship channel. The large deck has a hot tub for relaxing, watching tug boats, seals, eagles and windsurfers. It is surrounded by tall cedar and fir trees and a tall cliff with waterfalls. A private beach is a few steps away. Breakfast is served with fine china, crystal and warm Christian hospitality.

Hosts: Eric and Carolyn Feasey
Rooms: 4 (2PB; 2SB) $60-80
Full Breakfast
Credit Cards: C
Notes: 2, 5, 7 (over 6)

COSMOPOLIS

Cooney Mansion

1705 Fifth Street, 98537
(206) 533-0602

This 1908 National Historic Register home, situated in wooded seclusion, was built by Neil Cooney, owner of one of the largest sawmills of the time. It captures the adventure of the Northwest. Share the lumber Baron's history and many of his original "craftsman" style antiques. Enjoy 18 holes of golf (in backyard) or a leisurely walk around Mill Creek Park. Relax in the sauna and jacuzzi, curl up with one of the many books from the library or watch TV in the ballroom.

Hosts: Judi and Jim Lohr
Rooms: 9 (5PB; 4SB) $49-95
Full Breakfast
Credit Cards: A, B, D
Notes: 2, 5, 8, 10

COUPEVILLE

The Colonel Crockett Farm Bed and Breakfast Inn

1012 South Fort Casey Road, 98239
(206) 678-3711

The inn offers 135 years of Victorian/ Edwardian serenity in a farm-quiet island setting with pastoral and marine views. Period antiques enhance three large bed/sitting rooms and two smaller bedrooms. Common areas include an oak-paneled library, a wicker-furnished solarium, and a dining room that features individual tables. Separate owner's apartment. This 1855 Victorian farmhouse is on the National Register of Historic Places and has extensive grounds, walkways, and flowerbeds. No smoking.

Hosts: Robert and Beulah Whitlow
Rooms: 5 (PB) $65-95
Full Breakfast
Credit Cards: A, B
Notes: 2, 5, 7 (over 14), 10, 12

DARRINGTON

Sauk River Farm Bed and Breakfast

32629 State Route J30 NE, 98241
(206) 436-1794

The wild and scenic Sauk River runs through this farm nestled in a valley of the North Cascades. All season recreational opportunities await you. Wildlife abounds year round. The Native American Loft Room is a collector's delight; The Victorian Room offers pastoral privacy. Hallmarks of the farm are its views of rugged mountains, intimate atmosphere, comfortable accommodations, solitude for those seeking relaxation. Step back in time and sample Darrington hospitality with its Bluegrass music and crafters.

Hosts: Leo and Sharon Mehler
Rooms: 2 (SB) $40-60
Full Breakfast
Credit Cards: None
Notes: 5, 11

DEER HARBOR—ORCAS ISLAND

Deer Harbor Inn

P. O. Box 142, 98243
(206) 376-4110

For more than 70 years, thousands have enjoyed the solitude and natural beauty of Deer Harbor on Orcas Island. We offer eight quality guest rooms in a log cabin. There are two sitting and reading rooms and two beautiful view decks. Fine dining is available at the Deer Harbor Inn Restaurant. Sailing and fish-

---

year; 6 Pets welcome; 7 Children welcome; 8 Tennis nearby; 9 Swimming nearby; 10 Golf nearby; 11 Skiing nearby; 12 May be booked through travel agent

ing charters and small boat rentals are available, as well as hiking, fishing, and bird watching. Drive to the top of Mt. Constitution for a stunning view.

Hosts: Craig and Pam Carpenter
Rooms: 8 (PB) $65-85
Continental Breakfast
Credit Cards: A, B, C
Notes: 2, 4, 5

ELLENSBURG

Murphy's Country Bed and Breakfast

Route 1, Box 400, 98926
(509) 925-7986

Two large guest rooms in a lovely 1915 country home with a sweeping view of the valley. Full breakfast; close to fly fishing and golfing.

Host: Doris Callahan-Murphy
Rooms: 2 (S1.5B) $55
Full Breakfast
Credit Cards: A, B, C
Notes: 2, 5, 10

LACONNER

Ridgeway Bed and Breakfast

1292 McLean Road, PO Box 475, 98257
(206) 428-8068; (800) 428-8068

A perfect getaway! Enjoy the unique experience of this 1928 yellow brick Dutch Colonial farmhouse nestled in the heart of the Skagit Valley. Large windows offer an airy and open feeling with mountains and flowering fields in every direction. Queen and king beds,

homemade desserts, coffee or tea served in your room. Full farm breakfast. Orchard, flowers and two acres of lawn. A "Northwest Discovery," says *Evening Magazine* - KING TV, Seattle, Washington.

Hosts: Louise and John Kelly
Rooms: 5 (2PB; 4SB) $70-90
Full Breakfast
Credit Cards: A, B, C
Notes: 2, 5, 9, 10, 11, 12

LANGLEY—WHIDBEY ISLAND

Log Castle Bed and Breakfast

3273 East Saratoga Road, 98260
(206) 221-5483

A log house on a private, secluded beach features turret bedrooms, wood-burning stoves, porch swings, and panoramic views of the beach and mountains. Relax before a large stone fireplace or listen to the call of gulls as you watch for bald eagles and sea lions.

Hosts: Senator Jack and Norma Metcalf
Rooms: 4 (PB) $80-100
Full Breakfast
Credit Cards: A, B
Notes: 2, 8

LEAVENWORTH

All Seasons River Inn B&B

8751 Icicle Rd., 98826
(509) 548-1425

Come relax in the tranquil Cascade setting overlooking the Wenatchee River. Built as a bed and breakfast, all guest rooms are spacious, each with a sitting area, private bath and river view deck. Some rooms have jacuzzi tub. Antique decor, warm hospitality and a full gourmet breakfast offer a memorable getaway. Swim or fish from our beach or bike from the front door. One-half mile from skiing, golfing and hiking. Come for an experience that will call you back again and again.

Hosts: Kathy and Jeff Falconer
Rooms: 5 (PB) $85 (new room finished by 12/93!)
Full Breakfast
Credit Cards: A, B
Notes: 2, 5, 8, 9, 10, 11, 12 (with exceptions)

Pine River Ranch

19668 Hwy 207, 98826
(509) 763-3959

An exceptional inn with spacious, beautifully decorated rooms with woodstoves, decks and sunny sitting areas. A deluxe suite offers romantic seclusion. Fabulous food, hot tubs, acres to hike, stream fishing and lots of friendly farm animals. Enjoy private groomed ski trails with spectacular mountain views. Member of Northwest Best Places, AAA and Washington Bed and Breakfast Guild. Perfectly located two hours west of Seattle, minutes from the Bavarian Village of Leavenworth.

Hosts: Michael and Mary Ann Zenk
Rooms: 6 (4PB; 2SB) $65-125
Full Breakfast
Credit Cards: A, B
Notes: 2, 5, 7, 8, 9, 10, 11, 12

LOPEZ ISLAND

Aleck Bay Inn

Aleck Bay Road, Route 1, Box 1920, 98261
(206) 468-3535

The Aleck Bay Inn is located on Lopez Island, the Heart of the San Juan Islands, overlooking the Strait of Juan de Fuca on private Aleck Bay. Serene and secluded on seven acres with beach to stroll. Enjoy the view from the outdoor hot tub; most of the rooms have a fireplace.

Host: May Mendez
Rooms: 4 (2PB; 2SB) $79-129
Full Breakfast
Credit Cards: A, B, C
Notes: 2, 5, 9, 10, 12

MacKaye Harbor Inn

Route 1, Box 1940, 98261
(206) 468-2253

This Victorian beachfront bed and breakfast in the San Juan Islands is an ideal getaway, full of warmth and nostalgia. There is a sandy beach and extensive grounds on a tree-lined harbor. Wildlife frequents the area. Rowboat, kayaks, and bicycles are available.

year; 6 Pets welcome; 7 Children welcome; 8 Tennis nearby; 9 Swimming nearby; 10 Golf nearby; 11 Skiing nearby; 12 May be booked through travel agent

Excellent for small groups of five or six couples. The kitchen is available for guest use. No smoking.

Hosts: Robin and Mike Bergstrom
Rooms: 5 (1PB; 4SB) $69-109
Full Breakfast
Credit Cards: A, B
Notes: 2, 5, 10, 12

MONTESANO

The Abel House Bed and Breakfast

117 Fleet Street South, 98563
(206) 249-6002; (800) 235-ABEL

Gracious English home and gardens, built in 1908, welcomes guest with tea, full breakfast and attractively appointed rooms. "Dan the Cook" serves coffee and juice to your room for a morning wake-up call, and the resident bassett hound will greet you upon arrival each afternoon. We restrict smoking to our Billiards Rooms on the third floor.

Host: Victor J. Reynolds
Rooms: 5 (SB) $50-70
Full Breakfast
Credit Cards: A, B
Notes: 2, 5, 8, 9, 10, 12

Sylvan House

P.O. Box 416, 98563
(206) 241-3453

A Country hideaway, ten-minute hike to lake Sylvia State Park, hunting, fishing, swimming. Three story home, 1970 family home used as B&B for six years. High on a hilltop with a sweeping view of valley below. Gourmet food. Char-

ter member of Washington State Bed and Breakfast Guild. In Washington's State magazine *Destination Washington*. Four rooms: two queen, one twin, two baths. No smoking. High decks. Limited to older children. No pets. In several cookbooks and B&B books on West Coast.

Hosts: Mike and Jo Anne Murphy
Rooms: 4 (2PB; 2SB) $55-65
Full Breakfast
Credit Cards: None
Notes: 2, 5, 7 (older) 11, 12

MORTON

St. Helens Manorhouse

7476 Hwy 12, 98356
(206) 498-5243

Welcome to my 1910 Manorhouse atop a knoll, surrounded by lawns and walnut, chestnut, and fruit trees. Rooms elegantly appointed with carefully selected antiques and books. Breakfast is a special occasion prepared lovingly with local delicacies garnished with fresh mint and flowers. Served on 100-year-old china. Come relax under a tree or on a cozy porch surrounding home with comfortable seating, inviting conversation or peaceful napping. Close to fishing, water sports, hiking, skiing and glorious vistas. Come be my guest.

Hostess: Susan Dragness
Rooms: 4 (2PB; 2SB) $59-69
Full Breakfast
Credit Cards: D
Notes: 2, 4, 5, 9, 10, 11

NOTES: Credit cards accepted: A Master Card; B Visa; C American Express; D Discover Card; E Diners Club; F Other; 2 Personal checks accepted; 3 Lunch available; 4 Dinner available; 5 Open all

PORT ANGELES

Annikens's
Bed and Breakfast

214 East Whidbey Avenue, 98362
(206) 457-6177

Welcome to Northwestern hospitality
and a wonderful view of the harbor,
Victoria, BC, and the mountains of
Olympic National Park. Two comfortable rooms with shared bath adjoin a
lofty sitting rooms (additional bath on
main floor). Your homemade full breakfast always includes fresh fruit and gourmet coffee. We are just five minutes
from the Victoria ferries and the Park
Visitors' Center.

Hosts: Robert and Ann Kennedy
Rooms: 2 (SB) $55-60
Full Breakfast
Credit Cards: A, B
Notes: 2, 8, 9, 10

PORT TOWNSEND

Trenholm House

2037 Haines, 98368
(206) 385-6059

An 1890 Victorian farmhouse inn.
Original woodwork. Five guest rooms
and cottage furnished in country antiques. Gourmet breakfast, beautiful
lagoon and bay views make every stay
memorable. Members of the Washington Bed and Breakfast Guild, Olympic
Peninsula Bed and Breakfast Association, National Bed and Breakfast Asso-

ciation, and Chamber of Commerce.

Hosts: Michael and Patricia Kelly
Rooms: 6 (2PB; 4SB) $62-95
Full Breakfast
Credit Cards: A, B
Notes: 2, 5, 7 (over 12), 8, 9, 10, 12

REDMAN

Lilac Lea Christian
Bed and Breakfast

Redmond, 98053-5309
(206) 861-1898

Quiet woodland setting on dead end
road, next to 800-acre park. No smoking or consuming of alcoholic beverages on premises. Home unsuitable for
children or pets. Seventeen miles from
Seattle, one mile from bus. Private
second floor suite with private entrance
and private bath. Continental breakfast
served in suite. Two-year-old custom
built home. Rented to one party only at
a time. Antique furnishings. Close to
three national parks, ferry to Victoria,
BC. Wildlife abundant in area.

Hosts: Chandler Haight, Ruthanne Hayes-
Haight
Rooms: 1 suite (PB) $90
Continental Breakfast
Credit Cards: None
Notes: 5, 8, 9, 10, 11

SEABECK

Summer Song
Bed and Breakfast

P. O. Box 82, 98380
(206) 830-5089

---

year; 6 Pets welcome; 7 Children welcome; 8 Tennis nearby; 9 Swimming nearby; 10 Golf nearby; 11
Skiing nearby; 12 May be booked through travel agent

Summer Song, a whisper of an older time, a new breath of today, is a completely furnished cottage located on the shores of Hood Canal. A spectacular backdrop of the Olympia Mountains reflects on its moody waters. God has provided a peace and beauty in the middle of nature, and our guests are held on the tip toe of wondering, "Does the song of the sea end on the shore or in the hearts of those who listen?"

Hosts: Ron and Sharon Barney
Cottage: 1 (PB) $69
Full Breakfast
Credit Cards: A, B
Notes: 2, 3, 4, 5, 9, 10

The Walton House B&B Establishment

12340 Seabeck Highway NW, 98380
(206) 830-4498

A feeling of Grandma's house in this three story 1904 home filled with family antiques, operated by the third generation of Waltons. Old-fashioned double beds in two guest rooms with private baths. A wonderful view of mountains and Hood Canal with 350 feet of beach to explore. Movie theaters, restaurants, antique shops, museums, shopping mall six miles away. No smoking and no children under 16.

Hosts: Ray and Shirley Walton
Rooms: 2(PB) $65-75
Full Breakfast
Credit Cards: None
Notes: 2, 5

SEATTLE

Chambered Nautilus Bed and Breakfast Inn

5005 22nd Avenue Northeast, 98105
(206) 522-2536

A gracious 1915 Georgian Colonial is nestled on a hill and furnished with a mixture of American and English antiques and fine reproductions. A touch of Mozart, Persian rugs, a grand piano, two fireplaces, four lovely porches, and national award-winning breakfasts help assure your special comfort. Excellent access to Seattle's theaters, restaurants, public transportation, shopping, bike and jogging trails, churches, Husky Stadium, and the University of Washington campus.

Hosts: Bill and Bunny Hagemeyer
Rooms: 6 (4PB; 2SB) $77.50-97.50
Full Breakfast
Credit Cards: A, B, C, E, F
Notes: 2, 5, 8, 9, 10, 11, 12

Chelsea Station Bed and Breakfast Inn

4915 Linden Avenue North, 98103
(206) 547-6077

Chelsea Station consistently provides the peaceful surroundings travelers enjoy. Lace curtains, ample breakfasts, and comfy king beds share warm feelings of "Grandma's time." The nearby Seattle Rose Garden contributes beauty to the human spirit. With a cup of tea in the afternoon, Chelsea Station is a perfect place for relaxation and renewal. No smoking.

NOTES: Credit cards accepted: A Master Card; B Visa; C American Express; D Discover Card; E Diners Club; F Other; 2 Personal checks accepted; 3 Lunch available; 4 Dinner available; 5 Open all

Hosts: Dick and Mary Lou Jones
Rooms: 5 (PB) $59-104
Full Breakfast
Credit Cards: A, B, C, D, E
Notes: 2, 5, 8, 9, 10, 12

SEAVIEW

Gumm's
Bed and Breakfast Inn
Highway 101 and 33 Avenue South, P. O. Box
447, 98644
(206) 642-8887

This home features a large living room
with a great stone fireplace. Four guest
rooms are uniquely decorated with special thought to the guests' comfort. Sun
porch, hot tub, TV. Breakfast is served
in the Julie Anne Room, with three
French doors opening onto a spacious
deck.

Host: Mickey Slack
Rooms: 4 (2PB; 2SB) $65-75
Full Breakfast
Credit Cards: A, B
Notes: 2, 5, 7, 8, 10, 12

WHITE   SALMON

Llama Ranch
Bed and Breakfast
1980 Highway 141, 98672
(509) 395-2786; (800) 800-LAMA

Hospitality plus unforgettable delight.
Jerry and Rebeka share their love of
llamas on free llama walks through the
woods with each guest walking a
"llovable" llama. There are stunning
views of both Mt. Adams and Mt. Hood.
The ranch is located between the Mt.
Adams wilderness area and the Columbia Gorge national scenic area with
many varied activities close by. Picturesque views and photographic memories abound along with the serenity,
dignity, and beauty of llamas.

Hosts: Jerry and Rebeka Stone
Rooms: 7 (2PB; 5SB) $55-75
Full Breakfast
Credit Cards: A, B, D
Notes: 2, 5, 6, 7, 10, 11, 12

West Virginia

ELKINS

Tunnel Mountain
Bed and Breakfast
Route 1, Box 59-1, 26241
(304) 636-1684

A charming, three-story fieldstone home is nestled on the side of Tunnel Mountain, four miles east of Elkins, Stuart Recreation Area exit off Route 33. Five private, wooded acres overlook scenic mountains, lush forests, and the Cheat River Valley. Three romantic guest rooms are furnished with antiques and handmade comforters. The large common room has a fireplace. Activities include hiking, cross-country and downhill skiing, fishing, hunting, rafting, canoeing, golf, antiquing, festivals, tennis, caving, swimming.

Hosts: Anne and Paul Beardslee
Rooms: 3 (PB) $55
Full Breakfast
Credit Cards: None
Notes: 2, 5, 8, 9, 10, 11

HINTON

Sunset
413 1/2 Sixth Avenue, 25951
(304) 466-3740

Sunset—one full cabin separate from innkeeper's home—with porch overlooking New River in woods above historic Hinton. Kitchen (breakfast foods, barbecue supplies and snacks included), bath and private entrances. Located near Bluestone and Pipestream State Parks, sports and hunting facilities, and Amtrak depot. No pets, please. A private cabin in the bed and breakfast tradition.

Host: Jane S. Duffield
Rooms: 1 (PB) $50
Self Serve Full Breakfast
Credit Cards: None
Notes: 2, 3&4 (with notice), 5, 7, 8, 9, 10, 11

Tunnel Mountain Bed and Breakfast

NOTES: Credit cards accepted: A Master Card; B Visa; C American Express; D Discover Card; E Diners Club; F Other; 2 Personal checks accepted; 3 Lunch available; 4 Dinner available; 5 Open all

HUTTONSVILLE

Hutton House

Route 219-250, 26273
(800) 234-6701

Meticulously restored and decorated, this Queen Anne Victorian on the National Register of Historic Places is conveniently located near Elkins, Cass Railroad, and Snowshoe Ski Resort. It has a wraparound porch and deck for relaxing and enjoying the view, TV, game room, lawn for games, and a friendly kitchen. Breakfast and afternoon refreshments are served at your leisure; other meals are available with prior reservation or good luck! Come see us!

Host: Loretta Murray
Rooms: 7 (3PB; 4SB) $55-75
Full Breakfast
Credit Cards: A, B, C
Notes: 2, 5, 7, 8, 10, 11, 12

MATHIAS

Valley View Farm

Route 1, Box 467, 26812
(304) 897-5229

National Geographic's *America's Great Hideaways* calls Valley View Farm "Your home away from home," and it is just that. This cattle and sheep farm of 250 acres specializes in excellent food

and friendly hosts. Lost River State Park is nearby. Horseback riding and other recreation is available in season. Craft shops. Located on Route 259 near Mathias, opposite Stone Mennonite Church.

Host: Edna Shipe
Rooms: 4 (SB) $25 per person
Full Breakfast
Credit Cards: None
Notes: 2, 3, 4, 5, 6, 7, 8, 9, 11

MORGANTOWN

High Moon Stables/High Places Ranch Camp

1315 Dorsey Avenue, 26505
(304) 296-7433

We are dedicated to providing you with the opportunity to experience a time of quality relaxation, fun, spiritual growth and fellowship. This unique camp offers both outdoor camping and indoor farmhouse living. The farmhouse has four bedrooms and one bathroom and is intended for group use. Great for family retreats or group outings. Also available are modular homes for families, one of which is located on Cheat Lake. Kitchen utensils are provided, but you must supply your own food.

Host: Jo Ann Moon
Rooms: 2 farmhouses
No Breakfast
Credit Cards: None
Notes: 2, 3, 4, 5, 6, 7, 8, 9, 10, 11

year; 6 Pets welcome; 7 Children welcome; 8 Tennis nearby; 9 Swimming nearby; 10 Golf nearby; 11 Skiing nearby; 12 May be booked through travel agent

Wisconsin

ALBANY

Albany Guest House

405 South Mill Street, 53502
(608) 862-3636

An experience in tranquility, just 30 miles south of the capital dome in Madison. Enjoy king and queen beds in air conditioned rooms in a restored 1908 home. Relax on the wide, flower-filled front porch or light the fireplace in the master bedroom. Canoe or tube the Sugar River; bike, hike, or cross country ski the Sugar River trail. Visit nearby New Glarus, America's Little Switzerland, or Monroe, The Swiss Cheese Capital.

Hosts: Bob and Sally Braem
Rooms: 4 (2PB; 2SB) $50-70
Full Breakfast
Notes: 2, 5, 10, 11

Sugar River Inn

304 South Mill St., 53502
(608) 862-1248

Our turn-of-the-century inn, with many original features, has the charm of yes-

teryear. Christian fellowship. We are located in a quiet village in southern Wisconsin along the Sugar River. We have spacious lawn, canoeing and fishing in the back yard. We are minutes away from the bike trail. Comfortable and light, airy rooms await you, queen size beds, fine linens and afternoon refreshments and wake up coffee. We are near New Glarus, House on the Rock, Little Norway and the state capital in Madison. Cash or check. Children allowed by arrangement.

Hosts: Jack and Ruth Lindberg
Rooms: 3 (1PB; 2SB) $50-60
Full Breakfast
Notes: 2, 5, 7 (by arrangement), 10

BALDWIN

Kaleidoscope Inn B&B

800 Eleventh Avenue, 54002
(715) 684-4575

Baldwin, a quiet Dutch community, has flower-lined boulevards and authentic Dutch windmill. Massive ornate antiques and stained glass lamps adorn the B&B. Listen to the nickelodeon and spend hours viewing a col-

---

lection of 125 magnificent Kaleidoscopes (including a spectrasphere and a fountain scope). Close to St. Croix Meadows, Apple River Tubing, Crystal Cave State Parks, Afton Alps. Forty minutes from Minneapolis-St. Paul. Reservations recommended. Gift certificates available.

Hosts: Cherie and Chris Jacobsen
Rooms: 4 (1PB; 3SB) $55-75
Continental Breakfast
Credit Cards: A, B
Notes: 2, 5, 8, 9, 10, 11

Kaleidoscope Inn

BARABOO

Frantiques Showplace

704 Ash St., 53913
(608) 356-5273

A three-story Victorian mansion filled with a lifetime collection of nostalgia. A personal "tour" included. The suite contains a brass bed, TV, kitchen facilities, private bath and private entrance. Another suite features brass bed, oak furniture and private bath. A fireplace in the living room, down comforter quilts and an old-fashioned breakfast to complete your stay!

Hosts: Fran and Bud Kelly
Rooms: 2 (PB) $65-70
Full Breakfast
Credit Cards: None

Notes: 2, 5, 7, 8, 9, 10, 11

CEDARBURG

The Washington House Inn

W62 N 573 Washington Avenue, 53012
(414) 375-3550; (800) 554-4717

Built in 1884 and listed on the National Register of Historic Places, 29 guest rooms feature antiques, down comforters, whirlpool baths, fireplaces, and cable TV. Located in the heart of the Cedarburg historic district, within walking distance of area antique shops, fine dining, and historic Cedar Creek settlement.

Host: Wendy Porterfield
Rooms: 29 (PB) $59-139
Expanded Continental Breakfast
Credit Cards: A, B, C, D, E
Notes: 2, 5, 7, 8, 9, 10, 11

DEFOREST

Circle B Bed and Breakfast

3804 Vinburn Road, 53532
(608) 846-3481

Located ten miles north of Madison, Wisconsin. Enjoy a relaxed stay in the country on 160-acre farm with livestock. A very neat and well kept home and yard. Sitting deck in summer, cozy room in winter. Beautiful view of sunrises and sunsets. Antiques decorate the home. Wisconsin Dells, House on the Rock, and other activities nearby, also winter activities. Great hospitality and country breakfast. No smoking or pets.

Host: Donna Buchner
Rooms: 4 (2PB; 2SB) $65-75
Full Breakfast
Credit Cards: F
Notes: 2, 5, 8, 9, 10, 11

EAGLE RIVER

Brennan Manor—Old World Bed and Breakfast

1079 Everett Rd., 54521
(715) 479-7353

This castle in the forest evokes images of King Arthur with its suit of armor, arched windows, hand hewn wood work and a 30-foot stone fireplace. You'll stay in one of four antique-decorated rooms (private baths) that open onto a balcony overlooking the Great Rooms. There, wintertime guests gather to sip hot chocolate and munch popcorn after cross country skiing in the Nicolet National Forest or snowmobiling on 500 miles of trails. Situated on the largest freshwater chain of lakes in the world, the inn's frontage includes a beach, boathouse and piers for warm weather fun. A three bedroom guest house is also available. No smoking.

Hosts: Connie and Bob Lawton
Rooms: 4 (PB) $69-89
Full Breakfast
Credit Cards: A, B
Notes: 2, 5, 8, 9, 10, 11, 12

The Inn at Pinewood

P.O. Box 549, 1800 Silver Forest Lane, 54521
(715) 479-4114

Northwoods elegance at its finest. Warmest hospitality awaits you the minute you arrive at this delightful 21-room bed and breakfast. Eight romantic guest room, all with king size beds, private baths, balconies. Many with double whirlpool baths and fireplaces. Summers: swim, hike, fish, play tennis. Winters: ski, snowmobile, then relax by the fire in the huge stone fireplace. Reserve the entire inn for conferences and retreats. Scrumptious full breakfasts. Gift certificates available.

Hosts: Edward and Nona Soroosh
Rooms: 8 (PB) $65-95
Full Breakfast
Credit Cards: A, B
Notes: 2, 5, 7, 8, 9, 10, 11, 12

EAU CLAIRE

Otter Creek Inn

2536 Hwy. 12, 54701
(715) 832-2945

This spacious country-victorian inn has four guest rooms, all with private baths and three with jacuzzis. The magnificent decor and country antiques combine with warm hospitality and a crackling fire in the lounge to create a retreat you will long remember. The inn is located on a one-acre wooded lot where whitetail deer visit the backyard feeder daily, yet is five minutes from the malls, the university and over thirty restaurants.

Hosts: Randy and Shelley Hansen
Rooms: 4 (PB) $59-119
Expanded Continental Breakfast
Credit Cards: A, B, C

NOTES: Credit cards accepted: A Master Card; B Visa; C American Express; D Discover Card; E Diners Club; F Other; 2 Personal checks accepted; 3 Lunch available; 4 Dinner available; 5 Open all

Notes: 2, 5, 9, 10, 11

ELLISON BAY

Wagon Trail Resort, Restaurant and Conference Center

1041 Hwy. 22, 54210
(414) 854-2385

Wagon Trail's homestyle hospitality begins with comfortable year-round accommodations, from a large Scandinavian lodge to secluded vacation homes and cozy bayside cottages. Tensions melt in our indoor pool, sauna and whirlpool. Homemade specialties and a delectable buffet distinguish our restaurant, while Grandma's Swedish Bakery serves famous pecan rolls and Scandinavian treats. Miles of groomed hiking and ski trails criss-cross two hundred wooded acres.

Hosts: Mike and Miriam Dorn
Rooms: 45 (PB)
Both Full and Continental Breakfast
Credit Cards: A, B, C, D, E
Notes: 2, 3, 4, 5, 7, 8, 9, 10, 11, 12

ELROY

Waarvik's Century Farm Bed and Breakfast

N4621 County Rd. H, 53929
(608) 462-8595

Let the birds sing you awake on our 150-acre family farm. Choose your favorite era: 3 rooms in Grandma's house, a family suite at the folks' house, or privacy in your 130-year old pioneer's log cabin. Full Breakfast, shared baths, smoking on the porch. Near Elroy, where 3 bike trails meet. Open May through October.

Hosts: Mary and Muriel Warrvik
Rooms: 6 (1PB; 5SB) $40-70
Full Breakfast
Credit Cards: None
Notes: 2, 7 (in family suite), 8, 9, 10

FISH CREEK

Thorp House Inn and Cottages

4135 Bluff Road, P. O. Box 490, 54212
(414) 868-2444

A turn-of-the-century historic home has a bay view. Four romantic guest rooms (one with whirlpool), parlor with stone fireplace, and cozy library--all furnished with fine antiques and lots of authentic detail. Home-baked continental breakfast. Fireplace cottages furnished in country antiques are also available. We are located in the village of Fish Creek, the heart of the Door County Peninsula, just blocks from a state park.

Hosts: Christine and Sverre Falck-Pedersen
Rooms: 4 (PB) $70-130; 7 cottages (PB)
Continental Breakfast
Credit Cards: None
Notes: 2, 5, 7 (cottages only), 8, 9, 10, 11

FORT ATKINSON

The Lamp Post Inn

408 South Main, 53538
(414) 563-6561

We welcome you to the charm of our 115-year-old Victorian home filled with beautiful antiques, 5 grammophones for your listening pleasure. For the modern, one of our baths features a large jacuzzi. We are located 7 blocks from the famous Fireside Playhouse. You come a stranger, but leave here a friend. No smoking.

Hosts: Debbie and Mike Rusch
Rooms: 3 (2PB; 1SB) $60-85
Full Breakfast
Credit Cards: None
Notes: 2, 5, 7, 8, 9, 10, 11

HAZEL GREEN

Wisconsin House
Stage Coach Inn
2105 E. Main St., 53811-0071
(608) 854-2233

Built as a stage coach inn in 1846, the Inn now offers six rooms and two suites for your comfort. Join us for an evening's rest. Dine and be refreshed in the parlor where General Grant spent many an evening with his friend Jefferson Crawford.

Hosts: Ken and Pat Disch
Rooms: 8 (6PB; 2SB) $50-95
Full Breakfast
Credit Cards: A, B
Notes: 2, 3, 4, 5, 7, 9, 10, 11, 12

LIVINGSTON

Oak Hill Farm
9850 Highway 80, 53554
(608) 943-6006

A comfortable country home with a warm, hospitable atmosphere is enhanced with fireplaces, porches, and facilities for picnics. In the area, you will find state parks, museums, lakes, and the Chicago Bears' summer training camp.

Hosts: Elizabeth and Victor Johnson
Rooms: 4 (1PB; 3SB) $30-40
Continental Breakfast
Credit Cards: None
Notes: 2, 5, 6, 7, 8, 9, 10, 11

Annie's Bed and Breakfast

MADISON

Annie's Bed and Breakfast
2117 Sheridan Drive, 53704
(608) 244-2224

When you want the world to go away, come to Annie's, the quiet inn on Warner Park with the beautiful view. Luxury accommodations at reasonable rates. Close to the lake and park, it is also convenient to downtown and the University of Wisconsin campus. There are unusual amenities in this charming setting, including a romantic gazebo surrounded by butterfly gardens, a shaded terrace and pond. Air conditioned. Two beautiful two-bedroom suites. Double Jacuzzi. Full air conditioning.

Hosts: Anne and Larry Stuart

Suites: 2 (PB) $75-95
Full Breakfast
Credit Cards: A, B, C
Notes: 2, 5, 7 (over 12), 8, 9, 10, 11

PLAIN

Bettinger House Bed and Breakfast

855 Wachter Avenue, Highway 23, 53577
(608) 546-2951

In this 1904 two-story red brick home, Marie's grandmother, Elizabeth, a midwife, delivered over 300 babies. It is close to the American Players Theatre, Frank Lloyd Wright's Taliesin, and House on the Rock. Air conditioning, fully refurbished. Biking, canoeing, and downhill and cross-country skiing are nearby.

Hosts: Jim and Marie Neider
Rooms: 6 (3PB; 3SB) $45-55
Full Breakfast
Credit Cards: A, B
Notes: 2, 5, 8, 9, 10, 11, 12

PORT WASHINGTON

Grand Inn B&B

832 W. Grand Avenue, 53074
(414) 284-6719

Our home is a special turn-of-the-century Queen Anne Victorian house elegantly furnished with period and antique furnishings. Two of our oversize bedrooms feature queen size beds, sitting area and private bath with two-person whirlpools. Port Washington is a New England like lakeside community providing charters, swimming,

shopping and wonderful restaurants. Ten minutes from Cedarburg's shops.

Hosts: Joyce and Richard Merg
Rooms: 3 (PB) $75-99
Both Full and Continental Breakfast
Credit Cards: A, B, C
Notes: 2, 5, 8, 9, 10, 12

The Inn at Old Twelve Hundred

806 West Grand Avenue, 53704
(414) 284-6883

Midway between Milwaukee and Sheboygan, Port Washington is a quaint fishing village on the shores of Lake Michigan. Minutes to historic Cedarburg. Elegant late 1800s grand Victorian offering authentic decor and furnishings. beautifully appointed guest rooms (king suite with fireplace). Spacious enclosed porches. Enjoy croquet, horseshoes, tandem bicycle, picturesque gazebo in large private yard. Air conditioned. Restricted smoking.

Hosts: Stephanie and Ellie Bresette
Rooms: 3 (PB) $65-135
Both Full and Continental Breakfast
Credit Cards: A, B, C
Notes: 2, 5

SPARTA

The Franklin Victorian Bed and Breakfast

220 East Franklin Street, 54656
(608) 269-3894; (800) 845-8767

This turn-of-the-century home welcomes you to bygone elegance with

year; 6 Pets welcome; 7 Children welcome; 8 Tennis nearby; 9 Swimming nearby; 10 Golf nearby; 11 Skiing nearby; 12 May be booked through travel agent

small-town quiet and comfort. The four spacious bedrooms provide a perfect setting for ultimate relaxation. Full home-cooked breakfast is served before starting your day of hiking, biking, skiing, canoeing, antiquing, or exploring this beautiful area.

Hosts: Lloyd and Jane Larson
Rooms: 4 (2PB; 2SB) $60-80
Full Breakfast
Credit Cards: A, B
Notes: 2, 5, 7 (over 10), 8, 9, 10, 11

SPRING GREEN

Hill Street
Bed and Breakfast

353 Hill Street, 53588
(608) 588-7751

The 1900 Queen Anne Victorian has a turret room, hand-carved woodwork, queen beds, and air conditioning. Near House on the Rock, Frank Lloyd Wright's Taliesin, American Players Theatre. Biking, canoeing on the Wisconsin River, and cross-country and downhill skiing are all close by.

Host: Doris Randall
Rooms: 7 (5PB; 2SB) $50-70
Full Breakfast
Credit Cards: A, B
Notes: 2, 5, 7, 8, 9, 10, 11, 12

STEVENS POINT

Dreams of Yesteryear
Bed and Breakfast

1100 Brawley Street, 54481
(715) 341-4525

Featured in *Victorian Homes Magazine* and listed on the National Register of Historic Places. Your hosts are from Stevens Point and enjoy talking about the restoration of their turn-of-the-century home which has been in the same family for three generations. All rooms are furnished in antiques. Guests enjoy use of parlors, porches and gardens. Two blocks from historic downtown, antique and specialty shops, picturesque Green Circle Trails, university and more. Dreams of Yesteryear is truly "a Victorian dream come true."

Hosts: Bonnie and Bill Maher
Rooms: 4 (2PB; 2SB) $55-75
Full Breakfast
Credit Cards: A, B, D
Notes: 2, 5, 7 (over 12 or with approval), 8, 9, 10, 11, 12

Dreams Of Yesteryear Bed and Breakfast

Victorian Swan on Water

1716 Water Street, 54481
(715) 345-0595

Enjoy our city's central location. From here you can see the rest of Wisconsin. This restored 1889 home showcases crown moldings, beautiful woodwork and antiques, with comfort as the main ingredient. Stroll our riverwalks. Visit

---

our university, local brewery, the many golf courses, parks, bike and ski trails, but don't forget our delicious breakfast. Private baths, A/C and gift certificates.

Host: Joan Ouellette
Rooms: 4 (PB) $45-65
Full Breakfast
Credit Cards: A, B, C, D
Notes: 2, 5, 10, 11, 12

WAUPAN

The Rose Ivy Inn
228 South Watertown Street, 53963
(414) 324-2127; (800) 258-5019

Enjoy the romance and elegance of this beautifully restored Queen Anne Victorian home filled with antiques and lace. Visit nearby Horicon Marsh Wildlife Refuge, the "Little Everglades of the North." Free use of the inn's bicycles so that you can tour the historic Waupan area at your leisure. We offer gift certificates as well as many other amenities. We encourage you to check with us for more information about winter weekend Christian retreats.

Hosts: Melody and Ken Kris
Rooms: 4 (2PB; 2SB) $59-79
Full Breakfast on weekends/holidays,
Continental Breakfast weekdays
Credit Cards: A, B, C, D
Notes: 2, 5, 11

WISCONSIN DELLS

Historic Bennett House Bed and Breakfast
825 Oak Street, 53965
(608) 254-2500

The 1863 home of an honored pioneer photographer is listed on the National Register of Historic Places. We'll pamper you with elegant lace, crystal, antiques, romantic bedrooms, and luscious fireside breakfast. The private suite has a parlor, Eastlake bedroom, and shower bath. The English room has a walnut and lace canopy bed. And the garden room has a brass bed. Walk to river tours, antiques, and crafts. Minutes to hiking, biking, canoeing, four golf courses, five ski areas, five state parks, greyhound racing, bird watching, and Indian culture. Bennett, Rockwell, circus, and railroad museums are also near by. Gift certificates are available.

Hosts: Gail and Rich Obermeyer
Rooms: 3 (1PB; 2SB) $65-80
Full Breakfast
Credit Cards: None
Notes: 2, 5, 8, 9, 10, 11, 12

---

year; 6 Pets welcome; 7 Children welcome; 8 Tennis nearby; 9 Swimming nearby; 10 Golf nearby; 11 Skiing nearby; 12 May be booked through travel agent

Wyoming

CODY

Parson's Pillow

1202 14th Street, 82414
(307) 587-2382

Comfort, elegance and the sense of coming home are yours to enjoy as a guest of Parson's Pillow B&B. Antiques and turn-of-the-century lace surround you. Our 1902 former church has been caringly restored so that you might experience homestyle hospitality. Each room (4) is individually designed and a full breakfast is provided. Just boot steps from Buffalo Bill Museum and shops. Cody is the eastern gate (52 miles) to Yellowstone National Park.

Hosts: Lee and Elly Larabee
Rooms: 4 (2PB; 2SB) $65-75
Full Breakfast
Credit Cards: A, B
Notes: 2, 5, 8, 9, 10, 11

NOTES: Credit cards accepted: A Master Card; B Visa; C American Express; D Discover Card; E Diners Club; F Other, 2 Personal checks accepted; 3 Lunch available; 4 Dinner available; 5 Open all

Alberta

CANMORE

Cougar Creek Inn
P.O. Box 1162, T0L 0M0
(403) 678-4751

The Cougar Creek Inn Bed and Breakfast is in Canmore (pop. 6000) located in the Canadian Rockies. Canmore hosted the 1988 Winter Olympic Nordic events and is a quaint mountain community. Canmore's closest major city is Calgary, Alberta, which is 100 km east. Ten miles west is Banff, 25 more miles west is Lake Louise. The area's biggest attraction is the spectacular beauty of the rugged mountain scenery which invites all types of outdoor activity. Just to name a few: mountain biking, cycling, golf, tennis, fishing, hiking, heli-hiking, skiing and climbing. The rooms are quiet, and the setting is rustic. The guests have their own sitting area with a fireplace, color TV, games, books, magazines and a sauna. Breakfasts are known to be wholesome and hearty.

Host: Mrs. Patricia Doucette
Rooms: 4 (SB) $55-60 (Canadian)
Full Breakfast
Notes: 2, 3, 5, 7, 8, 9, 10, 11

NANTON

The Squire Ranch
Rural Route 1, T0L 1R0
(403) 646-5789

Welcome to our ranch in the lovely foothills of the Rocky Mountains. We have horses, cattle, goats, sheep, llamas, miniature donkeys, and bantam chickens. Yard, playground, and indoor activities are available. This is good country for riding, walking, hunting, and fishing. We have easy access to Fort MacLeod, Kananaskis, Waterton, and Banff. There is a small gift shop on the premises.

Hosts: Sam and Rosemary Squire
Rooms: 3 plus cabin (1PB; 2SB) $25-50
Full Breakfast (other meals upon request)
Notes: 2, 3 (restricted), 4 (restricted), 5 (restricted), 6, 7, 8, 9, 10, 11

---

year; 6 Pets welcome; 7 Children welcome; 8 Tennis nearby; 9 Swimming nearby; 10 Golf nearby; 11 Skiing nearby; 12 May be booked through travel agent

Timber Ridge Homestead

Box 94, T0L 1R0
(403) 646-2480

Timber Ridge Homestead is a rustic establishment in beautiful foothills ranching country about 70 miles SW of Calgary. We have good, quiet horses to help you see abundant wild flowers and wild life and wonderful views of the Rockies. Good plain cooking if you want it. To get here, go to Nanton, 50 miles south of Calgary, drive West on highway 533 for 4 miles, turn south and follow winding road into hills for twelve miles and the gate is on the right.

Host: Bridget Jones
Rooms: 3 (SB) $25 per person
Full Breakfast
Notes: 2, 3, 4, 7

NOTES: Credit cards accepted: A Master Card; B Visa; C American Express; D Discover Card; E Diners Club; F Other; 2 Personal checks accepted; 3 Lunch available; 4 Dinner available; 5 Open all

British Columbia

ABBOTSFORD

The Cliff House

36050 Southridge Place, V3G 1E2
(604) 852-5787

Our bed and breakfast is two miles from the U.S. Border. Set in a quiet location, The Cliff House Bed and Breakfast offers visitors a restful spot to spend the night or longer in Mountain Village at the home of Walter and Ina Friesen. The home away from home with its elegant traditional decor is equipped with a luxurious full bathroom, queen size beds and the use of our family room. No Pets, No Smoking!

Hosts: Walter and Ina Friesen
Rooms: 2 (SB) $55
Full Breakfast
Notes: 5, 8, 9, 10, 11

BURNABAY

An English Garden B&B

4390 Frances Street, V5C 2R3
(604) 298-8815; FAX (604) 298-5917

From Highway 1A or 99A, turn north on Willingdon Avenue to Frances which is two blocks south of Hastings Street. Turn left; our house is one block west of Willingdon. This white stucco bungalow offers a choice of accommodations. One room, with a view of the mountains, has a king size bed, an extra single bed, a TV and a private bath (with shower). The other has a queen size sofa bed, a TV, and a shared bathroom. We are fifteen minutes from most of Vancouver's tourist attractions and ten minutes from the top of Burnaby Mountain, with its spectacular view of the city. We pride ourselves in the full breakfast we serve. A quick phone call in advance would be appreciated. We have a cat; sorry, no pets permitted.

Host: Norma McCurrach
Rooms: 2 (1PB; 1SB) $60-75
Full Breakfast
Credit Cards: A, B, C
Notes: 5, 8, 9, 10, 11

COQUITLAM

Meckies B&B

2242 Park Crescent, V3J 6T2
(604) 469-7105

Meckies B&B is a very comfortable

---

year; 6 Pets welcome; 7 Children welcome; 8 Tennis nearby; 9 Swimming nearby; 10 Golf nearby; 11 Skiing nearby; 12 May be booked through travel agent

clean German home 30km from Vancouver. Enjoy our guest suite with king size bed, cable TV, fireplace and private bath. We serve a full nutritious breakfast. Our guests always appreciate our homemade jams, garden fresh fruits and German buns in addition to a traditional Canadian breakfast. We live in a quiet residential area with a park and a creek in our backyard. Convenient bus service to Vancouver.

Host: Gabriela Butz
Rooms: 1 (PB) $70 (US)
Full Breakfast
Notes: 2, 5, 7, 8, 9, 10, 12

Meckies B&B

FORT STEELE

Wild Horse Farm
Box 7, V0B 1N0
(604) 426-6000

Step back into a time of leisure and luxury at Wild Horse Farm, a secluded, historic, park-like 80-acre estate in the Canadian Rocky Mountains adjoining Fort Steele Historic Town. The log covered home was built by the New York Astors in the early 1900s with spacious high ceilinged rooms, five fieldstone fireplaces, antique furnish-

ings. Screened verandas invite you to relax in a setting which reflects generations of tradition and comfort. Awaken to hot tea or coffee brought to your room. Enjoy a leisurely gourmet breakfast later in the dining room.

Hosts: Bob and Orma Termuende
Rooms: 5 (2PB; 3SB) $48-87
Full Breakfast
Notes: 5, 7 (by arrangement), 8, 9, 10, 11, 12 (10%)

MILL BAY

Pine Lodge Farm Bed and Breakfast
3191 Muatter Road, V0R 2P0
(604) 743-4083

Our beautiful antique-filled lodge is located 25 miles north of Victoria. It is situated on a 30-acre farm overlooking ocean and islands. Arbutus trees, walking trails, farm animals, and wild deer add to the idyllic setting. Each room has en suite baths and shower. Also, a delightful cottage with two bedrooms and baths, living room, dinette, kitchen, and hot tub is available. Full farm breakfast. No smoking.

Hosts: Cliff and Barb Clarke
Rooms: 7 (PB) $75-85
Cottage: 1 (PB) $110-160
Full Breakfast
Credit Cards: A, B
Notes: 2, 5, 10, 12

NOTES: Credit cards accepted: A Master Card; B Visa; C American Express; D Discover Card; E Diners Club; F Other; 2 Personal checks accepted; 3 Lunch available; 4 Dinner available; 5 Open all

SOOKE

Ocean Wilderness Guest Accommodations

11009 West Coast Road, V0S 1N0
(604) 646-2116

Seven guest rooms on five wooded acres of oceanfront, with a breathtaking view of the Straits of Juan de Fuca, Olympic Mountains and forest. The original log house serves as a dining room and common area for the inn. The large, beautifully decorated guest rooms with private baths, Persian carpets and bed canopies are in the new wing. A silver service of coffee with a miniature vase of flowers is delivered to guest room doors as a gentle wake up call. A full breakfast is served daily and dinner can be arranged. The hot tub, tucked in a little Japanese gazebo, is a popular respite for weary vacationers. Book your time for a private soak.

Hosts: Marion Paine
Rooms: 7 (PB) $85-210 Canadian
Full Breakfast
Credit Cards: A, B
Notes: 2, 4, 5, 8, 10, 12

UCLUELET

Bed and Breakfast at Burley's

Box 550, 1078 Helen Road, V0R 3A0
(604) 726-4444

A waterfront home on a small "drive to" island at the harbor mouth. Watch the ducks and birds play, heron and kingfisher work, and eagles soar. In the harbor, trollers, draggers, and seiners attract the gulls. There is a view from every window, a large living room, fireplace, books, and recreation room with pool table.

Hosts: Run Burley and Micheline Riley
Rooms: 6 (SB) $40-50
Continental Breakfast
Credit Cards: A, B
Notes: 8, 9, 10

VICTORIA

AA-Accommodations West B&B Service

660 Jones Terrace, V8Z 2L7
(604) 479-1986; FAX (604) 479-9999

No reservation fee. Over seventy choice locations. Inspected and approved. Ocean view, farm tranquility, cozy cottage, city convenience, historic heritage! Assistance with itineraries includes Victoria, Vancouver Island, and some adjacent islands. For competent, caring service, call Doreen—7 days. Open 7am-10pm Monday thru Saturday and 2pm-9pm on Sundays.

All Seasons Bed and Breakfast Agency

P.O. Box 5511, Stn B, V8R 6S4
(604) 655-7173

All Seasons Agency specializes in waterfront and garden homes in Victoria, Vancouver Island and gulf islands. All homes inspected. Free brochure upon request. There is an accommodation style for everyone. Kate Cattrill, operator.

---

year; 6 Pets welcome; 7 Children welcome; 8 Tennis nearby; 9 Swimming nearby; 10 Golf nearby; 11 Skiing nearby; 12 May be booked through travel agent

Battery Street Guest House

670 Battery Street, V8V 1E5
(604) 385-4632

Newly renovated guesthouse, built in 1898 with four bright comfortable rooms, two with bathrooms. Centrally located within walking distance to downtown, Beacon Hill Park, and Victoria's scenic Marine Drive only one block away. A full hearty breakfast served by a Dutch hostess. No smoking.

Host: Pamela Verduyn
Rooms: 4 (2PB; 2SB) $55-80
Full Breakfast
Credit Cards: None
Notes: 2

Dashwood Seaside Manor

Number One Cook Street, V8T 5A7
(604) 385-5517

Enjoy the comfort and privacy of your own elegant suite in one of Victoria's traditional Tudor mansions. Gaze out your window at the ocean and America's Olympic Mountains. If you're an early riser, you may see seals, killer whales, or sea otters frolicking offshore. Watch an eagle cruise by. Help yourself to breakfast from your private, well-stocked kitchen. You're minutes away from the attractions of town. Stroll there through beautiful Beacon Hill Park.

Host: Derek Dashwood
Rooms: 14 (PB) $65-240
Self-cater Full Breakfast

Credit Cards: A, B, C
Notes: 2, 5, 6 (small), 7, 8, 10, 12

Elk Lake Lodge B&B

5259 Pat Bay Hwy (Route 17), V8Y 1S8
(604) 658-8879; FAX (604) 658-4558

Originally built as a chapel in 1910, the Elk Lake Lodge now offers 5 very comfortable and attractive guest rooms, catering to an informal warm Victorian hospitality. Located just 10 minutes from downtown Victoria. Across the road from beautiful Elk Lake, guests can enjoy the outdoor hot tub, a view from every bedroom, fresh flowers, comforters. Fresh baking daily. Coffee and tea served each evening with a charming fireplace on those chilly nights.

Hosts: Marty and Ivan Musar
Rooms: 5 (3PB; 2SB) $75-89 (off season rates available)
Full Breakfast
Credit Cards: A, B
Notes: 5, 7 (over 12), 9, 10, 12

Peggy's Cove Bed and Breakfast

279 Coal Point Lane, V8L 3R9
(604) 656-5656

Spoil yourself! Come join me in my beautiful home surrounded by ocean on three sides. Imagine a gourmet breakfast on the sundeck, watching sea lions at play, eagles soaring and if you are lucky a family of killer whales may appear. In the evening, spend a romantic moment relaxing in the hot tub under the stars. World famous Butchart Gar-

---

NOTES: Credit cards accepted: A Master Card; B Visa; C American Express; D Discover Card; E Diners Club; F Other; 2 Personal checks accepted; 3 Lunch available; 4 Dinner available; 5 Open all

dens, BC and Anacortes Ferries are only minutes away. Many consider Peggy's Cove a honeymoon paradise.

Host: Peggy Waibel
Rooms: 3 (1PB; 2SB) $95-150 (US)
Full Breakfast
Notes: 2, 5, 6, 7, 8, 9, 10

Prior House B&B Inn

620 St. Charles, V8S 3N7
(604) 592-8847

Formerly a private residence of the English Crown's representative, this grand bed and breakfast inn has all the amenities of the finest European inns. Featuring rooms with fireplaces, marble jacuzzi baths, goose down comforters, mountain and ocean views, sumptuous breakfasts and afternoon teas. Rated "outstanding" and "distinguished" by Northwest Best Places and American Bed and Breakfast Associations. Special private suite available for families!

Host: Candis L. Cooperrider
Rooms: 6 (PB) $85-210 Can.
Full Breakfast
Credit Cards: A, B
Notes: 2, 5, 7, 8, 9, 10

The Ridley's B&B

1786 Teakwood Rd., V8N 1E2
(604) 477-5604

The Ridleys are a retired couple who enjoy doing B&B. Hostess delights in preparing full breakfasts; host can provide helpful information about Victoria and Vancouver Island. Their home is located 3 blocks from University of Victoria, 15 minutes drive from down-

town. The house was built in 1979, open design, cathedral-type ceiling, all electric, with conservatory, fruit trees, flower gardens.

Hosts: Joanne and George Ridley
Rooms: 2 (SB) $50
Full Breakfast
Notes: 2, 5, 7, 8, 9, 10

Sonia's Bed and Breakfast

174 Bushby St., V8S 1B5
(604) 385-2700; (800) 667-4489 (for Washington and Oregon)

Sonia has queen and king size beds, private bathrooms with a big hot breakfast. The new suite looks out over the Straits of Juan de Fuca. A lovely walk to the Inner Harbour—Empress hotel. Close to everything. Shopping, good restaurants, Beacon Hill Park, bus at door. No smoking. Adults only.

Host: Sonia McMillan
Rooms: 3 (PB) 1 suite (PB) $55-125 (US)
Full Breakfast
Notes: 2, 6, 10

Top O'Triangle Mountain

3442 Karger Terr, V9C 3K5
(604) 478-7853

Our home, built of solid cedar construction, boasts a spectacular view of Victoria, the Juan de Fuca Strait and the Olympia Mountains in Washington. We are a relaxed household with few rules, lots of hospitality, and clean, comfortable rooms. A hearty breakfast is different each morning.

Hosts: Pat and Henry Hansen

year; 6 Pets welcome; 7 Children welcome; 8 Tennis nearby; 9 Swimming nearby; 10 Golf nearby; 11 Skiing nearby; 12 May be booked through travel agent

Rooms: 3 (PB) $60-85 Canadian
Full Breakfast
Credit Cards: A, B
Notes: 5, 7, 8, 9, 10, 12

WEST VANCOUVER

Beachside
Bed and Breakfast

4208 Evergreen Avenue, V7V 1H1
(604) 922-7773; FAX (604) 926-8073

Guests are welcomed to this beautiful waterfront home with a basket of fruit and fresh flowers. Situated on a quiet cul-de-sac in an exclusive area of the city, the house, with Spanish architecture accented by antique stained-glass windows, affords a panoramic view of Vancouver's busy harbor. There are private baths, a patio leading to the beach, and a large Jacuzzi at the seashore, where you can watch seals swim by daily. Near sailing, fishing, hiking, golf, downhill skiing, and antique shopping.

Hosts: Gordon and Joan Gibbs
Rooms: 3 (PB) $80-129
Full Breakfast
Credit Cards: A, B
Notes: 2, 5, 8, 10, 11, 12, 13

WHISTLER

Golden Dreams B&B

6412 Easy Street, V0N 1B6
(604) 932-2667; (800) 668-7055; FAX (604) 932-7055

Uniquely decorated Victorian, oriental and Aztec theme rooms feature sherry decanter, cozy duvets. Relax in the luxurious private jacuzzi and awake to nutritious vegetarian breakfast including homemade jams and fresh herbs served in the country kitchen. Short walk to valley trail to village activities and restaurants.

Host: Ann Spence
Rooms: 3 (1PB; 2SB) $65-95
Full Breakfast
Credit Cards: A, B
Notes: 7, 8, 9, 10, 11

Manitoba

WINNIPEG

Bed and Breakfast of Manitoba

533 Sprague Street, R3G 1J9
(204) 783-9797

Organized in 1980, B&B of Manitoba has a variety of hosts who add a unique flavor of ethnic and cultural heritage along with warm, friendly Manitoba hospitality. The inspected homes are located in urban, rural and popular resort areas. Call or write for a full color brochure, with detailed listing and descriptioin of each home.

---

year; 6 Pets welcome; 7 Children welcome; 8 Tennis nearby; 9 Swimming nearby; 10 Golf nearby; 11 Skiing nearby; 12 May be booked through travel agent

Nova Scotia

PARRSBORO

Confederation Farm

RR #3, B0M 1S0
(902) 254-3057

Our place is a berry farm along the Bay of Fundy, overlooking Cape Split. Clean beaches, a delight for collectors of driftwood and agates. Semi-precious stones such as amethyst are found in cliffs along the shore. Nature and historic folklore have been bountiful; your eyes will see the serene natural beauty that surrounds you. See the fascinating tidal bore and visit fossil cliffs at "Joggins" or enjoy a clam bake. There is also a private picnic park and a big barbecue cooker. Then there is a special Pioneer Farm Museum, with plenty of artifacts. There are many local festivals such as Rock Hound Round Up and Blueberry Festival. We particularly welcome guests and recommend the fabulous Parrsboro to Advocate scenic drive. Our place is open May 1 until November 1. Please reserve in advance, $20 deposit is required. Cash is required for full settlement.

Hosts: Julia and Bob Salter
Rooms: 4 (2SB) $40
Full Breakfast
Credit Cards: None
Notes: None

NOTES: Credit cards accepted: A Master Card; B Visa; C American Express; D Discover Card; E Diners Club; F Other; 2 Personal checks accepted; 3 Lunch available; 4 Dinner available; 5 Open all

Ontario

BRAESIDE

Glenroy Farm

Rural Route 1, K0A 1G0
(613) 432-6248

Beautiful, quiet farm setting just a one-hour drive from Ottawa. Situated in historic McNab township of Renfrew County in the heart of the Ottawa Valley, halfway between the towns of Renfrew and Arnprior. We live in an 1884 stone house that has been well-maintained by three generations of McGregors, the family who built the home and lived in it. We have a farming operation growing strawberries and corn and raising beef cattle. Located within driving distance of the Ottawa River raft rides, Storyland, Logos Land, Bonnechere Caves, and other attractions. Home of the 1994 International Plowing Match. No smoking or alcoholic beverages.

Hosts: Noreen and Steve McGregor
Rooms: 5 (1PB; 4SB) $35-50
Full Breakfast
Credit Cards: None
Notes: 2, 4, 5, 7, 9, 10, 11

ELMIRA

Teddy Bear Bed and Breakfast

Wyndham Hall, RR 1, N3B 2Z1
(519) 669-2379

Hospitality abounds in our gracious countryside 1907 schoolhouse, minutes from Elmira. The elegance and charm of our home is enhanced by Canadiana and old order Mennonite quilts and rugs. Beautifully decorated bedrooms. Private/shared guest bathrooms; lounge; complimentary refreshments; and full breakfasts.

Hosts: George and Vivian Smith
Rooms: 3 (1PB; 2SB) $65 (Canadian)
Full Breakfast
Credit Cards: A, B, C
Notes: 2, 5, 10

Teddy Bear Bed and Breakfast

---

year; 6 Pets welcome; 7 Children welcome; 8 Tennis nearby; 9 Swimming nearby; 10 Golf nearby; 11 Skiing nearby; 12 May be booked through travel agent

KAWARTHA LAKES

Windmere Farm Bed and Breakfast

Selwyn, RR3, Lakefield, K0L 2H0
(705) 652-6290; FAX (705) 652-6949

Windmere is located in the heart of the Kawartha Lakes, a water skier's and fisherman's paradise. Joan and Wally have an 1845 stone farmhome, set amid shaded lawns and a huge spring fed swimming pond. The older part of the house has high ceilinged rooms decorated with fine art and Victorian antiques. In the new wing, the accent is on wood, warmth and informality. Fresh baked bran muffins and homemade jams are served each morning; in the evening, tea and snacks are offered in the family room. Walking trails, golf courses, and parks are nearby.

Hosts: Joan and Wally Wilkins
Rooms: 4 (2PB; 2SB)
Full Breakfast
Credit Cards: B
Notes: 3, 5, 7, 9, 10, 11, 12 (10%)

LEAMINGTON

Home Suite Home Bed and Breakfast

115 Erie Street South, N8H 3B5
(519) 326-7169

Near Point Pelee National Park. Home Suite Home features 2 honeymoon suites, 2 additional rooms, large inground pool. Large traditional home decorated Victorian Country. Four and one-half baths, plush carpet and fine linen. In house air conditioning, hearty full country breakfast. Log burning fireplace for cool winter evenings. No smoking. No pets. Agatha is coordinator for Point Pelee Bed and Breakfast Association.

Hosts: Harry and Agatha Tiessen
Rooms: 4 (2PB; 2SB) $40-60
Full Breakfast
Credit Cards: None
Notes: 2, 5, 7, 8, 9, 10

NEW HAMBURG

The Waterlot Inn

17 Huron St., N0B 2G0
(519) 662-2020

Spend a night with us sometime. Two large and very comfortably appointed rooms, one under each of the 1840 peaks at the front of the house. These share a memorable marble shower, bidet, water closet, wet vanity and a sitting area lit by the cupola. A white iron double bed, a queen size sleeper in the living room and a large three piece bathroom. In the morning we'll feed you something, but you must catch the kitchen help first—but not too early!

Hosts: Gordon Elkeer
Rooms: 3 (1PB; 2SB) $65-85
Continental Breakfast
Credit Cards: A, B, C
Notes: 2, 3, 4, 5, 8, 9, 10, 11

NIAGARA FALLS

Gretna Green B&B

5077 River Rd., L2E 3G7
(416) 357-2081

NOTES: Credit cards accepted: A Master Card; B Visa; C American Express; D Discover Card; E Diners Club; F Other; 2 Personal checks accepted; 3 Lunch available; 4 Dinner available; 5 Open all

A warm welcome awaits you in this Scots-Canadian home overlooking the Niagara River Gorge. All rooms are air conditioned and have their own TV. Included in the rate is a full breakfast with homemade scones and muffins. We also pick up at the train or bus stations. Many people have called this a "home away from home."

Hosts: Stan and Marg Gardiner
Rooms: 4 (PB) $45 (Oct-April), $55 (May-Sept.) Canadian
Full Breakfast
Notes: 5, 7, 8, 10

OTTAWA

Australis Guest House
35 Marlborough Avenue, K1N 8E6
(613) 235-8461

We are the oldest established and still operating bed and breakfast in the Ottawa area. Located on a quiet, tree-lined street one block from the Rideau River, with its ducks and swans, and Strathcona Park. We are a 20-minute walk from the parliament buildings. This period house boasts leaded-glass windows, fireplaces, oak floors, and unique eight-foot-high stained-glass windows overlooking the hall. Hearty, home-cooked breakfasts with home-baked breads and pastries. Winner of the Ottawa Hospitality Award for April 1989. Recommended by *Newsweek*, January 1990, and featured in the *Ottawa Sun* newspaper, January 1992 for our Australian bread. Baby-sitting is available.

Hosts: Carol and Brian Waters
Rooms: 3 (1PB; 2SB) $45-65 Canadian

Full Breakfast
Credit Cards: None
Notes: 2, 5, 7, 8

TORONTO

Burken Guest House
322 Palmerston Blvd., M6G 2N6
(416) 920-7842; FAX (416) 960-9529

Lovely non-smoking home located in downtown close to all attractions. Eight guest rooms furnished with antiques, washbasin, telephone and ceiling fans. Continental breakfast served on deck in summer. TV-lounge, parking, maid-service.

Hosts: Burke and Ken
Rooms: 8 (SB) $60-65 (Canadian)
Continental Breakfast
Credit Cards: A, B
Notes: 5, 12

Toronto Bed and Breakfast
Box 269, 253 College St., M5T 1R5
(416) 588-8800; (416) 961-3676; FAX (416) 964-1756

Let us simplify your travel plans throughout Metro Toronto, Ottawa, Kingston and Niagara Falls! Now in its 15th year, Toronto's oldest and original bed and breakfast registry is serving the entire area. Our reservation service of quality inspected B&B homes provides a high level of safety, comfort, cleanliness and hospitality. Advance reservation recommended; free brochure on request. Traveler's checks, Visa, MC, AE, DC.

---

year; 6 Pets welcome; 7 Children welcome; 8 Tennis nearby; 9 Swimming nearby; 10 Golf nearby; 11 Skiing nearby; 12 May be booked through travel agent

Prince Edward Island

MURRAY RIVER

Bayberry Cliff Inn
Rural Route 4, Little Sands, C0A 1W0
(902) 962-3395

Located on the edge of a 40-foot cliff
are two uniquely redecorated post-and-
beam barns, antiques, and marine art.
Seven rooms have double beds, three
with extra sleeping lofts. One room has
two single beds. The honeymoon rooms
have a private bath. Seals, restaurants,
swimming, and craft shops are all
nearby.

Hosts: Don and Nancy Perkins
Rooms: 8 (1PB; 7SB) $35-70
Full Breakfast
Credit Cards: A, B
Notes: 2, 9, 10

O'LEARY

Smallman's Bed and Breakfast
Knutsford, Rural Route 1, C0R 1V0
(902) 859-3469; (902) 859-2664

We have a split-level house with a
garage on the west end and brick gate
posts. We have a racetrack behind the
house where some guests like to go for
a walk. There are churches, stores,
craft shops, tennis, golf, and lovely
beaches for relaxing. We live in a quiet,
country area on Route 142 off Highway
2. Come into O'Leary and go four
miles west.

Hosts: Arnold and Eileen Smallman
Rooms: 4 (SB) $25-35
Full or Continental Breakfast
Credit Cards: None
Notes: 4 (on request), 7, 8, 9, 10, 11

NOTES: Credit cards accepted: A Master Card; B Visa; C American Express; D Discover Card; E
Diners Club; F Other; 2 Personal checks accepted; 3 Lunch available; 4 Dinner available; 5 Open all

Victorian Village Inn

Box 44, C0A 2G0
(902) 658-2483

Circa 1880 Victorian located in tiny non-commercial seacoast village away from the hustle and bustle of business and tourist traffic. Inn is decorated and furnished with many Victorian and Canadian antiques to reflect its heritage. Small craft shop on premises. Several packagaes available from $250. Information on packages supplied on written request only.

Hosts: Erich and Jackie Rabe
Rooms: 5 (3PB; 2SB) $40-65
Continental Breakfast
Credit Cards: B
Notes; 4, 5, 9, 10, 11

Quebec

KNOWLTON

Auberge Laketree

R.R. 2, 687 Stage Coach Road, J0E 1V0
(514) 243-6604

Twenty room house, built 1965, unique view on private 6-acre unpolluted lake. Surrounded by mountains. No other houses. Boats canoes, rafts, large terrace for meals and lounging overlooking lake. House has large lounge, two fireplaces, library, artistically furnished. Existing as country inn for 20 years. Ten minute drive to unusual Victorian town of Knowlton.

Host: Mrs. Ursula Seebohm, proprietor
Rooms: 10 (3PB; 7SB) $70 (Canadian)

MONTREAL

Armor Inn

151 Sherbrooke Est, H2X 1C7
(514) 285-0140

The Armor Inn is a small hotel with a typical European character. In the heart of Montreal, it offers a warm, family atmosphere and is ideally situated close to Métro, Saint Denis, and Prince Arthur Streets. It is a 15-minute walk to Old Montreal, the Palais of Congress, and numerous underground shopping centers.

Host: Annick Morvan
Rooms: 15 (7 PB; 8 SB) $38-55
Continental Breakfast
Credit Cards: A, B
Notes: 5, 7, 12

Bed and Breakfast à Montréal

PO Box 575, Snowdon Station, H3X 3T8
(514) 738-9410

B&B Montréal is the city's oldest reservation service, established in 1980. This agency specializes in quality private homes, most offering private bathrooms. Locations are downtown or up to 10 minutes away with excellent public transit. All hosts speak English and will enhance your visit with their suggestions. Full Breakfasts are served and free parking is available.

NOTES: Credit cards accepted: A Master Card; B Visa; C American Express; D Discover Card; E Diners Club; F Other; 2 Personal checks accepted; 3 Lunch available; 4 Dinner available; 5 Open all

Casa Bella Hotel

264 Sherbrooke West, H2X 1X9
(514) 849-2777; FAX (514) 849-3650

The same owner has operated this charming hotel for 21 years. The 100-year-old European-style house has been renovated and is located downtown, near "La Place Des Arts," U.S. Consulate, Metro, bus, and within walking distance of Old Montreal, Prince Arthur Street, and shopping center. Rooms are comfortable for a low price. Parking is available.

Rooms: 20 (14 PB; 6 SB) $43-72
Continental Breakfast
Credit Cards: A, B, E
Notes: 5, 7

Manoir Sherbrooke

157 Sherbrooke Est, H2X 1C7
(514) 845-0915; FAX (516) 284-1126

The Manoir Sherbrooke is a small hotel with a European character offering a family atmosphere. It is convenient to Métro and Saint Denis and Prince Arthur streets. It is within walking distance of Old Montreal, the Palais of Congress, and numerous shopping centers.

Host: Annick Legall
Rooms: 22 (14 PB; 8 SB) $42-70
Continental Breakfast
Credit Cards: A, B
Notes: 5, 7, 12

Bay View Farm

NEW CARLISLE WEST

Bay View Farm

337 Main Highway, Route 132, Box 21, G0C 1Z0
(418) 752 2725; (418) 752-6718

On the coastline of Quebec's picturesque Gaspé Peninsula, guests are welcomed into our comfortable home located on route 132, Main Highway. Enjoy fresh sea air from our wrap-around verandah, walk, swim at the beach. Visit natural and historic sites. Country breakfast, fresh farm, garden and orchard produce, home baking, genuine Gaspesian hospitality. Light dinners by reservation. Craft, quilting, folk music workshops. August Folk Festival. Also a small cottage for $350 per week. English and French spoken.

Host: Helen Sawyer
Rooms: 5(SB) $35
Full Breakfast
Notes: 3, 4, 5, 7, 8, 9, 10, 11

QUEBEC

Bed and Breakfast Bonjour Québec

3765 Boulevard Monaco, G1P 3J3
(418) 527-1465

The first reservation service of Quebec represents 11 homes that were carefully selected to make your visit a genuine French experience. The Grande-Allee is reminiscent of the Champs Elysée in Paris. Historic sites, the St. Lawrence River, charming restaurants, and shops are within easy reach

year; 6 Pets welcome; 7 Children welcome; 8 Tennis nearby; 9 Swimming nearby; 10 Golf nearby; 11 Skiing nearby; 12 May be booked through travel agent

of every location.

Coordinators: Denise and Raymond Blanchet
Rooms: 22 (SB) $45-60 Canadian
Full Breakfast
Credit Cards: None
Closed November-April
Notes: 2

ST-MARC-SUR-LE-RICHELIEU

Auberge Handfield

555 Chemin du Prince, J0L 2E0
(514) 584-2226; FAX (514) 584-3650

Quintessentially French is this inn on
the Richelieu River in an ancient French-
Canadian village, where French is uni-
versally spoken. The somewhat rustic
decor of this venerable 160-year-old
mansion is complemented with antiques
and locally crafted furnishings. A marina and other resort facilities, including a health club, along with the outstanding regional cuisine make this a
most enjoyable holiday experience.

Host: Conrad Handfield
Rooms: 55 (PB) $55-145 (Canadian)
Full Breakfast
Credit Cards: A, B, C, E
Notes: 3, 4, 5, 7, 8, 9, 10, 11, 12

Hostellerie Les Trois Tilleuls

290 Rue Richelieu, J0L 2E0
(514) 584-2231

The Hostellerie Les Trois Tilleuls is a
charming inn on the banks of the
Richelieu River. The dining room features authentic French cuisine with an
extensive wine list of exceptional vin-
tages.

Host: Michel Aubriot
Rooms: 24 (PB) $84-350 (Canadian)
Full Breakfast
Credit Cards: A, B, C, D, E
Notes: 3, 4, 5, 7, 8, 9, 10, 12

NOTES: Credit cards accepted: A Master Card; B Visa; C American Express; D Discover Card; E
Diners Club; F Other; 2 Personal checks accepted; 3 Lunch available; 4 Dinner available; 5 Open all

Saskatchewan

GULL LAKE

Magee's Farm
Box 428, S0N 1A0
(306) 672-3970

Mixed working farm, some small animals. Modern cottage, fully equipped, accommodates up to 6 guests. Hosts are interested in photography, people and nature. Campers, hunters and bus tours welcome.

Rooms: 3 (2PB; 1SB) $35 (Canadian)
Full Breakfast
Credit Cards: None
Notes: 2, 3, 4, 5, 6, 7, 8, 9, 10

Puerto Rico

Beach House Inn

Calle Italia 1957, Ocean Park, 00911
(809) 726-9111

Small guest house located in a peaceful residential area not far from all the tourist and commercial points of interests. Ocean front located at the best beach area in San Juan. 85% of our clients are women. Continental breakfast included with rates. Lunch or dinner available upon request.

Hosts: Rosie Bernal or Addy Pietri
Rooms: 8 (PB) $50-75 (off season rates available)
Continental Breakfast
Credit Cards: A, B, C
Notes: 3, 4, 5, 6, 9

El Canario Inn

1317 Ashford Avenue-Condado, 00907
(809) 722-3861

San Juan's most historic and unique B&B inn. All 25 guest rooms are air conditioned with private baths, cable TV and telephone and come with complimentary continental breakfast. Our tropical patios and sundeck provide a friendly and informal atmosphere. Centrally located near beach, casinos, restaurants, boutiques and public transportation.

Hosts: Jude and Keith Olson
Rooms: 25 (PB) $65-90
Continental Breakfast
Credit Cards: A, B, C, D, E
Notes: 5, 7, 8, 9, 13

Tres Palmas Guest House

2212 Park Boulevard, 00913
(809) 727-4617

Remodeled in 1990, all rooms include air conditioners, ceiling fans, color cable TV with remote control, AM/FM clock radio, small decorative refrigerators, continental breakfast. Oceanfront, beautiful sandy beach; daily maid service; newspapers; magazines; games; ocean-view sun deck; fresh beach towels and chairs. Tourist information available. Centrally located ten minutes from the airport and Old San Juan.

Hosts: Jeannette Maldonado and Elving Torres
Rooms: 9 plus 3 apartments (11PB; 1SB)
$45-85; $45-60 off-season
Continental Breakfast
Credit Cards: A, B, C
Notes: 3, 4, 5, 7, 9

NOTES: Credit cards accepted: A Master Card; B Visa; C American Express; D Discover Card; E Diners Club; F Other; 2 Personal checks accepted; 3 Lunch available; 4 Dinner available; 5 Open all

Virgin Islands

ST. CROIX

Pink Fancy Inn

27 Prince Street, 00851
(809) 773-8460; (800) 524-2045; FAX (809) 773-6448

A small unique historic inn located a block and a half away from the town of Christiansted. From our inn, there are 20 restaurants, duty-free shopping and historic sites. All our rooms are on a courtyard with a tropical garden, a pool, hammocks and gazebo. Our rooms all consist of kitchenettes, cable color TV, telephone, fridge, air conditioning and ceiling fans. And to top it off, we have a twenty-four hour complimentary bar and expanded continental breakfast.

Host: Jens Thomsen-innkeeper
Rooms: 10 (PB) $90
Expanded Continental Breakfast
Credit Cards: A, B, C, E
Notes: 5, 7, 8, 9, 10, 12

ST. THOMAS

Danish Chalet

P.O. Box 4319, 00803-4319
(800) 635-1531; FAX (809) 777-4886

Thirteen minutes from the Cyril King Airport, overlooking Charlotte Amalie Harbor with cool mountain and bay breezes. Five minute walk to town with duty-free shopping, restaurants, and waterfront activities. Complimentary continental breakfast, sundeck, jacuzzi, $1 honor bar, free beach towels, in-room phones, air conditioning or ceiling fans. Can arrange day sails, sight-seeing trips, car rental, etc. Special honeymoon packages available. We have been in the hospitality profession for 47 years and welcome your visit.

Hosts: Frank and Mary Davis
Rooms: 13 (5PB; 8SB) $60-95
Continental Breakfast
Credit Cards: A, B
Notes: 2, 5, 6, 7, 8, 9, 10, 12

---

year; 6 Pets welcome; 7 Children welcome; 8 Tennis nearby; 9 Swimming nearby; 10 Golf nearby; 11 Skiing nearby; 12 May be booked through travel agent

Island View Guest House

P. O. Box 1903, 00801
(809) 774-4270; (800) 524-2023 reservations

This charming guest house is located midway between the airport and the town of Charlotte Amalie, on Crown Mountain, 545 feet above and overlooking the harbor. Freshwater pool, beach and restaurants are close by. Rooms have king, queen, and twin accommodations, most with private bath and balcony. Fans, air conditioning, telephone in room, laundry facilities available. Kitchen available upon request.

Hosts: Norman Leader and Barbara Cooper
Rooms: 15 (13PB; 2SB) $63-95 winter; $45-68 summer
Continental Breakfast; Full Breakfast available
Credit Cards: A, B, C
Notes: 3, 5, 8, 10, 12

Mafolie Hotel

P. O. Box 1506, 00804
(809) 774-2790; (800) 225-7035; FAX (809) 774-4091

Enjoy the world-famous view 800 feet above the town and harbor. The hotel was totally renovated in 1991. Mini-suites can sleep four and have TV, refrigerator, and king beds. The freshwater pool has a large deck; lunch is served all day. An excellent restaurant on the property serves seafood, steak, chicken, and pork--all grilled to perfection. Entree prices start at $13.50 and include the huge salad bar and baked potato or rice. Free transportation to Magen's Beach.

Host: Lyn Eden
Rooms: 18 plus 5 mini-suites (PB) $60-68 summer; $93-97 winter
Continental Breakfast
Credit Cards: A, B, C
Notes: 3, 4, 5, 7, 8, 9, 10, 12

NOTES: Credit cards accepted: A Master Card; B Visa; C American Express; D Discover Card; E Diners Club; F Other; 2 Personal checks accepted; 3 Lunch available; 4 Dinner available; 5 Open all